5·1·80

THE AMERICAN WIRE SERVICES

A Study of Their Development as a Social Institution

This is a volume in the
Arno Press collection

DISSERTATIONS IN BROADCASTING

Advisory Editor
Christopher H. Sterling

See last pages of this volume
for a complete list of titles.

THE AMERICAN WIRE SERVICES

A Study of Their Development as a Social Institution

Richard Allen Schwarzlose

ARNO PRESS
A New York Times Company
New York • 1979

**Publisher's Note: This book has been reproduced
from the best available copy.**

Editorial Supervision: Andrea Hicks

———◆———

First publication 1979 by Arno Press Inc.
Copyright © 1979 by Richard Allen Schwarzlose

DISSERTATIONS IN BROADCASTING
ISBN for complete set: 0-405-11754-X
See last pages of this volume for titles.

Manufactured in the United States of America

Publisher's Note: Any mispagination reproduced in the Arno edition
occured in the original volume. The text is complete.

———◆———

Library of Congress Cataloging in Publication Data

Schwarzlose, Richard Allen.
    The American wire services.

    (Dissertations in broadcasting)
    Originally presented as the author's thesis,
University of Illinois, 1965.
    Bibliography: p.
    1. News agencies--United States. I. Title.
II. Series.
PN4841.A1S3 1979   070.4'35   78-21738
ISBN 0-405-11774-4

THE AMERICAN WIRE SERVICES:

A STUDY OF THEIR DEVELOPMENT AS A SOCIAL INSTITUTION

BY

RICHARD ALLEN SCHWARZLOSE
B. S. , University of Illinois, 1959
A. M. , University of Illinois, 1960

THESIS

Submitted in partial fulfillment of the requirements
for the degree of Doctor of Philosophy in Communications
in the Graduate College of the
University of Illinois, 1965

Urbana, Illinois

PREFACE

At its best, a thesis is the embarkation upon a promising voyage with the expectation of charting unexplored seas. At its worst, a thesis is the manipulation of data and hypotheses to produce a dribbling of facts and assertions. I suspect the student usually envisages the former and his advisors and teachers tolerate the tedium of the latter. Despite the traditional claims of advancing the cause of science or drawing back the veil of secrecy, theses somehow must always apologize for omissions and limitations. In the final analysis, they are simply what could be managed under the expert policing of teachers, wives, and a host of personal doubts.

Originally this thesis was to combine a theoretical framework--a modification of the systemic perspective applicable to social institutions-- and a thorough examination of the wire services. In typical graduate student fashion, my hopes were wider than the realities of producing such a work would permit. While the description was to occupy the dominant role, the theory might detract, or worse two theses under the same cover would be unmanageable. Thus the framework has been picked over and the more important organizing concepts culled for this paper. A full theoretical exposition must await another time and place.

Slicing off an entire social institution for description, even if a large contributing literature had been available, requires more stamina than insight, and I confess to have run out of both with no more than two-thirds of my notes and tabulations committed to paper.

For tolerating frequent consultation and my propensity for voluminous undertakings, I wish to thank my advisor, Professor Jay W. Jensen. I

also want to express my appreciation to Professor James Carey for

reading this thesis and providing helpful and constructive criticism. A

special note of thanks goes to Miss Eleanor Blum whose help and coopera-

tion made my library research both fruitful and easy, and to Henry Schulte

and the many other journalists whose thoughtful responses to my comments

and questions made parts of this thesis possible.

    Finally, I owe a large debt of gratitude to my wife, Sally, for her

patience and understanding during these long months of researching and

writing. Her encouragement and faith at every step of the way have con-

tributed vastly to making this thesis possible.

Author's Note:

    The reader should understand that this study was undertaken to explore
the research potentials of a systemic model for institutional growth. The
wire services were a convenient communication institution on which to test
the systemic model. Most of the wire service history found in Chapters II
and III here is drawn from common secondary sources and is valuable primarily as a summary of that literature. The author's subsequent research on
19th century wire history will clarify, correct, and elaborate on this work.
    Material in Chapters IV through VII and in the Appendices, however,
represents previously unreported evidence, drawn from AP Annual Reports
(which unfortunately are no longer available at the University of Illinois
in the form and quantity that they were thirteen years ago), interviews
with wire service personnel, and the author's first-hand experience with
wire service news reports.
    The value of this dissertation after thirteen years is to be found
in the epistemological approach being proposed and tested here and in the
wire service information, primarily for the 20th century, which the
researcher now would have difficulty amassing.

                                                   R. A. S.

Evanston, Illinois
August 1978

TABLE OF CONTENTS

LIST OF FIGURES

Chapter I

INTRODUCTION

> Characteristic of organization,
> that of a living organism or a
> society, are notions like those
> of wholeness, growth, differen-
> tiation, hierarchical order,
> dominance, control, competition,
> and so forth.
> -- van Bertalanffy (1956)

Every day in the year thousands of American and foreign newsmen

and editors gather, edit, and schedule hundreds of thousands of words of

news and opinion for distribution over an intricately-woven network of tele-

graph and telephone lines to nearly every newspaper and broadcast outlet

in the United States. This continuous and continually changing stream of

stories, features, and photographs from here and abroad is the product of

the nation's largest continuous public communication organizations: the

major American wire services.

The purpose of this paper is to describe the historical trends and

contemporary conditions of the major American wire services, with the

goal of understanding how and why they first appeared and have developed

since, and what position they have come to occupy in society. In this

introductory chapter, the author will explain his reasons for undertaking

this study, describe the previous investigatory work in this field, sketch

in the organizing principles around which the study is planned, introduce

several research hypotheses, and outline the succeeding chapters.

The term "wire service" as used here refers to those national or

1

international organizations which continuously and simultaneously gather and distribute news and comment to local outlets instantaneously by means of radioed and wired telegraphy and telephony. "Wire service" is a modern term, coined to take notice of the twentieth-century technological methods by which these organizations attain their unique speed of transmission and volume of copy. These organizations previously were called news, or news-gathering, agencies, terms which reflected the earlier uniqueness they derived from widespread contacts with regional, national, or international fields of news sources. This condition is no longer confined solely to what is called here a wire service, and the term "news agency" more recently carries the connotation of possible governmental support or direction, a press-government relationship recently increasing in frequency. Finally, "press association" is often applied to large-scale collection and distribution of news, but it is the author's sense that this phrase refers to the genus of which "wire service" is a species. As such, the press association classification also includes all specialized or intermittent or periodic news and feature services for local outlets. The major American wire services forming the subject of this study are the Associated Press, United Press International, and their various local, regional, and national forerunners.

Essentially four reasons support the undertaking of this study. First, as will be noted in detail immediately below, investigators of the media of mass communication have almost completely ignored the American wire services as large-scale participants in the on-going communicative intercourse of this society. Conversely, the author's preliminary inquiries into the wires convince him of the possibility that they may occupy a central position and play a powerful role in communication between various sectors of this democratic society. Second, the author feels that there is a need at this time in communications research to draw together the few existing, though scattered and fragmentary, wire-service studies for an evaluation of where research on the wires has been, what it has and has not considered, and where it has yet to go to attain understanding of the wires. Growing out of this need to consolidate wire-service research, will be the third reason for this study: to suggest areas of future investigation concerning the wire services. Fourth, this study is undertaken partially as a vehicle by which the author may introduce hitherto unreported data on the structural, maturational, and relational aspects of the wire services.

Survey of the Literature

Existing contributions to the scholarly literature of wire-service research suffer, without exception, from one of three ills: possible or apparent bias, outdatedness, and incompleteness. By and large, the so-called primary sources of wire-service data fail for their bias (and many, additionally, for outdatedness). Autobiographies of past wire-service leaders, such as Kent Cooper, Melville E. Stone, Charles S. Diehl, and Hugh Baillie, [1] are filled with the bias and sentimental attachment to their respective organizations that one would expect to find in such works. Their most valuable contribution has been the explanation of historical wire-service mechanics and the revealing of leaders' policies and perspectives.

Several wire-service histories have been written by men closely related to the wires, including those of Joe Alex Morris, Cooper, and Oliver Gramling.[2] Slanted presentation is more subtle in this type of work, but the author has noted, no less prevalent. Like the autobiographies, these histories make for romantic reading, but as scholarly, objective works they are of little value.

Perhaps the only authoritative and factual historical sources are Victor Rosewater's history of collective news gathering,[3] which is now thirty-five years old, and Unesco's twelve-year-old historical and comparative study of news agencies.[4] More recent Unesco statistical descriptions update selective quantitative characteristics of major wire services,[5] but historical and operational details are omitted. These sources will be used extensively in this study, because of their reliability and as foundations upon which more recent historical developments are presented.

Finally, there exists a very large group of studies which either deal briefly with the wires from a broader framework (e.g., histories of journalism) or focus in detail on aspects of wire-service operation (e.g., correspondents, relations with industry and government, litigation, etc.). These works will be introduced at appropriate places in this study, their number being far too great for introduction here. They are largely reliable and represent that fragmented body of research which the author purposes to draw together into a unified description of the wires.

Special mention must be made of AP's <u>Annual Volumes</u>[6] as a source of raw data. They are the annual management reports to the AP membership, and although their promotional value to AP will be established later in this paper, their quantitative and explanatory contribution to the author's research has been great. He relies upon their contents for several statistical and personnel tables in Appendix B and for statements and explanations of policy throughout the following chapters. The author's reliance upon these reports has made this study somewhat over-balanced with AP material, but as will be noted from time to time, fundamental operational and policy similarities can be assumed to exist among all wires in a given time and place, and AP's longer and more illustrious history warrants primary attention.

Since this study is not a description of the mechanics of daily wire-service operation (and thereby assumes that the reader understands such mechanics), the author will simply note that several works provide adequate textbook explanations of wire-service mechanics. General introductions to the wires, with emphasis on local-editor handling of incoming wire-service copy, are given by Taylor and Scher, Brown, and Westley[7] while explanations of and instruction in wire-service reporting and writing are found in books by Flesch and Ault and Emery.[8]

Theoretical Framework and Organizing Concepts

Description of the wires' historical trends and contemporary conditions proceeds in this study under the general purview of the so-called

General System Theory (or simply "systems theory").[9] Assuming that the organism is a valid unit of identification and investigation, systems theory emphasizes structure and organization as a whole unit which exhibits the never-ending, dynamic processes of maturation or decay, processes relatively similar in both human and physical systems. Systems theory views the universe as strata of vertically and horizontally reciprocally interacting systems with units in one stratum acting as sub-systems of units in the stratum above. From this viewpoint, an investigator may ascend the strata considering, for example, in order: the individual, his committee or work unit, policy or work divisions, the production or service entity (e.g., a corporation, agency, etc.), the institution, the social order of several related institutions, and a society or civilization. A sense of the vertical interaction is noted in the following statement by Robert E. Park in his "natural history of the newspaper": The press "is the outcome of a historical process in which many individuals participated without foreseeing what the ultimate product of their labors was to be."[10]

In this study, vertical dynamics involves political and productive sub-systems' influence upon the corporation sub-systems' contribution to the wire-service system's trends and conditions.

A dynamic interaction among systems or sub-systems horizontally within a given stratum is also assumed. Here reciprocity of influence is thought of as flowing among individuals, committees or work units, divisions, and so on up to the various institutions in a given society. Edwin Emery's introduction to his journalism history makes this horizontal interaction the focus of his work and the basis of its title.

> The title, The Press and America, reflects the
> emphasis placed upon correlation of journalism history
> with political, economic, and social trends. In this
> interaction, the press has had its influence upon the
> course taken by our country. Conversely, the conditions
> and influences present in each historical era have cumu-
> latively determined the shape of the press. [11]

In this study, the author confines his horizontal perspective to interaction
at the institutional level, although reciprocity through the institutional
system originating in sub-systems will also be noted at times. Two types
of systematic relationships will be employed: (1) the "primary environmental institutions," those systems with which the wires have immediate
and daily contact (principally the local media subscribers to the wires and
the news sources from which the wires gather their news); and (2) the
"secondary environmental institutions," the entire field of institutions
which in the course of performing their generally assigned social functions
exchange influence with the wires as well as all other sectors of society.

Emerging from this discussion, then, are two sets of concepts
around which this study will be organized. Political and productive processes of operational growth will be concepts characterizing two vertical
phases of the wire services. The political process is here defined as that
set of individual and group contributors and of interactions leading to con-
ferral or assumption of power by sub-systems and by which policy is
made or changed The productive process includes that set of contributors
and interaction leading to creation and distribution of the wires' "goods
and services," i. e. , the daily news report in its various forms.

Again, the other organizing concepts, as noted above, are primary and secondary environmental institutions, and they supply the contributors to horizontal interaction with the wires.

In a sense, the production process of wire services includes or involves a third process, that of communication, in that what is produced is a communicative message. And while it must be understood that communication is the principal social function of the wire services, this third process has had to be omitted from this study, owing to time and space limitations.

Since historical trends in wire-service development are here considered as important as the wires' current conditions, much of this study will deal either with chronological or topical historical accounts. Systems theory postulates that systemic growth and change result from endogenous and exogenous interaction, guided by teleologic, vitalistic direction. Growth and change are made possible by the fact that human organisms (including institutions) are "open systems," and thus receive and give off influence constantly with their environment. Von Bertalanffy observes:

> Systems by their very nature and definition are not closed systems. Every living organism is essentially an open system. It maintains itself in a continuous inflow and outflow, building up and breaking down of components, never being, so long as it is alive, in a state of chemical and thermodynamic equilibrium but maintained in a so-called steady state which is distant from the latter. [12]

While, as noted above, this openness has definite implications for intra- and inter-system development and influence, it also gives specific direction to the mode of historical accounts proceeding under its aegis.

Consistent with systems theory, Jay W. Jensen formulates three requirements for the "critical acquisition of knowledge," particularly concerning the mass media: (1) a strict adherence to objectivity, in terms of both the investigator's possible predispositions and the nature of the data collected, manipulated, and discussed; (2) a regard for the nature of the institution's historical development and of the historical forces which shaped it; and (3) a regard for the "contextual" relationships of the institution, i.e., relations with its socio-cultural environment.[13] Of the third requirement, Jensen says:

> . . . while we may arbitrarily abstract the media from their socio-cultural environment in order to analyze them, so to speak, as things in themselves--their technical structure, their routines, and conventions--we all know that they cannot really be understood apart from the context of their environment.
> The social nature, function, and control of contemporary mass media cannot be fully understood except in their relationships to prevailing ideologies, to other institutional orders, to the power structure of society, and so on.[14]

It is this emphasis which leads Emery to comment about the title of his history (quoted above) and which is apparent in Theodore B. Peterson's introductory statement: "I have tried to explore the major tendencies in the magazine industry and social and economic forces that helped to shape them."[15]

The more traditional history, by comparison, is but a compendium of facts, dates, and names, arranged in a linear sequence, following this or that chain of events singularly and episodically to its present state or past termination. Although a thorough and accurate work (and one used extensively in the present paper), Frank Luther Mott's American

Journalism is an example of this latter variety, having as its purpose "to provide a comprehensive work, in which historical narrative is combined with some of the characteristics of a reference book . . . "[16]

Hypotheses and Chapter Outline

The author's interest in and study of the major American wire services extends back over four years of reading, data collecting, interviewing and handling of wire copy. In the course of this preparation and investigation, he has formulated five propositions to which he will address the findings and conclusions of this study. The hypotheses are divided into three categories, according to their areas of emphasis. (Roman numerals in parentheses indicate the chapters in which the hypotheses will be discussed. The symbols II-III and IV-V refer to the single concluding sections both for Chapters II and III and for Chapters IV and V.)

INSTITUTIONAL STATUS

1. The wire services over time have attained the status of a social institution, after having begun as a group effort within another social institution, the newspapers. (II-III, IV-V)

2. The wire services' operational patterns have continually resembled those of their secondary environment through constant interaction with this socio-cultural environment. (II-III)

POLITICAL AND PRODUCTIVE MATURATION

3. The wire services have increasingly attained political and productive stability (an essential characteristic of increased maturation) by virtue of decreases in the influence of exogenous forces and of decreases in the possibility of endogenous fragmentation and conflict. (IV-V)

PRIMARY ENVIRONMENT RELATIONS

4. The wire services have increasingly dominated the
   political and productive relations with subscribers in
   the primary environment. (VI)

5. The wires services have been increasingly dominated
   by news sources in the political and productive relations
   with the news sources in the primary environment. (VII)

The reader will note that these hypotheses as a group assert the

general proposition that the wires have risen to a place of significance in

American society and of dominance with respect to certain important insti-

tutions in society. If the following chapters can supply verification for such

a proposition, one major objective of this paper will have been achieved:

identification of a major communication institution requiring considerably

more research attention than it has commanded up to this time.

This study is divided into seven chapters beyond the present one,

having as their individual content the following: Chapters II and III (Wire-

Service History) present a chronological, "contextual" history of the major

American wire services, focusing upon the wires' interaction with their

secondary environment. A single section of discussion and conclusions at

the end of Chapter III accommodates both chapters. Chapter IV (Maturation

of Wire-Service Power Structures) presents the topical, historical develop-

ment of political patterns in terms of state and federal governmental control,

subscribers, and the decision-making bodies of the wires. Chapter V

(Maturation of Wire-Service Production Structures) is a topical, historical

treatment of revenue sources and expenditures, and includes considera-

tion of endogenous and exogenous forces' effect upon them. The discussion and conclusion section of Chapter V includes material from Chapter IV. Chapter VI (Wire-Service Relations with Subscribers) describes the potential subscriber field and some of its problems and presents political and productive trends apparent in the wire service-subscriber relationship. Chapter VII (Wire-Service Relations with News Sources) delineates wire-service, news-gathering facilities and presents political and productive conditions existing between these facilities and sources. Chapter VIII (Conclusions) summarizes findings, discusses hypotheses, probes the implications of findings for the wires' social role, and introduces areas of future investigation.

Footnotes are employed (appearing at the end of each chapter) only where sources are directly quoted, where source works are actually mentioned, or where the literature is in disagreement. Footnotes also perform the occasional function in this study of providing sources for additional study and giving supplementary or explanatory information not absolutely germane to the text. On the other hand, lists of sources are given in the text wherever possible to introduce presentations in which factual material has not been footnoted. Finally, while all cited works are included in the bibliography, several uncited sources also appear there as contributors to the author's research and presentation. An effort has been made, in fact, to compile a thorough bibliography on the wire services.

The reader will note that the paper includes three appendices, the use of which is an effort to avoid breaking or fragmenting the narrative or expository strain of the text. Appendix A contains a juxtaposed, chronological listing of wire-service, media, and environmental events and serves as a shorthand summation of and reference point for Chapters II and III. Appendix B contains the thirty statistical tables for material introduced in Chapters IV through VII, and Appendix C includes the mechanics of and responses to two samples used to gather data for Chapter VI.

Aside from the straight tabular matter appearing in Appendix B, the reader will find thirteen figures in the form of charts and maps inserted throughout the text to clarify and summarize various diverse or detailed portions of the presentation.

Footnotes

[1]Kent Cooper, Kent Cooper and The Associated Press (New York: Random House, 1959); Melville E. Stone, Fifty Years a Journalist (Garden City, N. Y.: Doubleday, Page & Company, 1921); Charles S. Diehl, The Staff Correspondent (San Antonio, Texas: The Clegg Company, 1931); and Hugh Baillie, High Tension (New York: Harper & Brothers Publishers, 1959).

[2]Joe Alex Morris, Deadline Every Minute: The Story of United Press (Garden City, N. Y.: Doubleday & Company, 1957); Kent Cooper, Barriers Down (New York: Farrar & Rinehart, Inc., 1942); and The Right to Know (New York: Farrar, Straus and Cudahy, 1956), both including sections of normative advocacy as well as accounts of AP's historical contacts with foreign news services and news sources; and Oliver Gramling, AP: The Story of News (New York: Farrar & Rinehart, Inc., 1940).

[3]Victor Rosewater, History of Cooperative News-Gathering in the United States (New York: Appleton and Company, 1930).

[4]Unesco, News Agencies: Their Structure and Operation (Paris: Georges Lang, 1953).

[5]See Unesco's World Communications: Press, Radio, Television, Film (Amsterdam: Drukkerij Holland, N. V, 1964) for the fourth revision of the organization's statistics on national and world communications systems.

[6]The Associated Press of Illinois, Annual Volumes (Chicago: The Associated Press), I-VIII (1894-1901), and The Associated Press of New York, Annual Volumes (New York: The Associated Press), I-LXIV (1901-1964), and "Preliminary Proceedings" (1900).

[7]Howard B. Taylor and Jacob Scher, Copy Reading and News Editing (New York: Prentice-Hall, Inc., 1951), pp. 99-117; Charles H. Brown, News Editing and Display (New York: Harper & Brothers, Publishers, 1952), pp. 110-131; and Bruce Westley, News Editing (Cambridge, Mass.: The Riverside Press, 1953), pp. 161-193.

[8]Rudolf Flesch, The AP Writing Handbook (New York: The Associated Press, 1951) among others by him, and Phillip H. Ault and Edwin Emery, Reporting the News (New York: Dodd, Mead & Co., 1959), pp. 216-232.

[9]The author's background in systems theory is gleaned from the following articles by its originator, Ludwig von Bertalanffy: "General System Theory," General Systems: Yearbook of the Society for the Advancement of General Systems Research, I (1956), pp. 1-10, and "General System Theory--A Critical Review," ibid., VII (1962), pp. 1-20. The author also relied heavily upon a recent modification of systems theory for application to

the communications field: James W. Carey, Communication Systems, and Social Systems: Two Economic Postulates Applied to a Theory of Communication Systems (Urbana, Ill.: unpublished University of Illinois Ph. D. thesis, 1963).

[10]Robert E. Park, "The Natural History of the Newspaper," Mass Communications, Wilbur Schramm, ed. (2nd ed.; Urbana, Ill.: University of Illinois Press, 1960), p. 8.

[11]Edwin Emery, The Press and America (2nd ed.; Englewood Cliffs, N. J.: Prentice-Hall, Inc., 1962), p. v.

[12]Von Bertalanffy, op. cit. (1956), p. 3.

[13]Jay W. Jensen, "A Method and a Perspective for Criticism of the Mass Media," Journalism Quarterly, XXXVII (Spring, 1960), pp. 262-263.

[14]Ibid., p. 263.

[15]Theodore B. Peterson, Magazines in the Twentieth Century (2nd ed.; Urbana, Ill.: University of Illinois Press, 1964), p. viii.

[16]Frank Luther Mott, American Journalism (3rd ed.; New York: The Macmillan Company, 1962), p. v.

Chapter II

WIRE-SERVICE HISTORY: EARLY DEVELOPMENT AND INSTABILITY

> Importance depends on endurance.
> What endures is identity of pat-
> tern, self-inherited. Endurance
> requires the favourable environ-
> ment.
> -- Whitehead (1925)

This is the first of two chapters devoted to the chronological and

"contextual" history of the American wire services. Although history,

except under the most superficial perspective, does not proceed episodically,

historical periods have been superimposed upon the account in Chapters II

and III in order to draw together more easily the wires' history and that of

the social and cultural environment. Choice of these periods is arbitrary

and reflects only the author's judgment as to significant turning points or

milestones in wire-service development. Moreover, the year 1893 as the

dividing point between the two chapters is also an arbitrary choice, made

primarily because of the year's central position in the wires' history in

terms of both arithmetic and developmental significance.

The principal general sources of wire-service history used in this

chapter are Rosewater, Mott, Emery, Unesco, AP's Annual Volumes,

and Alfred McClung Lee.[1] Other, less general, sources will also appear

from time to time to complete the account. While wire-service history

accounts for the bulk of these chapters, brief consideration of the social

and cultural environment is also required. Sources of this material are

Henry Steele Commager and Samuel Eliot Morison (for the long-range

16

view of trends and issues) and Richard Hofstadter and the University of

Maryland History Department (for specific dates and finer detail). [2]

Each of the five historical periods (three in this chapter, two in the

next) is divided into three parts: Social and Cultural Environment, a

description of the general social context; Media or Wire-Service History,

a factual and explanatory account without anecdotes and personality

sketches; and Period Summary, a joining of the first two sections with

discussion geared to better understanding of the wires' social role.

Conclusions and discussion of relevant hypotheses for all five periods ap-

pears at the end of Chapter III.

The reader's attention is directed to Appendix A which consists of

a detailed chart of chronological events presented in Chapters II and III.

It will serve as a shorthand summary of these two chapters and as a

reference of historical sequences useful throughout the remainder of this

study.

A. Pre-Wire-Service Media and Techniques: 1690-1848

1. Social and Cultural Environment

This period of pre-wire-service history, both generally and in terms

of communication media, encompasses the rise of this country to national

stability, exhibiting relatively effective institutions and a degree of inter-

national prowess and security. Throughout this period, however, the

dominant theme of growth and stability was accompanied by the strong

undertow of ideological and institutional conflict and interaction, accompanied by considerable contradiction within each of these sectors. Such contradictions have become a dominant theme in the often-compromising ways of American thought and action, even up to the present time, but because of their shifting alignments, multitude of spokesmen, and bases through the years, they cannot be adequately capsuled in this brief study. The give-and-take of the broader ideological and institutional coalitions stemming from them, however, must be a principal subject of these social and cultural sections.

In the broad context, colonial development was both an economic necessity for England, and a financial and political burden to her, particularly with England's conflicts in Europe tapping her strength throughout this period. Right up to the American Revolution (and probably one of the causes of that revolt), the British were forced to operate a seesaw colonial government, first imposing taxes in order to offset protection of the Colonies and then relinquishing control to the Colonists as disputes and warfare with France or Spain developed. By 1760, the Colonists had had a taste of self-government, and England was finally ready to incorporate the Colonies into the empire. The Americans pleaded for the federal theory, claiming colonial sovereignty over internal affairs and asking parliamentary protection in international matters, and the British emphasized the universality of crown-parliamentary sovereignty over all subjects in the empire (the unitary theory). Moreover, unrest in America was fed by England's espousal of the Lockean rationale for the 1688 Bloodless Revolution. Colonists asked why representative, contractual government based on natural law and the natural rights of mankind was applicable to

Englishmen but not to Colonists? The American Revolution was inevitable

and grew out of an uncommon unanimity of ideological thrust such as

America would not experience again for two hundred years.

The reaction to distant, centralized English government led the

new American freemen to the safe, colonial-style confederation of states,

whose inherent shortcomings and eventual replacement laid down the guide-

lines and protections with which the new nation's institutions developed

their structure, vigor and ability to serve society. The new constitutional

government provided the framework for institutional growth and strong

leaders protected and embellished the framework: Washington gave strength

and dignity to the unprecedented and often-feared office of the President;

Hamilton formulated a stable and workable economic plan for America;

John Marshall brought equality to checks and balances and national suprem-

acy to the federal system; and Jefferson and Jackson provided the place for

the common man in society and furthered the cause of civil liberties and

democratization.

By 1848, the United States had not only defended its borders but

had pushed them west to the Pacific, thence north and south as far as

military fortunes and "manifest destiny," tempered by a small amount of

prudence, would permit. To 1815 the nation regrouped following the Revo-

lution and carved out its institutional life, leaving its cultural origins and

its ideological fervor across the Atlantic or under a rock. After 1815

continental expansion, a factory system in full swing, the first influx of immigrant labor, the growth of cities, a rising democratization of politics, education, law, and religion, and the rise of the popular press contributed to an integrated national drive for stability and equilibrium of social forces.

The new American institutions of industry, science, and government spun merrily on their way, unmindful of the growing undertow of moral, ideological, and reformist unrest after 1815. Soon after 1848, the undertow would materialize as a series of deep, uncompromising splits over fundamental issues: north and south over slave labor, east and west over immigrant influx, business and government over depressions and panics, labor and management over working conditions, and Democrat-Republican and Federalist-Whig over uses of power, vested interests, and a wide array of possible answers to the above issues. The seeds of these problems had been in the American soil long before 1848, and in fact, some had been transplanted from Europe as far back as the seventeenth century.

2. Media and Techniques History

Within this environment grew the printed medium of communication with origins--like those of all colonial and post-Revolution life--stretching back to Europe. Also inherited, particularly from England, was an on-going discussion of press controls and freedoms, which the colonial editors and governors picked up and continued with renewed vigor. An opinionated press of political and economic values dominated journalism in America for nearly 150 years from the first American newspaper (1690), through the first New York City newspaper (1725), the first foreign-language newspaper (1732),

the first daily newspaper (1783), to the "official, " "national" newspapers
(Fenno's Gazette of the United States in 1789, Freneau's National Gazette,
and the National Intelligencer in 1800). The New York Sun's new concept
of reporting (1833) challenged the press of opinion, but the latter would not
die until after the Civil War.

Public officials, realizing as did the printers and writers the potential
power of the press to sway the small powerful group of political leaders and
businessmen who read the papers, sought continually to control the colonial
press for their own purposes. The Zenger trial, while backfiring on the
government, was only one of many instances in which public officials took
arbitrary measures to silence the printed opposition voice. The First
Amendment guarantee of free speech meant little nine years after its adop-
tion when Congress shackled the opposing Democrat-Republican press with
the Alien and Sedition Acts. Although Jefferson's repeal of the acts closed
the door on congressional regulation (except in time of war or national
crisis), Congress remained unapproachable for reporting purposes for many
years, in spite of the importance of the legislators' role. The saving grace
throughout the period, however, was the fact that the press continued to
represent all dominant viewpoints and often risked great penalties to break
down barriers to ignorance and inaccessibility, in and out of government.
The observation by Sidney Kobre about the post-Revolutionary newspaper
reflects its deep-seated, dynamic role in early American life.

The press played a significant role in founding the new
republic and in its subsequent development. The Revolutionary
War demonstrated that the newspaper possessed barely-tapped
persuasive power. With the growth of the new political parties,

the Federalists and the anti-Federalists turned to the
newspaper to fight political party battles in the early
decades of the republic. As the parties developed and
grew more powerful, so did the newspaper. The editors
not only mirrored the party battles, but aided the leaders
in consolidating and expanding economic life of the nation
and its cultural and social development. [3]

The press, therefore, matured in a growing, young nation, seeking

new techniques, outlets, and content, and structuring its developing en-

vironment as the latter, in turn, made new demands upon it. And within

this reciprocal process of early life, four trends gradually became dis-

cernible which led ultimately to the press technique known as news gather-

ing and to the institution known today as the wire service. It should be

noted that these trends not only led to development of news-gathering agencies

but also reflect the dominant characteristics of the emerging press institu-

tion in the pre-1848 years. In one sense, therefore, the wire services be-

came the outgrowth of the natural tendencies of their parent institution, the

press. The four trends are: the rise of daily newspapers, a more aggressive

seeking of news, certain communicative and transportation developments,

and a revision in the concept of news. Each had its effect on the other three,

and all responded to the changing needs and desires of the society in which

they were introduced.

While the first daily newspaper, per se, was the Pennsylvania Evening

Post and Daily Advertiser in 1783, the social need for daily intelligence had

preceded this newspaper by widespread use of interpersonal contacts in

taverns, coffee houses, inns, ordinaries, merchants' exchanges, churches,

and postmasters' offices. Domestic developments, world affairs, the con-

ditions of shipping, piracy, markets, raw materials, the labor market, etc., were increasingly sought as the early American desired to keep abreast of events which directly affected his rapidly growing institutional world. To fill this need, the daily political and mercantile newspapers began to take over where coffee houses and postmasters had carried the burden. The fact that the early daily press was opinionated did not diminish its general importance in society. (See Table 13, Appendix B for the rate of daily newspaper growth in this and following periods.)

Coupled with the growing activity of daily news dissemination was that of more aggressive news collection. Historically, national and international news was slow-moving, passed on by word of mouth, in letters, or by exchange newspapers mailed or shipped from distant points. News of the Revolutionary War came fast enough to convert weeklies into tri-weeklies and to tantilize public interest, developing in the community the newspaper-reading habit. Following the war, however, editors to maintain subscription lists and continue the more lucrative increased frequency of publication turned both to political and mercantile specialization and to more aggressive news-gathering techniques. The threat of rising newspaper competition made such activities all the more important, particularly since most newspapers concentrated on national and foreign news, unable to compete with coffee houses, etc., for dissemination of local news. The bulk of the national and foreign content of the newspapers at this time was gleaned from the pages of other newspapers, and editors naturally sought faster ways of receiving these newspapers. Overland routes followed the terrain and overland shipping developed slowly, the victim of adverse weather,

among other problems, Editors had to wait for technical improvements
and governmental direction to secure overland domestic news rapidly.
Their gathering of foreign news was impeded by the slowness of transatlantic ships. Even with the introduction of ocean-going steamships in
1838, the Atlantic crossing took three weeks. The only dent editors could
make in this cumbersome method of foreign news transmission was to meet
incoming ships with fast "news boats" which received the incoming foreign
newspapers at sea before the ships' time-consuming harbor entry and
docking procedure.

The practice of meeting ships with news boats, dating back to 1784
when the (Boston) Massachusetts Sentinel referred to such activities,[4] did
not reach an organized, regular basis until 1811 when Samuel Topliff, Jr.,
became proprietor of Boston's Exchange Coffee House reading room and
operated a news boat regularly in Boston harbor. Topliff's records, though
primarily for the coffee house patrons, were used extensively by Bostonian
newspapers as a source of up-to-date foreign news. A former Bostonian,
Aaron Smith Willington, began the same method in 1813 for the Charleston
(S. C.) Courier. An employee of that newspaper, James Gordon Bennett,
later became involved with similar news-gathering practices in New York
City, eventually employing them on his own paper, the New York Herald,
founded in 1835.

By 1821 there is evidence of New York City newspapers jointly and
singly meeting ships, although specific arrangements and procedures are
not definitely recorded until 1827 when a rivalry for harbor supremacy and

speed sprang up between the news boats of the Journal of Commerce and

the Courier. As the period progressed, faster boats and various combina-

tions of newspapers were employed to save New York City editors the ex-

pense of individual activity and the embarrassment of losing news to

competitors. Increased speed of news gathering, keener competition,

and improved printing methods continually pushed deadlines earlier. By

1848 most of the aggressive, competitive U.S. newspapers were morning

publications. In New York City, for example, the newspapers (whether

class- or mass-oriented) which most frequently engaged in harbor activities

were in the morning field.

Increasingly the association plan of gathering news appealed to the

economically-minded New York City editors. Several such associations

or cooperative pools were used between 1827 and 1848, with their fluctuat-

ing longevity dependent upon the whims of editors. None of these pools

seems to have been based on formal agreement. Sensing the association

trend in New York City journalism, a group of unaffiliated reporters es-

tablished the Independent Reporters Bureau in 1847 to aid newspapers in

gathering primarily domestic and local news on a free-lance basis. One

of the reporters, Dr. Alexander Jones, the following year became the first

general agent of the New York Associated Press.

Closely associated with the news aggressiveness of reporters and

editors, but slower to materialize, was the development of communica-

tions and transportation facilities to transmit news rapidly over great dis-

tances. Editors were quick to use any means which appeared to aid them gather news more quickly. Along with news boats, they used locomotives, the pony express, and homing pigeons to carry news and newspapers to the printing plants. As an increasing number of methods were tried, it became clear to editors that if they wanted an entire exchange newspaper, they had to sacrifice speed of transmission, but if they wanted speed, they had to settle for only a few important news items. On the one hand, tradition held out for awaiting the entire newspaper. Culling important bits of news at or nearer the source gave a sense of duplicating transmission efforts since the newspaper itself would arrive eventually anyway. But American journalism, on the other hand, was becoming a vigorous, highly competitive American institution and editors gradually shook off traditional vestiges, yielding to the contingencies of a changing communication structure. Speed of transmission became more important than volume to the editor, and out of this decision grew a new entity in the news-gathering field: the news dispatch, a single item of news with a specific transmission source and destination. The new concept, however, could not be immediately realized. Slow-moving land and ocean traffic still blocked full realization of the news dispatch's potential, and compromises between volume and dispatch transmission were necessary. Daniel Craig, for example, boarded incoming transatlantic ships at Halifax, Nova Scotia, secured a bundle of European newspapers, condensed their significant contents into brief, abbreviated messages, and sent these condensations to Boston and New York City newspapers by carrier pigeon.

Another manifestation of the news dispatch emerged with the development of the distantly-based newspaper correspondent. While most of the early correspondents were only stringers or junketing editors, their prin-

cipal task was to gather and send news to a specific newspaper. Moreover,

the value of a correspondent was largely determined by his ability to beat

other sources in delivering the news item to the newspaper office the

fastest way he could. (In the mid-twentieth century, by contrast, his

value is to interpret or background the raw-boned news which is con-

currently delivered by the wire services. Correspondents seldom place

much emphasis on speed now, having been pre-empted in this respect by

the wires.) Thus, the stringer began to replace the exchange newspaper

or page proof coming from important news centers because of the speed,

individuality, and exclusiveness of his dispatches.

Human communication over long distances had been limited, prior

to 1832, by man's ability to produce or hear sounds and to make or see

visual signals. Crude devices, such as bells, trumpets, guns, yodelling,

whistling, tom-toms, flares, torches, lanterns, and smoke, were used to

cover distances faster than a man or animal could carry a written or verbal

message. The late-eighteenth and early-nineteenth centuries, however,

saw several promising discoveries which might aid long-distance communi-

cation. Electrical experiments led to the harnessing and storing of elec-

trical charges in the battery by 1800, and within a quarter of a century the

principle of electromagnetism was discovered. The invention of the

electromagnetic telegraph by Samuel Morse in 1837 provided the first

really fast means of transmitting messages over long distances at a rapid

speed. The first telegraphed news dispatch in the United States was sent

on May 1, 1844, and within two years most New York City newspapers
were carrying columns of telegraph news. Telegraph systems spread
quickly across the settled country, reaching St. Louis and Charleston,
S.C., in 1847 and Chicago in 1848.

The fourth trend leading to the first news-gathering agency in
America and reflecting the changing character of the press institution
was the changing definition of news in the United States. For more than
a century prior to 1833, American newspapers had been politically or
economically oriented. They waged political wars and aided businessmen
and financiers, using only that part of the news which appealed to or was
of aid to the powerful and wealthy elite of American society. Jeffersonian
and Jacksonian democracy in the meantime was elevating the self-image
of the rising, immigrant-fed common man group, preparing it for its
place in the new democracy. In 1833, American journalism began a revolution of news content which affected the entire society. That news content
revolution had, as its first vehicle of expression, the New York Sun, the
first of the so-called "cheap" or "penny" newspapers in the United States.
Essentially two aspects of journalism were altered with the appearance of
the Sun: first, a previously untapped reader and consumer market of
laborers and common men in the growing industrial cities was reached by
the printed medium, and second, an entirely new definition and treatment
of news was devised to attract and hold the interest of this rising lower
and middle class group

Two theories for the rise of the penny press as related to the changing
news values in America have been advanced. Mott sees it primarily as an

economic and technological development, encompassing the rise of the
factory system, the improvement of printing techniques, the emergence
of a laboring class, the rise economic-bred class relations, the rise of
metropolitan industrial areas, and the beginning of popular education.[5]
Emery places more emphasis on political forces, including the rise of
the common man, labor class recognition in society, franchisement for
most, political backing for the penny press movement, and greater interest
by the labor class in government.[6] The environment appears to have included both sectors, as well as the old political-mercantile press, whose
stuffy treatment, opinionated presentation, partial coverage, and high
prices had asked for a counter-movement from somewhere within the newspaper institution.

Mott summarizes the characteristics of the new penny press news
approach as: (1) an increase of local or home-city news, (2) a greater
emphasis on sensational news, especially crime and sex, and (3) the appearance of what later is called "human interest" news--dealing with persons as flesh and blood human beings[7] Emery notes that the original
sensationalism of the penny press was a reader lure, a "developmental
phase." As time passed, the poor man's tastes improved as did his
reading, and members of other classes were drawn to the new press, thus
creating a demand for more sophisticated penny press content. Also,
Emery points out, the old partisan press had been the reader's ally in
good times and bad, but now the greater objectivity of the press alienated
itself from the reader.[8] In general, American society, however, was

becoming more impersonal, and the loss of a printed friend was not felt
for very long

The press was becoming a separate institution in American life, no
longer springing from the people's ideological and financial interests but
devising its own solutions and methods which responded both to its own
problems and to the new problems and conditions of society. Amid the
revolutionary turn of press content was the first hint of objectivity and
aloofness which in the mechanistic, Libertarian tradition of Locke, Milton,
and Jefferson was viewed as the linear channel of social communication in
which truth would prevail provided all statements of fact and opinion were
permitted interaction in the "free and open marketplace."[9] The desire of
the press, consequently, was increasingly to: inform, entertain, safe-
guard civil liberties, service the economic and political systems, and make
a profit.

3. Period Summary

By 1848, the young nation had asserted and won its independence and,
with adjustments, had attained a degree of institutional sophistication and
effectiveness. Meanwhile the underlying contradictions of background, region, and institutional necessity were beginning to make themselves heard
concerning the federal and state levels, business and labor, the north and
south, east and west, republicanism and democratism. The many debates
had not yet settled on key, life-or-death issues in 1848, and the nation
plunged vigorously ahead, eager for tomorrow's invention or the promised
land beyond the horizon.

In this active, but increasingly volatile, context, society managed to settle upon a cultural life style uniquely its own and consumed and produced the contents of a concurrently maturing press system. The medium reflected the democratic, metropolitan, diverse, industrial American trends in its own drift toward the common reader and the reader market, the large-city daily, objective reporting, and an awareness of competition As government, industry, agriculture, and religion continually grew to stability and readjusted the American power structure among them in this first period, each formulated its own institutional capacities and its social role vis-a-vis the others. The press concurrently was making strides toward assumption of its role as symbolic arbiter among the disparate, established institutions and growing ideologies whose fluid interaction comprised the mid-nineteenth-century American society.

B. Local Organization and Early Growth: 1848-1862

1. Social and Cultural Environment

The institutional edifice erected in the previous period, was shaken and seriously threatened in the fourteen years after 1848 by a surge of American ideological conflict and multiple reform movements. The question of slavery was only one symptom of a general social and cultural reorganization and reappraisal about to engulf the United States at the midpoint of the nineteenth century. While institutions fought to maintain their operations and influence, the issues and opinions would not be resolved, peaking with the Free-Soil party (1848), the 1850 Compromise, Stephen

Douglas's attempts to get the railroad to run through Chicago (1854), the Dred Scott case (1857), and the 1860 presidential campaign and election. What was worse, even the institutionalists found themselves divided and without compromise. There was increasing industrial growth and prosperity in the north and a continuing southern agrarian tradition, and the rising midwestern agriculture was quite different from that of the southerners Each sought its own place in U.S. economics and sought a place in culture for the rationales which supported its claim to economic superiority. None, however, would rise to a superior position for several years, and even then not without confronting the constant backwash of the subordinated sectors.

While America came unraveled politically, economically, and ideologically without much-needed compromise among various courses for social and institutional adjustment, American intellectuals found in the social unrest the opportunity to gain a foothold with a solely American culture. The European culture which Whitman, Thoreau, and Emerson had decried as worthy of abandoning was moving ahead on several fronts led by Marx, Mill, and Darwin, posing problems and solutions which Americans would not have time nor inclination to contemplate for several decades.

Pride and uncompromised principle ultimately led the nation to civil war and the sectionalism implicit in Lincoln's 1860 presidential victory became the rationale and motivation for a war which would only prolong American ideological divergence, further engrain sectional factionalism, and permit a postwar rebirth of institutional extremes requiring adjustment far into the twentieth century.

2. Wire-Service History

It shall be seen several times in this discussion that a particular isolated incident precipitated a significant wire-service development or innovation. But the momentary event or crisis serves only to push practitioners over a threshold to which internal and external forces have inched them for many years. So it was with the founding of the New York Associated Press in May of 1848. Superficially, the mutual assistance pact among six morning newspapers in New York City[10] was caused by the papers' dissatisfaction with the Mexican War coverage. Telegraph transmission of war news was expensive, slow, and sometimes even nonexistent. More generally, however, the trends toward daily newspapers, aggressive news gathering, technical developments, and objective reporting (all of which antedated 1848 and all discussed in the previous section) were simply joined or unified by the occurrence of the difficult-to-cover war. Other, more recent, trends migrating toward the NYAP were (1) press difficulties with the burgeoning telegraph industry, (2) successes of foreign news agencies, and (3) a radical revision of editors' thinking regarding ompetition, rising costs, etc., and possible new ways of gaining economic security in the rapidly changing journalistic situation.

The rapidly growing telegraph industry around 1848 was confusingly complex, individually aggressive, and viciously competitive, and although the telegraph and the press saw each other as potentially lucrative partners, their early contacts were complicated by misunderstandings, excessive self-interest, and often even news rivalry.[11] Was news collection the proper function of the telegraph companies and operators, the newspapers and their reporters, or independent news brokers? All three systems of news gathering were employed in one place or another across the nation during the early part of this period. The larger the city or the client-newspaper, the more likely it was that a reporter or a broker gathered the news and the operator merely relayed it. In smaller communities, however, the telegraph operator replaced the colonial postmaster as gatherer and disseminator of news and rumors.

Telegraphic rates, though reduced for press dispatches, were still high enough to cause constant controversy and to force reporters to use a cipher system of condensing entire paragraphs into single words. The composite words were not familiar to the telegraph operators, and thus increased the possibility of transmission errors as well as press-telegraph friction.

Most difficult of the early telegraphic problems to solve, however, was the shortage of lines. Single wires stretched across vast expanses, but the object of the telegraph entrepreneur was to control as much territory as possible, not to improve or duplicate existing facilities. Thus, several reporters filing dispatches at the same remote telegraph office had to vie for first position (and the consequent "news beat") on the only available line. Wires were deviously tied up, sometimes for hours, by reporters awaiting a news story to break. This was the principal cause of New York editors' dissatisfaction over the Mexican War coverage.

A final telegraph problem was the diversity of telegraph owners. Each owner employed his own policy toward the press, some favoring home-town newspapers, others bleeding all press clients. Although telegraph managers fought with each other, nearly all bickered with at least some segment of the press. It was not uncommon, therefore, for newspapers to finance friendly telegraph speculators in regions where existing telegraphic facilities were hostile to press interests. Thompson concisely states the press-telegraph relationship and its pitfalls around 1848.

> The press contended it was trying to adapt itself
> to a telegraph going through an awkward adolescence; the
> telegraph for its part, maintained it was having difficulty
> in serving an industry going through a revolution. Both
> were correct. [12]

An inherent, growing desire for economic security told both industries that greater cooperation within and between the two would solve many of these problems for both sides. The NYAP became the answer for some important members of the press in 1848. The much newer telegraphic industry, however, did not attain a similar unanimity in dealing with the press until about 1860 when two corporate giants (the North American Telegraph Association and Western Union) had replaced the dozens of small units. Six years later, Western Union emerged as "the nation's first great industrial monopoly and its largest corporation," thereby creating on the one hand telegraph's needed unified front, and on the other hand a new group of relational problems for American editors.

In the realm of foreign news agency successes, Unesco distinguishes between Charles Havas' news disseminating agency started in France in 1825 for private individuals (diplomats, businessmen, etc.)

and his reorganized service for newspaper clients, appearing in 1835. [13]

A true "news broker" (contracting stringers and operating the transmission system but not as a newspaperman), Havas refocused the news content of his carrier pigeon, semaphore, and newspaper-exchange system in 1836 to meet the needs of France's first "penny" newspapers. [14] By 1850, Havas was converting his system to telegraph, a process completed within nine years.

Bernard Wolff, a former Havas employee turned Berlin newspaper executive, followed Havas' example founding the Wolff Telegraphen Bureau, at first a service of stock exchange quotations but by 1855 a full-fledged news service for German newspapers. Another German and former Havas employee, Julius Reuter, moved to London in 1851 and established a commercial news service. Reuter's service was a blossoming newspaper wire by 1858. Agence Havas, Wolff, and Reuters in 1859 concluded competition-limiting, mutually exclusive territorial agreements for news exchange, dividing the world into three parts. White and Leigh describe the spheres of influence.

> Reuter got the British Empire, North America, a
> number of "suzerian" states along the Mediterranean-Suez
> lifeline, and most of Asia; Havas got the French empire,
> southwestern Europe, South America, and parts of Africa;
> Wolff got what was left of Europe, including Austria-Hungary,
> Scandinavia, and the Slav States. [15]

Thus, between 1836 and 1858 New York City editors witnessed from afar the successful domestic and international news-gathering techniques and cartel agreements of two broker-oriented and one-newspaper-oriented agencies. On the one hand, it must have been inspiring, but on the other,

American journalism was again under English threat. The NYAP no

doubt saw its bailiwick given to Reuter, watched as Europe came closer

with each successive attempt at a transatlantic cable, and must have seen

the eventual assertion of American journalistic sovereignty as necessary

to maintaining its own dominant position in this ountry.

Up to this point, six factors have been discussed as contributors

to the founding of the NYAP. Four were relatively long-standing trends or

manifestations: the rise of daily newspapers, aggressive news gathering,

communication and transportation improvements, and revisions in the con-

cept of news. Two of the more recent forces were: press-telegraph in-

compatibility and foreign news agency successes. The interaction among

these forces or trends, whether direct or indirect, is obvious. They in-

creasingly operated in concert to influence the editors' awareness of their

own problems and possible courses of action. In a word, the editors in-

creasingly acquired a propensity to protect themselves from the bloodshed

of the journalistic (and, indeed, the social) revolution in which they found

themselves. A propensity or predisposition to cooperate with colleagues

thus became the seventh trend, one partially realized in the pre-1848

associational efforts of New York City newspapers to gather news.

(Universal aggressiveness in news gathering is one important development,

but a desire to submit to cooperative agreements with contemporary com-

petitors for news collection, whether aggressive or suppressive, is quite

another important phenomenon.) Whether it had been the Mexican War, a

political campaign, a tragic flood in a remote area, or an active congres-

sional session, this propensity would have found a cause to dictate a NYAP creation within a few years after 1848. (Similar propensities were evident, by the way, in virtually every other sector of American life during this peak of institutional activity and growth and before the post-1850 reforms and attacks began.)

Six leading editors in New York City, therefore, formed two organizations. One was the Harbor News Association to operate a single news boat cooperatively. The other, an apparently nameless cooperative until 1856 when it was first called the New York Associated Press, secured domestic and local news for the six member newspapers. A central office was set up at Broadway and Liberty streets, and Dr. Jones conducted the cooperative's affairs from that office. Jones describes the office operation.

> We received and distributed the news, paid all tolls and other expenses necessary to conduct the business. We employed reporters in all the principal cities in the United States and Canada, and, on receiving it in New York, would make about eight or nine copies of it on manifold paper--six for the New York press, and the remaining copies for reforwarding to the press in other cities and towns. To this had daily to be added the New York local and commercial news, ship news, etc. The remuneration for services was made to depend chiefly upon what we could obtain from papers in other cities, such as Boston, etc., for the news of all kinds reforwarded, including the local intelligence. The agent had an office separate from the press, but centrally located, where he employed generally an assistant, besides one or two other parties either as clerks or aids, with an errand boy or two.
> In reporting congressional proceedings, the usual plan was to employ two reporters in Washington; one for the House of Representatives, and another for the Senate. The reports of the House would be sent by one line, and those of the Senate by the other.
> The plan upon which the members of the Associated Press acted in obtaining extra news was such that any one of them could order any particular kind of news, such as proceedings of conventions, etc., and the others were to exercise their option whether they would take it. If all should decline it but one or two, those one or two were expected to bear the whole expense. [16]

The first newspaper outside of New York City served by the NYAP
was the Philadelphia Public Ledger which began receiving the news service
in 1848 Many other papers up and down the eastern seaboard and west along
the new telegraph lines soon followed suit, paying a contracted rate for
service, rather than the pro-rated assessment of the six New York City
papers.

L. A. Gobright, first chief of the NYAP Washington, D.C., bureau,
describes his duties and viewpoint on news.

> My business is to communicate facts; my instructions do
> not allow me to make any comment upon the facts which I com-
> municate. My dispatches are sent to papers of all manner of
> politics, and the editors say they are able to make their own
> comments upon the facts which are sent to them. I therefore
> confine myself to what I consider legitimate news. I do not act
> as a politician belonging to any school, but try to be truthful
> and impartial. My dispatches are merely dry matters of fact
> and detail. Some special correspondents may write to suit the
> temper of their organs. Although I try to write without regard
> to men or politics, I do not always escape censure. [17]

In 1851 Jones resigned, complaining of the grueling demands of the
job of NYAP general agent. Daniel Craig, at that time still meeting ships
at Halifax and transmitting news by pigeon, replaced Jones and immediately
applied pressure on telegraph companies ultimately producing reduced
rates and improved facilities for the NYAP. Also in 1851, contractual arrangements with client-newspapers outside of New York City were tightened,
and the cost of service was increased. Without competition, the NYAP's
highhanded rules and price setting went unopposed and unquestioned. The
NYAP was still a novel journalistic innovation of increasing desirability
in America, albeit a small but effective monopoly of self-interested editors.

The growth of a new company or organization may be measured by any of a number of numerical or monetary indices or by the changing nature of its relationships with adjunctive organizations. In the latter realm, two developments indicate the rapid growth of the NYAP in this first period of its history. First, its relation with client-newspapers was continually restructured to afford the NYAP increasing control over its news report and the clients who bought that report. All the while many newspapers clamored for the new type of journalistic service, literally asking to be subjected to the NYAP's rigid regulations and increasing service charges in order to obtain reports of the mounting social turmoil and debate occurring at this time. Second, the NYAP was attaining enough power, via the first relationship, to extract special treatment and rates from telegraph companies, as shall be seen in a moment.

In connection with the first relationship, the NYAP undertook in 1856 the first of three major reorganizations in the nineteenth century. For the first time in eight years, a formal document spelled out NYAP policy and procedures. The NYAP was seeking the stability and continuity which established, lucrative social institutions exhibited. The NYAP was beginning to split off from the mainstream of American newspaper journalism, creating a subsidiary journalistic function or role. Though still operated by newspaper editors, the association wanted a news broker role just as two of its three European counterparts had had at their founding. Briefly, the 1856 reorganization contained the following points:

    1. Continuing incumbent officers' tenure (Gerard Hallock, president; Moses Y. Beach, secretary; George H. Andrews and

Frederick Hudson, executive committee members) at the pleasure
of a majority of the seven members.

2. Refusing additional memberships without unanimous
consent of existing members.

3. Permitting the sale of news to other newspapers on consent
of six-sevenths of the membership.

4. Requiring six-month notice for withdrawal from membership.

5. Expelling any member or subscriber who fails to pay
assessments for thirty days or otherwise violates regulations.

6. Requiring resale of all interests in the NYAP to other
existing members at two-thirds of the appraised valuation of visible
property when a membership is terminated.

7. Continuing the job of general agent as administrator of
NYAP, working under the direct supervision of the executive committee.

8. Listing the general agent's duties as:
   a. collection and distribution of all telegraphic communi-
      cation,
   b. collection of weekly assessments,
   c. payment of all bills and accounts,
   d. general supervision of the network of correspondents.

9. Maintaining correspondents in Washington, D.C., Albany,
N Y., and such other points as the executive committee designates.

10. Pooling among all seven members all news received by
each member.

11. Assessing members who used stories resulting from special
coverage orders the full cost of the coverage.

12. Prohibiting participating newspapers from making agreements with rival telegraphic news agencies in the United States and
from receiving any news from such agencies.

13. Providing stiff penalties for any employee found aiding a
rival association. [18]

Although the NYAP membership of the New York Courier was trans-

ferred to the New York World when the latter absorbed the former in 1859,

the number of NYAP memberships never advanced beyond seven. Each re-

organization in the nineteenth century was aimed at protecting the NYAP or

its successor from internal subversion and external competition, either

from rival news agencies (of which there was none in 1856, but many later

on) or from rivals to the telegraph companies with which NYAP did business.

By 1859, Craig had introduced news collection from inbound ships at Halifax rather than in New York harbor, with the increase in telegraphic facilities throughout New England and Nova Scotia.

Also by 1859 the United States Associated Press was rivaling the NYAP with news boat operation at Halifax. New Yorkers' first serious competition had to be crushed or the NYAP ran the risk of losing its unitary control on news service operations. The solution to the USAP problem was found in the steadily strengthening ties between NYAP and the American Telegraph Company, a rising giant in the new industry. The NYAP's growth had been rapid and widespread and its revenue had mounted well beyond the 1855 mark of $50,000 annually. Most of this revenue was earmarked for telegraphic charges, and Craig offered this growing business to American Telegraph in exchange for reduced rates and line priority over other news dispatches. The informal pact was still recent when the USAP appeared. Seeing an opportunity to increase its news dispatch revenue, American Telegraph threatened to terminate the agreement with NYAP and align itself with USAP. At the height of the controversy, American Telegraph's managerial personnel (responsible for the threat to NYAP) were replaced by stockholders sympathetic to NYAP and its potential power. The NYAP had weathered its bout with competition successfully, but it was obvious that the organization's continued dominance would depend in large part upon help from and close-knit affiliation with adjacent industrial institutions. The USAP continued its Halifax operation, although greatly subordinated and ineffective, until 1866 when the first successful cable made news boats obsolete. American Telegraph was soon absorbed by Western Union, the latter eventually becoming a close partner of the NYAP.

At the start of the Civil War, New York City members paid between $200 and $230 a week, New York City evening papers were assessed half as much, and all out-of-town clients were billed between $10,000 and $12,000 a year. Within the New York City morning field, the NYAP was still visualized simply as an extension of the newspaper staff, explaining in part why the NYAP members maintained such tight control over the organization. Elsewhere in the country, however, the growing number of NYAP clients[19] viewed the association increasingly as a necessary raw material, like printing and reportorial labor, ink, paper, etc. Outside of New York City, it was no longer thought of as the possession of seven New York newspapers; its product and the local readership it elicited had become important nationally. In a sense, it was "owned" by all users, because the act of subscribing to the NYAP was synonymous with providing a democratic service to the nation's population. The NYAP's extensive Civil War coverage served to enhance the value of the news report in the eyes of an anxious, war-engulfed population. But in 1862, New York's supremacy was about to be challenged by regional journalistic spirit precipitated by that very supremacy and by the quality and value of the news report which that supremacy had created.

3. Period Summary

This brief period witnessed the full realization of American institutional growth. Many technological and social developments reached full flower and, in turn, enhanced the power and stability of the institutions into which they were introduced. But this uninterrupted growth and self-attainment concurrently called forth institutional critics in increasing numbers, and the need for reform and compromising readjustment was evident everywhere.

A latecomer to the American scene, the wire service was at first only an appendage of newspaper journalism, established by and reacting to the changing needs of the mother institution and to the increased complexity of external conditions. By turning its increasingly significant product back upon the parent institution and upon the social and cultural environment as a growing necessity to their existence, it found reason to separate itself, formally and for the most part in practice, from newspaper journalism, seeking to attain an identity of its own, even if not at this early date an institutional identity. Moreover, the growing importance of its product would not stop with complete severance from newspapers in general; it pushed ahead, calling for abdication of its own seven New York crown princes.

C. Regional Organization and the Drive for Stability: 1862-1893

1. Social and Cultural Environment

The federal government won the Civil War but lost the struggle for Negro rights, for national reunification, for control over big business, for its own integrity, and for business and agricultural stability This period in the United States saw a new low of federal ineffectiveness in the face of its own graft and self-interest, or a rapidly expanding economic sector,

and of largely solidified southern race conflict. It was a period of unprecedented business growth that utilized monopolistic or cartel agreements to
advantage, capitalized on technological developments which would secure
industrial protection from competition, and disregarded the public's welfare, the demands of labor, and the need for a stable economy. As institutions grew, an ideological rationale (a subversion of Darwin's evolution
theory called "Social Darwinism") trailed along behind half-heartedly, an
unnecessary luxury for the head-strong industrialists.

As for government, the possibilities for reform and integrity in the
postwar period were pre-empted by the assassination of Lincoln and ascent
of congressional "Radicals." Governmental activity was cloaked in spiteful
revenge against the south and acquiescent support of northern industry.
Although big business did not actually govern the United States, politicians
and business magnates coalesced, with the formers' use of favors, financial
support, immigrant control, and a deaf ear to unethical, cutthroat competition. The Tweed Ring, scandal, and graft dominated governmental practice.

But the coalition soon had its repercussions. Violent strikes and
riots broke out, culminating in the organization of powerful and sometimes
ruthless labor unions The 1873 panic reached into the farmland by the
1890's, breeding the Populist brand of discontent over low commodity prices,
tight money, high costs, local graft, and the general reduction of agriculture
to a second-class economic role in the nation.

Both major parties were of about the same size throughout this
period, both advocating similar policies. The dominant Republicans were
supported by the large northern business sector; Democrats were experiencing

the beginnings of a long-term internal illness: north-south disagreement
and factionalism, with the northern faction sounding like Republicans and
wanting on the gravy train. The desire for reform grew, and Congress
reacted modestly, forming the Interstate Commerce Commission (without
sufficient power to act effectively) and passing the Sherman Antitrust Act
(on the negative and ineffective assumption that breaking up some existing
monopolies was better than regulating all business to avoid such arrangements in the first place). A conservative U.S. Supreme Court, operating
on the principle of dual federalism, further mitigated the effect of a growing ideological fervor by protecting big business under constitutional civil
liberties provisions, while failing to expand the same protection for individuals.

2. Wire-Service History

The year 1862 marks a drastic change in wire-service activity.
New York City editors' control over the policies of the NYAP had begun to
irritate client-editors across the country. Often the New Yorkers conducted
the service as if it were solely for their own benefit (which in fact, it
originally was), mindless of its growing national importance and of the vast
financial support of clients. Repeated attempts by clients to secure special
service or even service useful to evening or regional newspapers were re-
sisted in New York. The NYAP was to remain the sole property of New York
papers; clients could get along as best they could.

The NYAP's Civil War coverage, in particular, was treated as if it
were the sole possession of the seven New York editors, and western editors

at the height of the crucial conflict finally acted. In 1862 fifteen repre-

sentatives of nine large cities in seven midwestern states[20] met in In-

dianapolis and formed the Western Associated Press. The new organi-

zation had two objectives: first, to improve midwestern coverage for

its own regional members, and second, to gather strength for a final

confrontation with the NYAP to secure a more equitable arrangement on

costs and policies. The WAP incorporated under Michigan law in 1865

and established by-laws which, like the 1856 formal NYAP reorganization,

refused AP service to competitors and extracted sole allegiance to the

WAP from member newspapers. The WAP was permitted to place an agent

in the NYAP office to supervise the gathering and distribution of news for

the WAP members. Although an independent organization, the WAP still had

to rely on the NYAP wire for most of its important domestic and foreign news.

The WAP finally moved against NYAP in 1866 with the departure of

Craig as NYAP general agent. He somehow figured in the WAP revolt and

later aided WAP, but the literature is vague regarding how and why events

occurred as they did in 1866. In that year the WAP presented the NYAP with

the following "bill of particulars."

> 1. The news report was made wholly in the interest of the
> seven controlling New York City newspapers.
> 2. The pro rata charges to subscribers was based on the
> full delivered news report, much of which (e.g., arrivals and de-
> partures of ships in Eastern ports) was worthless to western news-
> papers.
> 3. The New York City editors, by controlling the report,
> made the commercial interests of the entire nation unjustly de-
> pendent upon those of New York City.
> 4. Much of the news accounts for which subscribers were
> assessed never reached subscribers' offices.

   5. The NYAP monopoly in press association operation prohibited or discouraged the establishment of new newspapers across
the nation. [21]

These were accompanied by an ultimatum demanding an egalitarian division

of labor between the NYAP and WAP, in collecting news, setting general

policy, and arranging for telegraph transmission contracts. The situation

was crucial for the WAP; the first successful transatlantic cable was near-

ing completion and its operation was to give the NYAP the cable-head power

to turn its back on the WAP. The NYAP turned down the westerners' ulti-

matum and replaced Craig with James W. Simonton. With Craig's help,

the WAP established an independent service to compete with the NYAP and

to deny the latter the revenue from weekly assessments. The WAP explained

its move to members in a letter, part of which read:

> By establishing competition, there will be a constant
> incentive to the rival organizations to excel in their legitimate
> functions of obtaining and forwarding news to the press ac-
> curately and promptly. The Western press shall receive news
> reports from all parts of the country and from Europe that
> shall compare favorably with those sent by the New York Asso-
> ciated Press. * * * It is provided that the new opposition
> association shall never exercise, or claim to exercise, any
> control over local associations or individual editors as to their
> right to receive news from other associations or parties in
> New York, or elsewhere, and the Western Associated Press
> is conceded the exclusive control of their news report within
> their own territory. [22]

The NYAP, however, needed the westerners' revenue, the WAP needed

the New Yorkers' access to the new Atlantic cable and to other reduced-rate

telegraphic facilities, and both needed the stability stemming from mutual

assistance. Early in 1867, therefore, the second major NYAP reorganization

of the nineteenth century made the two associations partners and added the

full cooperation of Western Union, which by then was the singular American
telegraphic giant. Provisions of the combine arrangement were as follows.

> 1. A territorial division (with boundaries set along the
> Appalachian range) for news distribution and collection.
> 2. The full and mutual exchange of news between the two
> organizations.
> 3. A specified aggregate payment to NYAP for the foreign
> news and special domestic news it gathered.
> 4. Respect for each other's territorial monopoly.
> 5. An exclusive agreement between NYAP-WAP and Western
> Union for priority of the formers' news on the latter's wires in ex-
> change for the formers' exclusive use of the latter's system. [23]

WAP's success in securing territorial autonomy and a degree of
freedom from oppressive, arbitrary assessments encouraged creation of
similar regional cooperatives elsewhere in the United States. Other such
organizations appearing during the period were: The New England Associated Press, covering New England, except for Connecticut; the Connecticut
Associated Press; the New York State Associated Press, including upstate
New York newspapers; the Southern Associated Press; the Northwestern
Associated Press, encompassing Minnesota and the eastern Dakotas with
headquarters in St. Paul-Minneapolis; and the California Associated Press,
including the Rocky Mountain States, California, Oregon, and Washington.
Each organization was relatively autonomous but gained the security of
mutual assistance pacts with the other associations. Often, however, regional problems or individual differences among managers of the various
associations created unstable conditions in the loose Associated Press confederation, as Swindler notes.

> During most of the 1870's and 1880's, newsgathering
> services were kept in a constant state of flux by alternate
> compacts for mutual assistance and exchange of news, and

surreptitious efforts to seize advantages over each other.
With costs mounting after each new shift in relations, and
with workaday news service in a chaotic condition because
of these errant rivalries, it was logical that leading publishers
should at length perceive that some permanent remedy was
essential, and that was one nationwide incorporation.[24]

The "permanent remedy" Swindler refers to signals the start of the

fourth historical period in 1892 and will be described later. In the mean-

time, the fragmented condition among the organization's regional and state

associations created a constantly changing situation. The "drive for

stability" noted in the title of this period had two simultaneous manifesta-

tions: first, the general desire of all regional and local organizations to

maintain under the Associated Press banner a monopoly of news-gathering

and news-distributing facilities in the United States, and second, the

individual desires of each organization to secure and maintain its own

territorial and membership autonomy. The continual state of flux created

within the AP organization by these contradictory drives was joined by two

additional problems for AP, both originating outside the organization:

first, a revolt of newspapers not included in an AP organization, and second,

the shifting tides of telegraphic competition. These two forces will now be

discussed briefly.

Two types of newspapers became enemies of the AP organizations.

One was the morning newspaper which could not secure an AP membership

because of AP's by-law barriers against admitting competitors of existing

members, and the other was evening papers which felt that AP's news re-

port was unduly biased by structure and content in favor of morning publi-

cations In 1869 the Hasson News Association was founded to serve evening papers; it was renamed the American Press Association in 1870. Its existence depended upon that of the Atlantic and Pacific Telegraph and the Southern and Atlantic Telegraph Companies, two of the few remaining telegraph firms opposing Western Union Also relying upon the Atlantic and Pacific Telegraph Company was the National Associated Press Company, which in 1877 absorbed the American Press Association. Soon after this, Atlantic and Pacific was swallowed by Western Union and NAPC was forced out of business. Several small local and regional news-gathering associatiations came and went during this period, but most could not meet the formidable combination of a national AP confederation and the powerful Western Union empire.

For several years following 1876, AP became the object of frequent congressional investigations and proposed dissolution bills. General Agent Simonton, repeatedly called to hearings in Washington to defend the AP, dwelled on four points: (1) the AP is not a monopoly; (2) the AP is a private business; (3) the AP has no franchise to operate from the government and thus no legislation within the power of Congress can take from it the tools of its creation; and (4) AP is independent of Western Union.[25] These satisfied a majority of congressmen. The principle of antitrust legislation and adjudication had not yet developed in America, and Congress' primary interest in the AP stemmed from political motives and from the uniquely significant impact of the "product" which AP handled. Another congressional motivation is found in the fact that in 1879 Western Union as a public utility granted AP its first leased wire, an arrangement which smacked of special

treatment from a utility for a private customer. No action was taken,
however, to retract the leased-wire agreement, and AP continued to
lease an increasing number of wires after that point, until within fifteen
years the bulk of AP's service was carried on such facilities.

The AP operation in 1877 (based on interviews with members of the
NYAP organization) was described in Harper's Magazine of that year as
follows.

> It collects news primarily for its own seven members,
> taking for the use of all a common dispatch, narrating con-
> gressional proceedings and any event of general interest, and
> reducing the cost to each by dividing between all the expenses
> of reporting and telegraphing. . . . It now sells news at stipu-
> lated rates to over 500 other papers published in every part
> of the continent.
> In well populated regions of the United States sub-
> associations are formed which give the local papers fuller
> details on local affairs than more distant papers would require;
> and in sparcely settled districts, where news items are not
> frequent enough to warrant the appointment of regular agents,
> the telegraph operators are authorized to employ men of ability
> in the interest of the association whenever any calamity, dis-
> turbance or excitement occurs. [26]

Melville E. Stone, AP's general manager from 1893 to 1921, describes the
type of news treatment used by AP between 1848 and 1882.

> All this while the Association had confined its energies
> to the gathering and distribution of what is known among news-
> papermen as "routine news"--shipping, markets, sporting,
> Congressional reports, and the "bare bones" of a day's
> happenings. The owners of the great metropolitan dailies who
> controlled it preferred to hold the management in leash so
> that they might display enterprise with their special reports
> of the really interesting events. The smaller papers, which
> were wholly dependent upon the Association for general news,
> could not afford extensive special telegrams, and therefore
> desired the organization to make comprehensive reports of
> everything. [27]

In 1880 evening newspapers again outnumbered AM's, and the way
was opened with this vast, untapped market for press associations wanting

to cater to PM's. In that year AP served only 355 newspapers (228 morn-

ing and 127 evening) of a total of 971 daily newspapers in the United States.

AP's dominance in the news-gathering field (in spite of serving only 36.6

per cent of the U.S. dailies) is attributable to its affiliation with the giant

Western Union and its position at the Atlantic cable head. In 1881, how-

ever, millionaire John W. Mackay underwrote the new Postal Telegraph

Company and two years later, Mackay and James Gordon Bennett, Jr.,

founded the Commercial Cable Company. Potential AP competitors had a

partner in these Western Union competitors.

In 1882 William Henry Smith replaced Simonton as AP general agent,

and the United Press appeared,[28] constituting a merger and reorganization

of the old American Press Association and the National Associated Press

Company, both of which had limped along after the demise of their earlier

telegraphic partners. In addition to having the backing of a telegraphic com-

petitor to Western Union and having the impetus of national organization and

a background of press work in the APA and NAPC, the old United Press was

firmly supported by several established evening metropolitan newspapers

in the East and Midwest, or by AM competitors of AP members. The group

included, for example, the Boston Globe, the Philadelphia Public Ledger,

the New York Daily News, the Chicago Herald, and the Detroit News.

Within three years UP's news service was fully as complete and as ac-

curate as AP's (with the possible exception of foreign news), and its

membership was expanding rapidly.

Although competition threatened AP, it still had one bargaining point:

its incoming flow of foreign news. The NYAP still controlled the transatlantic cable head in the United States, even though the Commercial Cable Company was soon to threaten this dominance and duplicate NYAP's reception of foreign news. The NYAP, however, had still another card up its sleeve: mutual assistance agreements with foreign news agencies. The Havas-Wolff-Reuters agreement of 1859 had given Reuters North America. The British agency, however, could bargain with AP for control of the United States, since the former was concerned primarily with Canada as the object of British cultural propaganda. Thus the agreement in 1872 between Reuters and AP (at least the New York City organization) for an exchange of news and respective territorial autonomy did not damage the British and became a valued possession first to the NYAP, and secondarily to the entire Associated Press confederation. Three years later a similar agreement linked AP with Havas, the principal supplier of news (under the 1859 cartel arrangement) to the South and Central American neighbors of the United States. Havas received assurances of exclusive operation in Latin America, and the NYAP received the all-important exchange of news arrangement with the French agency. By 1887 these three agencies, plus Wolff, completed a formal cartel arrangement which confined AP to the continental United States but gave it access to the news reports of the three foreign news agencies.[29]

The NYAP, therefore, remained the pivotal organization in the AP confederation having news-exchange agreements with foreign agencies, controlling the cable head and controlling news coverage in some important Eastern cities. At this juncture with regional demands increasing and competition on the rise, the NYAP could see its best interests served by working both sides of the street: keep the AP organization fragmented so that its

own control would prevail and maintain sufficient client following and news

report sales to turn a large profit. WAP members, on the other hand,

held out for a unified national organization which would assume control of

these NYAP assets in the name of all American journalists. This, WAP

said, was the only way to combat the UP threat. While the NYAP played

the AP against itself to mitigate the threat of the WAP proposal, it was

also working another street on the other side of town. It sought a secret

mutual assistance agreement with the old United Press, using as its strongest

bargaining points its foreign cartel agreement and its relatively large domes-

tic news-gathering organization. The NYAP, by far the most conservative

of the AP organizations, feared that any upheaval might spell disaster, and

thus it wanted to avoid conflict with UP while the more vigorous and liberal

WAP wanted to unify and kill off UP. Western Union, as the third party in

the 1867 reorganization of AP, sided with WAP, hoping that UP's demise

would also kill Mackay's Postal Telegraph Company, a potential threat to

Western Union's dominance.

William Henry Smith, coming to the NYAP after a stay with WAP as

manager, understood the westerners' position and presented it to the New

Yorkers' along with Western Union's threat to abandon the NYAP in deference

to the WAP's unification proposal. The New Yorkers could see that they had

only one choice. To take either the active, defiant role or the passive, non-

committal role would have angered many, perhaps all, parties involved; a

compromise was called for, consisting of a joint committee to direct AP's operations. The committee included two NYAP members, two WAP members, and a chairman chosen from the NYAP. Lasting ten years (until 1892), this arrangement continued to favor NYAP dominance and to advance NYAP's goals of peaceful, if underhanded, resolution of the UP problem. This joint proprietory smoke screen was lifted by the WAP in 1892 as shall be seen in the next period.

3. Period Summary

The similarities between AP business activities and relations with the government and those of established institutions in this country are striking during this period. In the industrial sector, the period was dominated by combinations and trust empires, welded together by contracts, secret agreements, mergers, and absorptions. If immediate satisfaction could not be attained through cooperation or sheer force of power, mercenary, cutthroat competition or the pulling of political strings eventually brought the weaker party to its knees. Industry's law of "survival of the fittest," had as its corollary: cooperation with others and help from politicians make one more fit.

The conservative NYAP, for the most part, held the greatest power among the wire services during this period. Its support, as a growing industrial empire, was derived from agreements with the growing Western Union and the large foreign news agencies and from control over the transatlantic cable head, many wealthy eastern newspapers, and many growing regional Associated Press organizations, although these regional organizations were not always easily controlled. The NYAP operated successfully

from a position of power, vis-a-vis the more liberal WAP, giving in
slightly on small points in order to maintain strength on the broader level.
The New Yorkers met competition from both WAP and the old UP with
conciliation, secret agreements, and special favors, but always from a
position of growing strength. Although AP's cutthroat dismemberment
of competition came shortly after the end of the present period, these de-
ployments of force and negotiations for support indicate NYAP's desire to
survive in the business jungle and evidence NYAP's resemblance to other
business enterprises at this time.

The period is also marked by a lack of political action in the public
interest, despite many provocations in both the political and economic
spheres. Dual federalism held off public utility and antitrust action for
the most part, and congressional investigation of NYAP-Western Union
ties was satisfied by General Agent Simonton's assertion of the rights of
AP private property, the naturalness of mutual assistance contracts, and
the unmonopolistic character of AP's operation.

The wires however, had one unique source of strength throughout
this and other periods. Whether the industrialists and politicians dominated or were under attack from reformers, the news report was increasingly an interesting and salable commodity because of such news, and the
wires gained added strength and institutional stability from such a commodity, regardless of environmental institutions' ups and downs.

In 1893 a thorough reorganization of the American wire services
occurred and with it the start of the wires' modern period of technological

growth, relative stability, and increasingly untroublesome competition. This modern period is described in Chapter III.

Footnotes

[1]Op. cit. for all except Lee's The Daily Newspaper in America
(New York: The Macmillan Company, 1937). Because of the numerous
references made in this study to AP's Annual Volumes, the author will
employ an abbreviated citation which distinguishes between the Illinois or
New York corporation and notes the volume number, year, and pages.

[2]Henry Steele Commager and Samuel Eliot Morison, The Growth
of the American Republic (5th ed.; New York: Oxford University Press,
1962), I & II; Samuel Eliot Morison, An Hour of American History (Rev.
ed.; Boston: Beacon Press, 1960): Richard Hofstadter, Great Issues in
American History (New York: Vintage Books, 1958), I & II, and American
Civilization: A History of the United States, Wesley M. Gewehr, Donald C.
Gordon, David S. Sparks, Roland N. Stromberg, and Herbert A. Crosman,
eds. (New York: McGraw-Hill Book Company, 1957).

[3]Sidney Kobre, Foundations of American Journalism (Tallahassee:
Florida State University, 1958), p. 130.

[4]Ronald R. Fett, America's Role in International News Exchange:
A Study of the AP, UP, INS, and "Voice of America" Since World War II
(Urbana, Ill.: unpublished University of Illinois Master's Thesis, 1949), p. 1.

[5]Mott, op. cit., pp. 215-216.

[6]Emery, op. cit., p. 217ff.

[7]Mott, op. cit., p. 243.

[8]Emery, op. cit., pp. 214, 219-221.

[9]For a discussion of the "Libertarian tradition" and a comparison of
it with other press theories, see Fred S. Siebert, Theodore Peterson, and
Wilbur Schramm, Four Theories of the Press (Urbana, Ill.: University of
Illinois Press, 1956), esp. pp. 39-71. For the "contextual" relationships
between Libertarianism and the broader philosophic environment, see Jay W.
Jensen, Liberalism, Democracy and the Mass Media (Urbana, Ill.: unpublished University of Illinois Ph.D., thesis, 1957), esp. pp. 74-106.

[10]The six morning newspapers originally forming the NYAP (and their
founding dates) were: one political paper, the Express (1836); two mercantile papers, the Courier and Journal (merged in 1829) and the Journal of
Commerce (1827); and three penny papers, the Sun (1833), the Herald (1835)
and the Tribune (1841). A seventh morning paper, the Times, was included
in the NYAP at its founding in 1851. It was the fourth penny paper in the organization.

[11]This section on the telegraph industry and the press is based on Robert L. Thompson's Wiring a Continent (Princeton: Princeton University Press, 1947), esp. Chapters 14, 22, and 30.

[12]Ibid., pp. 220-221.

[13]Unesco, op. cit. (1953), pp. 11-12.

[14]Unesco reports that the first "cheap" newspapers in France were Emile de Girardin's La Presse and Dutacq's Le Siecle, both founded in 1836. Cheap newspapers came to Great Britain in 1855. Ibid., pp. 9, 11.

[15]Llewellyn White and Robert D. Leigh, "The International News-Gatherers," Mass Communications, Wilbur Schramm, ed. (2nd ed., Urbana, Ill.: University of Illinois Press, 1960), p. 77.

[16]Alexander Jones, Historical Sketch of the Electric Telegraph: Including Its Rise and Progress in the United States (New York: G. P. Putnam, 1852), pp. 136-137, 139.

[17]Quoted in Gramling, op. cit., p. 39.

[18]Paraphrased and summarized from Rosewater, op. cit., pp. 88-91.

[19]Unfortunately, the literature does not record conclusively and with agreement the number of clients for the NYAP during its early years. Several sources, including objective ones, leave the impression, however, that NYAP subscribers probably exceeded two hundred. It must be remembered that most of the clients (as well as all of the members in New York City) were morning newspapers, since the news report was geared to AM deadlines and production problems.

[20]Representatives at the Indianapolis meeting were from: the Louisville Courier and Journal, St. Louis Republican, Chicago Tribune, Detroit Free Press, Cleveland Herald and Leader, Pittsburgh Commercial, Dayton Journal, Cincinnati Gazette and Commercial, and the "Indianapolis papers." (Rosewater, op. cit., p. 114, quoting from the 1876 Western Associated Press Report.) Only western Pennsylvania was included in the WAP. Eastern Pennsylvania, as represented by the Philadelphia Public Ledger, remained loyal to the NYAP.

[21]Paraphrased and summarized from Rosewater, op. cit., p. 118.

[22]Quoted in ibid., pp. 120-121.

[23]Lee, op. cit., p. 508.

[24]William F. Swindler, "The AP Anti-Trust Case in Historical Perspective," Journalism Quarterly, XXIII (March, 1946), p. 45.

[25]Rosewater, op. cit., p. 165.

[26]William H. Rideing, "The Metropolitan Newspaper," Harper's Monthly, LVI (December, 1877), pp. 55-56.

[27]Stone, op. cit., p. 210.

[28]This United Press organization is commonly referred to by journalism historians as "the old United Press" to avoid confusing it with the United Press Associations, founded by E. W. Scripps in 1907.

[29]Before the turn of the century, AP was attempting to get out from under the territorial confinement of this agreement. The next chapter reveals that in 1934 AP was able to break the cartel agreement completely and thereby to open the way for its own international service twenty years after Scripps' UP had made the leap.

Chapter III

WIRE-SERVICE HISTORY: MODERN COMPETITION AND TECHNOLOGY

> ...civilizations are not static con-
> ditions of societies but dynamic
> movements of an evolutionary kind.
> They not only cannot stand still,
> but they cannot reverse their direc-
> tion without breaking their own law
> of motion.
> -- Toynbee (1935)

Like the larger human system Toynbee refers to in his A Study of
History, the American wire services were to progress both despite and because of competition and internal strife. In this chapter, the history of wire
services in the United States is continued from 1893 up to the present day.
The section on Discussion and Conclusions at the end of this chapter summarizes material found in both Chapters II and III.

D. National Organization and the Rise of Competition: 1893-1914

1. Social and Cultural Environment

The absence of any degree of ideological influence since the end of
the Civil War had only increased the need for an ideological reappraisal of
gigantic institutional power. Various third parties appeared early in the
1890's to expose social ills and give voice to one or another of the increasingly apparent reform movements in the country. Some reforms were even
very drastic in the increasingly conservative American climate, having
been borrowed from European socialism or communism. The Democratic
party in 1896 assimilated some of the Populist party's platform, but did

so principally in an attempt to regain political power rather than to carry out the Populist reforms. A brief and intoxicatingly glorious war with Spain, however, intervened, diverting Americans' attention from their domestic problems. No national figure could tackle these problems again until Theodore Roosevelt abruptly became President in 1901.

The paradox of the Roosevelt "progressive era" is that the house cleaning stayed within horizontal layers of government with many federal, state, and local reformers working in isolation. These progressives, and those of the next two decades, were simply adhering to the contradictory Populist notion that liberal, even Socialist, reforms could best be conducted at the local level, i.e., under the states' rights banner. The notion had its limitations if a thorough revamping of the American life style was to be accomplished. Fragmented, spotty, and uncoordinated, the Populist-bred reform movement fell far short of the needed adjustments.

Yet despite the U.S. Supreme Courts' continued dual federalism to protect what it saw as the economic mandate written into the U.S. Constitution, some antitrust litigation was successful, the Pure Food and Drug Act was passed, and the Hepburn Act strengthened the Interstate Commerce Commission. There did seem to be a gradual, plodding drift to liberal reform in federal action which transcended the more radical give-and-take of a "crash-program" ideology versus self-interested institutions. On the other side, however, there was an internationalism about Roosevelt which rewrote "manifest destiny" in the language of neighborhood imperialism. While "trust-busting" at home, he built a political trust abroad at the expense of Latin Americans.

Roosevelt observed tradition, declined a third term, and left the Republican progressives and old guard at each other's throat. A Democratic progressive, Woodrow Wilson, pledged himself to more reform (by now, a popular political slogan and a guarantee of election victory) and won in 1912. The Democrats, grateful to have both a winner in Wilson and a strong popular platform for a change, moved quickly to solidify their gains, producing: the lowest tariff since the Civil War, ratification of the income tax amendment, the Clayton Antitrust Act which favored labor, and the Federal Reserve Act to improve the banking system and seek a degree of regulation of the national economy. But war again intervened. Many reform measures had to be scuttled; war demands swung emphasis back to institutional potentials and output; the Democrats were caught short of full entrenchment with an unrealized peacetime program and an unrealistic and short-lived plea for U.S. neutrality.

2. Wire-Service History

The secret NYAP-UP alliance produced the third and final major nineteenth-century reorganization of the Associated Press. Suspicions of such a connection were aroused when western AP editors found their own AP news dispatches appearing in competing newspapers under the UP logotype. An investigation disclosed a web of news-exchange agreements and interlocking stock arrangements which essentially was causing western AP members to work against themselves. The most flagrant of the NYAP-UP abuses had newspapers paying large sums to the competing wire service

(e. g. , AP member paying UP) to guarantee that the local competitor newspapers would not receive the competing news report.

The WAP, humiliated by and indignant about the findings, summarily assumed full control of the AP organization, announced the establishment of a national wire service headquartered in Chicago, and sought inclusion of all existing AP associations, except the NYAP. At the same time the WAP, which now had attained its long-sought vested interest and unique assets, conducted discussions with the NYAP and UP in an effort to arrive at a satisfactory cartel arrangement which would protect WAP's new-found power. By assuring UP that it now spoke for the entire AP organization, the WAP infuriated NYAP members, who saw their dominance in AP slipping away. The prospect of losing AP power brought internal struggle among NYAP members over the group's next move. The New York Sun and Tribune finally took matters into their own hands and bolted the AP organization, affirming full allegiance to the UP. While UP waited for the rest of the NYAP members to make up their minds, it held WAP at bay on the cartel proposal. The latter, impatient with both NYAP and UP and eager to proceed with its national plans, conferred with regional AP organizations and secured tentative agreement for merger into a national organization. In September of 1892, the national organization was completed and steps were taken to secure AP's incorporation under Illinois law. The first stockholders meeting of the new AP firm was held in December, the same month in which the remaining NYAP members joined UP.

Later that month, the new national Associated Press and United Press reached a cartel agreement (pressed by AP for its own protection) staking out

territorial sovereignty (UP's was east of the Appalachians and north of
Virginia), calling for an exchange of one-half of each company's capital
stock, exchanging directors, dividing the news-gathering function, and
agreeing to exchange all news. It is interesting to note that now the reorganized WAP was the conservative group, attempting to avoid open conflict, while UP assumed the liberal stance, having nothing to lose by full-
scale war and everything to gain. Within a matter of weeks, UP was
raiding AP's territory, signing up client-newspapers for its news report.
It felt its assigned territory was too small. But on the other hand, AP's
quick reorganization had been a shock to its system. Newspapers were
apprehensive initially about affiliating with either organization, fearing
the prospect of reparations if they ultimately found themselves tied to the
loser. Melville E. Stone, named general manager of AP in July, 1893,
describes AP's secondary position in the field in 1893 caused by this ap-
prehension.

> (AP's) outlook was certainly not inviting. Against them
> was arrayed the wealth of the entire Eastern journalistic field
> and they had apparently been cut off from all relations with the
> foreign news agencies. There were but sixty-three members.
> None was very rich and several were not even well-to-do.
> And three or four were under well-grounded suspicion of dis-
> loyalty. [1]

Although UP had been the aggressor, AP soon found its vested interests
not large enough to avoid conflict, that is, it lacked sufficient newspaper
support and doubted its continued participation in the world news agency
cartel. AP, therefore, declared unconditional war on UP in 1893 and sent
Stone to London to try to regain a place in the world cartel. Contrary to

rumors that UP had taken over NYAP's place in the cartel, Stone was able

to sign for the AP. This development was enough to convince many pre-

viously uncommitted editors of AP's ultimate invincibility; AP's ranks grew

quickly.

Stone relates the motives of those in charge of the AP when war was

declared on the UP.

> My friends felt it unsafe to leave so important a business
> under a privately owned, money-making control. We took it
> for granted that the need of an intelligent, well-informed elec-
> torate in a self-governing people must be admitted. * * * This
> business of news gathering and purveying had fallen into private
> and mercanary hands. Its control by three men was quite as
> menacing as that of the governmental autocrats of ages agone.
> * * * A national cooperative news-gathering organization owned
> by the newspapers and by them alone, selling no news, making
> no profit, paying no dividends, simply the agent and servant of
> the newspapers, was the thing. * * * This was the dream we
> dreamed. [2]

This romanticized version seems to overlook the fact that AP and its clients

had to fight or die. Although they held the key to foreign news coverage,

they were still a minority of the American press. (See Table 13 of Appendix

B and membership totals below for a comparison.) Also, there was no as-

surance that Reuters, Wolff, and Havas would continue indefinitely to recog-

nize them as the international representative of American journalism. A

later AP general manager, Kent Cooper, looks back to 1893 and comments.

> The new organization planned to take into its member-
> ship every existing newspaper in the country. * * * There
> was then no patriotic motive for establishing a truly united
> nation. This unity developed without the members of the new
> association ever having thought of it. What they wanted to do
> was to kill the privately owned United Press, and they did. [3]

With war declared, no territory was sacred and each wire raided the

opposition's camp seeking members. The confusion of two small agencies

scrambling for national dominance was considerable during 1893, but by
the end of 1893 AP had begun to emerge as the stronger of the two. Two
factors seemed to make this so: (1) AP's extensive coverage of the Russo-
Japanese War beginning in 1894 demonstrated AP's eagerness to cover
difficult news events, and (2) AP's financial potential and actual operating
base was broader than UP's, as Stone explains.

> The members of the Associated Press promptly
> assembled and subscribed to a large guaranty fund to
> provide for the deficits, while the four or five New York
> papers behind the United Press were compelled to con-
> tribute in like manner in order to hold their clients to any
> degree of allegiance.[4]

The following figures from AP's Annual Volumes of that time indicate the
extent to which AP's membership and financial support increased during
the crucial six-year period of the conflict:

Date	AP Clients and Members	AP Stockholders
Dec. 13, 1892	9	9
March 16, 1893	63	
Aug. 1, 1893	207	
Feb. 14, 1894		90
Dec. 13, 1896	381	124
Feb. 1, 1895	397	132
May 13, 1896	418	
May 7, 1897	685	171
May 18, 1898	709	176

On April 7, 1897, United Press declared bankruptcy and discontinued its
wire service. The deciding factor seems to have been AP's incoming
foreign news, both from the cartel and through its own facilities. The
AP management was jubilant over the victory, as the following board of
directors statement in its 1897 report to the members indicates.

It is our privilege and pleasure. . . to announce that
the ideal of the Associated Press has been accomplished.
It now includes in its loyal membership all the established
newspaper properties of the country, with comparatively few
exceptions. And it is a matter for mutual congratulations
that the contest which has for nearly four years divided the
press of the country has been brought to a conclusion which
already commands general acceptance as permanently assuring the best interests of the whole American press. [5]

When UP died, AP's directors provided AP memberships for all

previous UP newspapers, regardless of existing AP members' franchise

rights.[6] But some longstanding AP members resented the abridgment of

their rights after having faithfully and expensively supported AP during the

hard fight, bringing legal action against AP for alleged breach of contractual

provisions. Most of these suits were settled in AP's favor, but a few long-

time AP members left the organization as a result of the policy. Most

former AP members stayed with AP because there were only weak alter-

native wire services and because AP vigorously demonstrated its value to

newspapers the following year with extensive coverage of the Spanish-

American War. The war was a newspaperman's delight being close at

hand, not particularly dangerous for the nation, and a source of great

interest and emotion for the reader. AP commissioned special boats,

detailed a detachment of correspondents to the scene, relieved AP's assist-

ant general manager, Charles S. Diehl, from office responsibilities to

devote full time to directing the coverage operation, and became journal-

istically entrenched in the post-UP war years with a blaze of journalistic

enterprise.

Only the New York Sun held out against the AP in the New York area,

relying on its own Laffan News Bureau, created in 1888 to supplement the

Sun's UP news service. When UP disappeared, Laffan became one AP

opponent, although a small one. Others were established for evening

papers by E. W. Scripps. Scripps had been a staunch supporter of UP,

but found himself without a national and international news wire with UP's

demise. AP offered to accept some of Scripps' newspapers, but not all

of them, into membership. Scripps saw a need for an afternoon wire

service, convinced that AP had never altered its original morning-news-

paper bias. The biggest factor, however, was Scripps' future newspaper

expansion plans and the restrictions the AP franchise rights would impose

upon these plans. Joe Alex Morris, a former foreign editor and a his-

torian for the new United Press Associations, explains Scripps' motives.

> Perhaps more important was the fact that (Scripps)
> intended to start a score or so of newspapers and he was
> bitterly opposed to the Associated Press policy of granting
> exclusive franchises to member newspapers. If he were
> a member of the agency, this policy would prevent him--
> except under special circumstances--from becoming a
> competitor of an established Associated Press newspaper,
> which was what he intended to do in a number of cities. [7]

Scripps, therefore, organized or took control of three regional news-

gathering and distributing organizations: Scripps-McRae Press Associa-

tion, for midwestern newspapers, founded in 1897; Scripps News Asso-

ciation, for Pacific Coast newspapers, also founded in 1897, and Publishers

Press Association, an independent eastern agency with which Scripps se-

cured news-exchange agreements in 1898. Scripps reorganized these three

agencies in 1907 under the name of United Press Associations and named

Roy Howard general manager the following year. This new UP became AP's

first national competition since the decline of the old UP in 1897.

In spite of the vacuum of national opposition to AP, many small regional or special news agencies, such as Laffan, operated throughout this period, and the AP in order to protect what it hoped would be a closed national monopoly prohibited the AP members from exchanging news with these smaller outsiders. Laffan was considered particularly "antagonistic" to AP because of its former affiliation with the old UP and its present tie with the New York Sun, the only truly belligerent New York newspaper. The Chicago Inter-Ocean, disregarding AP warnings, continued to receive Laffan news reports and sued AP for breach of contract when the latter cut off its news report in 1898. The case reached the Illinois Supreme Court in 1900, where AP was held to be affected with the public interest and was enjoined from refusing service to any newspaper, under this quasi-public utility construction, which could afford to pay the weekly assessments. In effect, AP was at the mercy of a court which had previously been impressed by Munn v. Illinois (1877), in which the federal courts upheld the Illinois General Assembly's attempt to regulate private business concerns in the public interest. Since AP's charter was granted by the State of Illinois, regulation of the wire could be imposed by either the legislature or by judicial construction if the wire's operations were held to constitute a business in which the public has a definite and positive interest. This finding was, indeed, the court's understanding of AP.

AP was not disturbed about payment to the Inter-Ocean of $40,500 in damages for breach of contract, but it did worry about its future control over its own organization. If, as the Illinois Supreme Court had held, AP was a public utility in the eyes of the incorporating governmental unit,

then governmental regulation was inevitable, and it might not stop with

determining AP's membership. Regulations could extend to shaping the

news report, censorship for political reasons, propaganda, and so forth.

First and foremost, however, in the AP directors' minds was the

possibility of losing control over AP's operations. The board spoke of

the decision's damage to journalism and of AP's innocence with regard

to Illinois' incorporation laws.

> The scheme of organization of The Associated Press,
> adopted in 1892, . . . was intended to be a scheme of coopera-
> tion which would at once call forth the best energies of the
> management, bring into membership strong, healthful news-
> papers, and put under close check all of the agencies employed
> for the collection and distribution of information to be published.
> There was no law in existence in Illinois or elsewhere in
> 1892, which . . . was precisely adapted to our needs. Under
> the circumstances, an incorporation was effected under the
> general laws of Illinois, and an earnest effort was made to
> bring the Association in harmony with its provisions. [8]

New York State, in the meantime, had enacted an incorporation

law specifically for membership organizations, the implication in the litera-

ture being that AP had lobbied for its passage and that its final wording was

singularly aimed at securing AP incorporation in New York. An amendment

to the law, passed in Albany within two years after the 1900 Illinois Supreme

Court decision, exempted such membership corporations in New York State

from being considered a public utility by the state courts. The connection

between this amendment and requests from AP representatives is obvious

and open in the AP records.

In any event, AP moved to New York City in 1900 after an absence

from that city of only eight years, received a corporation charter, and began

delivering its news service from the Western Union office on October 1,
1900. For the next fourteen years, AP's operation proceeded without
observable difficulty. Opposition arose in the form of two rivals, but AP
was serving 801 newspapers in 1910 and was well ahead of competition in
delivering a complete and factual service. Both competitors, as will be
noted in a moment, were national in origin and potentially a real threat to
AP. But it is interesting to note that AP's management had come to real-
ize after 1897 that its "dream" of a national, all-inclusive wire-service
cooperative was never to materialize, regardless of how many opposing
wire services it crushed as it had the old United Press. Although AP could
count among its membership most of the wealthy and powerful daily newspapers in the United States after 1897, it could never entice more than 20
or 30 per cent of the total daily newspapers to its ranks during this period,
nor could it effectively keep new wire-service competitors from appearing
on the scene. Scripps stepped in, for example, immediately after the
death of the old UP, and other agencies were constantly appearing and dis-
appearing from the field. AP turned its attention to producing a better news
report, increasingly accepting the fact that it would probably always have
to share the wire-service field with other organizations.

One competitor, Scripps' United Press Associations which at the
1907 reorganization was serving 369 newspapers, had surpassed the 400
mark within three years and by 1914 (when AP had 909 members) listed
over 500 clients. Scripps' investment in one of two large and powerful
national newspaper chains both required and aided in the support of UP. A

similar situation occurred in the other great national chain, that of William

Randolph Hearst. Although more closely aligned with AP's organization

than Scripps (Hearst held more AP memberships than any other publisher

and at one time even attempted to gain control of AP through a proxie

battle), Hearst still faced two major problems with AP: (1) like Scripps, he

could not secure AP memberships for all of his newspapers, and (2) he

was not content to receive the dull, objective AP news report. He wanted

color, human interest, special assignments, etc. Thus, in 1909 Hearst

inaugurated International News Service for morning papers and National

Press Association for evening papers. Two years later the two were merged,

making INS responsible for both cycles. In 1917, the cycles again were split,

the new Universal Service handling the AM news report and INS moving the

evening report. But again in 1928 the two sides of the wire were merged

under the INS logotype, and Universal was given Hearst's supplementary and

special services.

3. Period Summary

For two historical periods, wire-service development has closely

resembled developments in the social and cultural environment at large.

The cyclical alternation between institutional growth and ideological read-

justment had strongly favored the former during most of the two periods, and

wire-service growth, also, appeared continuous and inclusive of business

devices found in the environment. (Although the question of when institution-

alization of wire services occurred will be discussed in response to a specific hypothesis at the end of this chapter, it is worthwhile to note here that the process appears to have occurred during the last decade of the nineteenth century. Previous similarity to actual environmental institutions derives from the wires' institution-like structure which, while involved in a maturation process, differed from a real institution only by degrees of size and influence.)

Between 1893 and 1914, however, the progressive movement in society sought out AP through the Illinois Supreme Court's decision that the wire was vested with a public interest and must conduct its operations as a utility. But AP, fresh from a glorious victory over a strong rival and still basking in the light of relative national dominance, evaded the reform movement by another legalistic, contractual dodge, very reminiscent of its earlier "drive for stability."

Three factors set AP apart from its environment in this period: (1) the persistent rise of competition continually postponed AP's realization of a complete national dominance--a condition which it still has not attained; (2) the rapidity with which important environmental news event occurred during the period to give AP and its competitors an opportunity to strengthen their new institutional position through their unique and "untouchable" product; and (3) the ascent to institutional status early in this period which gave the wires an impetus as newcomers to such a position for resisting anti-institutional trends in the environment.

The drive for stability in the preceding period had, in fact, attained that stability by midway through the present period, giving renewed strength

to the wires' claim of importance and immunity in a democratic society.
Far beyond 1914, the magic words of "freedom of the press," "governmental intervention," "censorship," etc., allowed the wires, particularly
AP, to avoid the reforms started elsewhere in American society before
1914 and picked up again in new forms in 1929. Throughout, moreover,
the situation is complicated by the environmental forces of news events
which increasingly entrench the wires' position and fail to influence directly
their structure and function.

E. International Organization and the Technological Impetus: 1914-1964

1. Social and Cultural Environment

The final period of this study encompasses a half-century of fast-
moving events both in and out of journalism. Necessity dictates a brief
treatment of both the wires and their environment, permitting the exposition of only the few dominant themes of each.

World War I dominates the start of this period with considerable
pro-Allied sentiment in the United States. President Wilson actively
sought U.S. pacifism, but was backed to the wall by repeated Allied and
Axis efforts to involve this nation. America's entry into the war, at first
based on motives of securing the peace and restoring human rights, became for Wilson, and Americans in general, a crusade with extremist
goals of hate the Huns, unconditional surrender, making the world safe
for democracy, etc. After the Americans rid themselves of disease abroad
in 1918, their fired-up superpatriotism led to a grand inquisition at home
which continued for several years.

Like the Civil War, World War I gave America a chance to begin again with a fresh slate on human relations and democratic government, but petty politics, an industrial boost from the war effort, new special interests, and a propensity for extracting reprisals at home and abroad obliterated high goals and ideology, turning the United States to a secure isolationism, turning down the "entangling" League of Nations, and beginning a purge of Socialists, Communists, Catholics, Jews, Negroes, foreigners, free opinion, and constitutional guarantees. Prosperity and a new institutional materialism gained acceptance. The war had increased incomes, spending, and the emphasis on material goods, and the Republicans swept into the White House on promises of isolationism and continued prosperity. President Harding allowed Americans to turn themselves inward again and forget the horrors of war, and he introduced policies of graft, contract favors to some big business and special interest favoritism, all of which were throwbacks to the post-Civil War era.

Under governmental protection, institutional forces in America were again dominated by big business, and now industry had the additional boost of access to wartime inventions. The depressed farmer and liberal reformer again raised their voices in objection as in the 1890's, but their effect was slight. Many reformers, particularly those with an artistic bent, even gave up in America emigrating to Europe in search of a more liberal, more diversified climate American reform, however, came quicker than most expected, prompted by the 1929 Depression.

Unlike the progressive movement of almost thirty years before, the new reform surge was allowed to run its course before war again intervened.

The new movement was definitely not a Populist one in that it included strong national programs which cut vertically through all levels of government. Industry, agriculture, and banking were restricted, antitrust cases increased, public works projects replaced private initiative, labor received some legal status, and welfare provisions for individuals of all ages were made. The economy was being rebuilt with federal controls as part of the super-structure. Franklin Roosevelt's "New Deal" was based on sections of the liberal ideology which sought mitigation of private institutional dominance and private individual deprivation via imposition upon society of the so-called welfare state. But for any ideological movement which is allowed to run its course, the means of operational realization themselves produce a degree of institutional dominance. Indeed, any ideological reform seeks to replace the dominance of one institution with that of another. And so, in the New Deal, private dominance was partially offset by a public dominance manifested in increased governmental controls and a mushrooming federal bureaucracy. But the ideological undercurrent prior to 1929 did have its chance in that year as no other has had in American history.

Perhaps the two most difficult problems facing the United States at the turn of the century were the farmers' constantly depressed condition and the Negroes' suppressed status. No reform movement, however lengthy, in this century has effectively solved these problems. The former is difficult because, although the nation continues to need farm commodities, the agrarian economic structure was replaced soon after the Civil War by an industrial one for directing the national business condition. The latter

elicits the most sacred and conflicting of America's ideological contrac-
tions: majority rule versus minority rights, the rights of private property
versus the rights of human beings, and federal intervention versus
sovereign states' rights.

World War II has erased isolationism as a tenable American
stance with the subsequent East-West cold war and a potentially powerful
United Nations serving as checks against its return. Administration
foreign policy has begun to replace domestic issues (except for the two
mentioned above) as dominant political and intellectual themes in the United
States. A postwar boom, based on wartime inventions, a war-fostered,
higher standard of living, and a postwar rearmament program, has again
allowed institutions to outstrip ideology, creating what C.P. Snow calls
"two cultures." An extended period of military development and improvement (nearly a quarter of a century since the start of World War II) has
made partners again of industry and government. Although certain reformist checks reduce graft and favoritism in governmental contracts and
operations to a large extent, materialism, negativism, and increasing
bigness are the hallmarks of the newest alignment. A rebirth of ideology
to adjust the so-called cultural lag seems imminent, but its precipitating
crisis is difficult to foresee, although it is increasingly ominous as the
power of institutions increases.

2. Wire-Service History

The year 1914 begins this final period because it was then that two
shakey, but eventually significant, innovations were made in wire-service

operation. One was the introduction of teletype transmission of news copy, and the other was a request from South America for an American news-service report and the resulting scramble to settle on an international operations policy.

Telegraph had remained essentially unchanged since its 1844 beginning in this country. While some minor improvements were made in equipment and a degree of operator proficiency had been introduced, news continued to be transmitted by dots and dashes which had to be converted into letters and words. Even the infrequent, limited use of radio prior to 1914 embodied the Morse or International codes. The system had attained an average speed of thirty-five words per minute, and widespread use of leased wires assured constant access to transmission facilities, but the human element continued to plague the wire services. The labor union movement had reached Western Union's operators, and wire-service telegraphers devoted the first decade and a half of this century attempting to secure, by demands and strikes, the same privileges for themselves. Moreover, the possibility of errors in transmission was prevalent, and the sheer number of operators needed to work the many sending and receiving points in the wire-service network made telegraphic transmission no small financial burden. (At least one operator was required in each city with a subscribing newspaper; two were employed where both cycles of the report were received. In addition to these men, operators had to man the sending stations on both trunk and regional wires.)

The teletype device, introduced in 1914 by AP for transmission on an experimental basis to newspapers within New York City, was simply a consolidation of a typewriter mechanism (in both sending and receiving stations) with a device for transmitting electrical impulses along connecting telegraph or telephone wires (or even through the atmosphere by radio). Early models were not dependable, but within a year UP was using a refined teletype outside New York City, and the race to convert Morse telegraph to teletype was on, to be completed in the mid-1930's. The innovation raised transmission rates to sixty words per minute, reduced operator manpower to a single sender for each trunk or regional wire, and permitted reception of a greater volume of cleaner, more uniform, and more immediately usable news copy in the newspaper office.

The four-party world news cartel had proved to be the protective shield by which AP attracted newspaper members and fought off the old United Press. In 1914 (and up to 1934) this cartel arrangement remained in effect, but the former AP asset became a source of intra-AP struggle and eventually a liability for the wire service. General Manager Stone, who had renewed the agreement in 1893 at a crucial time in AP's fight with the old UP, was convinced of the cartel's importance to AP. The young, ambitious AP traffic department chief, Kent Cooper, could see it only as a source of restriction to AP expansion and as a source of dubious news about America directed toward Europe and Latin America. Cooper later discussed the negative implications of the cartel.

> Tragically for our country . . . the restraints that The Associated Press so willingly accepted had placed the United States, as a nation, in an inferior position abroad, and the cartel knew it. Each member of it except the Associated Press was more or less responsible to and motivated by the government of its own country.

Not only did these three news agencies prevent The Associated Press from sending its news abroad, but correspondents of Reuters, Havas, and Wolff, stationed in the Associated Press office in New York, could and did pervert AP news into dispatches that misrepresented and disparaged America before the rest of the world.

I disliked the idea of the Associated Press having exclusive access to and being an outlet for the propaganda-tainted announcements of foreign governments, which in effect set The Associated Press up as the exclusive mouthpiece in America for these governments. [9]

Jorge Mitre, publisher of the wealthy Buenos Aires newspaper La Nacion, had become dissatisfied with the biased Havas treatment of early-World War I news. His discontent led him to ask AP for its direct service, as a more objective source of news. Stone automatically refused to consider the request because the cartel agreement gave South America exclusively to Havas. Cooper fumed about letting the opportunity for expansion slip away. After getting no AP reply, however, Mitre contacted UP. The United Press had become as complete a wire as AP, in many instances surpassing the stoggy, dull AP style with bright, human interest reporting and writing. Not bound by the cartel, and actually eager to extend its reporting facilities into the international field because of its competitor's cartel agreement, UP had no restrictions against beginning South American service, which it indeed did in 1916. INS, to a lesser extent, was also in the international field at this time, although Hearst's personal editorial comments on international affairs often closed foreign governments' doors to INS reporters.

Two years after UP moved into South America, Cooper, still fighting with Stone and the cartel, surveyed the Latin American situation, found anti-French German press influences strong throughout the continent,

and returned to New York to negotiate with the director of the war-weakened

Havas. Playing on the postwar anti-German French sentiments, Cooper

persuaded Havas to allow AP to serve South American papers. Further

foreign expansion for AP, however, had to wait until 1934 while UP service

made what headway it could internationally under the confining pressures of

growing world tension, a domestic Depression, and the growing threat or

promise of radio competition at home. UP's big South American benefactor,

the Buenos Aires La Prensa, was persuaded by UP's Roy Howard to take his

wire in competition with La Nacion's move to AP in 1918. La Prensa's

owners, the wealthy Paz family, asked and received from UP special detailed

European coverage at great expense to the paper. Stephen Vincent Benet,

telling the UP story in Fortune Magazine in 1933, explains how La Prensa's

special news demands brought new integrity to UP's principally human

interest, often sensationalistic, news service.

> Unipressers started flooding the South American wires
> with the drama, death, color, and romance of the War--the
> tried product, gobbled by newspaper readers from Massachu-
> setts to Oregon. There was only one difficulty. The South
> Americans didn't like it at all.
> They demanded terse truth, a truly informed international
> viewpoint, the underlying economic and social significance be-
> neath the rainbow paint. So UP reversed its policy and gave
> them what they wanted. With one hand it wrote and delivered
> the heart throbs and personalities for which North Americans
> clamored; with the other it filed an authoritative, sedate, and
> encyclopedic report for the countries south of the Canal.
> As La Prensa's authoritative news poured past the eyes
> of UP's wire editors, they themselves became interested.
> * * * Hesitantly they began to try out some of this sort of
> news on their clients in the U.S. They began to stress econom-
> ics as well as people, background as well as personalities,
> underlying significance as well as obvious drama. And . . .
> they educated themselves toward a broader point of view.[10]

UP service to European clients began in 1921 and in 1924 UP formed Acme Newspictures, a mailed-feature service to newspapers in the United States. United Press was moving in all directions to serve its growing number of subscribers, backed by the power and vigor of the huge Scripps-Howard organization. It remained the underdog in terms of U.S. newspaper clients, but its potential expansion appeared limitless by comparison with AP's.

The Associated Press, on the other hand, clung to many traditions which made it outdated in 1921 when Stone was replaced by his personal choice, Frederick Roy Martin. Not only were the administrators (except for Cooper) retaining vestiges of bygone days, but the bulky, slow-moving policy-making process which involved many publishers across the country could not keep up with the times. It was a major progressive step in 1915 when AP (under threat of possible antitrust action from U.S. attorney general) permitted its member to receive news reports from other agencies. The members, however, remained committed to giving their local news only to AP, and the franchise rights remained in effect. The news report was a stuffy, lack-luster, and unappealing thing to newspaper readers. AP could not decide whether sports constituted legitimate news. By-lines were forbidden on AP stories. Members squabbled over whether AP should serve the infant communications industry, radio. About three-fourths of AP's revenue went to Western Union without attempts being made to seek less expensive routes and to use competitive bidding. Progressive AP members argued for reform, and the old guard held back, wherever policy was made or discussed: on the board of directors, in the annual meetings, and within the administrative management.

Martin lasted four years as general manager, perpetuating Stone's managerial policies, but in 1925 he resigned and was replaced by Cooper whose chief claim to AP fame had been making good a promise to save $100,000 in transmission costs per year if given a free hand in his department. With Cooper at the helm, AP came alive with a spirit of growth and innovation which rivaled, and ultimately even surpassed, its UP competitor. AP led the way in wire-service expansion and technological development from 1925 to Cooper's retirement in 1948. Some problems had to be resolved by the membership (e.g., the membership franchise right, radio competition, etc.) and thus were out of Cooper's hands (although he freely expressed his opinion on them from time to time), but for the most part the AP after 1925 was Cooper's creation. Oswald Garrison Villard, a former AP director and editor of the New York Evening Post, criticized as editor of The Nation, Cooper's changes in AP policy in 1930.

> Melville E. Stone must be turning in his grave if he is aware of the kind of sob stuff that is now appearing in the Associated Press--banal and pathetic stuff of the kind to shame a college sophomore despite the fact that the rules of the AP urge "a simple narrative style" and deprecate fine writing.
> Mr. Kent Cooper . . . has to face an intense, rapidly growing, and successful competition from the virile and liberal United Press. He has broken with tradition after tradition of the service--the comic strips are his latest venture. So the Associated Press has long since abandoned its original conception of being a service devoted exclusively to the gathering of news; it is now engaged in the merchandising of purely amusement features. Side by side with a vast deal of really admirable and altogether praise-worthy reporting . . . it disseminates a line of trivial and often nauseating human-interest stores wholly devoid of any news value. [11]

Cooper, more a businessman than a newsman, saw the value of a loyal membership and staff and the need to buttress the organization against

possible future difficulties, e.g., economic recessions, members' loss of
the franchise rights, etc. He explains his progressive policies.

> I wanted members to take more pride in their Asso-
> ciated Press service so that they willingly would pay for the
> striking improvements I had planned. With more money, I
> could make The Associated Press a more attractive place
> for competent men to work. A well-rewarded staff would
> produce a better news service, which in turn would increase
> membership loyalty--indeed, such a firm loyalty that when
> the members lost their so-called exclusive franchise rights,
> as I then feared one day they surely would, not one of them
> would resign his membership because of that loss, since by
> that time the service might be so valuable as to be indis-
> pensable to them. [12]

The growth of American wire services, with AP generally the front-
runner, from 1914 to the present may be classified under four headings.

Membership
1. Rapid expansion of domestic and foreign newspaper clients.
2. AP nullification of the world cartel agreement (1934).
3. AP creation of foreign subsidiaries to facilitate news distribution--
   the Associated Press of Great Britain Ltd. (1932),
   The Associated Press of Germany (1932),
   La Prensa Asociada, Inc. in Latin America (1939). [13]
4. Formation of the Associated Press Managing Editors Association
   to improve the news report and to create more membership
   loyalty to AP (1933).
5. Revision of the AP assessment scheme to make payments among
   members more equitable (1922).
6. Stimulation of interaction with members and clients and of their
   loyalty by use of state and regional organizations and meetings,
   both in AP and UP.
7. Expansion of service to outlets in new media beginning with radio
   in which UP and INS took the lead (1935).

News Report
1. Establishment of complete, full-page market tabulations (1929).
2. Establishment of a balance between hard-core news reports and
   human interest writing (beginning in 1918 in both wires).
3. Introduction of interpretative reporting as a wire-service
   function (1950).
4. Introduction of photo service--
   a. mailed service (UP's Acme in 1924)
      (AP's Newspictures in 1928),

      b. wired photography (AP's Wirephoto in 1935)
                   (INS's Soundphoto in 1935)
                   (UP's Telephoto in 1936),
      c. wired facsimile (UP in 1953)
                   (AP's Photofax in 1955).
5. Improvement and expansion of coverage of special interest,
    specialized news fields (e.g., science, religion, medicine,
    the arts, farm and industrial news, sports, etc.)
6. Emphasis increasingly placed in governmental news, par-
    ticularly that originating in Washington, D.C.

Organization
1. Reduction of operating costs by prudent planning and innovation
    of new devices wherever possible.
2. Departmentalization of the wire-service operation to improve
    service and reduce costs.
3. Permission for unionization extended to reporters and operators.
4. Establishment of a pension program for employees (AP in 1918).

Technology (news collection and distribution)
1. Transmission speed increased--
    a. mail to wire,
    b. Morse to teletype (1914-1935),
    c. cable to radio,
    d. wired photography to wire facsimile,
    e. human to computer tabulation of statistics (1963).
2. Transmission distance increased--
    a. wire or cable to radio,
    b. radio to communications satellite.
3. Readiness of product for clients' use increased--
    a. teletype to teletypesetter (1952),
    b. wired photography to wired facsimile. [14]

Throughout this period, wire services have been at the scientific

fringe, innovating whatever developments would be useful to their operation,

sometimes even financing and urging scientific developments aimed at solv-

ing particular wire-service problems. Cooper's prodding of American

Telephone and Telegraph to create a device to send wired photographs is

an example of this, as is AP's establishment of experimental laboratories

in 1935 and of Press Association, Inc., in 1941 as a subsidiary to hold

patent rights for devices developed in the laboratories. As technology came

to the wires, so did the possibility of expansion into new mass communications media and into geographic areas of the globe previously difficult
to reach, if not for AP prohibited by the cartel.

There is no precise starting point for this dynamic new twentieth-
century growth pattern of the American wire services. Wars, as before,
provided reader interest, wire-service business, technological advances,
and the opening of foreign subscriber markets. But, at the same time,
technology and improvements in foreign coverage made possible better war
coverage and increased reader interest while increased membership provided the market for and financial support of such vast coverage undertakings.
Meanwhile a vast array of wartime and peacetime institutional developments
at home and abroad (e.g., a Great Depression, new types of political conditions and processes, the unique needs of radio and television, etc.) revised
the wires' image of what a news report should contain. Increasingly this revision has carved out for the wires a function of broker or shaper of mass
society's messages to itself.

Although wire services have progressed rapidly and ingressed deeply
into the social fabric since 1941, there is no reason to believe that these
trends have found culmination. The computer-teletypesetter linkage promises
to create increasing control by wires over the content of client-newspapers,
and, in turn, over the product consumed by the reader. High-speed writing,
editing, and routing of news stories by computers has gained only a foothold
in journalism at this writing Developments in facsimile, electro-chemical,
and computer-printer transmission are bound ultimately to supplant teletype

and teletypesetter alone because of the former's superior speeds, ease of handling, and fidelity. Finally, point-to-point and broadcast transmission will probably be replaced by the use of communication satellites because of the latters' freedom from the atmospheric disruptions which frequently plague signals transmitted parallel to the earth's surface or refracted by the ionosphere. The importance of these speculations lies in the fact that as specific aspects of wire-service operation today are considered in subsequent chapters, it must be remembered that whatever the wires' condition is now will probably be amplified many times technologically in the next few decades.

Organizational development of the wires in this final period requires special attention because of its implications for the wires' ingression into their social and cultural environment. Period IV (1893-1914) includes the rise of competition in the American wire-service field producing by the start of this period AP, UP, and INS in a national competition from two distinct viewpoints and within a dichotomous spectrum of organizational structures. AP has remained the cooperative news-gathering agency, making some of its decisions through the process of membership consultation and desiring only enough "profit" to provide a cushion against unforeseen future difficulties or expensive coverage situations. UP and INS, on the other hand, have continued as private agencies, serving client-newspapers as a grocer serves the housewife and hoping to turn a large profit for the private management. Each position accuses the other of being detrimental to American journalism. AP has said that UP and INS do not give the

editor a voice in policy decisions and are in business only to make a profit;
UP and INS said that AP's decision-making machinery is slow and conservative, producing a stodgy and impotent news report and that its club-
biness and restrictive membership regulations have resulted in factionalism,
loss of competitive spirit, and monopolistic practices in American journalism.

In point of fact, none of these accusations has, at the present, very
much validity. AP editors have had a decreasing role in the wire's decisions
regarding administration, innovation, and finances. (See Chapter IV for a
study of AP's changing power structure.) All wire services have come to
rely heavily on clients' usage and suggestions in determining the form and
content of their news reports. They go out of their way to seek editor
advice on the "product," e.g., the APME, state and regional meetings,
personal visits to newspaper offices, etc. Profits of any large scale are
unheard of in competing wire services; it is commonly accepted that UP
(and now United Press International) has not been a money maker for the
Scripps-Howard organization. Scripps describes the beginning deficit situation of UP.

> The early days would have been critical had it not been
> for the fact that I owned so many of the newspapers that were
> its clients that its financing was a simple matter. * * *
> I imagine that in founding the new United Press, the Scripps
> papers actually paid out several hundred thousand dollars more
> than they would have paid out had they been members of the
> Associated Press. However, notwithstanding these compara-
> tively large payments, I felt that the investment, bad as it was
> financially in one way, was a good one because it secures . . .
> freedom from the temptation of one huge monopoly. * * *
> It is quite possible that I am the only man in the country who
> could have performed this service. [15]

Although UP has become somewhat more solvent in recent years, unexpected coverage situations will always drain off large portions of the profits, and UP's policy of charging for its service what the market will bear necessarily makes it undersell AP's fixed pro-rata assessment in the many areas where the two compete vigorously for clients. INS had been in financial difficulty for several years and the disclosures before the Senate Foreign Relations Committee in 1963 of INS publicity involvements with right-wing Latin American governments[16] indicate the possible facts surrounding the INS demise in 1958 and assimilation by UP. Individuals in INS had been conducting a pro-rightist propaganda campaign. Discovery within the organization could have produced such chaos that restoration of INS's good name would have been impossible. More likely, however, UP uncovered the INS operation and "persuaded" INS officials to sell what was already a deficit wire service. In any event, UP, INS, and UPI have not been big profit makers. The number of administrators with five- and six-digit salaries in AP is about as large as those in UPI, and neither wire has much additional cream after these salaries and necessary costs have been skimmed off of the top.

UP's contention that AP's wire report is stodgy and slow moving is invalid in light of the repeated editor suggestions acted upon by AP to improve its report. Also, with the rise of independent administrators, AP's news coverage and distribution structures have become much more flexible. A subsequent discussion (see Chapter VI) will bring out editors' impressions of the wires' respective images. It will be asserted there that these impressions are based on traditional stereotypes rather than on actual news report conditions. The reports are very similar in every respect, whether one looks at content or form.

The one UP claim which was valid before 1945 concerns the restrictiveness of AP memberships. Loss of the so-called franchise right which Cooper had wanted to offset with loyalty and excellence came in 1945 in a decision of the United States Supreme Court. Although the United States v. Associated Press antitrust action of 1942-45 will be described in Chapter VI, it will suffice here to say that the liberal Chicago Sun, with New Deal backing, petitioned the U.S. Justice Department to enjoin AP from denying it AP membership on the grounds that such a denial (and the by-laws permitting such a denial) was a violation of the Sherman Antitrust Act. AP news was necessary to all newspapers desiring it, the Sun said, and the franchise right unduly restricted interstate trade and competition among newspapers and wire services. Both the New York City Federal District Court and the U.S. high court held for the government, and in 1946 AP was forced to permit unrestricted membership to newspapers. At the same time, but not because of the court's decision, AP broadened its definition of associate membership to include all radio and television outlets.

The net effect of the antitrust decision has been to improve the condition of all parties involved (although some old guard factions of the AP would probably disagree). Newspapers and broadcasting outlets now have a wider choice of news reports, and the two wire services are placed on an equal footing in terms of their competition. AP is no longer hampered in its domestic growth, and UP (and many newspapers) no longer must compete

with a closed group of monopolistic editors. (Evidence of this contention
is presented in Chapter VI.)

3. Period Summary

The interesting aspect of wire-service history in this most recent
period has been that the wires have continued to grow and thrive institu-
tionally, in large part due to their continuing coverage of institutional and
ideological struggles in the environment. The pre-1914 struggle for survival, the drive for economic and structural stability, and the 1890's acquisition of institutional status, led the wires to a point of equilibrium and
strength in 1914 which permitted them to feed on the developments (newsworthy and technological) in their environment, touched by the ideological
hand of the reformer only twice: the AP antitrust decision and the Senate
Foreign Relations Committee's disclosures regarding INS and UPI.

The paradox of this historical trend has been that the wires have
weathered large and small crises which have dealt devastating blows to
virtually every other institution and ideology in their environment, and they
have done so simply by telling their environment about itself and its crises.
In return, this relaying process has strengthened the wires as institutional
entities. In one important sense, therefore, this paradox sets wire services
apart from their environment--probably strengthened, but at least untouched,
by the ebb and flow of institutional and ideological interplay. They have
emerged as brokers of society's messages to itself.

Discussion and Conclusions

Implicit in the above brief accounts of the wires' social and cultural
environment is the notion, popular in some circles, of a cyclical thrust of
historical events. It is the notion of society's oscillation between institutional and ideological dominance, roughly equivalent to the Italian concept
of power (see, for example, Machiavelli, Pareto, and Mosca) as alternat-
ing between "lions" and "foxes." Although the author does not wish to argue
for the universal and exclusive validity of the so-called Italian school, or of
any other, he asserts that in the present study these notions serve as a useful framework for understanding many diverse historical occurrences easily
and for comparing wire-service history with that of its environment. Some
would argue that this oversimplifies the problem of historical understanding.
They would say that whatever the terms used (institutional-ideological,
lions-foxes, hawkers-heroes, or rentier-speculator), they cannot represent
between them all facets of history.

Although these persons may well have a valid criticism, they overlook
two considerations. First, the shortcomings of dichotomous alternatives
may be resolved in the future by refinements yielding various gradations or
continua, tending increasingly to be more realistic in their emphasis on the
relational-interactional trends interposed between the crude, alternative
peaks one is now forced to use. Second, an essential aspect of present
systems theory holds that throughout the cyclical swings of society, there
is a direction in which events move. Nothing is repeated in exactly the
same form and content, and each cycle accumulates for the social structure

and culture some new forms and contents from the dominant institutional
and ideological conditions through which the cycle has passed. Such a
scheme is consistent with the dictates of Toynbee and yields the types of
contextual, dynamic historical perspectives utilized by Emery, Park,
Jensen, and others cited in Chapter I.

This type of perspective, used throughout the preceding historical
account, is also the basis for Figure 1 (see next page), which summarizes
the cyclical trends of the wires and their environment from 1690 to 1964.
It should first be noted that Figure 1 has overcome the fragmenting effect of
historical periods. While specific periods are marked off in the figure, they
represent tendencies toward dominance or superordination, backed up by the
notion of relatively continuous cyclical motion, rather than by the notion of
discrete historical episodes.

One important feature of Figure 1 is immediately evident. Obviously,
the wire services were latecomers to the American scene in comparison with
other types of corporate or institutional phenomena. But whether one considers the beginnings of wire services to be 1811, 1848, 1856, or the 1890's,
he cannot help but note that the wires' historical, cyclical course has not
been comparable to that of their environment, except perhaps belatedly.
Environmental oscillations between ideological and institutional tendencies
toward dominance have been frequent and continual, but the institutional
(or quasi-institutional) dominance of wire-service activities was unremitting
up to 1945. This does not mean that wires have not taken on characteristics
of the broader environment. On the contrary, their pursuit of certain

Figure 1. Historical Ideological and Institutional Trends: 1690-1965

Social and Cultural Environment	American Wire Services
1690-1760 - Ideology & Institutions Growth of both under influence of many diversified internal & external influences & forces.	
1760-1790 - Ideology Fresh start after Revolution. Creation & direction of new styles of life.	
1790-1815 - Institutions Standardization & expansion of operation; establishment of operational rationales.	1811-1856 - Institution (Nprs.) Experimentation to improve news gathering; cooperative idea tried and made standard usage.
1815-1850 - Ideology & Institutions Institutional operations & rationales conflict; reforms advocated.	
1850-1861 - Ideology Conflicts & various reforms cannot be compromised or settled.	1856-1862 - Quasi-institution (Wires) Formalized NYAP breaks wires away from newspaper institution; separate growth begins.
1861-1865 - Institutions (Civil War)	
1865-1873 - Institutions (Postwar) Political-economic coalition brings out worst in both; industry replaces agriculture as dominant.	1862-1897 - Quasi-institution Vested interests protected; cartels & mutual assistance pacts signed; regional conflicts are prominent.
1873-1901 - Ideology & Institutions Political-economic extremes; conflict & disorder are prominent; reforms are called for in various sectors.	1897-1925 - Institution Real institution for first time in 1890's; new aggressive coverage (wars & abroad) gives wires' an important place; "quiet" competition begins.
1901-1914 - Ideology Progressive-Populist reforms started.	
1914-1918 - Institutions (World War I)	
1918-1929 - Institutions (Postwar) Old Pol.-Econ. coalition returns.	1925-1945 - Institution Technological, geographical, content, new-media growth is rapid.

Figure 1 (continued)

Social and Cultural Environment	American Wire Services

1929-1941 - Ideology & Institutions
  Welfare-state reforms create new,
    more powerful political institution.	

1941-1945 - Institutions (World War II)	

1945-1965 - Institutions (Postwar)
  New Pol. -Econ. coalition produces
    positive aid, militarism, material-
    ism, massive contracts, bigness
    in both.
	1945-1964 - Ideology & Institution
	  Above growth continues; concern
	    over wires' power grows; re-
	    forms are US v. AP & hearings
	    on INS & UPI deals with right-
	    wing regimes.

environmental characteristics and their utilization of environmental phenomena have, in fact, been the principal determinant of this continual institutional dominance.

In part, this long-standing, non-cyclical condition appears to be the result of the unique product or service offered by the wires. On the one hand, the wires' activities are protected from abridgment by the First Amendment to the U.S. Constitution, a protection which has successfully shielded the press in general from external interference and from internal breaks with tradition. On the other hand, the press thrives on opportunities to cover all types of ideological and institutional crises and conflict--the very phenomena which alter the environment. Wars, for example, have been occasions of great success or of further institutional entrenchment for the wires: the Mexican War led to the creation of the NYAP; the Civil War strengthened the NYAP and helped to create widespread regional AP organizations; the Spanish-American and Russo-Japanese wars entrenched the AP of Illinois and New York State, respectively; and World Wars I and II prompted international expansion and technological innovation. Thus, while other sectors of American society were undergoing agonizing reforms and crises, the wires remained aloof, becoming stronger rather than weaker in times of controversy simply because of their coverage of that controversy.

Two hypotheses from Chapter I are wholly or partially relevant to the historical accounts in Chapters II and III. Each will be discussed separately.

1. The wire services over time have attained the statue of a social
   institution, after having begun as a group effort within another
   social institution, the newspapers.

Verification of part of this hypothesis must await presentation of
material in Chapters IV and V, because of the diverse elements here defined as constituting a social institution. That definition is: a relatively
standard pattern of beliefs and actions directed at solving a unique problem
for society. Patterns of beliefs can be known only through their representation in the organization's statements and actions, since no reliable mea-
suring device of a system's thoughts has as yet been developed. Patterns
of action, in the organization of this paper, are the elements of the political
and productive processes, and introduction of these processes necessarily
requires material discussed in Chapters IV and V.

Other questions raised by the hypothesis and by the definition of a
social institution can be dealt with here. Standard patterns are those which
exhibit spatial and temporal consistency. And while the patterns themselves
and their temporal consistency are relevant after the next two chapters,
spatial pattern consistency (patterns used by all organizations purporting to
constitute a social institution and by each organization's sub-systems) is
relevant here. The preceding chapters show that no such consistency was
apparent until sometime in the 1890's and after all regional Associated Press
organizations had been combined into one single unit, all operating similarly
and under the same set of policies and procedures, those originating at the
central headquarters in Chicago (and later New York City). The unanimity
of Scripps' three regional wires was also apparent after 1897 and was only

reorganized in 1907. Prior to the 1890's, the NYAP often had confronta-
tions with clients, burgeoning regional AP groups (e.g., the WAP), the
telegraph companies, and in 1893 even some of its own New York membership. Reorganizations in 1856 and 1867 did not solve the factionalism within
AP's ranks and only the 1893 reorganization overthrew the NYAP's power
(the source of much of this factionalism) and opened the door to the possibility
of spatial unification. In fact, it was this possibility which apparently motivated the WAP's move to shift the base of power from New York to Chicago.
Whatever the actual patterns of action involved, 1897 marked the beginning
of spatial consistency for Scripps' UP forerunner and, with the death of the
old UP, for AP.

The problem the wire services attempted to solve was the national
and international collection and the national distribution of news as supplier
for local outlets. (If an older tradition of mutual assistance pacts allows one
organization's solution to involve reliance on foreign wires, such a pattern
does not detract from the solution.) Pragmatically speaking, and almost by
definition, the problem has remained unique in that only wire-service organizations have come forward to attempt solutions for it. Radio-television
networks, news magazines, and many newspaper press services have succeeded in solving varying degrees of the problem, with certain emphases
(selective, interpretative, opinionated, backgrounding, etc.), and by certain
technical means, but only the wire services have provided a complete solution (in terms of speed and volume), in the sense that society knows of nothing
more complete in the news-gathering field today.

Essentially, the problem was solved long before 1893 (The reader is reminded of descriptions by Harper's Magazine, Alexander Jones, and L. A. Gobright, quoted in the previous chapters.), and it is probably this early solution which sustained the organizations through their nineteenth-century turmoil and crises. The "standard" unified solution, however, was not forthcoming until after 1893, as noted above. In effect, the problem itself helps to define a wire service, along with the wire's utilization of certain technical devices which enhance its speed and volume. In light of these considerations, therefore, a newspaper, for example, could solve this problem for itself and for a relatively large national clientele of newspapers (with requisite speed and volume) and be considered in the wire-service institution, in addition to being in the newspaper institution. In fact, UP, INS, and UPI have had their beginnings in newspaper chains, and AP grew out of the cooperative association of New York City morning newspapers. Newspapers (themselves a social institution which solves a communication problem primarily for local society) devised a supplier of news, one which ultimately attained an identity of its own. Whether this separate identity can be called a social institution will be answered in the concluding section of Chapters IV and V.

2. The wire services' operational patterns have continually resembled those of their secondary environment through constant interaction with this social and cultural environment.

Certainly it cannot be denied that the wires' early history in New York City resembled the newspapering techniques for aggressive news gathering which had preceded the wires' development. Wires became possible because daily newspapers were increasing in number, developing communication and transportation techniques had proved useful to newspapers previously, and all of newspapering was more aggressively seeking news through individual and cooperative effort. Moreover, the rise of the penny press not only augmented the trend toward more daily newspapers, but it also established an emphasis on non-political and non-mercantile news upon which a wire-service supplier for many newspapers of various persuasions could most easily base its report. Thus, the early patterns of wire-service operation were established by the parent-newspaper institution during the latter's pre-wire-service gropings for a solution to this problem of national and international news collection.

After the wires became somewhat separate entities (in 1848) they still reflected the needs and techniques of American newspapering as they sought the continued patronage of newspapers and were administered by newsmen. Their presence, in turn, was reflected by the newspapers which increasingly relied upon them and were influenced by the wires' writing style and subject matter. And while this interaction has continued even to the present day, the wires were beginning also to resemble their closest ally, the telegraph companies. Both parties, through cooperation and compromise, supported each other's growth and increasing stability Following the Civil War, both resembled, through their own interaction and that with other sectors of the environment, the larger politico-economic environment in various ways: avoiding governmental interference, advocating and utilizing the sanctity of private property, using mutual assistance agreements and secret agreements, and building large trusts or monopolies through mergers, absorption, and cutthroat competition. Later (1893-1914) the public utility concept involved in the Inter-Ocean case and its circumvention by a move to New York resembles the dichotomy and conflict between the antitrust concept and the dual federalism of the Supreme Court.

Until 1945 when the Supreme Court opened the Associated Press, the wires had resembled their environment when the latter was at the peak of its institutional domination. At other times, the wires have ridden out ideological conflict by the simple process of reporting such conflict to an anxious, interested American public and institutional sector. As noted above in connection with Figure 1, the recent postwar period shows some signs of a breakdown in this ability to assimilate institutional patterns and to feed on ideological conflict by remaining aloof. Future developments will tell whether, indeed, there has been such a breakdown. Clearly the press in America (including the wires) is an adjunct of the business sector, and thus it reflects trends in this sector through interaction with it.

Footnotes

[1]Stone, op. cit., p. 214.

[2]Ibid., pp. 215-216.

[3]Cooper, op. cit. (1959), p. 6.

[4]Stone, op. cit., p. 218.

[5]Illinois AP, Volume, IV (1897), p. 3.

[6]Franchise rights (or protest rights) allowed AP members to determine whether a competing local newspaper could receive the AP news report. Going back to the 1856 reorganization of NYAP, these rights could only be waived by the newspaper involved or successfully sidestepped by a large vote of the entire AP membership. This by-law provision is discussed in detail in Chapter VI.

[7]Morris, op. cit., p. 19.

[8]Illinois AP, Volume, VII (1900), pp. 3-4.

[9]Cooper, op. cit. (1959), pp. 263-264, 267.

[10]Stephen Vincent Benet, "The United Press," Fortune Magazine, VII (May, 1933), pp. 72, 94.

[11]Oswald Garrison Villard, "The Press Today: II. The Associated Press," The Nation, CXXX (April 23, 1930), p. 488.

[12]Cooper, op. cit. (1959), pp. 95-96.

[13]Originally the British and German subsidiaries were developed to facilitate AP newsphoto collection abroad, a wire-service operation not limited by the cartel agreement among AP, Havas, Reuters, and Wolff. Thus, their incorporation date precedes the 1934 demise of the cartel agreement. They assumed news distribution duties abroad after the cartel was broken.

[14]Sources for this list are many and varied. The principal ones are: Cooper, op. cit. (1959), pp. 162-164; Mott, op. cit.; and various numbers of the Associated Press of New York, Annual Volumes, op. cit.

[15]Quoted in Morris, op. cit., pp. 20-21.

[16]For a discussion of these disclosures, see James A. Wechsler's "Propaganga in the News," The Progressive, XXVII (August, 1963), pp. 10-15.

Chapter IV

MATURATION OF WIRE-SERVICE POWER STRUCTURES

> In order to understand the organic
> laws of a political system, it is
> necessary to examine it as a whole
> and seek to discover not only the
> true functions of each part, but
> also its influence upon each other
> part, and its relation to the equi-
> librium of the complete organism.
> -- A. Lawrence Lowell

While the last two chapters presented the chronological history of

the wires in terms of social and cultural interaction, this chapter and the

next one give detailed, topical historical accounts which depict systemic

maturation more or less vertically, i. e., in terms of political and produc-

tive processes. The aim of Chapters IV and V is to identify trends in these

processes, ending with relatively definite descriptions of these processes in

their present state.

The dynamics of systemic interaction are also found occurring at the

intra-institutional or inter-sub-system level. Whether one talks of politics

as the populating of power positions or as the making and executing of policy,

the process is on-going, reciprocal, and everchanging, based not only upon

the contributions of participants, but also on the traditions and history of the

process itself. V. O. Key emphasizes this dynamic aspect of power.

> Politics as power consists fundamentally of relation-
> ships of superordination and subordination, of dominance
> and submission, of the governors and the governed. * * *
> The power relationship may vary from brute force to the
> most gentle persuasion. * * * The power relationship is
> reciprocal, and the subject may affect the ruler more pro-
> foundly than the ruler affects the subject. [1]

For purposes of this study, power and the political process include the legal framework within which the wires operate, membership influences upon the wires' structures, and the quasi- and extra-legal developments within the actual policy-making structure of the wires.

Each of these three aspects of wire-service politics will be discussed under separate headings in this chapter: (1) State and Federal Legal Guidelines, in which corporation law and court decisions affecting the wires' political structures are discussed; (2) Membership-Subscriber Influence on Wires' Politics, in which membership types and voting privileges are discussed; and (3) Politics at the Decision-Making Level, in which the interaction among the board of directors, the general manager, and the administrative staff is examined.

Although both Chapter IV and V contain summary discussions, the introduction of hypotheses relevant to both chapters is postponed until the end of Chapter V. This is done because material in both chapters can be visualized as complementary phases of the same systemic maturational process. But more importantly, the same hypotheses apply to both chapters, and discussion of these hypotheses will be more meaningful if both political and productive findings are combined in a single, overall treatment of maturation.

State and Federal Legal Guidelines

Individual or partnership ownership of business organizations was common in 1848 when the New York Associated Press was formed. The practice by states of granting corporation charters under a general incorporation law (as opposed to the earlier and sometimes grossly unfair practice of incorporation by special legislation) did not become widespread in the United States until the 1850's or 1860's. Add to this the fact that the six, and later seven, New York City editors considered the NYAP an extension of their newspaper staffs, and it obvious that the NYAP had little reason to seek a corporation charter in 1848, or for many years thereafter. It will be remembered that the first Associated Press organization to secure a charter was the Western Associated Press (from Michigan in 1865). Other AP regional organizations and various competitors of the NYAP also received corporation charters after 1865, but the NYAP never applied for a charter, presumably feeling that such a charter would impair the New York editors' control over what they felt was their personal private property. Consequently, the NYAP--the one organization which must be considered as the most powerful of the AP group before 1893--was never directly tied to state government control through the incorporation procedure.

It will be recalled that during the 1870's and 1880's Congress investigated AP's operations at various times, but the literature indicates that any congressional action which might have been taken would, at best, have been indirect (e. g. , through limitation of AP access to congressional news, control of Western Union, etc.).   In fact, no governmental pressures appear to have been applied to the AP at that time, nor did the incorporating states act as a force on regional or state AP organizations, or on the private competing wire services.

The first corporation charter for AP's controlling group was granted by the state of Illinois in 1892 in accordance with "An Act Concerning Corporations" passed by the Illinois General Assembly on April 18, 1872. In the application for a charter, the purpose of the AP of Illinois was:

> . . . to buy, gather, and accumulate information and news; to vend, supply, distribute, and publish the same; to purchase, erect, lease, operate, and sell telegraph and telephone lines and other means of transmitting news; to publish periodicals; to make and deal in periodicals and other goods, wares, and merchandise. [2]

Two conditions about this application and description are worth noting. First, AP because of its own internal power struggle found it advantageous to incorporate in Illinois. That state in 1892, however, had only a general corporation law, pertaining primarily to private, profit-making firms, even though AP was a cooperative membership venture. Thus, neither AP's application nor the state charter was actually appropriate in the situation. Second, AP's application is vaguely worded, including many seemingly unjournalistic activities, e.g., publishing, erecting and operating telegraph and telephone lines, etc. AP felt insecure about its future. It relied heavily on telegraph transmission and at the moment was facing the formidable old United Press in the East. It wanted to allow itself latitude for expansion into adjacent operating fields if future conditions required it.

It was this second condition--an AP attempt to provide for expansion or at least for protection in the future--which led to the Illinois Supreme Court's Inter-Ocean decision in 1900 that AP was impressed with the public interest. The public utility concept applied to AP on the basis of the so-called Granger cases (Munn v. Illinois, 1877) and was occasioned by the

phrase "to purchase, erect, lease, operate, and sell telegraph and telephone lines" in the statement of purpose. In effect, the court was saying
that AP's purpose included an element of common carrier operation and
thus had to observe the public interest in its policies. (The court held that
it was not in the public interest for AP to punish a member, the Chicago
Inter-Ocean, for trafficking with a competing wire service.) As Chapter III
indicates, this situation was truly threatening for AP, so much so that AP
felt obliged to terminate its Illinois charter and search elsewhere for legal
status. Illinois, through its incorporation laws (which actually did not apply
to the AP type of organization) and through its courts (which focused on a
purpose which AP had never actually undertaken) was threatening AP with
strict control as a public utility.

New York State had recently enacted a corporation law specifically
for membership organizations, and it was under this law that an AP charter
was approved on May 22, 1900--the charter under which AP still operates.
Chapter III indicates, as does the literature, that AP found much cooperation
among New York legislators in securing a charter which was tailor-made for
a cooperative, membership organization. For example, on April 19, 1901,
the New York Legislature amended its membership corporation law to permit incorporation of concerns gathering and distributing news. This extension of the membership law appears expressly aimed at insuring the legality
of AP's charter. In fact, much of the descriptive wording of the amendment
appears to have been taken from AP's statement of purpose in its charter
application. A comparison of relevant portions of the two documents (with

similar or identical passages underlined in each) will indicate the legislative assistance aimed solely at AP.

APIs Application-Purposes (1900)

. . . to gather, obtain, and procure
by its own instrumentalities, by exchange with its members and by any
other appropriate means, any and all
kinds of information and intelligence,
telegraphic and otherwise, for the use
and benefit of its members and to
furnish and supply the same to its
members for publication in the newspapers owned or represented by them,
under and subject to such regulations,
conditions and limitations as may be
prescribed by the By-laws; and the
mutual cooperation, benefit and protection of its members. [3]

Amendment-Membership Corp.
Law (1901)

Any corporation heretofore or
hereafter organized under this
article, for the purpose of gathering, obtaining and procuring information and intelligence, telegraphic or otherwise, for the use
and benefit of its members, and to
furnish and supply the same to its
members for publication in newspapers owned or represented by
them, may admit as members
thereof other corporations, limited
liability companies, joint stock and
other associations, partnerships
and individuals engaged in the same
business or in the publication of
newspapers, periodicals or other
publications, upon such terms and
conditions not inconsistent with laws
and with its certificate of incorporation, as may be prescribed in its
by-laws. [4]

In 1900 in New York State, AP's purposes were stated even more
broadly than in Illinois eight years before, but without specific transmission
references which might again render AP a public utility. On the other side,
the state's amendment not only included AP, but in places referred only to AP
by using AP's self-description to describe those organizations now included
in the membership law. This was not special legislation in the sense that it
applied only to AP; other membership corporations dealing in news gathering
and dissemination might apply for a charter later. At present, however, AP
was the only such membership organization in the country. AP's board of

directors noted the legislature's specific inclusion of AP as follows

> The New York Legislature has enacted a bill reorganizing the validity of our present organization under the "Membership Corporation Law," and authorizing corporations to hold membership in such an organization, questions having arisen on both of these points. [5]

Thus, AP was relieved of further infringement by states upon its private domain, the nature of its work, and the control of its operation. AP was never again to be threatened with revision of its legal status as a corporation by a state.

Chapter III notes that subsequent legal interaction with governmental units was only with the federal government, once in 1915 and again in 1945. In both instances AP's legal, corporate structure was untouched, but it was approached regarding its relationship with members and potential members in connection with the precepts of antitrust legislation. Since this relationship involves the added step of primary environmental components, a discussion of these two instances will be deferred until Chapter VI. Only one aspect is relevant in the up-coming section and will be only briefly introduced there.

Membership-Subscriber Influence on Wires' Politics

Within the realm of primary environmental components, i.e., mass communications outlets and other agencies served directly by wire services, a distinction must be made between members and clients, particularly in the case of AP. In terms of democratic institutions, the member would be a represented voter, recognized as having power to vote for representatives in the policy-making process if not himself having the possibility of being a representative. The client, on the other hand, has no voice in the decision-making process and exists, in the eyes of AP, only to the extent that he receives, uses, and pays for the AP news report. Another privilege extended to members, but not to clients, is that of investing in the organization via stocks or bonds, which in turn gives the member even more votes. Since membership in AP is largely a financial status, based in part upon past involvement and upon AP tradition, and since the membership-client dichotomy has changed from time to time, its various stages of development will be presented below in chronological order.

Between 1848 and 1892, the NYAP group continued in primary control of the Associated Press organization (by virtue of various possessions, agreements, and strategic geographical location). The AP "membership," therefore, consisted of six newspapers (1848-51) and then seven papers (1851-92). All other newspapers in the AP organization, regardless of longevity of affiliation, size of weekly assessment, or membership in regional or state organizations, were simply clients, receiving the news report but having little to say about policy. The period from 1862 to 1892 is depicted in Chapter II as encompassing a trend toward increasing ingression of the WAP upon the NYAP's control, but WAP never attained equal status (i.e., membership status) with the NYAP in the disposition of such operations as the all-important eastern seaboard coverage, foreign news exchange, etc. Even in 1882 when WAP held an excellent bargaining position, the joint proprietory committee's membership favored the NYAP, three to two.

"Membership" in the AP of Illinois after 1892 was contingent upon the purchase of AP stock. Only stockholders could vote for directors or help formulate policy in AP's annual meetings. AP actively sought to increase the number of stockholders between 1892 and 1900, but not so much because of the democratizing effect such an increase would have for the organization as because of the increased operating revenue and sound financial base it would provide the organization. Figures showing the growth of stockholding "members" between 1892 and 1898, relative to the membership-client totals are listed in Chapter III.

When the New York corporation was formed, the stockholding principle was abandoned in compliance with the state's membership incorporation law. All recipients of the news report were considered members and all could vote for directors, were eligible to become directors, and could participate in annual meetings. Stockholders' investments were honored by converting shares into bonds with an additional vote awarded to bondholders for each twenty-five dollars in bonds up to one thousand dollars. Consequently, although every member had a voice, those who had supported the old organization or who had chosen to support the new one financially had a larger voice in AP affairs. This differentiation continues today and is a matter of constant controversy.

In 1936 the board reported that bond subscribers numbered over 50 per cent of total membership. [6] In 1942, a federal district court, however, found that only ninety-nine out of 1,247 AP members held bonds with a face value of one thousand dollars or more, and therefore the accompanying forty

extra directorship votes. This is 7.9 per cent of the membership and
represents a bondholding group which held 3,960 extra votes as compared
with a total of only 1,247 voting members.[7] The court further found that
the bondholder vote completely controlled the selection of AP directors,
pointing out that between 1937 and 1942 the number of votes cast for each
nominee for director by bondholders greatly exceeded general membership
votes. Forty-five of the seventy nominees during this period received ten
or more times as many bondholding votes as they did membership votes.
In only two instances between 1900 and 1942 had the bondholding vote differed
from the popular vote in the election of directors.[8] Bondholding apparently
has perpetuated in the New York corporation the strength exercised by stockholders in the old Illinois organization.

An infrequently used classification of membership until after World
War II was associate member Begun in 1937 as part of a general overhaul
of the by-laws,[9] the classification contained thirteen clients in 1942.[10]
Associate members receive as much of the news report and supplemental
services as they desire (similar to regular members), pay less for the
service than members, and are not obligated to furnish local news to AP,
but are not allowed to vote or participate in AP's formal power structure
in any way. This classification was greatly expanded following World War
II to accommodate radio and television stations and foreign subscribers of
all types not wishing regular membership or prohibited from such membership status by AP's by-laws. Associate membership in AP is similar to
the client status of most subscribers to United Press International (and its

UP and INS predecessors), in terms of having no formal power in the decision-making process of the wire service. They do, however, exercise informal pressure upon the organizations in two ways. First, the wire desires as large a number of members and associate members or clients as it can recruit. Thus, their new or continued affiliation with a wire becomes an important objective of the latter. (See Chapter VI.) Second, clients' use of all or part of the news report, particularly if they also receive the competing wire, is carefully watched by the wire as a measure of the wire's previous news dissemination success and as an indicator of future changes in the wire's report.

The rank-and-file subscribers of AP, therefore, have continually been divided within the formal power structure between the powerful few (NYAP members, stockholders, and bondholders) and the powerless many (members of regional AP organizations, clients, and other regular and associate members). Between 1848 and 1892, as Chapter II has pointed out, the NYAP controlled as much of the AP organization as it could. This was sufficient to allow the New York six or seven to set the all-important policies despite the growing power and unrest of regional AP organizations. From 1892 to the present, stockholders and bondholders have dominated the "legislative" machinery of AP by controlling the election of directors. These findings lead to two questions: Do directors consult with members before formulating policy? What is the advantage of regular membership over associate membership?

A careful reading of AP's annual reports indicates that the membership is not consulted on most issues. Although the board is obviously aware of the necessity of explaining its actions to the membership and for main-

taining a favorable image among the members, directors operate ordinarily

without benefit of initiative and referendum. To a large extent, however,

the board seems to reflect the predisposition of the larger and more lucra-

tive members in the organization, those more likely to have the all-powerful

stockholder and bondholder votes. The next section will reveal that wealthy

large-city newspaper properties have continually been over-represented on

the board since 1892. Thus, there appears to be a board-stockholder and a

board-bondholder linkage which taints AP policy with the predisposition of

powerful AP members. In such a situation, constituency consultation would

be unimportant as long as the inherent predisposition of the two groups re-

mains relatively coincidental. This, in fact, appears to have been the case

throughout most of AP's modern history and on most important policy de-

cisions. While the aristocratic newspaper properties and the board act as

one (either by agreement or by unrecognized monolithic predisposition), the

latter's role has been to explain, rationalize, and hide its decisions, vis-a-

vis the membership as a whole.

One notable exception, however, developed over the difficult issue of

whether AP should service outlets of the new and growing radio industry.

By the early 1930's it was evident to the board and AP administrators that

the membership was at cross-purposes over the question, that no board or

administrative action would be acceptable to a safe majority of the members,

and that the organization's stability could best be maintained by taking no

initial stand and by conducting a referendum. In this way both the board and

the administration would absolve themselves of responsibility for the organization's final radio policy. Various pressures upon AP as an organization and upon its members as individuals made this truly a dilemma of
complex dimensions: (1) some newspapers (many of them wealthy AP
members) owned radio stations and wanted radio news service from AP;
(2) many newspapers had no radio outlets and for one reason or another
(e.g., fear of losing advertising revenue, circulation, or newspapers'
uniqueness as a timely news medium) did not want AP to aid the threatening
young opponent; (3) sponsored, commercial radio was increasing which if
tied to newscasts would cheapen and commercialize the AP news report;
(4) the increase of chain-radio and network activities threatened to create
independent news-gathering agencies competing with AP; and (5) UP and
INS were eager to serve radio stations and, with radio support, might
overtake AP as America's leading news-gathering service.

AP members were fined frequently for violating the AP board's early
policy of prohibiting AP news (whether out of the AP news report or from
the newspapers' own staffs) to be broadcast. Many large and aggressive AP
members with broadcasting outlets fought this policy during the late 1920's,
opposed by both large and small members without stations and confronted
with an uncertain AP board. The board's policy fluctuated on both the policy
and its enforcement during the late 1920's, but by the early 1930's membership conflict was acute, and a firm hand had to be applied in order to maintain control. By this time, the earlier advocates of AP service to radio
stations were strongly opposed by members disturbed by the growing size

and economic strength of radio. The inherent and always potential diffi-

culty of a democratic institution--deep-rooted disagreement based on

multilateral commitments or self-interests--had emerged, and the policy-

making machinery, unable to unravel the complex problem, turned in 1933

as a last resort to the will of the majority, hoping that this display of

democratic procedure and its resultant mandate would not be fatal to the

organization as a whole.

The referendum, in the form of a mailed questionnaire, elicited

a response of 92.1 per cent of the 1,197 domestic members. The results

are presented below under various significant categories and in descending

order of strength of membership sentiment.

Per Cent	Chain-Network Radio	AP Members' Radio	Radio In General
78.7%		I broadcast no news	
74.4	. . No AP Bulletins*		
69.5	. . No AP news at all		
69.0		Assess bdctrs**more	
66.9		AP Bulletins & local news only	
57.2		No news bdct at all	
54.3			No AP news at all. [11]

---

*One important question in the referendum concerned whether AP's Bulletin
service, an abbreviated timely service, should be offered to radio outlets
and/or whether it should be distinguished from the general news report.
**Abbreviation for broadcasters, referring to AP members with radio outlets.

Outside of the large group which did not broadcast news at all, the largest

majority sentiment was a consistent "no" to chain- or network-radio use of

AP news in any form. The next group approved of AP members using AP

bulletins and their own local news and paying an additional assessment for the privilege. The smallest two groups (although still representing a majority opinion) denied both AP members and all radio outlets the use of AP news. Not shown above, but perhaps most important, is the fact that 70.4 per cent gave the board power to decide AP's radio policy. Thus, the members had said that the board should permit only AP members to use only AP bulletins and their own local news reports and to pay an additional assessment. Sponsorship of AP newscasts, it was assumed by the board and the members alike, was out of the question. This was the essence of the board's policy set that same year[12] and reaffirmed again in 1935 and 1936.

By 1936, United Press had announced it was selling its news report for a broadcast sponsored by Standard Oil Company. AP held firm to its non-commercial policy saying "any sale of our news to commercial corporations not only would be contrary to the provisions of the By-laws but violative of the principles and spirit of the organization."[13] By this time, AP had become more concerned with the activities of its competitors, and the AP members had begun to resign themselves to the fact that radio was growing despite their opposition. General newspaper pessimism engendered by the Depression had given way to new optimism, prompted by rejuvenated advertising revenue and circulation figures. The board was in a position to assume a commanding role over the issue. In 1939, therefore, it pushed through AP-member sponsorship of AP newscasts, in 1940 it gave the general manager authority to contract with individual radio stations and with broadcasting networks, and in 1946 it secured associate memberships for all radio and television outlets.

The final question, concerning the advantage of regular membership over associate membership, now requires attention. Since the former is more expensive than the latter and yet carries so little actual status in AP's power structure for most newspapers, one might expect that a realistic publisher would prefer the less expensive associate membership. For some regular members, however, their status is a protective device. Only regular members could hold protest rights and many holders of such rights would rather keep them and protect their local power than gain power in national journalism. Currently only regular members can purchase bonds and thereby secure additional directorship votes. In another sense, the organization's constant emphasis (although somewhat less than accurate) on cooperative journalism and the democratic ideal of elective representation has created a need among publishers to participate, even though their single voice probably is no more effective in AP's structure than it is in American political structure.

Politics at the Decision-Making Level

As noted above, the internal structure of AP consists principally of three components: the board of directors, the general manager, and an administrative staff. Each will be described separately and then brought together in a synthesis of the internal structure over time.

According to the by-laws, AP has been governed by a board of directors since 1892 when the board consisted of the original nine stockholders and in-corporators of the Illinois firm. Within three years the board was expanded to eleven directors, and by 1896 these eleven were divided into three groups of three-year staggered terms, two groups of four directors and one of three. Election of directors was by stockholders during AP's annual meeting, and the board's principal functions were: (1) to set general policy for and to oversee the operation of the organization's news-gathering and distributing facilities; (2) to set the assessment rates and determine an assessment formula equitable for all members; (3) to hire and oversee the top administrator, the general manager; and (4) to receive and decide upon applications for client and member status. An executive committee of directors conducted the detailed study work and made recommendations to the board. The committee began with three members, increased to four in 1894, and was expanded to five in the next year.

Officers included a president who was a director selected by the board (and traditionally re-elected year after year until he indicated he no longer wanted the position), first and second vice-presidents who are non-director, AP members selected by the board (usually for one-year terms as training periods for possible future directorship service), a secretary and an assistant secretary, who were generally the general manager and assistant general manager, respectively, and a treasurer who was an administrative specialist performing the same function under the general manager within the administrative hierarchy.

The board was increased to fifteen directors in 1900 with the incorporation in New York, five directors elected to three-year terms by the members each year. The functions and officer positions remained essentially the same, and the executive committee fluctuated between five and seven directors. In 1937, the number of directors increased to eighteen, the additional three specifically coming from cities with populations of less than 50,000. This was in response to a long-standing demand by rank-and-file members for more equitable representation of the membership on the board. In 1942, directors were limited to three three-year terms, a move to end membership complaints that some directors had overstayed their usefulness to AP and that the board had become a club of tradition-bound friends. During the 1960 annual meeting, former Board President Robert McLean (himself a long-term director and officer) addressed the members about rescinding the 1942 limitation. His plea, as yet unheeded, was for experience on the board.

> It seems to me that no business of a comparable size would deny itself the services and the experience, the background, knowledge and ability of those well and able to serve, who are prepared to continue to serve. Hence I think it highly desirable, and I advocate that we start to reelect to the Board some of those who have served on the Board before. [14]

The legal functions of the board today are not appreciably different from those of 1893, as Article IV of the 1962 by-laws indicates in enumerating board powers.

> The affairs of the Corporation shall be managed by eighteen Directors. . . to make contracts; to fill vacancies in their own number until the next annual meeting; to elect and remove officers and agents; to engage and discharge employees; to fix the compensation of officers, agents and employees; to borrow money; to issue bonds . . . to expend the money of the Corporation for its lawful purposes. [15]

Elsewhere in the by-laws, the board is empowered to receive applications for membership and to act upon them, to apportion the costs of news gathering

and distribution among members and clients, and to penalize members who
violate the by-laws.[16]

Two important issues have been raised above in the historical description of the board: its representativeness as a nationally elected legislative body and the longevity of its members. These will be the principal
points of inquiry here with regard to the board.

Representativeness of the AP board can be considered in several
ways. The first question to resolve is what are the constituent units which
the board represents? One, according to the controversy leading to the 1937
increase in directors, is the population of the city from which a director
comes. Others which also seem feasible for consideration are newspapers,
cities, and states. All four units will be investigated.

Table 1 (see Appendix B) presents a sample of boards (except for
the first one, chosen on a decennial basis) arranged and augmented to elicit
the representativeness of the boards in terms of the members' hometown
populations. An index of population representativeness is calculated for each
board (according to a method described in a footnote to Table 1). The smaller
the index number, the less representative is the board of small communities
or the more representative is the board of very large cities. According to
the table, representativeness of the board was more than twice the theoretical minimum in 1892-93 (2.22), which is understandable considering that in
light of historical events the board was drawn from a small region of the
nation (primarily the Midwest) and could not have access to newspapers on the
populous East Coast. The 1900-01 board, on the other hand, comes closest

to the theoretical minimum representation (1.12), due largely to a con-
certed effort to integrate eastern papers into the new eastern corporation.
Three directors (Seitz, Reid, and Ridder) are from New York City newspapers, and other populous eastern cities represented are Philadelphia,
Baltimore, and Boston.

Three trends are apparent in Table 1: (1) a relatively steady increase from 1.12 to 4.35 between 1900 and 1930; (2) a decline of lesser
proportions from 4.35 to 2.69 between 1930 and 1950; and (3) a large increase from 2.69 to 6.65 between 1950 and 1960. In other words, two
peaks of population representativeness are revealed by this sample: 1930-
31 and 1960-61. It is interesting to note that the post-1930 decline occurred
after the board was expanded to eighteen members for purposes of making it
more representative of less populous areas. It appears as though this 1937
commitment to represent three small communities permitted relinquishing
of a previous commitment for general representativeness on the board. The
other fifteen directorships became more big-city after 1937.

In general, the trend has been from low to high representativeness.
The first four boards average a 2.29 population representation and the last
four average 4.27, nearly twice the first four.

Closely tied to population representation is the longevity of directors
from some areas or units as opposed to others. Aside from population differences, per se, within given boards, what is the long-term composition of
all AP boards with respect to general types of constituencies? Or rephrased,
do some newspapers, large cities, or populous states receive disproportionately high and enduring representation in the long run, similar to the so-called

safe congressional district? Tables 2, 3, and 4 present data on the long-term representativeness of these three "constituent" units among AP board members and officers. All three tables include all directors or officers who have served since 1893.

(Any unit with less than a three-year representation on the board was represented either on an interim replacement basis or as a vice-president. Because of this, such short durations on the board are not considered in this discussion as significant and are eliminated.)

Of the total 112 newspapers listed in Table 2, 82 (or 73.2 per cent) have three-year stays on the board or more, of which nine (or almost 11 per cent) have been represented at least half of the 71 years between 1893 and 1964. This shows a long-term representation for some newspapers. On the other hand, one-third of the 82 newspapers have been on the board at least 13 years (18.3 per cent of the 71-year period).

An even more limited representation can be noted in Table 3 in terms of city constituences. New York City has had directors 22 years more than there have been boards; Philadelphia falls short of continuous aggregate representation by one year. (Several of these long directorship periods, of course, are caused by overlapping terms.) Only 61 cities (78.2 per cent of the 78 cities listed) are represented three years or more. Eleven cities (or 18 per cent) are represented for one-half of the total 71-year period, and one-third of the cities (20 cities) are represented for at least 20 years on the board (or 28.2 per cent of 71 years).

Finally, state representation on the board (Table 4) includes four states (New York, Pennsylvania, Missouri, and California) with more years of representation than there have been years of the board's exist-

ence. New York comes within twelve years of doubling the board's life

span. Sixteen states (or 51.6 per cent of the 31 states with three-year

representation on the board) have been represented at least half of the

total 71 years, and the top one-third of the states has been represented

at least 53 years (or 74.6 per cent of the total 71 years).

An additional feature of Table 4 is the comparison of each state's

rank order by representation with its rank by membership totals in seven

selected years. This comparison, made in terms of the relative disparity

between the two rankings for the state, is transferred to Figure 2 (see the

next page). The figure shows over- and under-representation only where

the state's two rankings differ by at least three places. The twelve states

listed in Table 4 as having no board representation are among the twenty-

two states shown as under-represented in Figure 2. Thirteen states are

over-represented by the above standards, and sixteen are relatively properly

represented, in terms of their AP membership totals.

At first glance, Figure 2 reveals no inequalities of representation

occurring in one region, as opposed to others. (The four regions sketched

on the map are AP's so-called Grand Divisions, used for selecting nominat-

ing and auditing committee members.) Calculating the percentage of total

states in each region with unequal representation, the following rank orders

result: Over-Representation--Southern, 30.8%; Western, 27.3%; Eastern,

23.1%; and Central, 16.7% and Under-Representation--Southern, 53.8%;

Central, 50.0%; Eastern, 30.8%; and Western, 27.3%. No region is obvious

either for its over- or under-representation. In a regional framework, only

Figure 2. Representation on AP's Board Compared with Membership

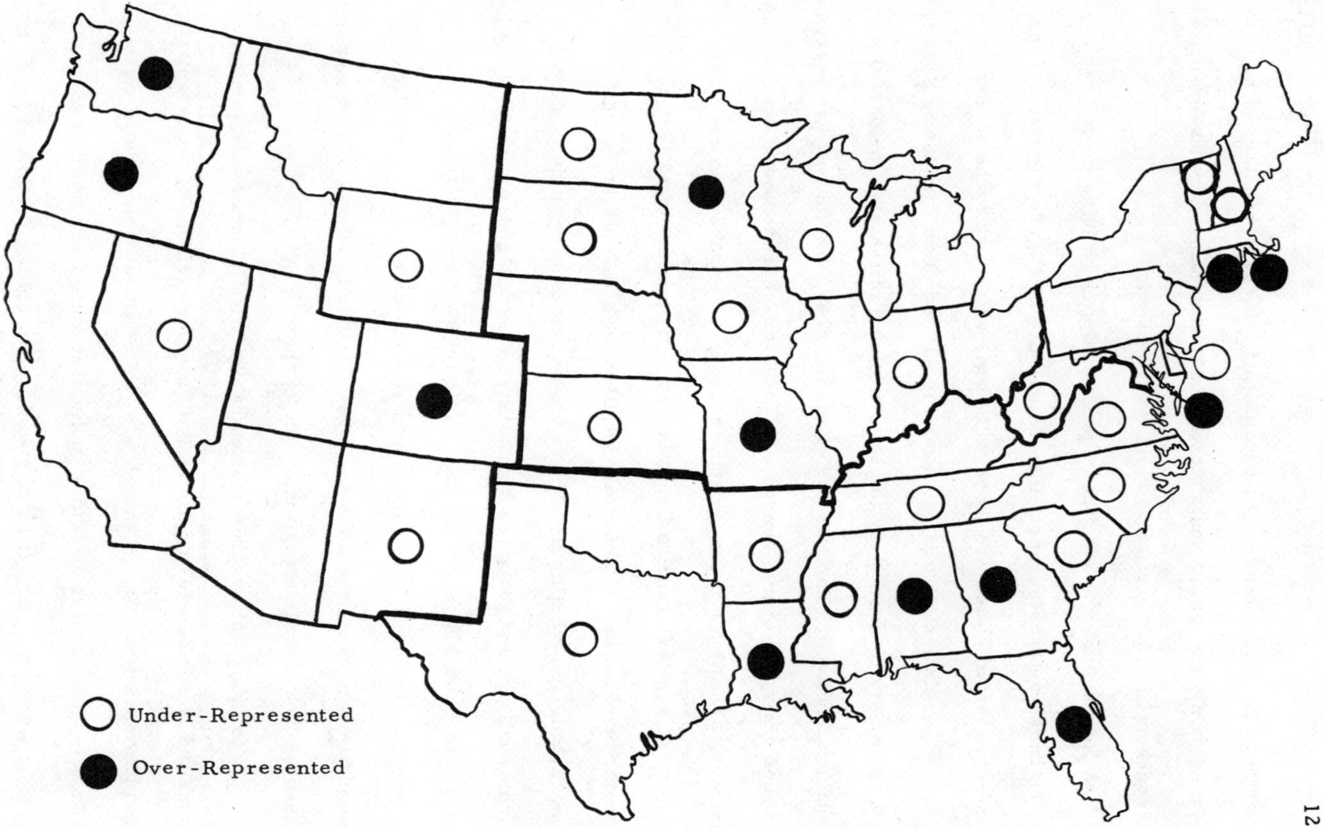

○ Under-Represented

● Over-Represented

the Southern Division stands out as exhibiting a large percentage of both

extremes. Only two of the South's thirteen states (Kentucky and Oklahoma)

are represented in proportion to their membership.

A long experience with these data and the underlying directorship

and membership cases suggests the significance of Figure 2. Many of the

under-represented states are those with many small newspapers, not

productive of relatively large revenues for AP and often fluctuating greatly

in total membership from year to year but virtue of the smallness of the

newspapers involved. The Dakotas, Kansas, Iowa, and Indiana are particu-

larly good examples of this condition. The over-represented states, on the

other hand, are for the most part dominated by newspapers in one or two

large cities, e.g., Denver in Colorado, St. Louis and Kansas City in

Missouri, St. Paul and Minneapolis in Minnesota, Atlanta in Georgia, etc.

Another factor contributing to over-representation is the individual zeal of

particular editors and their resultant desire to attain board positions and to

acquire a voice in AP policy-making. Often, however, this zeal is con-

currently manifested in statewide domination by the editor's newspaper.

These matters of representation will again be discussed and will be sum-

marized in the concluding section of this chapter.

Up to this point, representation has been considered solely in terms

of so-called constituencies or districts. Another element of representation

is the individual director. Although it would be impossible without first-

hand knowledge to report directors individual activities, motivations, and

viewpoints while in office, it is important to fill out the picture as much as possible about the longevity of individual directors within the framework

of constituency representation. Table 5 lists all directors and officers

of AP from 1893 to 1964, rank ordered according to their longevity on the

board. (It should be remembered that after 1942 directors were limited

to three three-year terms. This limitation makes post-1942 data less

meaningful in terms of longevity and not comparable with pre-1942 figures.)

Twenty-eight directors (or 25.2 per cent of the total 111 directors listed)

have served four or more terms on the board, and 83 (or 74.8 per cent)

have served 11 years of less. Thirty-seven directors (or 33.3 per cent of

the total) served more than three terms on the board, and the remaining

66.7 per cent served nine or less years. Finally, 55 directors (or almost

50 per cent) served nine or more years on the board.

Although ideally the most equitable representation would include

the election of a new director each time a term expired, a three-term stay

on the board appears to be the midpoint, separating high-longevity from

low-longevity directors. While nine years on the board seems like a long

time, compared with the many potential directors whose constituencies are

unrepresented, it is not an unreasonably long stay when compared with those

of directors appearing at the top of Table 5. Using seventy-one years as

100 per cent, Noyes was a director 74.6 per cent of the time; Howell, 60.6

per cent; and Robert McLean, 56.3 per cent. The significant fact about

these figures is that as many directors have low longevity as have high

longevity, using nine years as the dividing point. Consequently, the 1942

three-term limitation was aimed at the past longevity of only one-third of

the directors (i.e., those serving ten or more years on the board) and not
at a tradition permeating most of the fifteen and later eighteen directorships.

Having noted that low longevity is as prevalent as high longevity on
the board, one could ask whether low-longevity directors are confined to a
particular period between 1892 and 1964. It could be supposed that the recent emphasis on limiting directorships might cause a general increase in
awareness of the problem and a concurrent increase in the number of short-
term directorships. Raw data (not easily presented in table form) allow
comparison between longevity and a director's first appearance on the board.
Using longevities of from three to eight years and eliminating directors
serving at this writing, the author found the following grouping of starting
points among ten-year periods for this group of short-term directors.

```
1892-1900 - 10     1921-1930 - 2
1901-1910 -  2     1931-1940 - 3
1911-1920 -  5     1941-1950 - 2
```

Two periods stand out as having created low-longevity directors: 1892-1900
and 1911-1920. Apparently, two opposite trends were developing simultaneously on the board: one was the establishment of long-term directors, and
the other was the frequent replacement of short-term directors. Both
trends, of course, were decreasing up to 1942 when the artificial limitation
was imposed.

With respect to the first trend suggested above, twelve of the first
twenty-four directors listed in Table 5 (fourteen or more years on the board)
began their long directorships in the two periods above shown to have high

degrees of low-longevity directors as well. Pursuing this line of analysis

one step further, with the help of raw data, the author arranges the first

twenty-eight directors in Table 5 (twelve or more years on the board) ac-

cording to the beginning of their first term. (Numbers in parentheses are

high-longevity directors whose service carried over from previous periods.)

1892-1900 - 9	1921-1930 - 6 (6)
1901-1910 - 3 (9)	1931-1940 - 4 (9)
1911-1920 - 3 (7)	1941-1950 - 3 (8)

The dual trends noted above must be modified in light of these figures to

include only the 1892-1900 period. A renewal of short-term directorships

occurred in 1911-1920, and a renewal of long-term directorships occurred

in 1921-1930. Total high-longevity directors, new and carry-over ones,

remain relatively constant up to 1950 (fluctuating between ten and twelve),

but there is a marked reduction in new long-term directorships after 1930

(twelve years before the three-term limitation was imposed).

Between the extremes of high and low longevity, however, many

directors have come and gone since 1892. Table 6 shows the number of

directors replaced each year between 1901 and 1963. (The period between

1892 and 1900 is excluded here because of the difficulties imposed by the

various total directorships comprising the board during this period.) It can

be seen from this table that a relatively constant and low rate of change oc-

curred on the board between 1901 and 1940. On an average, slightly more

than one director was replaced each year (actually eleven new directors in

each ten-year period) until after 1940 when the three-term limitation began

to impose wholesale membership changes. Between 1950 and 1960 two directors per year were replaced on the basis of averages. In a three-year period (1950-52), however, twelve or two-thirds of the total eighteen directors were replaced. In another three-year period (1959-61) ten of eighteen directors were replaced. These periods are nine years apart and the former is nine years after the three-term, nine-year limitation had gone into effect.

The 1942 limitation appears to have increased periodic fragmentation on the board. The author does not suggest that such fragmentation is particularly good or bad. Theoretically, the best representation, from the constituents' viewpoint, would have six new men on the board each year. Continuity in matters of policy-making and implementation, on the other hand, would benefit the corporation, at least from the standpoint of experience with and knowledge about the firm's operations, hidden pitfalls, traditions, etc. Thus, the question of common-man representation versus expertise, of direct or agent democracy versus indirect or delegate democracy, emerges with respect to AP, as it does concerning all democratic institutions.

Another glance at Table 5 will reveal that high-longevity continuity of directorships on the board has also been the basis for most of the important offices, particularly board president and executive committee positions. These, also, have tended to become more fragmented over time. After 1900 and the fluctuating condition of the Illinois corporation, presidential terms have tended to become shorter: Frank B. Noyes, 38 years (1900-38); Robert McLean, 19 years (1938-57); and Benjamin M. McKelway,

5-1/2 years (1957-63). The present president, Paul Miller, of course, cannot be considered here. Again, increased fragmentation and a more representative board seems to be the trend. A concluding section will discuss in detail the changing condition and role of the board, vis-a-vis the membership, the general manager, and the administrative staff.

It is clear from the historical account in Chapter III that the appointment of Kent Cooper as AP general manager signaled a drastic revision in the role of that office and in the aims and operations of AP as a whole. Some general agents during the nineteenth century (notably Daniel H. Craig, 1851-66, and James W. Simonton, 1866-82) were very aggressive AP leaders at a time when AP's very existence was constantly threatened by environmental pressures and radical changes. Melville E. Stone (1893-1921) became increasingly conservative, however, during his tenure, and his hand-picked successor, Frederick Roy Martin (1921-25), simply continued Stone's policies. The differences between Stone and Cooper are many, in places very striking. Cooper makes this unmistakably, and at times unmercifully, clear in his volumes of advocacy and autobiography. Cooper's own drive to create the world leader in news gathering was fed by a personal intuition about innovation and business and by a zealous desire to reverse the policies and principles of his first AP superior and his arch antagonist, Melville E. Stone.

Cooper's accomplishments while AP general manager are noted in Chapter III, and it remains for this section to indicate his rise to power and the trends begun during his administration. His respect for Stone was offset by what he felt were Stone's painfully detrimental policies and irreversible

blindness about AP's deteriorating realities: excessive costs, outmoded

news ideas, lack of aggressive drive to improve the service, and gross in-

efficiencies in the organization's administration. Of Stone, he says:

> When I first met the general manager of the AP, he
> was sixty-two years old--very old, I thought--and he had
> no idea of quitting though plainly he was a tired man, old
> beyond his years. The position had lost its glamour for
> him. [17]

This 1910 observation was followed by "evidence" of Stone's ineffectiveness

within the organization: "As I found out later, some aggressive younger

men in The AP membership had formed a special committee to investigate

the effectiveness of Mr. Stone's administration. It had completed its re-

port, which contained many recommendations." [18]

After being named general manager, Cooper fought conservative board

members, a conservative president (Noyes), and the general inertia of a

growing but old organization in his unending desire for success. His drive

and vision are indicated in the following accomplishments which Cooper

attributes to himself.

> First, to enlarge the scope of (AP's) news coverage to
> include information, pictures and news features that interest
> everybody and thus tremendously widen the circle of news-
> paper readers.
> Second, having done so, to make the product lift that
> enlarged circle of American readers out of their isolation
> into an awareness of how large the world is and acquaint
> them with human activities and aspirations everywhere.
> Third, to make it the world's greatest news and news
> photo agency with its news, pictures, and news features
> available through The Associated Press, not alone to the
> people of the United States, but to as many in every country
> in the whole world as could be reached, hopeful that the truth
> would contribute to mutual international understanding. [19]

In 1930, many conservative AP publishers were not quite as willing as

Cooper was to see AP change in the ways he describes above. Of these

opponents, he says:

> . . . some of America's greatest newspaper publishers . . .
> were guardians of the organization's welfare and not pro-
> moters of change, the latter of which I, to them, was a
> radical example. They had, however, become my personal
> friends in spite of the fact that most of them felt I was making
> too many changes in The Associated Press too rapidly. Yet,
> though some Board members wanted me to slow down, not
> one of them ever told me he wanted me to give up trying to
> convince him. [20]

One of Cooper's early innovations was a mailed-newsphoto service,

a service which many conservative AP members opposed as being not within

the realm of newspapering or news gathering. While Cooper was pushing

for this new service and making it available for the first time in 1927, he

already had his eye on the next innovation--electronic, wired photography.

He describes his rationale for the newsphoto innovation as follows.

> I convinced myself that it was as much the obligation
> of The Associated Press to deliver the news in picture form
> as to deliver the news by telegraphing words, since pictures
> often had proved to be the best way of telling the news.
> Obviously this meant that sooner or later The Asso-
> ciated Press, if it was to thrive, ought not only operate its
> own news photo service for its newspapers, but also arrange
> instantaneous country-wide distribution of the pictures by
> wire. [21]

Membership and board objections were many, but Cooper, the politician,

finally won his battle.

> I hesitated, however, to give future sending of pictures
> by wire as the real reason for wanting to establish a news
> photo service. I did not in my first year as general manager
> want to arouse fears in the Board that the establishment of a
> picture service was merely the inexpensive first step toward
> the second and more costly one of sending pictures by wire.

> I knew there would be members of the Board who
> would object to an Associated Press picture service on the
> ground that the organization had built its substantial,
> eminently dignified reputation as the reliable transmitter
> of news by words alone. [22]

Cooper won his battle for AP Newsphotos, Wirephotos, AP News-

features, departmentalization, a larger administrative organization, world

news gathering and distribution, interpretative reporting, service for radio

stations, and many other innovations. And each new addition brought more

of a realization by the members and directors that their organization could

both support the improvement and benefit from it. Each innovation further

entrenched Cooper as a source of power and policy in the organization, be-

cause each innovation required additional administrative personnel who

answered primarily to Cooper and took at least their first orders from him.

Two trends were evident: (1) Cooper was increasing his control over policy

decisions and the setting of organizational goals, and (2) Cooper was building

an administrative organization to handle new areas and services.

Relatively faithful as an index of the rise of the general manager is

the content and organization of the AP Annual Volumes. Figure 3 summar-

izes the trends of the board's and general managers' annual reports within

the Volumes.

Between 1900 and 1911 the board presented the principal report to

the members on AP's operations and growth during the previous year.

Stone's only presentation was the financial and leased-wire statistics in

lengthy, dull tables. The 1912 departmentalization of AP's headquarters

took both the finances and transmission facilities out of Stone's direct control

Figure 3. Summary of Annual Reports: 1900-1963

Periods	Report & Position in Vol		Avg Pages	Remarks
1900-11	Board	1	3.6	Actual report of operations
	Stone	2	18.8	Statistical tables only
1912-25	Board	1	4.9	Actual report of operations
	Stone & Martin	0	--	
1926-37	Board	1	1.8	Gives membership growth
	Cooper	2	3.3	Gives operational growth
1938-52	Board	3	3.6	Outdated membership growth
	Cooper & Starzel	5	18.7	Actual report of operations
1953	Transition issue - does not relate to other Volumes.			
1954-63	Starzel & Gallagher	1	22.6	Actual report of operations
	Board	4	4.0	Outdated, limited report.

and left him with no report of his own. The board, however, continued to
report to the members on AP's development and operations. From 1926 to
1937, Cooper as new general manager split the reporting responsibilities
with the board The board reported primarily on membership expansion
and the financial condition, a report addressed to the membership, and
Cooper took almost three times as much space to report organizational
develop (the principal activity of AP during this period) to the board. In
1929 the board stopped writing an up-to-date report for the Annual Volume.
The volumes always have contained the previous year's minutes, actions,
etc., and after 1929, the previousyear's board report to the membership
(presented at the annual meeting in April) was reprinted one full year later
in the next Annual Volume. (Thus, the board's report on 1962 membership
growth and finances appears in the 64th volume, appearing in 1964 and

covering 1963 events, including the annual meeting during which the 1962 board report was presented.)

This outdated presentation to the membership by the board has continued, with only a couple of exceptions, up to the present time. After 1937, the manager's report was moved farther back in the book for fifteen years, but it had four advantages over the board's: (1) it was not partially hidden in the minutes of the annual meeting as was the board's report; (2) it was up to date, covering the entire previous year; (3) it included all AP developments inside and outside the organization, while the board continued to concentrate primarily upon financial, membership, and legal matters; and (4) it was being embellished gradually to attain an identity all its own by the use of several typographical and content devices: (a) use of larger body type than is found in most other portions of the book; (b) use of bold-face paragraphs; (c) use of sub-heads set in larger type; (d) categorization of the report for easier finding of specific information; and (e) elimination of the words "report to the Board of Directors" from the first page of the report.

Starzel took over the report in 1950, two years after being named general manager, and three years later pictures appeared in the Annual Volume for the first time. Seven of the total nine pictures in that issue were in Starzel's report to the membership; the board's report had no pictures. Beginning in 1954 a picture appeared on the cover of the book, and the general manager's report took over the first position in the volume, using about half of the average 18.9 pictures appearing per issue since then. A picture of the board appears about every other year, but it is separated from the other pictures, inserted among the now greatly abbreviated minutes of the board's meetings for the previous year.

If the <u>Annual Volume</u> is any indication, the general manager and his staff have gained ground in terms of the apparent importance of their work. If one wants to set a precise year in which this gain was manifested, it would probably be 1942 when Cooper no longer reported "to the Board."

Part of the general manager's strength has stemmed from a growing body of executives, operational chiefs, and departmental heads. As the organization has grown in size, the general manager and his lieutenants have assumed an increasing responsibility for the success of AP activities. The administrative staff, then, has emerged as the third significant component in AP's internal power structure.

The administrative sector has grown, subdivided, and reorganized several times since 1912 in an excellent example of the internal growth or maturation pattern of a thriving system. Table 7 summarizes the history of the three AP administrative strata: executive, operations, and departments. The relative position of strata in Table 7 and the operational content of each will serve as a framework for evaluating the administrative rise of AP. At the outset, a brief description of historical developments is in order.

As of December 31, 1894, AP's list of salaries included five persons as comprising its executive sector: General Manager Stone; Charles S. Diehl, assistant general manager; J. R. Youatt, auditor; P. H. Kerby, secretary; and Charles G. Gaither, bookkeeper.[23] The first three appeared as executives in the list of AP officials for that year; the other two were not mentioned elsewhere. The arrangement had not changed appreciably when Cooper joined AP as a traveling transmission inspector in 1910. One of Cooper's first suggestions to Stone was a reorganization of AP to "departmentalize" its functions. The system had been paralyzed by an inefficient code of responsibility--too much responsibility for some men, not enough for others; the system was decaying from within. Cooper describes the situation.

> The treasurer leased the wires. The bureau correspondents hired the operators. I reflected upon the tripod organization then existing in the A. T. & T., comprising three departments under the general manager--commercial, plant, and traffic. I thought it should be news, traffic, and finance in The Associated Press. [24]

In 1912 Stone finally agreed to Cooper's departmentalization idea under pressure from Directors McClatchy and Ochs, naming Cooper as chief of the traffic department, Youatt as treasurer, and Charles E. Kloeber as chief of the news department. The board in its next report to the members said the departmentalization was done to increase effective operation within and cooperation among departments and strata and to provide many savings of effort and expenditure. Also, it was meant to enable the general manager to "secure prompt and thorough investigation of all matters demanding it."[25] This last comment apparently was aimed at reaffirming Stone's general control over the newly diversified and reintegrated system and reassuring members that the organization had not grown too large too rapidly. (It should be noted that the three administrative arms established in 1912 are called departments by the board, Stone, and

Cooper. The author, although using their terminology here, recognizes
that in a broader historical perspective the three arms created then were in
the operations stratum, as indicated in Table 7, rather than in the more
specialized and diversified departmental stratum.)

The financial arm has remained unchanged up to the present time,
the treasurer heading up a relatively small group of accounting experts.
Traffic, earlier in the century, continually presented new problems. Under
Cooper, the department sought equitable contracts with and treatment for
telegraphers. In 1914 it was beginning to experiment with teletypewriter
equipment and beginning the difficult task of converting the entire system
from Morse to teletype. And while it was innovating, it had to maintain
facilities and personnel for delivering the news report economically. The
problems of technological innovation and transmission maintenance were to
require various additional reorganizations of administrative personnel as
time went on. Finally the news report following 1912 was undergoing many
revisions and additions as competition, AP members, and new types of
coverage situations demanded more from AP's news staff.

The news department, in fact, was the first to show any major
reorganization. Emphasis was placed on strengthening AP's day wire for
afternoon newspapers. (AP had traditionally been thought of in the industry
as primarily an AM wire beginning in 1848 with its founding by six morning
newspapers in New York.) In 1923 a general shift in emphasis toward the
day side coincided with a revitalization of the afternoon newspaper in American journalism. A general night editor was added to the department's

hierarchy and a "superintendent of markets and elections" was named to improve the tabulation of statistical news [26] General news supervisors were used between 1920 and 1937 to oversee development of the news report and generally to trouble shoot within the department.

From 1912 to about 1925, the growth of the news report and the news department was matched by the national need for improved national gathering and distributing of news. On the one hand, the news-gathering divisions into which the United States had been divided were including more bureaus of greater news source significance. In 1921, for example, eight bureaus were added within AP's four geographical divisions and three were dropped. [27] While continuing to some extent up to the present day, this reorganization of news-gathering facilities was very evident during the first three decades of this century. Apparently AP was feeling its way along the route of expanded news coverage and a more diversified field of news sources, nationally. On the other hand, the traffic department was moving ahead with creation of state and regional distribution circuits which were fed from centralized state or regional points and which included both national and state-regional news segments. By 1921, AP's board could report the existence of thirty-eight state circuits and six regional circuits, operating day and night. [28]

With this huge technological and reporting expansion, AP was due for another reorganization of its hierarchy. In 1927 and 1928 the reorganization of the news department, both nationally and in the New York headquarters, was accomplished. On the national level Cooper abolished the

four geographical divisions "which were then satrapies, each of them
presided over by a superintendent, "[29] and made approximately forty
domestic bureau chiefs responsible directly to him for the news they
handled.[30] In the headquarters, Cooper departmentalized specialized
news staffs by naming editors for sports, Newsphotos, foreign news, and
Newsfeatures, including the already existent market and election superintendent, and naming a general news editor to oversee the various departments. Throughout the system, Cooper emphasized the need for
specialists to fill reporting posts. Cooper explains why the adjustments
were made.

> The specific advantages have been quicker action on
> administrative problems, more direct contact between the
> members and the General Manager, and through the General
> Manager, with the Board of Directors more prompt collec-
> tion and distribution of news, broader opportunities for a
> larger number of members of the staff, and the inspiration
> for better work which such opportunities afford.[31]

Table 7, under "Department Editors," indicates when other equivalent editorships were created, most of them growing out of technological or
geographical expansion originating elsewhere in the AP system. By 1931,
the day and night wires had been separated again with renewed fervor, each
wire coming under the management and scrutiny of a different individual.
Within two years Cooper was claiming success for the "good natured rivalry,"
pointing to the fact that the day side stressed brevity in writing, clearness
of presentation, accuracy, and speed while the night side had made progress
in developing fresh copy, new stories, and new angles in night leads.[32]

Up to 1938, the AP administrative structure existed primarily at the
first and third levels of Table 7 (i. e., the executive and departmental

positions). The many assistants in the former directed various innovations
and expansion programs on behalf of the general manager while department
editors supervised coverage. Perhaps operational chiefs had functioned
since 1912 (e.g., the original traffic, news, and finance chiefs), but the
continual addition of positions and expansion of the scope and size of the
organization had kept these positions in a state of flux, never finally emerging as what they may actually have been from a historical viewpoint. In
1938, however, Cooper made the last of his organizational realignments,
including a strengthening of the second stratum. In that year he foresaw
the eventual expansion of AP service to radio and television outlets and to
international dimensions. He did not foresee World War II and postpone-
ment of these and other grand plans until about 1944.

Between 1938 and 1949 AP's administration leaned heavily on a
structure of four operational chiefs, inserted between existing executive and department positions and superimposed upon existing functions of
both strata. In a sense, therefore, the operational policies of the second-
stratum chiefs extended into the two existing, well-defined strata, classi-
fying or reorganizing the work of both assistant general managers and
executive assistants, on the one hand, and of departmental personnel and
editorial heads, on the other hand. Pointing out that more than one
hundred persons had reported directly to him prior to 1938, Cooper made
the following operation chief assignments:

    1. Byron Price, Executive News Editor, in charge of the news
        report;

2. Lloyd Stratton, Assistant General Manager, to handle
    "special administrative details" and the Newsphoto
    and Newsfeature operations;
3. W. J. McCambridge, Assistant General Manager, in charge
    of traffic and membership operations;
4. Alan Gould, Executive Assistant, in charge of personnel. [33]

(Note that each of these men held titles in either the first or third stratum.

Their power was being extended from their own original position in the

hierarchy to affect policy and operations between the first and third strata.)

By 1943, these four classifications of operations had emerged as mutually

exclusive spheres of activity. News, Newsfeatures and Special Services,

Traffic and Membership, and Personnel and Promotion became the organiz-

ing loci of the second stratum and for the first time were unmistakably de-

fined in the Annual Volumes. An organizing stratum had been inserted

between executives and department editors strengthening ties between the

first and third strata. With more than one hundred persons reporting to

Cooper, the need for an intervening stratum to relay messages and to act

on behalf of each stratum toward the other apparently became compelling.

Frank J. Starzel, Cooper's successor, gradually abolished the

operational chief stratum between 1949 and 1954, returning to the two-

strata designation of executive positions (general manager, assistant

general managers, and executive assistants) and departmental heads

(general news editor, and editors for Newsphotos, foreign, business, sports,

radio, Newsfeatures, and Wide World Photos). Wes Gallagher's only change

has been the addition of a deputy general manager (apparently the ranking

assistant general manager) and a manager of research and development (at

the departmental level). Despite the more recent absence of operational chiefs, their functions continue to be performed somewhere in the ad-

ministration. Since AP has continued to grow since 1949 and many of the

technological innovations continue to be directed by executive personnel,

the responsibility held previously by the second stratum has probably

once again come to rest in the executive positions. Moreover, the raw

data would seem to indicate that the bulk of AP's day-to-day operations--

the routine gathering of news and constructing of a news report--is directed

principally from the departmental level of AP's administration. To seek

verification for this statement one must look into the conditions in three

aspects of AP's administrative operations: trends of stability and longevity

within each stratum, trends of upward mobility within the hierarchy, and

the apparent activities and functions of present day executives in AP's or-

ganization.

Table 8 presents only the raw data useful in determining the degree of

stability and longevity of administrative personnel within each stratum. Its

presentation here is principally to complement Table 5, in which similar in-

formation is given for directors. Table 9, however, summarizes Table 8

and gives some insight into the conditions of stability, longevity, and mobility

in AP's administrative structure. Three conditions are immediately apparent

from Table 9: (1) 77.2 per cent (or 61 out of 79 persons) experience no

mobility, and 62 per cent (49 out of 79) could have moved upward, but did

not; (2) the greater the mobility and the higher the position one attained in

the administration, the higher was his average longevity; and (3) the range

of longevity among the seven possible mobility configurations is relatively

similar. Figure 4 (see next page) schematically portrays Table 9 to a
scale of approximately one square centimeter per man in each sector.
The figure reveals the increasing mobility as one considers each seceding
sector. Only 20.5 per cent of the departmental stratum attained higher
mobility; 50 per cent of the operational chiefs did so, or received mobile
personnel from below; and 58.6 per cent of the executive level received
mobile persons from below.

If the AP administration has become increasingly strengthened, and
more particularly, the bulk of responsibility has, as suggested above,
come to reside in the departmental stratum, a relatively high degree of
stability must be evident, particularly in the lowest level. The aggregate
data used up to this point cannot yield this type of evidence, but specific
individual cases can. The departmental backbone of the administration
has shown increasing stability since its introduction in 1927, and it has
been enlarged and subdivided over time. Starzel and Gallagher have been
content to rely on it rather than on the operational chiefs of Cooper's invention. At this writing, only two department editors, General Business
Editor James F. Tomlinson and World Service Editor Watson S. Sims
have less than ten years of service as editors, but both have probably
worked within the AP organization many years before attaining these posts.
The other six departmental heads have terms ranging from ten to twenty-
six years, and average 18.2 years of service in their present posts. All
of these departmental positions are editorial positions. Thus, they constitute the core of responsibility for AP's principal product--the news
report in its various forms and contents.

Figure 4. Relative Mobility and Longevity of Administrative
Personnel

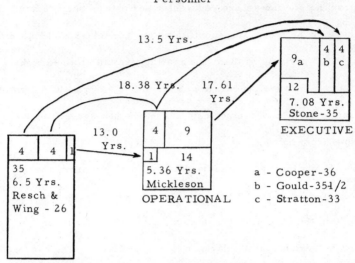

13.5 Yrs.

18.38 Yrs.   17.61
Yrs.

13.0
Yrs.

9a	4 b	4 c

12
7.08 Yrs.
Stone-35

EXECUTIVE

4	9
1	14

5.36 Yrs.
Mickleson

OPERATIONAL

4	4	1

35
6.5 Yrs.
Resch &
Wing - 26

a - Cooper-36
b - Gould-35-1/2
c - Stratton-33

DEPARTMENTAL   SOURCE: Table 9, Appendix B.

Moreover, the predominant business activity of the administration
traditionally has come under the jurisdiction of operational chiefs and
executives, and it is here that the greatest mobility has occurred. In
fact, the last three general managers attained their highest rank, not so
much because of their abilities as reporters and editors, but because of
their capacities for conducting a business, more precisely for administer-
ing traffic or personnel operations. Cooper was traffic chief from 1912 to
1920; Starzel was the same for a while before being added to the executive
stratum; and Gallagher was personnel chief from 1950 to 1954. From these
positions all three became either executive assistants or assistant general
managers in the executive stratum, serving apprenticeships for the post of
general manager. They had all been rank-and-file AP employees at one

time; the organization seems to prefer choosing leaders from its own

ranks.

The question seems to be, however, whether the man is made a

departmental chief (and thereby assumes the large responsibility for con-

ducting routine product construction, without much possibility of ascend-

ing to new positions of large responsibility) or whether he skips department

editorships and moves directly into the operational or executive strata

(and thereby assumes the large responsibility for innovation, distribution,

business, or the like). This is illustrated by the backgrounds of the two

top executives in AP at this writing.

Wes Gallagher, General Manager	Harry T. Montgomery, Deputy Gen. Mgr.
1940 - In Europe covering WWII	1937 - Asst. City Editor, NYC Bureau
1945 - Covered conclusion of WWII	1942 - Cable Desk Editor, NYC
1947 - Chief of German operations	1947 - General Business Editor (DEPT)
1950 - Personnel Chief (CHIEF)	1950 - Traffic Chief (CHIEF)
1953 - General Executive (EXEC)	
1954 - Asst. General Manager (EXEC)	1954 - Asst. General Manager (EXEC)
1952 - General Manager (EXEC)	1962 - Deputy General Manager(EXEC)

Gallagher moved into the administrative and executive sectors without

stopping at the departmental level. Montgomery is one of only four men who

have occupied all three strata and may well have attained his highest rank in

the organization.

The feeling one gets from talking to the men in AP's administration,

particularly those in the executive stratum, and from reading the recent

Annual Volumes is that each executive and editor operates primarily in his

own sphere, developing or maintaining his own policy and conducting the

operation of his sphere in his own way. The organization has become very large, complex and fragmented in recent years. Board meetings are increasingly taken up with reports of chiefs and editors in all strata. When the board acts, its decisions are based largely on the reports it receives from those heading up the department directly affected by the decisions. Moreover, the board's reliance on administrative specialists seems to be shared by other administrative personnel.

While AP growth continues, most of its operation is routine gathering and packaging of the news product. Responsibility for this has been delegated primarily to department heads. Thus, while editors carve out spheres of control and responsibility in a complex network of diverse operations, their power becomes further entrenched. The high longevity of most present day departmental editors testifies to their power in the organization both as regards making decisions and influencing executives and directors in the higher decisions which perpetuate or increasingly entrench the editors and their operations.

During a two-hour interview with one of the six occupants of the present day executive stratum, the author found that the administrator had relatively little knowledge about present operations outside his own bailiwick --the development of a computer system for market tabulations, and ultimately perhaps for linkage of computers with the teletypesetter system. Response to most of the author's questions concerning areas outside his own specialty was usually the shop-worn "party line" which AP uses to promote its service both to newspapers and the reading public. It was not a case of disclosing secret information as much as it was simply of not being versed on other aspects of AP. The following representative excerpts

from the interview will illustrate his responses. The questions and answers

are followed by the author's comment on the nature and shortcomings of

the executive's responses.

QUESTION: What type of reporting qualifications and
background does AP look for when it hires reporters?

ANSWER: The same as any newspaper. Advanced training
in specialty areas is good.

COMMENT: He has skirted the issues of liberal arts
versus journalism college training, American versus foreign
national, number of years of practical experience, etc. In
typical bureaucratic fashion, he appears not to know what
types of men write the copy or what types AP would like to
have. These decisions are made by bureau and departmental
heads, and although this executive purports to speak for the
entire AP, he has no idea what is going on in these other administrative spheres.

Q: Do you find it necessary to train or retrain some or
all of the news men?

A: I don't know. Check with the public relations director
on that when you see him later. I guess it depends on the individual.

C: The question has a dual purpose: to try to dig beyond
his first answer and to probe for any endoctrination programs.
The answer is straight forward and supports the author's comment above. The fact that the author was referred to the public
relations man indicates how little information passes from one
sphere to another in the administration and how futile further
pursuit of this type of information would be.

Q: What has been the effect of the electronic media on AP's
operations, on its news concept?

A: The added service [referring to AP's radio-television
news wire] simply required a new wire--a wire handled differ-
ently. It's written to be read and heard.

C: The answer emphasizes only the additional service gained
from and staff needed for the new outlets. To the executive, the
electronic media represent a newer market which must be met
with a special type of product. The problem of competition from
network news departments' growing news-gathering effort is not
mentioned. Problems arising from the dichotomous, largely
opposite news concepts employed by the print and broadcast news
media are not mentioned: newspapers no longer can compete on

the basis of speed and broadcast media have no use for
background, interpretation, features, completeness, etc.
These divergent concepts tend to pull the reporter and
editor in opposite directors at once, since all staffers
are producing and covering for both media at once.

Q: What effects have the UP-INS merger had on AP?

A: Given the structure of AP, we'd want the competition. Think it out. We're doing the best we can; we want
a full report and would get it anyway. But the existence of
competition keeps us on our toes. Without competition AP
would not gain. INS was a poor third. This contributed to
the fact that in the long run the merger was of no real effect
to us.

C: Having thought it out, the author notes that without
competition AP's definition of a "full report" might change
radically. Without competition AP could afford to lay off
excess staffers, save on some transmission costs, and
reduce or perhaps even eliminate some bureaus. Without
UPI, only the superficial or narrowly focused news-gathering efforts of networks, magazines, and individual newspapers would serve as a check on AP's report. If the effect
on content of declining local newspaper competition is any
criterion, it must be expected that AP's report would decline in local and regional news, speed of transmission,
completeness of stories, and perhaps even some degree of
objectivity. Finally, if AP is "doing the best (it) can" and
"would get (a full report) anyway," what sort of competition
could help "keep (AP) on (its) toes?" If, in other words, AP
is already doing its best, no amount of competition can make
it do better, and without competition, AP's best would
probably cost AP much less.

Q: But isn't UPI a much more imposing competitor to
AP now because of a larger staff and more clients?

A: As I said before, competition is good for us. It's
more of an opportunity for AP than anything else.

C: If AP is already doing the best it can, then why will
opportunities (coming from UPI competition) be of any value
to AP? These statements are purely promotional. They are
a business man's double-talk, which in the case of AP is a
luxury afforded by the wire's unequalled position in the field.
(UPI executives, the author noted, talk of competition with
AP in very different terms. They talk of strategy to outwit
AP, of enterprise, of new types of copy which AP does not
have, etc.) The AP executive, by the way, contradicts these
statements on competition below.

Q: What should the role or function of a wire service be today? I'm thinking particularly of the wire's operation with respect to the cold war and the democratic process in this country.

A: The report should be good, accurate, and representative of the day's news. We hit enterprise material hard. We're ahead of the opposition on it now. The service should inform the people of what's going on. It should write so that the public can understand what's going on. We don't monkey around with such things as moral reform in the United States. Groups often tell AP to cover them more, but we couldn't start doing this. There'd be no end to it if we got started, if we got off target.

C: In the first sentence he responds with AP's worn-out promotional slogan. In the third he contradicts his comments above by showing concern for the "opposition" and for wanting to stay ahead. ("Enterprise material," by the way, usually boils down to milking old stories and news events and does not necessarily lead to a news report which is "good, accurate and representative of the day's news.") In the fourth and fifth sentences, he frames the report in terms of a product of salable and useful dimensions to a consumer market. Here is where the thrust of the question could be discussed, but he skirts the issues of domestic and foreign public opinion and policy-making, of covering diverse foreign cultures for Americans and foreigners, and of treating some types of stories as more important than others. In the last three sentences, he contradicts his first notion. Although it is not here assumed that moral reforms are always daily sources of news, their existence (if not their actions) does make them a vital part of any report which purports to be "representative of the day's news." The author's question here is a very important one (implying concern about the wire's ingression into human communication and human values) and its broad political and philosophical possibilities are untouched by the executive in favor of answers which sound like advertising copy or which imply that AP's "target" is a bland, inoffensive product, structured for sale to the widest possible consumer market. [34]

In general, the executive's comments in these areas can be characterized as contradictory, ignorant of AP operations, and largely superficial. His answers were most explicit (not shown above) regarding technological advances, particularly computerization of the system.

Under such circumstances it seems evident that most of the day-to-day operation of the service is conducted and directed by specialists, without the general manager or his executive staff taking a role. In fact, AP's size and diversity seem naturally to mitigate Gallagher's close contact with all facets of the operation, in contrast to Cooper who until World War II was personally directing all innovations and most news report production. Even Gallagher's right-hand man, Montgomery, is specializing in one particular technological development. At best, the general manager can supervise only on the frontier, while the rest of the AP organization is conducted from mutually exclusive, relatively autonomous loci of power.

In one sense, the Associated Press, like other great corporations has surpassed the point at which managers and directors have any real responsibility or decision-making power. The assets of AP--the intangibles of news, meaning, and reputation--will outlive and transcend managerial direction, spurred on by the growing inertia of an increasingly stable and fragmented administrative structure and by outside relationships more than by internal pressures and policy. Andrew Hacker makes this point.

> The corporation . . . is power--the power of productive assets--without a human constituency. It has interests to promote and defend, but they are the interests of a machine more than those of the people who guide, and profit from, its workings. The managers who sit astride the corporate complexes do indeed have power; but it is the power bestowed on them by the resourses of the enterprises they tend. Executives come and go, and their terms of office in the top positions are surprisingly short. But the productive assets remain, continually developing new interests to be safeguarded and new demands to be fulfilled. [35]

Clearly, the trend toward administrative autonomy was begun in 1938 when Cooper noted the difficulties of keeping track of one hundred persons and consequently inserted a stratum of liaison chiefs between himself and departmental heads, bureau chiefs, etc. An intra-administration relationship was continued by this move, but one of the components was changed. By 1954, when the last of the second stratum had been eliminated by Starzel, the relationship had disappeared completely, the executive level performing innovative and developmental functions (not to mention the public relations and titular leadership functions always required of such persons), and the departmental level performing the fundamental, hardcore functions of producing, selling, and moving the product. Although this most recent condition is still new, the new procedural trend seems to be as follows. The executive branch assumes responsibility for the technological or symbolic innovation, developing it, and making all of high-level contacts across industrial and political boundaries to facilitate it. Then, it is turned over to either a new or an existing department for integration into AP's total picture, for expansion among AP's members and clients, for refinement and changes as conditions require.

Summary Discussion

In summary, the last three sections have presented data indicating trends in the conditions of the three sources of power regarding AP: secondary environment (government), primary environment (members and clients), and internal components (the board, general manager, and administrative staff). In general five trends emerge as dominating the political history of AP from 1893 to 1964: (1) because of the antagonism of one state government and with the help of another one, AP attained a high degree of stability with and immunity from state governmental inter- ference early in its history; (2) the board has been dominated by a few wealthy, bondholding and stockholding newspaper properties, in light of No. 3 (below) relevant more in AP's earlier history; (3) the board has be- come increasingly fragmented and less powerful; (4) the general manager- ship grew to a peak of power and has begun to decline; and (5) the adminis- trative staff is now attaining a peak of power in the organization. (Federal involvement, as a component in AP's secondary environment, over the question of franchise rights and membership applications is purposely de- ferred until Chapter VI.)

Figure 5 (see next page) summarizes the principal events and changes in AP's political history which indicate which of the three internal power components dominated the given relationship. Compiled from data presented in this chapter and the previous one, Figure 5 seeks to pinpoint periods of domination for each of the three components. As the summary in the figure indicates, the locus of power has moved from the board through the general manager to the administration, at least in terms of crude, quantitative indices. Appropriately, the trends are not so clearly defined that periods of transition (1908-25 and 1937-54) are not discernable. While the figure does illustrate the general trends suggested above, it cannot be considered the sole summary of this chapter. The trends have many subtle ramifications not appearing in the figure and requiring qualitative exposition.

Figure 5. Summary of Power Relations: 1893-1964

Year	Power Structure Event or Change	M-B	B-G	G-A
1893 -	Board hires general manager (Stone)	m-B	B-g*	
	Board makes all major policies	m-B	B-g	
	Large membership needed for success	M-b		
	Board needs membership backing	M-b		
	Board writes major report	m-B	B-g	
	Board enters world cartel	m-B		
	Board needs members' financial aid	M-b		
1894 -	Board directs war with old UP	m-B	B-g	
1895 -	Grand Divisions are set up	M-b	b-G	
1897 -	Board's policy wins war with UP	m-B	B-g	
	Board opens membership to all nprs.	m-B		
	Old AP members battle Board's policy	M-B		
1898 -	Spanish-American war coverage good	m-B	B-G	
1900 -	Board Representativeness is low	m-B		
	New corporation affirms AP's system	m-B		
	Membership stockholding eliminated	m-B		
	Noyes named President	m-B	B-g	
	Members given franchise rights	M-b		
1893-1908 - BOARD Dominates: 6-20-2-0**		6-13	7-2	0-0
1908 -	Membership Committee probes Stone	M-b	B-g	
1910 -	Board Representativeness is low	m-B		
	Board Longevity is low	m-B		
1912 -	Three administrative Chiefs added		b-G	
1914 -	Service to South America is denied	m-B	B-g	
	Teletype service is started		b-G	
1915 -	Members may receive other services	M-b	b-G	
1917 -	World War I coverage is good		b-G	
1918 -	South American Service is started		b-G	
1920 -	Board Representativeness increases	M-b		
	Board Longevity is high	m-B		
1921 -	State & Regional systems developed	M-b	b-G	
	Martin named general manager		B-g	
1908-1925 - BOARD-GEN. MGR. Dominate: 4-7-7-0		4-4	3-7	0-0
1925 -	Cooper named general manager		b-G	
1926 -	Board & gen. mgr. write major reports		B-G	
1927 -	Four department heads are added		b-G	G-a
1930 -	Board Representativeness is high	M-b		
	Board longevity is high	m-B		
	Board gives Cooper initiative to act		b-G	
1931 -	Day & night wires are separated		b-G	G-a
1932 -	British & German subsidiaries formed		b-G	G-a
1933 -	Radio issue left to membership	M-b		

Figure 5 (continued)

Event			
1934 - Cooper Breaks with world cartel		b-G	G-a
1925-1937 - GEN. MGR. Dominates: 2-2-11-0 2-0		1-7	4-0
1937 - Three small-town directors added	M-b		
1938 - Four administrative chiefs added		b-G	G-A
Miller named president		b-G	
General Manager's report is major		b-G	
One department head is added			g-A
1939 - Laboratory consolidates innovations			g-A
Board decides policy on radio service	m-B		
1940 - One department head is added			g-A
Board representatives is decreasing	m-B		
1942 - Directors limited to three terms	M-b	b-G	
1945 - Members lose franchise rights	m-B		
1946 - Associate memberships created	m-B		
One department head added			g-A
Foreign service is begun		b-G	G-a
1947 - One department head added			g-A
1948 - Starzel is named general manager			g-A
1950 - Board representativeness is low	m-B		
Board longevity is low	M-b		
1952 - TTS & Radio transmission are added			G-A
1937-1954 - GEN. MGR. & ADMIN Dominate: 3-5		0-5	3-8
3-5-8-8			
1954 - Annual Volume loses significance			g-A
General Manager writes major report		b-G	G-A
Administrative chiefs are dropped			g-A
1960 - Board representativeness is high	M-b		
Board longevity is low	M-b		
1963 - Computer system is added			G-A
1954-1964 - ADMIN. Dominates: 2-0-3-4 2-0		0-1	2-4

---

*Only those relations directly involved in or affected by the event or change are given here. The capitalized initial indicates which contributor to the relationship benefitted by the event or change, i.e., gained a degree of superiority in the relationship.

**These figures represent the total instances of superiority in each period for each of the four primary power components in AP's structure. Summarized, these figures are as follows:

Period	Yrs.	Evts/Year	Mbr.	Bd.	G.M.	Admin.
1893-1908	15	1.9	6	20	2	0
1908-1925	17	1.1	4	7	7	0
1925-1937	12	1.3	2	2	11	0
1937-1954	17	1.4	3	5	8	8
1954-1964	10	0.9	2	0	3	4

Early modern history for AP was a nightmare of instability, struggle, and potential destruction, originating both inside and outside the organization. The AP was incorporated on a regional base, without benefit of many wealthy and influential newspaper properties. Illinois' incorporation law did not exactly cover AP's structure, and AP's competitive situation, coupled with its reliance on adjunctive industries required a broad statement of incorporation purpose. Stockholders had to be courted for their financial support, and once recruited, they made their personal desires and goals those of AP in general. This was the first period of many short-term directors and simultaneously the starting point for some important and powerful long-term directorships. The addition of two more directors and incorporation of staggered terms did little to improve the board's partial state of flux created by these short-term directors. Within this context, the organization struggled along, relying on the policies of a dominant, but often desperate and unsettled, board of directors.

Incorporation in the friendlier state of New York gave the AP two new starting points. First, it insured no further state interference. AP's secondary environment thus was largely removed as a political threat which could compound AP's internal difficulties of organization and growth. Second, it permitted a fresh approach to the election of directors and to the board's composition. All members were given the vote, although pre-1900 stockholding interests perpetuated large-newspaper dominance of elections through bondholding. Meanwhile, the board was set at fifteen directors elected for staggered, three-year terms, supposedly by and from the entire nation. Early board composition, however, reflected a cosmopolitan, aristocratic viewpoint among newspaper publishers. By any standards, the board dominated AP during the initial stages of the New York corporation's development.

Technological opportunities, a conservative general manager, a new liberalism among some powerful newspapermen and AP members, a keen, growing competition with UP and INS, and a vigorous, critical, and ambitious young administrator named Cooper were the most important of many factors leading to the first shift in political dominance in AP. While Stone and Martin continued the tradition of bowing to the board's wishes, the board was experiencing (in 1911-20) a period of many short-term directorships and of general indecision over such issues as extending service to South America. This was followed by a decade signaling the start of long directorships principally occupied by strong liberal elements in American newspapering. Simultaneously, World War I furnished the technology and a broader vision upon which the first group of true AP administrators could act.

Cooper's ascent to the top position in 1925 began to bring down the curtain on the board's dominance of AP. While overt signs pointed to a sharing of responsibility between the board and Cooper, Cooper continued building a hierarchy of administrators and supplementary services, just as he had done as a junior executive before 1925 with the state and regional circuits, teletype, South American service, etc. Each new service meant another department or chief or executive to develop and direct it, and each new administrative post usually meant that a new service or innovation was going onto the drafting board. Cooper organized and re-organized his administration to attain the greatest efficienty and effective-ness, depending on AP's size and recent operation--at one point receiving information from and directing as many as one hundred administrators, and at a later time dealing primarily with only four.

The board by 1930 had become fairly well representative of various-sized population centers, but this advance in AP democracy was neutralized by the board's new policy of relying upon the general manager and his lieu-tenants. The directors learned of AP's operations from the administrators, whose jobs, power, and department's continued existence depended upon how favorably they could influence the board's decisions on general expansion and alteration plans.

By 1938 the administration was becoming too large for Cooper's per-sonal scrutiny, and operational chiefs were added. In effect, Cooper was freed of many policy decisions and the two lower strata of administrators were emancipated to expand their control over policy decisions. The ad-ministration was being separated from its creator and was assuming an identity of its own. Simultaneously, the membership was reacting to a second wave of long-term directors (begun between 1921 and 1930). A move to increase representativeness of the board (i.e., the 1937 addition of three directors from communities of 50,000 population or less) seemed to create the opposite effect: representativeness declined between 1930 and 1950.

Perhaps the voting membership (which still consisted primarily of wealthy, bondholding publishers) felt that the 1937 move had relieved them of the burden to elect small-town directors on their own initiative.

Five years later a three-term limit was placed on directors, and the turnover of directors doubled. Fragmentation of the board, the offices, and the executive committee became the rule, and as many as two-thirds of the directors were being replaced every nine years. All of these measures to improve the composition of the board would probably have reduced its power through fragmentation, if it had not already declined. Improvement of the board had become "window dressing" to sustain the image of a cooperative news-gathering agency in the eyes of the members. The real locus of power was now straddling the executive and administrative sectors of the organization.

Again a world war gave AP administrators a new technology and a broader perspective permitting their individual and collective power to become further entrenched. Cooper's liaison stratum declined soon after his departure, and the break between the executive personnel and the administrators in the departmental stratum was made clean and wide. In its most recent condition, AP's principal activity has been the gathering and disseminating of news, i.e., the maintenance of ground already gained. AP's improvements and changes in the service have been relatively few in the last decade and have made relatively little impact upon the wire's basic product-- the news report and key supplemental services. What few innovations have been introduced in the last ten years have had their initial impetus from the executive stratum (which still performs this vital developmental function),

but their actual implementation has been conducted by administrators at

the departmental level. The difference between this and previous periods

is that the innovations have been fewer and of less influence on AP's basic

news report.

V. O. Key's observations about recent governmental trends seem

more than coincidentally applicable to changes in AP's power structure

since 1893.

> The administrative services have, in terms of the dis-
> tribution of both formal governmental power and informal
> political influence, been the chief heirs of the declining repre-
> sentative bodies. * * * With almost a monopoly of information
> in its sphere of interest, the administrative organization is
> able to release or withhold data in such a fashion as to main-
> tain, if not to expand, their activities and to assure the re-
> tention of administrative arrangements they regard as satis-
> factory. * * * Departmental policy tends to harden into a
> tradition that resists alteration. The institutional pattern of
> ideas comes to be set in a certain fashion, and it tends to stay
> that way. [36]

Whether the democratic institution is a governmental body or a wire service,

expansion and the assimilation of new functions seem to lead naturally toward

systemic maturation. The "healthy" system is that which maintains an

equilibrium between the two trends, initiating either or both when necessary

but in any case making the most of either manifestation for the continued

effectiveness of the system in its relations with its socio-cultural environ-

ment.

(The reader is reminded that since the same hypotheses are relevant

to both Chapters IV and V, they will be introduced at the conclusion of the

next chapter.)

Footnotes

[1] V. O. Key, Politics, Parties, & Pressure Groups (5th ed.; New York: Thomas Y. Crowell Company, 1964), pp. 2-3.

[2] Illinois AP, Volume, I (1894), p. 4.

[3] New York AP, Volume, "Preliminary Proceedings" (1900), p. 1.

[4] Ibid., I (1901), p. 42.

[5] Ibid., p. 4.

[6] Ibid., XXXVII (1937), pp. 3-4.

[7] United States v. Associated Press, et al., "Findings of Fact and Conclusions of Law" (New York: Southern Federal District Court, 1944), sec. 126.

[8] Ibid., secs. 127, 130-132.

[9] New York AP, Volume, XXXVIII (1938), pp. 16-20, 30-36.

[10] U. S. v. A. P., et al., op. cit., sec. 4.

[11] New York AP, Volume XXXIV (1934), p. 26.

[12] See ibid., pp. 49, 57-58 for the specific provisions of the radio policy.

[13] Ibid., XXXVII (1937), p. 4.

[14] Ibid., LXI (1961), p. 44.

[15] Ibid., LXII (1962), pp. 98-99.

[16] Ibid., pp. 95-105.

[17] Cooper, op. cit. (1959), p. 44.

[18] Ibid.

[19] Ibid., p. 8.
[20] Ibid., p. 170.
[21] Ibid., p. 131.

[22]Ibid.

[23]Illinois AP, Volume, II (1895), p. 20.

[24]Cooper, op. cit. (1959), p. 45.

[25]New York AP, Volume, XIII (1913), pp. 3-4.

[26]Ibid., XXIII (1923), p. 77.

[27]Ibid., XXI (1921), pp. 110-111, and ibid., XXII (1922), pp. 97-98.

[28]Ibid., XXII (1922), p. 5.

[29]Cooper, op. cit. (1959), p. 163.

[30]The so-called Grand Divisions continue up to the present time.
In some ways the expanded job of domestic news gathering has reinstated
bureau organization on a division basis. Primarily, however, the divisions
organize membership participation on the annual nominating, credentials,
and auditing committees and organize various aspects of the Associated
Press Managing Editors Association and its work.

[31]New York AP, Volume, XXIX (1929), p. 6.

[32]Ibid., XXXIV (1934), pp. 9-10.

[33]Paraphrased and summarized from ibid., XXXIX (1939), p. 36.

[34]Interview by the author, December 27, 1963, in the executive offices
of the Associated Press, New York City. That portion of the interview reproduced here is as close to being verbatim as the author's notes permit.

[35]Andrew Hacker, ed., The Corporate Take-Over (New York:
Harper & Row, Publishers, 1964), p. 6.

[36]Key, op. cit., pp. 692-693, 695, 709.

Chapter V

MATURATION OF WIRE-SERVICE PRODUCTION STRUCTURES

> The new instruments which tech-
> nology has given the press have
> enormously increased the range,
> variety, and speed of mass com-
> munications. The changes in the
> press are closely related, partly
> as cause and partly as effect, to
> the technological and industrial
> changes elsewhere.
> -- Hutchins Commission (1947)

Production as an organizing concept in this study refers to those processes contributing to the daily construction and dissemination of the wires'
news reports. Essentially it is the business and economic (i. e., manufac-
turing and distribution) sector of the wires' total operation. As noted in the
introductory chapter, the author avoids describing the mechanics of daily
news gathering, editing, and distributing which in a more comprehensive study
would rightfully belong within this organizing category. Also omitted is consideration of the product itself, the communication message in its various
forms.

The raw data of this chapter are financial records of the Associated
Press, studied to understand how forces and events in the primary and
secondary environment affect the wires and their productive process. This
chapter also includes consideration of the effect of internal policy-making
upon production. The sections in this chapter are: (1) Revenue Sources and
Changes, in which financing is seen in terms of membership growth and
disposition, assessment formulas, stocks and bonds, and other forces, and

166

(2) Expenditure and Deficit Trends, in which organizational policies and exogenous influences are examined. A separate summary discussion of productive trends and conditions precedes introduction of hypotheses for both Chapters IV and V.

(The author regrets that a similar study cannot be made of UP, INS, or UPI, but these organizations have published revenue and expenditure figures only infrequently in the last few years and with no breakdown of operational categories and no indication of surpluses or deficits.)

Revenue Sources and Changes

The Associated Press has two major sources of revenue: (1) the sale of stocks or bonds and (2) the weekly assessment, the monetary return for sale of the news report and/or supplementary services to members and clients. Incorporation of the AP in Illinois in 1892 included provisions for stockholding in the corporation. Chapter III describes AP's reliance on stockholder investment as one of the determinants of AP's ultimate success in its war with the old United Press. The strength of AP was measured not only by the number of newspapers paying weekly assessments but also by the number of those newspapers willing and able to purchase shares of AP stock. At $50 per share, the original $30,000 in capital stock (held by the nine incorporators)[1] was increased to $100,000 in 1894.[2] Figures in Chapter III relate the rise of stockholders in AP to 176 by May 1898, although it must be noted that most of the large stockholders were large metropolitan newspapers and were the principal sources of power in the

organization. No dividends or profits were declared during the Illinois
corporation's eight-year existence as a matter of policy.

When AP incorporated in 1900 under the New York law, however, it
was required by that law to eliminate all forms of stock which potentially or
actually produced profit for the stockholding members. Since the bulk of
the stockholders were large and influential newspapers whose weekly assessment payments were very large, the new organization felt obligated to honor
their stock investments as much as it legally could. A bond issue was thus
authorized for $150,000 to which stockholders of the former Illinois cor-
poration were given first chance to subscribe.

The power of stockholders and bondholders is discussed in the previous
chapter, and it is in the power structure where their influence has been felt
by virtue of their augmented voting power rather than in the creativity structure. Although their support of AP from 1894 to 1897 was important to the
young and growing organization, AP's post-1900 structure makes production
contingent upon assessments rather than continued activity of stocks and bonds.

Three factors determine the size of AP's annual revenue based on
assessments: (1) the number of members paying assessments, (2) the degree
to which subsidiary or supplementary AP services are offered or subscribed
to, and (3) the condition of AP's assessment formula. Table 10 (see Appendix
B) compares percentages of annual increase or decline of revenue (derived
from assessments) with percentages of AP domestic and foreign membership
increase or decline, where available. Unfortunately, the latter figures are
supplied by AP and these become difficult to find when membership totals begin

to drop. Consequently, the comparison is less than complete, and a few
of the important occasions, when a definite change in revenue conditions
occurred, cannot be analyzed. In general, however, it appears from Table
10 that only large changes in the membership figures have had any influence
upon the degree of revenue change (1897 and 1945-46), and even this influence does not appear always, as in the cases of 1916 and 1947. Regardless
of whether large changes in membership have a concurrent influence on
revenue in every case, AP is well aware of the fact that the larger the
membership and clientele totals, the larger and more stable will be its
assessment-based revenue.

The second factor may be more important than the first, in terms
of its changing effect upon revenue. Early in the century the AP board
was greatly disturbed by the large number of members receiving only
"pony" service (i.e., an inexpensive, 500-word telephone report of the
day's top stories), as opposed to the full day or night cycle of telegraphed
news. The board's interest was to entice the pony service recipients to take
the full report. Its reports between 1904 and 1922 constantly refer to the
lack of leased-wire growth in relation to that of pony service and to the fact
that continued member reliance on the latter crippled AP financially. Continued growth and refinement of the system and its product, the impetus of
World War I, and the steady rise of teletype service and improvements
eventually converted both pony and Morse service to the new teletype circuits.

Moreover, by the mid-1930's when the above conversion was completed, AP was offering several supplementary services (e.g., Newsfeatures,

Newsphotos, Wirephotos, etc.) receipt of which required additional
assessment payments. Offering a new service, of course, does not in
itself insure its immediate acceptance by members and clients. The
latter must have a basic optimism about their own future and a general
propensity to speculate if they are to subscribe to the new service. Table
10 presents no explicit data related directly to this phenomenon. It will
be noted, however, that the general long-term increase of revenue occurs
at a higher rate than that of membership in AP. With the possible exception of the early 1930's (i.e., during the Depression and the initial thrust
of radio), publishers' optimism since 1893 has remained relatively high,
based on such general long-term newspapering trends as technological
advances in the industry, declining competition, increasing chain operation, and rising advertising revenue and circulation. Since it will be noted
below that Table 10 clearly shows the points at which effects of a revision
in AP's assessment formula are felt by revenue, the general high rate of
increase in revenue for the remainder of the period (vis-a-vis membership
increases) must be attributed to the continually high propensity of AP publishers to avail themselves of AP's increasing number and diversity of
supplementary services.

The third factor--the condition of AP's assessment formula--is, of
course, the important determinant of periodic revenue increases. AP's
pride in its cooperative structure stems primarily from its adherence to
and its success with the practice of pro-rata assessments. Beyond the
necessity for distinguishing between various types of service (leased wire,

pony service, supplementary, etc.), some distinction was necessary
earlier in AP's history between large newspapers and small ones and
between those easily reached by telegraph wires and those more distant.
Transmission costs traditionally are a wire service's largest expense
(usually about one-half of total annual expenditure - compare Tables 11
and 12 for the period 1893-1935). During AP's first thirty years when
its leased-wire network and membership were still growing, transmission costs were the primary determinant of a newspaper's weekly
assessment, unless the newspaper was fortunate enough to share the expense with several local competitors or was close to an AP trunk line or
division bureau. The farther the newspaper was from the headquarters
or regional relay point, the more leased wires and Morse operators were
needed to move the report to the paper's office and thus the higher the
assessment paid by the newspaper. Figure 6 rank orders large-assess-
ment newspapers in 1900 (New York corporation) according to weekly
assessments, and compares this order with the number of newspapers
among which the transmission toll was pro-rated, the population of the city,
and the distance of the city from a trunk or relay sending point. (All assessments are for morning papers.)

Included in Figure 6 are most of the nation's wealthy AM newspaper
properties, due principally to their occupation of the morning field in
generally large cities. Newspapers in these thirteen cities paid the highest
weekly assessments of any papers receiving AP in 1900. Clearly no one
factor accounts for the respective assessments. Apparently, in 1900 the

Figure 6. Assessment Determinants: 1900[3]

Assess. Per Npr	City	AM Nprs	Wire Miles	Pop. Rank	Tot.AM Assess.	Tot. Rank	Assess Determinant
$270.00	Seattle	1	879	--	$270.00	10	Few nprs, long distance
230.00	San Francisco	3	762	10	690.00	4	Long distance
	New York City	6	1	1	1380.00	1	Many nprs, population
201.25	Denver	2	606	24	402.50	7	Long distance
175.52	Kansas City	2	254	22	351.04	8	Long distance
154.00	Chicago	5	341	2	770.00	3	Population
139.12	St. Louis	3	295	4	417.36	6	Population, distance
134.93	St. Paul	2	412	8	269.86	11	Long distance
115.00	Salt Lake City	2	507	--	230.00	12	Long distance
	Pittsburgh	4	230	12	460.00	5	Many nprs
	Baltimore	3	97	6	345.00	9	Population
	Philadelphia	7	92	3	805.00	2	Many nprs
103.12	Cleveland	2	125	7	206.24	13	None

the formula at the top end of the assessment scale was based on two sets of
factors. The fewer the newspapers and/or the longer the transmission distance, the higher the assessment. Examples are Seattle, San Francisco,
Denver, Kansas City, St. Paul, Salt Lake City, and St. Louis to a lesser extent.)

If transmission distances were not particularly great, on the other
hand, the formula considered the city's population and/or the total number
of morning papers in the city. It is interesting to note, under this second
consideration, that although the pro-rata principle should in theory operate
to the advantage of AM newspapers in cities where many morning papers
operate, AP's scale does not adjust these papers' assessment downwards
enough to fully compensate for the large number of AM papers. In other
words, although Philadelphia has seven morning papers, its total AM assessment ranks second, while Chicago with five AM papers ranks third in total

assessment. The cities' population ranking and individual newspaper assessment are exactly the opposite. Apparently, the formula allows the pro-
rate principle to operate to AP's benefit first (in terms of aggregate weekly
revenue) and second to the members' benefit (individual weekly assessments)
where many newspapers are involved.

In general, the figures indicate an inequality of assessment with
the burden falling upon large-city newspapers, those with many competitors
and/or those most distantly located from New York or a relay point. Population in 1900 played a relatively minor role as a determinant of assessments.

The Annual Volumes indicate that general upward revisions of the
assessment formula to cover increasing costs or to equalize the formula
were made on five occasions. The effect of these revisions appears in
Table 10 as unusually large percentages of annual revenue increase, in relation to recent rates of change.

1913	4. 6%
1919-20	48. 2
1923	11. 1
1942	3. 7
1952	9. 1

Table 10 also indicates that a sixth revision may have occurred in 1960 (8. 4
per cent). Although no mention of a revision at this time was made in the
annual reports, this seems reasonable since AP attempts to revise its
assessment every ten years in connection with the new U. S. Census report.

A brief look at AP's remarks about these revisions will indicate
somewhat of their causes and of the formula changes over time. In 1911 the
board reported that the assessment revision was being conducted on the basis
of the 1910 U. S. Census Bureau report and that a deficit of $54, 902. 93 would

be cleared away within a year. It was also implied that part of the increased revenue derived from the revision would serve as the basis for a
reserve fund to guard against future deficits caused by unusually expensive
coverage or operational situations. [4]

This reserve fund helped AP through World War I coverage, but as
Table 11 reveals, AP had a $152,588 deficit in 1918. Another revision
was needed. The board justified the new increase on three grounds: (1) to
restore gradually the war-depleted emergency reserve fund, (2) to pay
necessary increases in salaries of editors, and (3) to meet higher costs of
everything "entering into the conduct of our business."[5] The revision was a
large one, but AP had grown rapidly during the final years of the war and
was emerging as a much larger and more energetic institution in the postwar
years. Postwar prosperity made editors optimistic, and this optimism led
them to want larger and more diversified AP news reports.

Another aspect of the 1919 revision was Cooper's pressure as traffic
department chief and later as assistant general manager to enlarge leased-
wire facilities, introducing the state- and regional-circuit concept into news
distribution. The so-called "side wires" not only provided newspapers with
much-needed state and regional news, but also gave the organization its first
real geographical, transmission basis for applying the principle of pro-rating
expenses. Cooper believed that the pro-rata principle should be used more
effectively and equitably than it had in the past (vis-a-vis the disparities
noted above in connection with the 1900 assessments) and his state- and
regional-circuit concept permitted a communal pooling of financial and news

resources for the mutual aid of all circuit members. The new assessment

formula used after 1919 was primarily Cooper's invention to "proportion

assessments more equitably among the members."[6]

By 1923 (the third major revision), the state and regional circuit

had developed sufficiently and the new U.S. Census figures were available

to facilitate both the new formula and an upward revision in the rates. The

board spelled out the characteristics of the new formula in 1923, dividing

the assessment into three types:

1. WIRE CHARGES - leased wire costs
   a. a pro-rated portion of state or regional circuit's pro-
      rated portion of the feeder, truck line.
   b. a pro-rated portion of the entire cost of operating the
      state or regional circuit.
   c. with pro-rated portions "a" and "b" (above) weighted
      according to population of the city.
   d. day-wire subscribers paying 57% of the aggregate and
      night-wire subscribers paying the remaining 43%.
2. GENERAL CHARGES - expenses of the organization
   a. apportioned among the newspapers according to their
      states' respective proportion of the total U.S. popula-
      tion.
   b. day-wire subscribers paying 46% of the aggregate and
      night-wire subscribers paying the remaining 54%.
3. LOCAL CHARGES - salaries & expenses of all locally-based
                   operators, manifolders, and messengers,
                   pro-rated among the newspapers served.[7]

By the late 1930's, AP's freedom from the world cartel became

somewhat of an unexpected burden on the organization, in light of heightened

tensions in pre-World War II Europe. After an initial expenditure to cover

itself in the foreign news field after leaving the cartel (a 24.1 per cent in-

crease in 1934 and a 17.2 per cent increase in 1935), AP continued concen-

trating on domestic news until 1939 when Nazi Germany invaded Poland and

the last few frantic rounds of prewar negotiations and conferences proceeded.

In that year AP's foreign news collection expense increased by more than
one-third, growing to over one million dollars for the first time in its
history. (See Table 12.) Revenue declined 0.4 per cent and expenses increased 0.2 per cent, leaving a deficit of $68,092, the first AP deficit
in fifteen years (and the first of Cooper's administration). Although membership figures are not available for this period, one can assume that
either membership declined (thus prompting the omission of membership
totals from annual reports), or members' optimism declined, causing
them to drop supplementary services. Cooper called 1939 "one of the most
exacting years as respects expenses," pointing out that UP and INS had imposed wartime levies on newspaper clients, and said that since AP had not
had a general assessment revision in twenty-five years, one was due.[8] The
board awaited the 1940 U.S. Census report to compute the assessment, and
announced in 1941 that the revision was underway and would be imposed the
following year.[9] Table 10 indicates that the revision increased revenue by
3.7 per cent in 1942, and a concurrent expense reduction of 0.5 per cent
left a surplus of $611,282 that year, the largest surplus in AP's history.
Part of the expense reduction was due to declines in AP's membership and
part caused by cutbacks in foreign and news distribution operations.

Upward assessment adjustments in the early 1950's and 1960's appear
to have occurred, although neither the board nor the general manager mentioned the latter, and the former was only hinted at. Apparently the organization feels it would have less of an effect upon membership numbers and AP's
image for members to make the decennial revision regular and unannounced.

One contributing factor to the de-emphasis of assessment revisions
and schedules is the apparent disproportionately heavy revenue load recently carried by domestic newspaper members, vis-a-vis associate
members in foreign countries and other media. Table 12 reveals that in
1963 total expenditures were divided among operational headings as follows:

```
Domestic News Collection & Distribution.... 54. 4%
Foreign News Collection & Distribution..... 16. 5
Supplemental Services ................... 27. 2
Administrative Salaries.................   1. 9
                                        100. 0%
```

Immediately, the question arises: how much of each of these operational expenditures is covered principally by domestic assessments? A
UPI staffer has told the author that AP's report is created first and foremost for AP's domestic members and particularly for newspaper members, and that clients (i. e., associate members) in foreign countries and
other media receive only a tailored or abbreviated version of this report.
Certain AP practices would seem to support this contention. Associate
memberships are not limited by pro-rata assessments; they can be acquired at whatever price the market will bear--usually a price propor-
tionally less than a membership assessment, all things considered and held
equal. Keen competition with UPI in areas where associate memberships
are numerically strong for AP helps keep that market price down. Moreover, AP's position as a strong world wire service, measured by its outlets,
their number and geographical scope, can now be maintained almost completely by keeping or increasing its associate members (its full membership
having remained limited to the relatively stable and unchanging newspaper

population of the United States). This, of course, would make AP want to offer associate memberships at the lowest possible price.

Although it is impossible to separate distribution from collection expenses in the new operational categories (categories, by the way, introduced in 1946 with the advent of the world and radio service, perhaps to conceal the very thing the author is trying to describe at this point), it can be assumed that transmission expenses still amount to about one-half of the total annual outlay, as it did earlier in AP's history. Yet one-half of the 1963 Domestic News Collection and Distribution total exceeds the total Foreign News Collection and Distribution for that year, while figures in Table 14 show that half of AP's total outlets are foreign, or worse, that about 78 per cent are associate members, foreign and domestic. Clearly, full members, while paying a pro-rata assessment which is probably equally divided among them, are supporting the AP organization to a much larger extent (given the distribution element of domestic expenditures) than the associate members (given their larger numbers and their immunity from the artificially, arbitrarily set pro-rata schedule).

An interesting departure from the general increase of revenue was AP's Depression policy of the early 1930's. AP's Depression figures, combined from Table 10, 11, and 13 in Appendix B, are as shown on following page.

The entire AP organization cut back its operation up to 1934, during the period in which critical financial pressure was felt by the news dissemination media in general. Table 12 indicates that every operation category was

Year	Revenue	Expenses	Deficit Surplus	AP's Mbrshp	Total U.S. Nprs. [10]
1929	6.8%	6.9%	$ 0	2.7%	0.3%
1930	6.1	3.7	231,661	1.3	-0.1
1931	-1.8	0.4	6,246	0.6	-1.0
1932	-10.6	-11.7	123,758		-0.5
1933	-12.6	-11.9	45,342		-0.1
1934	2.8	1.3	11,263	1.9	0.9
1935	16.3	15.9	141,959	1.4	1.1
1936	10.3	9.0	277,116	1.6	2.0
1937	3.6	6.6	0	2.4	-0.3

affected by the cutback. The least affected category was domestic news coverage which itself experienced an 11.7 per cent reduction in 1930. The first hint of Depression-induced trouble came from outside the AP organization in 1930-31 with the decline in the number of daily newspapers. Revenue declines for AP in 1931 are apparently attributable to publishers dropping supplementary services; membership changes were slight, but still increasing. The weaker papers suffered most from the Depression, feeling the pinch in advertising revenue and circulation figures, some finally succumbing to the squeeze. Many of the stronger papers weathered the declines until 1938-39 when a general realignment of newspapers occurred, only partially created by the Depression.

In 1931, the board, despite declining revenue, announced a modest expansion of operations to assume news-gathering responsibilities dropped by member newspapers. (It appears, however, as though this announcement was partially aimed at creating an optimistic attitude among members.)

> In large number, members in varying degrees have suspended their individual efforts at news collection in the foreign, and domestic and regional fields and have more fully utilized what The Associated Press news report affords. Members operating on this basis have effected

economies in other expenses than The Associated Press
assessment. This year the management is operating with
reduced income and it hopes without loss of efficiency.[11]

Table 12 indicates that reductions in that year were principally adminis-

trative (leased-wire service, -3.4%; salaries, -2.7%; and general ex-

penses, -15.8%) while increases were in news-gathering operations

(incoming service, 1.5%, and foreign service, 8.2%). Apparently,

newspapers had not yet started dropping from AP's membership ranks in

1931, but editors had started dropping AP's supplementary services and

relying more heavily on AP's hardcore domestic and foreign news reports.

The pessimism exhibited by cutbacks in extra service appears related to

declines in advertising revenue for U.S. newspapers in general. Mott re-

ports that a small decline was experienced in 1930 (15 per cent), but that

in 1931 the drop had reached 24 per cent, or twice the greatest general

circulation decline experienced during the Depression.[12]

In 1932, advertising revenue was down to 40 per cent below 1929,

and it hit bottom in 1933, 45 per cent below 1929. In these two years, AP's

board took more positive steps to retain its membership (which apparently

was beginning to decline) by cutting back expenses in all categories except

domestic news. Concurrently, it reduced assessments and paid assessment

refunds to members. In these two years assessment reductions totaled

$1,184,220.48, and refunds amounted to $1,391,066.78.[13] The end of refunds

and assessment cuts came in 1934 with a 16.3 per cent increase in revenue and

a 15.9 per cent increase in expenditures occurring in 1935. Impetus for re-

instatement of 1930 conditions came from Cooper, who even during the difficult financial times optimistically sought expansion of the service as a guarantee

of increased membership and members' loyalty. He reports his success

at reclaiming lost ground in 1934.

> At a board meeting in October . . . I reported that the
> assessment reductions and the refunds to the members, not
> only had halted the progressive development of the general
> service . . . but that in my opinion they had brought about a
> retrogression.
> I said that in continuous contacts with members, I had
> not found one who felt that the reduction to him had increased
> his interest in The Associated Press. The attitude was just
> that the reductions were welcomed. Some, however, did not
> know or had forgotten that any decreases in their assessments
> had been made.
> Considering this, I told the Board, I had reached the
> interesting conclusion that continuation of striking improve-
> ments in the service would have done more to enhance mem-
> bership appreciation than was accomplished by reducing
> assessments and salaries. . . . The Board at that session
> approved my recommendations (and) . . . I acted accordingly
> and promptly aimed for new achievements. [14]

Here the policies of the board and Cooper were apparently in conflict:

the board of newspaper publishers believed that loyalty could be attained

through assessment reductions, and Cooper as an administrator with re-

sponsibility for the jobs and salaries of many employees believed that con-

tinued growth and optimistic policies could best command loyalty. The actual

feelings of the members cannot be ascertained, but the reversal of AP policy

in 1934 was based on Cooper's report to the board. And the reversal came

none too soon. AP broke with the world cartel in 1934, inaugurated the con-

troversial Wirephoto system in 1935, and ran into its own financial troubles

in 1939 with outdated assessment rates and war clouds in Europe.

Expenditure and Deficit Trends

Expenses respond to three factors, but unlike revenue, the factors are somewhat different and their interplay is much more difficult to understand. The factors are: the domestic and foreign events requiring coverage; the momentary condition of technological and content innovation, and a vast number of arrangements and agreements, contractual and otherwise, with suppliers.

The continual existence of and pressure from competition has caused AP through the years to spend much money on news coverage, more so probably than if there were no other wire-service reports with which to compare AP's. Although wires attempt to locate full- or part-time correspondents in the major news centers of the world (an expensive arrangement in itself), no one reporter can adequately cover a foreign revolution or an election, a natural or man-made disaster, or any one of a number of other "banner stories." Although news coverage problems will be discussed in Chapter VII, it should be pointed out here that no amount of planning or even stockpiling of funds will insure adequate control over the coverage of a large and involved story. United Press International reportedly lost hundreds of thousands of dollars attempting to cover the violence and political maneuvering in the Republic of Congo following that country's acquisition of independence in 1960. [15]

The assassination of President Kennedy in 1963 provides a good example of the extent to which a wire service must go to cover an important, emotional, and complex news event, whether pacifying the readers of a one-wire newspaper or the wire editor of a two-wire paper. AP has listed 153

reporters, editors, and photographers who concentrated on the assassina-

tion story during the four days of its peak.[16] AP also claims to have moved

more than a quarter of a million words in the first four days under 133

different datelines and 96 different by-lines and to have moved 248 Wire-

photos.[17]

Coverage situations the magnitude of the Congo and the assassina-

tion, therefore, play a very pronounced role in shaping and altering,

drastically and quickly at times, the otherwise relatively stable condition

of a wire service's expenditure structure. As competition among the world's

wire services heightens and violence becomes the principal ingredient of a

"successful" daily news report, more and more such situations have come

to demand the all-out effort of the wires, and the wires, in turn, have

learned to weather an increasing number of these situations with relatively

little stress. Earlier wire-service history, however, was written in part

on the basis of unique coverage situations, and much of the expenditure

structure was explained to members in terms of the difficulty of or improve-

ment in covering particular events. In effect, these observations make firm

a connection between a largely internal systemic phenomenon (the expendi-

ture structure) and a largely external set of activities (secondary environ-

mental occurrences). The connection, far from causal, includes as many

influences flowing from the wire's value system for defining news and success

in news reporting as influences flowing from the environmental news events.

Large internal expenditure adjustments (i.e., increases of 10 per cent

or more and all decreases) are measured by overall expenses (see Table 11) by expenses within operational categories (see Table 12), and by annual

surpluses or deficits (see Table 11) wherein the element of revenue-

expense interaction is introduced. These, then, are the quantitative

aspects of structural changes in AP's expenses. Qualitative explanations,

where available, are furnished by the board or the general manager in

their respective annual reports. Taken together, these data, presented

below in chronological fashion, yield considerable understanding about

AP's productive process and growth since 1892.

Large deficits between 1893 and 1896 result largely from AP's

war with the old United Press. In 1895, the board referred to the conflict

and then confessed its inability to hold the line against deficits.

> After all had been done to reduce expenses that
> seemed at the time wise to do, there still remained an
> estimated monthly deficit of about $7,000. * * * The
> figures show that the contest with The United Press has
> cost the Association $209,414.82--a large amount, but
> a small price to pay for the independence of the American
> Press.[18]

The struggle's end brought increases in foreign coverage, salaries,

and general expenses amounting to 19.7 per cent in 1897. The following

year saw AP exerting its full organizational strength on coverage of the

Spanish-American War. Foreign news expenses were up more than 200

per cent in 1898 and general expenses increased by nearly one-quarter. The

war "involved some novel problems to the newsgatherer and taxed the in-

genuity and resources of this organization as they had never been taxed before,"

said the board.[19] This experience showed AP its potential strength as a

foreign news gatherer and the next twenty years saw AP moving into foreign areas wherever it did not conflict with its three cartel partners. Three

such areas were Russia, the Far East, and the Pacific Islands. The board

justified foreign expansion on a new trend in reader habits calling for foreign

news, a trend found in the Spanish-American War.

> Your board desires to impress upon your attention
> a change that has been going on in the demands of the reading
> public, and hence of the members. Until the outbreak of the
> Spanish-American war, interest in news from the foreign
> field was limited, and the expenditures for service by cable
> were comparatively moderate. Suddenly, however, not only
> were the operations of the American army and navy in the
> Philippines and the Antilles of the greatest moment, but a
> keen desire was awakened for detailed information from
> every point on the globe. * * * A marked increase in the ex-
> penses of the Association has been inevitable. . . . [20]

The Russo-Japanese War of 1904-5, a struggle of relatively minor

importance in America, became almost a domestic issue of the first order

in AP's report, because AP had found an area not disposed of elsewhere

within the cartel. The expense of covering this war was great (a 26.3 per

cent increase in 1903-4 and a 14.8 per cent increase in 1904-5), but AP

believed both its world and domestic positions would be enhanced by the

effort   The board comments.

> . . . the expenditures for the year exceeded the income by
> $43,279.22. This was due to the heavy burdens imposed by
> the Russo-Japanese war and the disturbed condition of affairs
> in European Russia. Your Board fully anticipated such a
> result, and the deficit occasions therefore neither surprise
> or alarm. . . . The news service covering the closing weeks
> of the conflict was exceptionally excellent and correspondingly
> expensive. In reporting the peace conference at Portsmouth,
> N.H., the Association achieved a distinct triumph. The dis-
> turbances in European Russia . . . tested the capacity of the
> organization in an unusual fashion, but happily, the require-
> ments of the service were met in every case and the dispatches
> presented such a view of the situation as, for comprehensiveness
> and truthfulness, has rarely been surpassed. [21]

The frequent deficits during the next ten years resulted from several causes, most of them associated with strengthening and expanding the service. In 1909, for example, the deficit was attributed to enlarging the staff and improving working conditions.

> The increased expenses during the year were
> partially due to an enlarging and strengthening of the
> working personnel, and to the physical betterment of
> all the central offices and partly to the reporting of a
> number of unusual news events.[22]

Much of this expansion was, in turn, caused by the gradual realization by AP that its dream of a purely cooperative organization in which members would share the burden of news gathering was not going to materialize. Stronger competition from UP, decreasing news-gathering participation by AP members, and a rising demand by members for a more comprehensive report appear to have been the key factors. The board tells the members its dilemma.

> . . . the Associated Press is now called upon to (handle
> important domestic news events) largely through its own
> staff correspondents. Much of this news in former years
> was received through the special reports of members in
> their respective home fields. The demand, however, of the
> membership for a comprehensive report and more rapid
> handling of important news occurrences has made it necessary
> for the management to send staff men to report many of these
> happenings. This has caused a greater expenditure than
> formerly, but in turn has resulted in a much more satisfactory
> and altogether quicker reporting of news in which the press
> of the entire country is interested.[23]

Covering three political campaigns in 1912[24] led AP to establish a reserve fund in 1913 to attempt to meet the large expenses of such coverage emergencies. The following year, however, World War I burst forth and AP's long-sought stability of surplus-deficit balance and expenditure was to be unobtainable until 1919. AP spent more money on war coverage between

August 1 and December 31, 1914, ($258,551.42) than it had throughout all

of 1913 on foreign coverage ($224,543.90).[25] Foreign service expenses,

according to Table 12, almost doubled in 1914, increased by 20.7 per cent

in 1915, and after reaching a plateau of more than $500,000 that year,

remained relatively constant until the United States became totally involved

in 1918, when it increased by 41.8 per cent. All other categories were

showing occasional declines and very few large increases during this period.

Between 1918 and 1923, AP's postwar expansion is measured pri-

marily in increasing leased-wire and salary expenses. It will be remembered

that during this period, regional and state circuits were being established,

teletype had begun to replace Morse transmission, and AP was extending

service to South America. Cooper became general manager in 1925 and

thus began an era marked by increasing stability of expenses. Prior to

1925, Stone and Martin had some relatively large increases in expenses,

coupled with at least three declines in total expenditure: 1899, 1905-6, and

1913. Apparently the pre-1925 policy permitted across-the-board reaction

to an external coverage emergency and retraction of such an effort after

the emergency had passed. First the emergency elicited increases

in the appropriate operational category (e.g., foreign news in 1898,

1904-5, 1914, and 1918, domestic news in 1911-12, etc.), and after the

emergency had passed the overall expenditure picture was reduced approxi-

mately the pre-emergency conditions. The propensity to expand the service

was there sufficiently to make AP move into the Far East and the Pacific
areas when an emergency occurred and to expand European coverage after
World War I, but in most cases AP's philosophy before 1925 was one of
reaction, a negative type of expansion which had to await crisis or external
opportunity to manifest change.

Cooper's philosophy, on the other hand, was a positive one: create
the opportunity, push for the innovation rather than waiting for it to materialize, permit a relatively high level of general and constant expansion and improvement. Stone and Martin had fifteen deficits in thirty-three years, a
rate of about 48.5 per cent. This percentage is a reliable indicator of the
number of years AP was caught short by some external condition. It must
be remembered, however, that those first thirty-three years included some
of the difficult instances of AP's long history: stiff competition, a shoestring beginning, a world war, and major changes in AP policy and technology, just to mention a few.

Cooper's twenty-four years included fewer drastic increases and decreased in overall expenses (except for the unique case of the Depression),
and had only two deficits (1939 and 1948, both explained below), for a rate
of only 4.2 per cent. The way was cleared for Cooper's positive philosophy
by the assessment increases of 1918-19 and 1923, which he claims to have
had a prominent part in acquiring. Martin's deficits in 1922 and 1924 appear
caused by over-extending some of the operational categories during the postwar years of prosperity and expansion. Under Cooper's direction, there
appears to be no less interplay among the operational categories, but the

overall expenditure rates were more consistently increasing and at a more

constant rate. After 1925, AP's growth was greatly accelerated in all

aspects of its work. Supplementary services were added and expanded

(with a separate operational category for it replacing general expenses

in 1936), the collection and distribution of foreign news was introduced

on a large scale, technological innovation was actively sought and utilized,

and several domestic crises and the news-producing New Dealers in

Washington prompted some large increases in domestic coverage.

By 1939 the old 1923 assessment formula was no longer producing

enough revenue to sustain AP's operations, particularly in the face of im-

pending war in Europe. Cooper admitted that 1939 was a bad year for the

organization; he experienced his first deficit as general manager that year.

A reduction in general expenses in 1942 is attributable to cutbacks in World

War II coverage in a year which was both defeating for the U.S. war effort

and somewhat slow-moving for war news production. The surplus that year

($611,282) is the largest in AP's history. Cooper's second deficit came in

1945 ($347,076) and was prompted by the massive war coverage effort and

by the concurrent extension of postwar news gathering and distribution

abroad.

World War II had delayed AP's post-cartel expansion of such facilities,

but Cooper resumed the expansion program before the end of the war. Cooper

explains his timing.

> Since The AP no longer had cartel restrictions, I
> instituted plans for The Associated Press world service, the
> execution of which had been my fondest dream. They had not
> fully developed when World War II broke out and interposed

delay. As the tide of war turned favorably toward America and its allies, however, I gave Lloyd Stratton, an assistant general manager, the opportunity to investigate the field open to the development of The Associated Press world service.[26]

Cooper's design called for following on the heels of occupation forces through Europe, Africa, and Asia, offering the service to new and re-appearing newspapers before other world services or national agencies had a chance to enter the field and take command.

Reorganization and redevelopment of the staff to cope with the complex problems of reconversion and peace-making were well underway by the end of 1945. Overseas the staff expanded its operations into former enemy or enemy-controlled areas, (and) continued to wage war against the lingering barriers of censorship existing chiefly in Russia's sphere of influence.[27]

Table 12 shows that the 38.4 per cent increase in expenses that year origi-nated in every operational category affected by world expansion; only domestic news collection had a relatively small increase over 1944.

Under Starzel and Gallagher, the Associated Press has again shown signs of instability, in that nine of the fifteen years (or 60 per cent) between 1949 and 1963 have produced deficits. This period has seen, as one unstable factor, considerable fluctuation in AP's international service. Factors af-fecting the equilibrium of international service are more diversified and complex than those determining the extent of stability within a single nation. International politics, competition with UP, INS, and UPI, competition with foreign national wire agencies (many of them governmentally operated and therefore "required reading" for the nation's newspapers), the difficulties of collecting, constructing, and distributing a news report for widely scattered

and highly diversified clients are a few of the more thorny problems which
confronted AP.

Advancing technology has led AP through various stages of improving
on its foreign news transmission. Starzel, in announcing the introduction
of radio teletype in 1956, indicated the number of technological conversions
necessary through the years to improve and extend transmission abroad.

> The growth of world service reached another significant
> stage. From Morse wireless to cable, to Hellschreiber, to
> leased wires, to radio teletype, has been its history of trans-
> mitting everything from an abbreviated to a complete news re-
> port, prepared and emitted from New York, San Francisco,
> London, Frankfurt. Unification and instantaneous transmission
> of the world report at New York became possible with the global
> use of radio teletype, east-west, north-south. [28]

When such an innovation is multiplied by the number of sending, relaying, and
receiving machines necessary for global transmission, the job of conversion
becomes massive and very expensive. Moreover, the expense is increased
by world transmission rate increases and by the individual rate schedules
and changes of each national or regional wire or cable organization with which
AP must deal.

To inaugurate service for just one newspaper in a previously unserved
nation requires a large expenditure to extend news distribution facilities,
install equipment, augment the bureau (if a news-gathering office is already
in the country), or to establish a bureau, perhaps provide for translation of
the report into a different language, etc. The problem for AP is compounded
by the fact that over several years, service to a given country may be started,
stopped, and started again several times. Although reports are often sketchy
about annual additions to and subtractions from AP's list of foreign countries,

partial lists indicate that in the years 1950, 1951, 1952, 1955, and 1956 service was started to twenty-five countries. In 1951, 1952, and 1955 service was discontinued to fourteen countries. Several countries appeared more than once in these years: Ethiopia and Paraguay started and stopped AP service in one year; the Netherlands stopped and started again in four years; Guatemala stopped and started in one year, Nicaragua in two years; and the Virgin Islands stopped, started and stopped again in six years.[29]

The complexity and magnitude of foreign news distribution is revealed by these comments from a former bureau chief stationed in an European capital.

> The size of a bureau is determined by two factors: the amount of business done in the country and the amount of interest by outside countries in that one. In the country where I was located, AP had only three newsmen and no operators in its bureau. It transmitted its copy by Telex, by which the sender is charged so much per minute. AP didn't sell much there; thus it was a small operation. UPI, however, had six newsmen and five operators and filed on a leased wire anytime it wanted to. The larger size was due to the fact that UPI had many more subscribers than AP and had to process the incoming news report for its subscribers. The outgoing report is gathered and transmitted in English. The incoming report is transmitted in English by the London bureau. The local bureau usually makes arrangements for translation into the native language and employs a good many natives as operators, messengers, etc. A better rapport is established if reporters are not natives.
>
> There is always pressure from the government. If you transmit what it doesn't like, it can cancel the use of your service in its country's newspapers. * * * The bureau chief has to see to it that the clients in his country are happy. I had to keep running messages across Europe and into London tracking down foreign stories with local angles that my clients could use. The clients would ask for what they wanted, and I would send a list to London and queries to the bureaus involved in covering the stories. About once or twice a week I'd travel the country trying to sign up new clients.[30]

These remarks indicate the multitude of considerations which affect a wire's local stability in each country actually or potentially served by a news report.

The Starzel-Gallagher period of instability, however, was not wholly dominated by expansion of problems with the world service. Table 12 shows that other categories were expanding just as rapidly. Between 1949 and 1963, total increases were as follows: Domestic News Collection and Distribution, 69.2%; Foreign News Collection and Distribution, 74.4%; Supplementary Services, 111.3%; and Administrative Salaries, 64.7%. This period is marked by a general expansion of facilities and introduction of new technology which were no more speculative than Cooper's activities, but which were of such a nature and origin as to be much more risky in the long run and more costly initially. In most cases the initial expense has ultimately paid off for AP (e.g., teletypesetter, Photofax, expanded market tabulations, etc.), but in one or two instances it has not, as in the case of news film distribution for television stations.[31]

Speculation in the post-World War II period has been more risky and costly than before the war for several reasons. First, the organization is now international, requiring a much larger initial investment to innovate a technological advance. Second, AP's addition of world and radio services brings AP and UPI more in line as direct competitors, making any innovation an immediate necessity in the new competitive situation. Third, an increasing number of innovations is based on electronic devices, the cost of which (whether as equipment rental, a patent-right arrangement, or original research and development) is much higher. Fourth, the wires often must depend upon outside corporations which are much more powerful, resourceful, and expensive than the wires in areas of technological advancement and innovation. Fifth, and in a somewhat different area, the postwar years and the cold war tensions have created coverage situations of so diverse a content and location that the wires must choose between over-expanding their staffs to accommodate all possible future emergencies, or continually shifting staffers from one area to another. Both have employed the latter approach primarily, and it has proved to be very costly for them. In all probability, however, the former alternative would have been even more expensive.

The positive, innovative policy which Cooper inaugurated in 1925, therefore, remains in effect today. The difference, however, between Cooper's period and that of Starzel and Gallagher has been in the nature of the innovative process and the types of innovations themselves, rather than in the policies of the respective administrations. Moreover, the nature of news gathering and distributing has become more complex and voluminous while concepts of news and news values are defined by both the wires and their uncontrollable environment, rather than by the wires alone.

Given these changes and the relative stability of AP s innovative policy, one must finally look at the most recent condition of AP's revenue and expenses to glean some understanding of how these postwar trends have actually affected AP's creative process. The pro-rata structure continues to function, and the formula for assessments remains essentially as it was introduced in

1923--based on population and the number of newspapers sharing a facility.

Cooper was able to weather his first decade conclusion (around 1929) with-

out difficulty, even though the assessment rates had been established six

years before. His second decade conclusion (1939) posed the twofold

problem of outdated assessment rates and increasing world tensions. A

gradual reduction in annual surpluses began in 1948 with Starzel in command,

turning into an increasing deficit in 1950. Apparently, the factors noted

above as affecting innovation and general news activities were beginning to

outweigh the increasingly outdated 1940 assessment rates. Deficits between

1955 and 1959 mounted gradually to a record $419,376 in the latter year,

again due to the inability of the 1950 assessment to cover the rising costs of

innovating and carrying on the expanding business of the wire.

In light of political findings in Chapter IV, some of the recent high

frequency of deficits is probably attributable to the propensity of an ex-

panding administrative staff to view the organizational productive structure

principally from individual or departmental standpoints. The increasing de-

partmental autonomy, coupled with increasing difficulty in pinpointing

responsibility and with the increasing desire by department heads and per-

sonnel to perpetuate or strengthen individual spheres of influence, lead

ultimately to economic fragmentation at the organization level, even though

a multitude of budget administrators may perform miracles at the departmental

level. Often budgets are exceeded or disregarded because of a sincere belief

or decision that this or that expenditure will benefit the organization as a whole

--not an atypical phenomenon when operations become autonomous, self-perpetuating, and jealously protected entities. But even the most sincere enthusiasm or calculated development may result at year's end in a heightened deficit burden for the organization.

One final characteristic of the data in Table 12 must be noted. The author sought correlations among the percentages of rise or decline for the various operational categories on the assumption that an initial large-scale activity in one category might simultaneously, or within a year or two, set off similar or opposite reactions in other categories. No such correlations, however, could be found which have not already been described here or which had any long-term consistency over several similar situations.[32] The only correlation found is the one implied above: when overall expenses rise markedly or fall at all, the change is attributable to concurrent and similar changes in one or several of the categories. (This is, of course, only common sense, since the total expenditure is but the sum of category expenditures.) Failure to find any long-term, consistent interrelatedness among the categories leads to the conclusion that each aspect of AP's operations is handled under separate sets of assumptions and criteria, each set geared to different internal and external pressures. As noted above, this autonomous handling of individual operations has become institutionalized and more rigidly structured by the rise of the equally autonomous organizational units. In sum, the categories respond to environmental conditions and to the individual beliefs and policies of administrators rather than to each other or to some overall set of policies guiding the organization as a unified whole.

Discussion and Conclusions

In this chapter it has been found that external pressures and events exert a large influence on productive activity, even when anticipation of such external contingencies forces the wire to operate beyond the bare minimum level required for effective routine production.

Figure 7 summarizes productive activity on the basis of revenue and overall expenditure declines and increases (over 10 per cent). If AP's revenue policy was revised in 1923 to become more equitable and its expense policy was made more flexible in 1925, the figure can be divided between 1924 and 1931 for purposes of reading and understanding. In the first half of the figure, revenue changes occur only when many members are added or the assessment formula is revised drastically. Expenses, however, fluctuate greatly, responding to coverage situations and innovations within the framework of Stone's and Martin's negative or reaction policy. This is borne out by the activities within the various operational categories, as the previous discussion indicates. Moreover, the period produced deficits in 48.5 per cent of the years included. Only four of these deficit years appear in Figure 7 (1895, 1918, 1922, and 1924). Thus, even when extreme conditions do not appear under the revenue or expense headings, deficits occurred 52.4 per cent of the time (eleven of the twenty-one years not appearing in Figure 7).

In general, this early period under Stone and Martin reflected a reaction policy of attempting to maintain a structure close to the daily routine news collection and distribution requirements. The failure to make allowance

Figure 7. Summary of Extreme Productive Activity: Relevant
Years (Revenue & Expenses)

Large Rise-Any Decline			Large Rise-Any Decline In Operational Categories:					
Rev.	Exp.	Year	IS	FS	LW	S	GE	Forces & Activities
20.3		1895	-1.6		16.7	-0.5	-5.6	War with old UP Large deficit Assessment increase
30.8	19.7	1897		16.0		16.5	95.8	Old UP defeated Assessment reduced Membership up 63.9%
18.7	24.3	1898	-14.7	200.7	11.1		-7.4	Span-Amer. war
	-4.8	1899	23.2	-30.3			-12.6	Span-Amer. war over Philippine Insurrection Large surplus
	13.0	1903-4		26.3			473.0	Russo-Japanese War
	-3.0	1905-6	-6.8	-26.9				War is over Large surplus
	-1.0	1913	-18.3	-5.9		-1.4	-11.6	Reserve Fund created Large surplus Assessment increase
	16.6	1918	-8.5	41.8	15.5		-8.9	U.S. in World War I South Amer. service Large deficit
17.6	12.9	1919	39.0	-6.7	20.7	10.2	-3.3	Wire mileage up 25% Assessment increased Staff returns to AP World War I over
	11.1	1922		15.7	10.3	13.4		Postwar prosperity
11.1		1923	118.3	-3.7	18.9	-65.0	38.6	Assessment increase Move to Madison Ave. Salary reorganization Large surplus
	10.8	1924	12.4				11.7	Large election coverage Employee's Reserve Fund
-1.8		1931			-3.4	-2.7	-15.8	Depression Npr. revenue affected
-10.6	-11.7	1932		-29.9	-9.3	-11.5	-15.1	Assessment reduced Assess. refunds made Salaries cut 10% Large surplus

Figure 7 (continued)

Rev.	Exp.	Year	IS	FS	LW	S	GE	Forces & Activities
-12.6	-11.9	1933	38.9	-11.3	-20.4	-7.9	13.9	Assessments reduced Assess. refunds made Npr. Circ. affected New Deal coverage
16.3	15.9	1935	18.7	17.2	13.4		12.2	Assessments restored New Deal activity
							SS	
10.3		1936		-2.1	-25.3	-3.7		Assessments restored Large surplus
-0.4		1939	-0.2	33.8	-0.1	12.2		Membership decline European War coverage
	-0.5	1942		-4.7	-3.5		11.4	Assessment increased Largest surplus World War II goes badly
-1.3		1943	11.4	42.2	-11.9		-0.1	Some membership loss No deficit
32.0	38.4	1945		76.8	45.6	44.4	27.5	Large deficit World War II wrapup Domestic membership rise Push for foreign clients
13.7	11.2	1946				13.1	22.6	No deficit World War II is over Domestic membership rise Push for foreign clients

for emergency news conditions and the innovation and expansion processes

allowed deficits to occur almost as frequently as surpluses. Large addi-

tions to the membership, particularly early in the period, yielded large

increases in revenue, and assessment revisions of large proportions in

1919 and 1923 produced other large revenue jumps. The factor of increased

use of supplementary services was not very critical in this period because

such services did not exist. Other revenue increases--the consistently low

degree of continual annual increase--averaged 3.7 per cent for the remaining

calculable years, and most of this was due to newspapers shifting from pony

to leased-wire service.

When artificially created changes resulting from the Depression are

eliminated from Figure 7, only five of ten years after 1924 remain (1939,

1942, 1943, 1945, and 1946). Both of Cooper's deficit years appear: 1939

as a decline in revenue, apparently due to a drop in membership, and 1945

as large increases in both revenue and expenses, but with the latter exceed-

ing the former because of world service expansion and World War II coverage.

The Cooper period between 1925 and 1948 (without the Depression-oriented

activities) reveals the first loss in revenue due to post-Depression and mid-

world war newspaper instability and to outdated and unrevised assessment

rates. The period saw the positive policy of aggressive innovation and high-

level coverage expenses which was shaken only when assessments became

obsolete, the organization was undertaking a massive expansion program, or

world news conditions became extreme.

On the whole, the Cooper period brought a reversal of AP's earlier

instability and added to the structure a consistently high-level rate of revenue increase by virtue of an increasing range of supplementary services offered by AP. This base increase averaged 5.4 per cent over the fifteen years of Cooper's reign (as compared with 3.7 per cent for Stone and Martin). Stability was high and annual deficits were low during the period.

Since 1948, no revenue or expense changes have been large enough to register on Figure 7, but the Cooper policy of high-level activity within the productive structure has continued to prevail. Many large problems which Cooper faced (obsolete assessments, introduction of radio and world services, and the reporting of a world war) have not affected Starzel's and Gallagher's administrations. Increasingly, however, the continuing policy of aggressive innovation and relatively high readiness for emergency news conditions has been affected adversely by outside factors, owing to the new nature of wire-service innovations, a new diversity of news content and sources, and a growing autonomy of departmentally administered budgets. This effect shows not in extreme changes of revenue and expenses (and thus not in Figure 7), but in the deficit rate which in the post-1948 period has risen to 60 per cent. Moreover, the continual growth rate based principally on addition of supplementary services has slipped from Cooper's 5.4 per cent average to a 4.6 per cent base. There probably are fewer new areas which AP can assimilate as supplementary services than there were in 1925, and development of such services from the ground up seems to have slowed somewhat. On the other hand, a saturation point appears to be poised on the horizon, with respect to existing supplementary services--a saturation point the approach of which is creating a decline in AP's base rate of revenue growth. The actual dimensions of this phenomenon, however, remain to be seen in the future.

Two hypotheses pertain to Chapters IV and V. Each will be discussed separately.

1. The wire services over time have attained the status of a social institution, after having begun as a group effort within another social institution, the newspapers.

In connection with Chapters II and III, it was noted that chronological history of the wires points toward attainment of standard spatial consistency and national solution of a unique problem during the 1890's, probably around 1897. Also, pragmatic consideration points to the unchallenged success of the wires' solution to this problem. Finally, Chapters II and III show the wires' institution-like resemblance to environmental institutions, including the press and telegraph industries in particular and the adjunctive business sector in general.

Patterns of action (which reflect unmeasurable patterns of belief) in the political process have shown legal standardization after the 1900 move to New York State. Also, political patterns (i. e., policy-making and the populating of power positions) have shown temporal standardization beginning in 1900 with the final reorganization of the wire's principal political sub-system, the board of directors. Temporal standardization refers to utilization of patterns consistently until, in the natural growth of a system, a new pattern becomes standardized, through operational necessity and the vitalistic reintegration of sub-systems. In this sense, AP has had three such standardized periods dominated by: the board, 1900-25; the general manager, 1925-54; and the administration after 1954. Each sub-system has come to power and has standardized political patterns of action in response to the momentary needs of the total system. The systemic reintegration which has accompanied their ascent to dominance has rendered previous patterns formally obsolete. Thus, although Chapters II and III locate attainment of institutional status in the 1890's, probably 1897, standardization of political and legal patterns was not attained until about 1900.

Productive processes have apparently been standardized since 1893, reflecting in their periodic reintegration the individual perspectives of general managers and of sub-system interaction, rather than inherent, fundamental change: Stone and Martin, reaction policy; Cooper, positive policy; Starzel and Gallagher, positive policy complicated by cold war and innovative difficulties. The potentially useful tools of adjustment to meet momentary productive crises (stocks or bond issues, assessment increases or reductions, and reallotment among expenditure categories) have been present since 1893.

It appears from material presented in Chapters II-V that the wires have indeed attained, by this writing, the position of a social institution in the United States. In fact, this status increasingly appears also to accrue to them abroad by virtue of their increasing ingression into the communication processes of foreign societies. In the final analysis, the important question is not when precisely the wire services attained institutional status by virtue of temporal and spatial standardization of operational patterns. Rather, the question is whether they have this status now, and if, as indicated

here, they do have such status, one is automatically led into a wide realm
of questions concerning their impact upon society and society's total communication process. Many of these questions will be posed in Chapter VIII.

    2.   The wire services have increasingly attained political and
        productive stability (an essential characteristic of increased
        maturation) by virtue of decreases in the influence of exogenous
        forces and of decreases in the possibility of endogenous frag-
        mentation and conflict.

Stability of the wires was not attained quite as early nor as easily as

institutional status in society. In political affairs, the AP could not find

internal stability of policy until Cooper was named general manager and had

taken control over significant policies from the board. This move success-

fully eliminated the endogenous fragmentation and conflict potentially apparent

in a board of individual newspaper publishers. The subsequent shift of power

to the administrative sector of AP, has eliminated the small potential threat

of individual instability or personal self-interest within general managers.

At present, stability has become so prevalent in the AP that the assets of the

corporation and the autonomy of individual departments sustain the organiza-

tion's day-to-day operation. Potentially, conflict among departments is a

threat, but long-standing policies and procedures in the wires (as within any

newspaper organization) dictate standard patterns of priority and hierarchy.

Exogenous forces in the political process were successfully circum-

vented with the 1900 move to New York City, and recent governmental inter-

vention (the 1945 Supreme Court case) involved relational rather than matura-

tional phenomena of the wires. (See Chapter VI.)

Productive stability has not been so easy to attain. Stone's and
Martin's reaction budgetary policy made AP vulnerable to any exogenous
news coverage emergency. Endogenous stability was, however, AP's
saving grace, accomplished through several large upward revisions in the
assessment schedules and through absence of large membership declines.
Cooper's period brought AP to the peak of its productive maturation. Membership and bondholding increases, standard assessment increases, introduction of many supplementary services and technological innovations, and
a generally high-level, positive budgetary policy, eliminated exogenous and
endogenous influences almost completely. (Only in two instances--1939
when war came swiftly to Europe and 1945 when war coverage was at its
peak and AP had begun its world service--did the Cooper policy fail to
accommodate such influences. It is, however, asserted that these are extreme influences by any standards.)

Although Starzel and Gallagher have attempted to continue Cooper's
positive policy, new exogenous forces have come into play: innovation of
techniques has become a complicated process involving much more money
and many more external suppliers and manufacturers, and cold war news
coverage has been complicated by the diversity of news sources and content.
These trends are relatively new, their full dimensions remain to be seen,
and they only begin to cast shadows of doubt over the assertion that maturational stability has been attained by the wires. Chapter VIII will again take
up the question of recent news coverage and innovation problems and explore
their possibilities in terms of the wires' future.

Footnotes

[1]Incorporators, each holding fifty-six shares of stock, were de Young, Collier, Scripps, Driscoll, Perdue, Hesing, Barr, and Knapp, with Lawson holding ninety-six shares. These men also constituted the 1892-93 board of directors and are listed with their complete names and newspaper affiliations in Table 1, Appendix B. Illinois AP, Volume, I (1894), p. 4.

[2]Ibid., p. 5.

[3]New York AP, Volume, "Preliminary Proceedings" (1900), pp. 150-161.

[4]Ibid., XII (1912), p. 2.

[5]Ibid., XX (1920), p. 5.

[6]Cooper, op. cit. (1959), p. 162.

[7]New York AP, Volume, XXIII (1923), pp. 6-7.

[8]Ibid., XL (1940), p. 56.

[9]Ibid., XLII (1942), p. 25.

[10]Percentages of rise and decline for total United States newspapers are taken from Table 13, Appendix B.

[11]New York AP, Volume, XXXII (1932), p. 6.

[12]Mott, op. cit., p. 675.

[13]New York AP, Volume, XXXV (1935), p. 9.

[14]Cooper, op. cit. (1959), p. 187.

[15]Conversation with the author.

[16]The Associated Press, The Torch is Passed (New York: The Associated Press, 1963), p. 99.

[17]Saul Pett, "How The Associated Press Covered the Kennedy Tragedy," The AP World, XVIII (Winter, 1963-64), p. 5.

[18]Illinois AP, Volume, II (1895), pp. 4-5.

[19]Ibid., VI (1899), p. 3.

[20]Ibid., VII (1900), p. 3.

[21]New York AP, Volume, VI (1906), p. 3, and VII (1907), p. 3.

[22]Ibid., X (1910), p. 2.

[23]Ibid., p. 3.

[24]In 1912, Theodore Roosevelt led the progressive faction out of the Republican party, formed the Progressive party, and conducted his own convention. Unlike most third-party or splinter-party movements, the Progressives had a popular following which actually surpassed that of the Republicans, and thus warranted extensive national press coverage.

[25]New York AP, Volume, XV (1915), p. 3.

[26]Cooper, op. cit. (1959), pp. 269-270.

[27]New York AP, Volume, XLVI (1946), p. 96.

[28]Ibid., LVII (1957), p. 25.

[29]Ibid., LI (1951), pp. 72-73; LII (1952), p. 90; LIII (1953), pp. 84-85; LVI (1956), p. 13; and LVII (1957), pp. 23-24.

[30]Interview by the author, September, 1963.

[31]Like AP's developing radio policy of the 1930's, AP newsreel service for television stations was first offered to AP newspaper members with television outlets. Minutes of the October 3, 1947, meeting of the board report: "The Board unanimously authorized the Executive Director [Cooper] to establish a newsreel for use by AP member stations, the cost of which is to be underwritten by subscribing AP member stations." New York AP, Volume, XLVIII (1948), p. 69. By April, 1948, however, the service--a totally new medium for news presentation for AP--was discontinued, apparently preempted by television network news activities.

[32]Although avoiding a full-fledged factor analysis of category percentages' interrelatedness, the author constructed frequency matrices to elicit (a) concurrent, like change; (b) concurrent, opposite change; (c) subsequent (one or two years hence), like change; and (d) subsequent, opposite change. Checking the various frequencies of occurrence, the author found no combinations or sequential chains occurring relatively frequently, vis-a-vis others. Also no one or two categories exhibited a significantly high frequency of change, vis-a-vis other categories. A careful examination of Table 12 in Appendix B will indicate the diversity of combinations occurring and the lack of consistently high or low occurrences of change within particular categories.

Chapter VI

WIRE-SERVICE RELATIONS WITH SUBSCRIBERS

> Nearly nine-tenths of all American
> communities are free to read the news
> according to one newspaper, . . . pro-
> vided always that nothing of national
> scope may ordinarily be presented by
> any newspaper anywhere that has not
> pleased Hearst, Scripps-Howard or
> the Associated Press to call news.
> -- Vance (1945)

Investigation in Chapters IV and V focused upon the maturation of

political and productive processes primarily within the confines of wire

services Although primary and secondary environmental factors were

introduced intermittently during those discussions, care was taken to con-

fine the scope of inquiry to the impact of all factors upon the wires' struc-

ture and process trends.

This chapter, along with the next one, shifts focus, giving latitude

to perspective and introducing the dynamic interaction as the most signifi-

cant phenomenon in which the wires participate. In the present chapter

wire service-subscriber relations are viewed from the perspective of both

political and productive interaction. Consideration is initially given to the

historical and contemporary conditions of the wires' total potential sub-

scriber field.

A small group of studies which might appear in this chapter are

concerned with the subscribers' uses of the news report, e g., the so-

called gatekeeper studies. But the author omits them because they would introduce aspects of the communicative product itself, an entity not within the scope of the present study.

The changing profile of communication media outlets has been the object of considerable discussion and analysis in recent years. New media have emerged to challenge and mitigate the stability and effectiveness of more traditional forms, labor unions and raw materials suppliers have exacted their sometimes painful toll to permit media outlets to continue operation, and news values and content have changed with the addition of each new medium, giving rise to many questions about the role and effect of news dissemination in a democratic society. Through it all the wire services have continued to grow and prosper, increasingly performing and changing the news-gathering function for the media in general, and establishing relations with each new medium.

Subscriber Trends and Problems

Table 13 (see Appendix B) depicts the growth patterns of those daily news outlets in the United States which potentially could use the product provided by the major American wire services. The growth of the daily newspaper was sporatic until about 1880, after which growth was relatively constant until declines in 1905 and 1911 foretold the coming newspaper declines. Emery summarizes the social and technological pressures which spurred daily newspaper increases between 1870 and 1900.

> The nationwide financial and industrial expansion which took the name of "big business" transformed the big city newspaper into a corporate enterprise rather than a personal venture. Increasing mechanization, spurred on by inventive

genius, revolutionized the printing processes just as it had other industrial processes. The tremendous growth of the cities permitted larger newspaper circulations, which were in turn made necessary by larger investments and operating expenses. And a steady increase in the number of urban communities, as population expanded and the economic benefits of industrialization spread across the country, offered a host of new publishing opportunities which were seized upon quickly. [1]

It is no coincidence that the Associated Press--created originally as the "personal venture" of individual New York newspapers--experienced some of its most difficult crises during this period of thirty years when daily newspaper totals almost quadrupled. The point has been made before that the Associated Press product had outgrown its small NYAP base and structure, and this increasing potential and actual market for the AP product only heightened the need for a broader perspective than the NYAP would supply.

The peak of newspaper growth was reached, according to Table 13, in 1916 with 2,461 dailies operating in the United States, and after that the total began to fall as the interplay between new newspapers and suspensions and as the general trend toward reduction of competition often created an annual net decline. Particularly after World War I, the new trend in journalism toward reduction of competition was developing. Emery finds that the impetus for nineteenth-century growth also sowed the seeds for twentieth-century decline among newspapers.

But the forces which created the modern mass news-paper--industrialization, mechanization, and urbanization--made for less individuality and more standardization of the product as the twentieth century unfolded. . . . Variety of competitive appeal tended to decline in the cities and towns of a standardized civilization. Competition for the mass

market in the urban centers, and other socio-economic
pressures stemming from technological change, led to an
inevitable contraction of newspaper publishing. * * *
These trends were toward suspension of some competing
newspapers, merger of others with their rivals, concentration of newspaper ownership in many cities and towns,
and creation of newspaper chains. [2]

Table 13 shows that periods of postwar decline were 1919-21 and 1924-28,

bringing the total to below two thousand dailies. The Depression created

four years of decline, but an eight-year, pre-World War II and a wartime

decline of 245 dailies was the devastating blow which brought daily news-

paper totals to the level at which they stand today.

These declines in AP's newspaper foundation no doubt contributed

to the organization's decision near the end of World War II to branch out

into other media and into the world field. United Press and International

News Service had never made it a policy of confining themselves to so

narrow a base and therefore probably encountered fewer difficult years for

this reason than did AP. One is reminded of the account in Chapter V of

AP's attempt during the Depression to salvage membership totals by re-

ducing assessments and refunding payments. AP's lifeline at that time

was connected only to the faltering newspaper industry.

Radio appeared in 1921, but growth was slow, not overtaking news-

papers in total numbers of outlets until 1949. The postwar growth of FM

radio and television aided AM radio in overtaking newspapers in total num-

bers in 1948. By 1963 newspapers accounted for only one-quarter of the

total daily news outlets in the United States. Emery finds that inter-media

competition has not in itself created the stagnant condition of newspaper totals. Rather, this condition seems to originate simultaneously in the

overall socio-cultural environment and in the self-defeating ownership

practices of publishers.

> Competition among the media, in the years after the
> rise of radio and television, was intense, both for advertis-
> ing revenues and for attention from the reader, listener, or
> viewer. But the effects of inter-media competition upon the
> fortunes of any one were less important than were the effects
> of general changes in the country's economy, fashioned in
> turn by a great depression, a world war and a postwar boom
> . . . . The socio-economic pressures inherent in modern
> American society, which had brought about concentration of
> newspaper ownership throughout the twentieth century, con-
> tinued to have their effects, both on newspapers and other
> media. Competition for the mass market encouraged further
> standardization at the expense of individuality--common de-
> nominators for mass readership, listenership, or viewership
> to win mass advertising. Failure of individual enterprises to
> keep pace with the requirements of a modern socio-economic
> situation also continued to play a part. And increasingly
> heavy investment costs in both publishing and broadcasting
> lessened ability to compete. . . . Big-time radio and tele-
> vision, like big-time newspaper and magazine publishing,
> was conducive to concentration of ownership--and radio and
> television proved to be easily adapted to chain operation.
> Finally, the natural tendency of publishers to become interested
> in new communications agencies, and their desire to spread
> their investments into radio and television, led to extensive
> interlocking ownership among the media. [3]

A new and expanding diversity of outlets permits the wire services to straddle

all media here and abroad in an attempt to guard against the repercussions of

excessive declines in any one.

Similar figures for world outlets would be useful to this study, but

they are almost non-existent. Unesco, however, has compiled some recent

world figures which are comparable to particular annual totals in Table 13.

Representing 1960-62, the world figures in summary are as follows. [4]

Region	Daily Newspapers		AM-FM Radio		Television	
Africa	226	2.9%	367	2.9%	20	1.4%
N. America	2161	27.5	5809	46.0	724	50.5
S. America	765	9.7	1784	14.1	59	4.1
Asia*	1736	22.1	1233	9.8	160	11.1
Europe*	2407	30.6	2789	22.1	358	24.9
Oceania	114	1.4	244	1.9	21	1.5
U.S.S.R.	457	5.8	407	3.2	93	6.5
	7866	100.0	12633	100.0	1435	100.0
U.S. (1961)	1761	22.4%	4328	34.3%	530	36.9%

*Excluding the U.S.S.R.

The world growth of news media outlets has been rapid since World War II, at least to the extent that newsprint supplies, literacy rates, costs to individuals of radio receivers and television sets, political and economic upheavals, etc., have permitted. It is obvious from the above figures that an American wire service is restricting its potential number of subscribers to a relatively small percentage of outlets by confining its distribution to the United States. At best, under such a limitation, the wire could hope to distribute to only 30.2 per cent of the potential global market (6,619 out of 21,934 outlets).

Table 13, moreover, shows a leveling off tendency among U.S. newspapers, and a lesser similar trend among AM radio and television stations Only FM radio totals have recently increased, and much of this since about 1960 is attributable to the innovation of multiplex broadcasting. Indeed, the growing market of daily news outlets is not in the United States, or even in Europe, but rather in the developing countries of Africa and

Asia, where millions of people in hundreds of populous centers remain untouched by daily accounts of the world's news. These developments have thrust the American wires into an international situation in which cold-war and general political configurations affect the wires' fortunes at least as much as the quality, speed, or salability of their service. The implications of these configurations and of the resulting press-government relations internationally will be discussed in detail in Chapter VII.

Returning to the domestic picture, which is the principal frame of reference for this chapter, the trends in daily news outlets noted above by Emery and in Table 13 have been studied and described in detail by Raymond B. Nixon in recent years.[5] Nixon's work reveals some current trends in domestic outlets, the effect of which cannot help but touch the wires' daily and long-term conditions and success.

Focusing initially on conditions among newspapers, Nixon finds the total number of newspapers having stabilized since World War II and more particularly since 1954 with the small number of suspensions and mergers balancing the number of new papers as the net change remains relatively small annually. (Table 13 shows that since 1954 newspaper totals have fluctuated within the narrow limits set by 1,765 and 1,751.) The important trends in newspapering, according to Nixon, have been in ownership and competition. He says ownership is "more intensive and less extensive,"[6] meaning it is increasingly local and regional rather than national. The number of chain ownerships is increasing, but the average number of newspapers per chain has not fluctuated significantly since 1910.

The decline in competition among newspapers has been striking, according to Nixon's statistics. "One daily is now the prevailing pattern in cities up to 100,000 population, whereas in 1945 it was the rule only in cities up to 50,000," Nixon reports.[7] Only sixty-one cities had competing dailies in 1960 while the remaining 95.8 per cent has only one newspaper voice, a condition called "one of the ugliest impacts of decimation of our daily press," by Ernst.[8] The one-newspaper cities include situation in which two newspapers are published by the same firm and two newspapers share printing and perhaps business and advertising facilities, i.e., the so-called "Nashville plan." Nixon lists five reasons for the decline of newspaper competition: (1) the decline of partisanship in the U.S. press; (2) the growth of objective reporting among American newspapers; (3) the desire of advertisers for larger circulations and less duplication of readership; (4) the growth of suburbs; and (5) the growing competition from the electronic media.[9] Of the second reason, Nixon observes:

> As newspapers have become more and more alike in their reporting of the news, and presenting both sides of controversial issues, there has come to be little more reason for two competing newspapers than there would be for two competing telephone companies.[10]

One cannot help but recall the emphasis wires placed on objective reporting and the fact that journalistic objectivity in general has been listed frequently as a major wire-service contribution to newspapering. In one sense, then, the wires have created an atmosphere through their news report which has reduced the potential market of subscribers for that news report.

In a more positive sense, however, the rising electronic media have been the wires' salvation in terms of continued growth into potential fields. Nixon shows that when all media are considered, there are 3,324 competing voices in 1,106 cities, while only 355 cities have single voices. "Most of the latter are so close to a large city that the absence of any locally competing voices appears to be of little importance," Nixon says.[11] He points out that the wires have played a role in keeping monopoly publishers in line because of the wires' increased saturation of all media outlets since World War II.

> . . . nearly all radio and television stations subscribe to a wire service and read late bulletins or summaries of news over the air. Even this much news serves as a sword of Damocles over the head of any "monopoly" publisher who might be tempted to grossly distort or to withhold news that he has received from the same wire service.[12]

Thus the competition among media outlets extends not only to advertising revenue and the attention of the public, but also to seeking and using the latest news from the wire-service reports. Timeliness has become the broadcasters' domain while completeness and depth have developed as the editors' bastion. Both are obtainable on most stories only with the help of the wires. The picture, therefore, emerges of wires increasingly becoming a significantly important supplier of all media outlets at the local level. Although network radio and television news departments prepare the large news packages for the local broadcasters, even they rely upon wires for their news "tips" and some of the actual reports (although rewritten) used on their broadcasts. In addition to the small news packages taken from the wires, local broadcast outlets must rely solely on the wires for state and regional news.

These changing quantitative considerations, then, form the backdrop for study of the wire service-subscriber relationship. The description of that relationship which follows will proceed first in terms of political interaction and then as a productive interaction.

Political Interaction and Trends

In Chapter IV some important aspects of the wire service-subscriber relationship are discussed from the viewpoint of their impact upon the internal structure of the wire services. These conditions and trends have also played important roles in shaping and altering the wire-subscriber relationship, taken as a separate entity. Board membership initially consisted largely of big-city, wealthy newspapers which could afford the luxury of buying AP stock. Later, when the stock prerequisite for voting and representation was dropped, the bondholder gained control of the election machinery, and a limiting of representation to directors from relatively large newspaper properties was again noted. By the time cities of less than 50,000 had been permitted three guaranteed directorships, board positions had been limited to three terms, and representativeness of the board actually had attained a broad base, the board had lost much of the actual control over the routine operations of the organization, yielding to a growing administrative staff and personal spheres of influence. Earlier, when the board-membership relationship might have benefited the members, only a few participated to any degree. Later the relationship became more universal but less meaningful as it dealt decreasingly with hardcore problems and issues.

It was also noted in Chapter IV that members were usually not consulted on key questions of expansion, innovation, and change. The only outstanding exception--the radic issue--had created such unrest and potential conflict within the organization, that men in power felt it advisable to use a referendum and thereby to relieve themselves of responsibility for the final decision. Finally, AP ties with regular members have strengthened in recent years, not because of the increased democratization of AP's policy-making machinery, but rather because of the organization's need for financial support in the fact of rising competition, foreign instability, and the less lucrative and permanent, though growing, associate memberships. Although it is difficult to pinpoint inequalities in the expenditure and revenue schedules when expense categories are arranged so that news distribution cannot be isolated for examination, gross figures seem to indicate disproportionately high assessments for regular members (i.e , domestic newspaper subscribers).

Legal interaction between AP and clients is sketched in Figure 8 (see the next page) which is compiled from several sources. [13] The figure will serve as a reference point for and summary of the following discussion. Unfortunately for AP, the service was started in 1892 on a shoestring, without either a large membership roster or an immediate and adequate source of revenue to support routine operation, much less to finance a "war" with the old United Press. Thus, in the early years (i.e., before the 1897 demise of UP) the membership and AP depended heavily upon each other. This helps explain, for example, why the board apparently had a relatively strong power position early in the organization's history: the AP organization had to yield to its cooperative structure (and, therefore, to its membership) if it hoped to grow and to emerge as nationally dominant. Several

Figure 8. AP-Subscriber Power Relations: 1893-1964

	1893-1900 Illinois Corp.	1900-1945 New York Corp.	1945-1964 New York Corp.
Subscriber:			
Apply	To Bd. of Dirs.	To Bd. of Dirs.	To Bd. of Dirs.
Approval	Bd. of Directors & Local Board	Bd. of Directors & Protest right waived	Bd. of Directors
Recourse	Ask Bd. of Dirs. overrule Local Bd.	4/5ths vote in annual meeting.	None necessary
Holder	Publisher by name	Publisher to 1932 Newspaper after '32	Newspaper
Types	Series A-report & on Local Board Series B-report	Member-report & vote Assoc. Mbr-report (after 1937)	Member-report & vote Assoc. Mbr-report
Withdraw	Majority vote of Bd. of Dirs.	6-month notice	6-month notice
Options:	Stockholding	Bondholding	Bondholding
Privileges:	All Subscribers-- Receive report Withdraw from AP Series A-- On Local Board Stockholders-- Votes	All Subscribers-- Receive report Withdraw from AP Bondholders-- Extra Votes BEFORE 1928: 'Charter'Member-- Protest right Vote Regular Member-- Vote AFTER 1928: Regular Member-- Protest right Vote	All Subscribers-- Receive report Withdraw from AP Regular Member-- Vote Bondholders-- Extra Votes

Figure 8 (continued)

Duties:

| | All Subscribers--
Pay assessment
Obey by-laws
Attribute to AP
News to AP only
Obey Antagonism
ruling | All Subscribers--
Pay assessment
Obey by-laws
Attribute to AP
News from AP only
(up to 1915)
Regular Member--
News to AP only
Give up Exclusive
news if asked. | All Subscribers--
Pay assessment
Obey by-laws
Attribute to AP
Regular Member--
News to AP only |

other aspects of this early balance of organization and membership power
grew out of the same dependence, and as the following discussion notes,
they remained a vital and dominant part of the relationship long after AP's
victory over UP (some even to the present time).

Two types of membership were available in 1892. Series A memberships, at a more expensive assessment, gave the newspaper both the
news report and a seat on the "local board" which consisted of AP newspapers in a given city who passed on the application for AP membership
of any of their competitors. Series B memberships included only the receipt of the news report. The arbitrary denial of AP news to local competitors by local-board members was often avoided by the general feeling
among AP members that a large clientele led to a stronger AP, vis-a-vis
the eastern UP opponent. The death of UP might have brought a tight-fisted
refusal by AP publishers to allow competitors to receive the AP report,
but the directors stepped in and liberalized the admission procedure to accommodate as many old UP members as possible. Such a policy, the
board said, would strengthen AP financially and strategically. Many Series
A members, however, disagreed for personal reasons and some even
brought suits against AP claiming abridgment of contractual provisions.

Essentially one sees here two branches of the same organization
(even two branches of journalism) bickering over ultimate distribution of
power. The board, representing and supported by the stockholding newspapers (most of which were wealthy enough not to feel the effect of local
competition as much as others) proclaimed through the board they controlled,

on the one hand, an open-door policy for new members.

> The Board is committed to the general policy of ad-
> mitting all newspapers qualified for membership . . . unless
> the report from the members of the local board presents
> some conclusive objection affecting the interests of the asso-
> ciation as a whole. [14]

(Note the emphasis of the above statement lodged in the last few words.

The board, obviously, and the wealthy newspapers, more interestingly,

were committed to a strong national wire. Their individual futures as

well as their local competitive situations could best be secured through a

strong AP, particularly in the event that another national wire appeared.)

The less firmly and financially settled rank-and-file members,

on the other hand, objected in part to this philosophy, which although

acknowledging the existence of local boards did not in fact heed the ob-

jections they raised to specific applicants. Inevitably rebellion among

some of the more aggressive members against the board's policy took

the form of breach of contract suits between members and AP. The

board reports in 1898.

> Not a little litigation has resulted from the effort
> of your Board to place The Associated Press upon a broad
> basis of permanent efficiency. It is peculiarly gratifying
> to be able to report that in every case that has thus far
> gone to a hearing, the courts have sustained the contentions
> of our counsel. [15]

Litigation failed in most cases against AP (primarily for lack of clear-cut

contractual wording), and members could either accept local competitors

carrying AP's news report or leave the only major American wire service

operating on a stable footing at the moment.

UP's death, however, brought AP into a bright spotlight of critical

scrutiny. If AP was to be the nation's only wire service (and its strength
at that time seemed to indicate this), should it not be open to all applicants
in the spirit of the First Amendment guarantee of press freedom? Although
the board had liberalized its policy, the local boards remained in existence
and potentially capable of choking off local competition by refusing wider
distribution of AP's report. The board reports on state legislatures'
attempts in 1898 to gain a wide-open AP membership, somewhat like an
enfranchised public utility.

> During the year an effort has been made in a number
> of states to secure legislation hostile to The Associated
> Press. Acts to compel all press associations to admit to
> membership any applicant have been passed in Kentucky,
> Tennessee, and Texas and measures of like character are
> under consideration in other legislatures. Believing, as
> we do, that all such attempts must ultimately fail . . . we
> have waited patiently for some effort to enforce these statutes,
> but thus far without result. [16]

Although AP's internal strife over membership policies and the
potential threat posed by such state laws may have contributed to the organization's move to New York State and its revised legalistic structure
in that state, the immediate impetus was a court ruling on the legality of
the two final items in Figure 8 for the period 1893-1900 (receipt of news
from AP only and use of the antagonism ruling).

An antagonism ruling by the board cited a belligerent organization
(newspaper or news agency) whose activities were deemed by AP as detrimental to AP's best interests. While the citation might have eventually
affected the opponent, its immediate purpose was to prohibit AP members
from having any relations with the cited antagonist. Early in AP's war with

the old UP, the AP board cited four New York City papers as antagonistic--
the Daily News, the Sun, the Tribune, and the Herald--because three (as
former NYAP members) had defiantly bolted the AP at a time when it
needed them for eastern strength and because all four were very strong
financial supporters of the old UP. The board's antagonism announcement
read as follows:

> We have . . . made every effort to hasten the present
> contest with The United Press to its logical conclusion--that
> of membership in The Associated Press of such of its mem-
> bers and clients as are desired in our association and the rele-
> gating of the remainder to such a secondary service as they
> may find themselves able to support. In the prosecution of
> this purpose the board deemed it wise and necessary as a war
> measure to declare the four New York newspapers . . .
> "antagonistic" to the Associated Press. . . .[17]

When the end was in sight for the UP and AP was on the verge of its long-
sought national dominance, AP dropped antagonism as a principle in favor
of membership for the wealthy New York "antagonists." On April 3, 1897,
just three days before UP's death, the Tribune and the Herald were granted
AP memberships.[18] The Daily News received an AP membership on May
25, 1897, cancelled its affiliation on December 14, 1898, and was denied
readmission in 1899, vetoed by the New York World through local-board
channels.[19] The Sun, however, shocked by the loss of UP but indignant
about what it considered AP's excessive wartime tactics against UP, announced that it would rely on its Laffan News Service.[20]

Traffic between the Chicago Inter-Ocean and the Laffan agency, as
described in Chapter III, led to the Illinois Supreme Court's verdict that
AP was a public utility and could not restrict the Inter-Ocean's relations

with other agencies. AP's use of the antagonism rule and the stipulation that members could not receive news from other agencies had boomeranged, and AP moved to New York State. As was the case with the broad statement of the Illinois corporation's purpose (which might never have been used to its fullest extent) these alternative devices to regulate AP members for the furtherance of the AP organization might never have been deployed had the board not felt its position was threatened by UP and, more significantly, feared a threat from within its own membership. After 1897, AP was interested in strengthening its position in its relations with members in order to gain two advantages: (1) continued large membership and new-found, politico-economic strength originating therein, and (2) mitigation of the possibility of new wire-service competitors.

The changeover to New York headquarters and jurisdiction did not soften AP's desire to control the wire-membership relationship. Swindler finds this in a comparison of old and new by-law provisions and notes that much of this impetus for AP control grew out of desires by a few wealthy publishers to run AP (from seats on the board and by virtue of large assessments and bondholdings) as their personal property and to control their local competitive situations through the admission machinery of AP.

> The New York charter had provided virtually un-
> limited freedom for the new association to regulate its
> membership as it saw fit. * * * The former supposed bene-
> fits of the Illinois corporation were asserted in stronger
> language. A resolution was offered at the first meeting of
> the new AP, forbidding the use by rival press associations
> of any facilities in the same "office or building" with AP
> operators. Another highly significant feature was the im-
> portant "right of protest" which was written into By-Law
> III (6). * * * These provisions show the determination of old-

line AP publishers to reap the fullest possible benefits from
the type of newsgathering entity they had fought through so
many legal difficulties to attain. [21]

As Figure 8 notes, the important changes in 1900 were: (1) the addition of

p rotest rights held by so-called Charter Members and overruled only by

a four-fifths vote of the entire membership; (2) the conferring of regular

membership (before 1937) upon all report recipients (and the converse,

that no outlet could obtain the report without a regular membership); and

(3) the sale of bonds giving additional votes in lieu of stockholding and of

the previous sole voting privilege attached to the stocks. The antagonism

ruling was dropped since it had been the initial point of contention among

AP, the Inter-Ocean, Laffan, and the Illinois Supreme Court. The stipu-

lation was made, however, that AP members could receive news only

from the AP.

Of the original 603 members of AP's New York corporation, 278

had held positions on local boards in the old Illinois AP and, thus, had

held veto rights over the admission of local competitors. These 278 news-

papers were given the protest rights in the new organization covering

areas averaging radiuses of 150 miles from their city of publication. [22]

Significant power patterns of the old Illinois AP were being retained, not

particularly because the organization as a whole would benefit directly

from it (although protest right holders usually paid large weekly assessment

bills), but because these publishers saw a chance through AP to maintain

some control over the AP organization, its competitors, and their own

local situations.

The protest right was first challenged in 1914 when the New York Sun, still a strong opponent of AP, filed the brief of a complaint against AP with United States Attorney General T. W. Gregory and with the judiciary committees of both houses of Congress (which were then studying ways of strengthening the Sherman Antitrust Act). The Sun contended that AP violated the Sherman Antitrust Act by prohibiting members from trafficking with other agencies and by permitting use of protest rights. Gregory dismissed the protest right matter but suggested that the organization drop its ban on members' relations with competing agencies as a possible antitrust violation. This was done in 1915, the board pointing out that the penalizing provision of the ban had been a "dead letter" since 1900. (Maybe so within the AP, but apparently the provision had affected Laffan's success in the wire-service field.) The protest right, however, was thus upheld by the U.S. attorney general and a small group of members were allowed to continue guiding the fortunes of AP, not to mention the shape of competition in their own localities. Continuation of protest rights, however, created internal factionalism: protest right holders collectively sought to confine AP membership growth for individual, local reasons while rank-and-file members, AP's growing administrative staff, and the increasingly liberal and representative AP board saw expanded membership as a source of strength, vis-a-vis UP and INS.

A clash of factions over the membership versus protest right issue was averted during the initial stages of U.S. involvement in World War I by high-handed administrative and board action. In 1916 American newspapers clamored for AP service (but not without members', and particularly

protest right holders' opposition). Cooper relates how he and Board
President Noyes worked together to reduce the size and effectiveness of
protest rights. They contacted protest right holders individually, press-
ing for cooperation with AP over the prospect of wartime enlargement of
membership. The board reports.

> During the year the co-operative character of the
> organization has been very effectively illustrated by the fact
> that nearly a hundred of the members holding protest rights
> covering more or less extended territory beyond the point of
> publication have generously waived them to enable the
> Directors to elect a very considerable number of new mem-
> bers. A very limited number have shown an unwillingness
> to make any such surrender. [23]

Table 14 shows that membership jumped 11.3 per cent that year, surpassing
the one thousand mark for the first time in AP's history. It should be noted
that reference is made to territory waivers, not to waivers within the city
of publication. The organization as a whole, and particularly the growing
administrative sector, was interested in expansion, strength, and stability
and saw the protest right as a potential limitation of these goals.

Cooper and Noyes reduced the territorial radius from 150 miles to
10 miles between 1916 and 1926 permitting what Table 14 reveals as a membership increase of almost 22 per cent during a decade when total newspapers declined almost 19 per cent, according to Table 13. Such attempts
as this one by Cooper and Noyes may have <u>reduced</u> the effectiveness of the
protest right, but until the right had been <u>eliminated</u>, the threat of conflict
persisted. In 1923 the board sought again to mediate between protest right
holders and non-holders to perpetuate postwar membership growth.

The Board records with satisfaction that less than a
half dozen members who hold protest rights are exercising
those rights beyond ten miles from the city of publication. It
believes it is for the best interests of the organization that
the comparatively few holding such rights since the year 1900
should not exercise them, and appreciates the cooperative
spirit of the great majority who have waived them in the common interest. [24]

Rosewater points out that the board had assumed an anti-protest right

posture and that during this period the protest rights were held generally

in disfavor and had declined in number.

Appreciating the standing invitation to adverse criticism,
the directors themselves initiated a policy aimed to restrict
the exercise of protest. No new protest right was to be granted,
"unless there are special and peculiar reasons." The precedent had been laid down early, that papers wishing to maintain
exclusive service in their protest territory would be charged on
the population of the entire area. By a campaign of persuasion
and pressure and extension of the practice of imposing this sur-
charge, not on the city, but on the particular publisher declining
to execute a requested waiver, more than 100 members who had
protest privileges covering more or less extended territory beyond
the point of publication, were induced to forego their rights in
order to facilitate admission of a very considerable number of
new members.
    Within the association, a deaf ear had been consistently
turned to all appeals for new protest rights, and steady pressure
had been applied to curtail the area over which the existing
privilege extended in the several cities. Protest rights, generally
speaking, were regarded with disfavor and discountenanced, and
their number, never more than a third of the membership, had
been shrinking absolutely, as well as relatively, in total membership. [25]

Despite these efforts, the protest right issue again became critical

in 1924 with respect to William Randolph Hearst's refusal to waive protest

rights in connection with two membership applications. Aside from the

competition which Hearst's INS afforted AP, Hearst, the publisher, dabbled

in AP memberships and local newspaper properties and competition as in AP memberships and local newspaper properties and competition as others would in stocks. Sometimes he was the focal point of internal AP struggle because of his applications for membership. (In 1900, for example, Hearst sued AP attempting to secure two memberships.[26])

Sometimes, however, he found himself on the inside of AP, fighting admission of a competitor and the sentiment of many of his AP colleagues, which was the case in 1924. Hearst was a large AP member and protest right holder, as Cooper relates.

> Hearst once owned more newspapers which were represented by membership in The Associated Press than any other individual, and the aggregate amount he paid for them while a member of The Associated Press for sixty years, he paid a total of many millions of dollars in weekly assessments for Associated Press service to his newspapers.
> Hearst felt that instead of being appreciated as The Associated Press' biggest financial supporter and catered to as such, there was deep antipathy toward him among some AP Board members whose newspapers were competitive with his. This strained relationship had started before the turn of the century. Twenty years later, when this was all but forgotten, litigation over the theft of Associated Press news by an employee of the Cleveland News on behalf of Hearst's International News Service rekindled a mutual ill feeling.[27]

Hearst threatened AP's equilibrium in 1924 when membership applications from the Baltimore Sun and the Rochester (N. Y.) Times-Union ran headlong into Hearst's Baltimore News and Rochester Journal and Post-Express franchises. The applications were automatically denied by the board when Hearst refused to waive his protest in both cities. The applications failed to obtain the necessary four-fifths vote of the membership that year.

Questions concerning interpretation of by-law provisions for a quorum and for whether it was four-fifths of the total membership or of those voting led to a second vote later that year. Both votes upheld

Hearst's protest, but both were close, one failing to make four-fifths by

two votes, which meant that a majority, at least, had voted against

Hearst's protest. Before the second vote, Hearst distributed a handsome

volume to AP members presenting his side of the case. Although claim-

ing that Hearst had "more at stake as an individual holder and owner of

Associated Press memberships than any other man in that organization,"[28]

the book emphasized the possible threat to other protest right holders if

Hearst's protest was overridden.

> . . . this is the first time, in the history of the Corporation,
> that members (having rights of protest) have been seriously
> asked to strike a direct blow at the property rights of another
> member, and an indirect blow against their own. * * * It
> would set a precedent full of menace to the property rights of
> all newspapers represented in the membership of the Asso-
> ciation, for what the Corporation may do to the News, it may
> do to any other member. . . .[29]

The two applicants in later years secured their place in the AP, but

the 1924 quarrel and Hearst's "plea to every member of the Associated

Press to preserve the asset value of his property,"[30] may well have pro-

vided the impetus for creation of a study committee four years later to

adjust the AP bond program and the protest rights. The committee recom-

mended and the membership agreed that: (1) a new bond issue should be

conducted, allowing all members to purchase a limited amount and receive

added votes for the purchases, and (2) all members should be given the

protest right. Rosewater comments that the bond proposal sustained and

strengthened the AP "aristocracy."

It was really a strange denouement, that objection to
a privileged class of bondholding members in position to
monopolize the voting power, and demand for revocation of
these special prerogatives, should have led the members into
voting themselves as a whole the same privileges. [31]

As for the protest right proposal, Rosewater strongly disapproved, noting

the curious reversal in AP policy and sentiment.

The policy was here completely reversed--instead of
being enjoyed by a limited few, protest rights were to belong
to one and all--instead of making it easier to gain admission,
it was to be more difficult--instead of leaving the directors
free to act on many cases, no application whatsoever could be
granted, without waiver of protest, except by the next to impossible overriding four-fifths vote of the members. The
trend in the arena of American journalism has been to consolidation and extermination, and to a diminishing number of
dailies, a trend whose continuance this tighter shutting of the
door to Associated Press service must further and stimulate. [32]

An AP membership became even more prized as a result of this move. Not

only was the news report worth receiving, but the franchise right became a

valuable asset to a newspaper wishing to hinder local journalistic competi-

tion or to enhance its own financial resources.

Speculation and investment in AP memberships became more preva-

lent, patterned after Frank Munsey's earlier activities. Munsey's purchase

of the New York Globe in 1923 was reportedly for two million dollars, and

the object of the purchase was "to get its Associated Press franchise for

the Sun to make the Sun structurally sound," according to Cooper. [33] The

Federal District Court of New York City found in 1944 that many large-city

newspapers paid large sums of money to acquire AP memberships and

franchise rights, some carrying their AP memberships on the books at values

upwards of one million dollars. [34]

One would guess that the 1928 by-law revisions concerning bonds and franchise rights tended to return the AP-subscriber relationship to the dominance by the subscribers, in whole or in part. Clearly the new bond issue, though meant to distribute investment and extra voting power more equitably, tended in practice to enhance the position of the already wealthy and power AP members. In theory, the redistribution was untenable, for as Rosewater points out, objection to privilege is not resolved by making privilege available to all. Universal protest rights pointed to individual, local considerations dominating AP membership growth and organizational improvement. Unlike the bond revision (in which practice mitigated the superficial democratization of the organization) the egalitarian granting of franchise rights to all members, however, did not, in practice, stifle membership expansion. Between 1928 and 1940 the AP membership roster grew 26.5 per cent, according to Table 14, despite the simultaneous decline of 6.1 per cent in total newspapers, noted in Table 13. Moreover, these membership gains were accomplished despite the Depression which descended one year after the revision and had side effects until the late 1930's.

The net effect of the new bond issue was felt in the election of directors, but after the internal locus of power had shifted to the general manager and his administrative staff (see Chapter IV). Universal franchise rights appear statistically to have had a negligible effect upon the organization; the AP organization continued, apparently its controlling role which dated from about 1916.

The threat of franchise controversy, however, was finally eliminated by the events which followed the Chicago Sun's application for AP
membership in the morning field on October 2, 1941. Only the Chicago
Tribune had a morning membership in Chicago at that time, and its publisher, Col. Robert R. McCormick refused to waive his protest right.
(Two other Chicago papers, the Daily News and the Herald-American held
morning franchises by virtue of earlier acquisitions of or mergers with
AP properties, but both were afternoon papers and agreed to waive their
protest right in favor of the Sun.) The Sun sought recourse through the
U.S. Department of Justice after failing a membership vote, 684 to 287. [35]
On August 28, 1942, the Justice Department filed an antitrust suit against
the AP, its directors, their newspaper properties, and AP membership in
general. The government accused AP of being . . .

> . . . continuously engaged in a combination and conspiracy
> in restraint of trade and commerce among the several states
> in news, information and intelligence; they have been, and
> are now parties to contracts in restraint of such trade and
> commerce; all in violation of . . . the "Sherman Anti-Trust
> Act" and . . . the "Clayton Act." [36]

In summary form, the government's logic ran as follows:

I. Importance of News
   A. Newspapers supply a necessary public service; they affect
      the national interest.
   B. Democracy operates on news and opinion.
   C. Newspapers are the chief medium for disseminating such
      news and opinion.
II. Importance of Wire Services
   A. Newspapers must have access to all news.
   B. Some news can be gotten only through wire services.
   C. Each wire service has its own character and extent of
      coverage.
   D. Economics do not permit more wire services or newspapers
      performing the function of wire services.
   E. All newspapers must have access to all wire services.

III. Importance of Associated Press
    A. As a wire service, AP "ranks in the forefront in public reputation and esteem" for two reasons:
        1. AP's size of operation exceeds UP's and INS's in terms of:
            (a) annual expenditure for news collection and distribution,
            (b) length of news report,
            (c) size and quality of its physical facilities,
            (d) size of its staff,
            (e) number and dispersion of its news bureaus,
            (f) number and dispersion of its contributing members.
        2. AP's cooperative character is an "invaluable" guarantee of news reporting without political or sectional bias.
    B. All newspapers should have access to AP's news report. [37]

The government suit contended that in order to gain this open access to AP's news report, the government was petitioning the courts to enjoin AP for four by-law or contractual provisions. The government's charges and pleas for relief can be summarized as follows:

I. Protest Rights:
Use of protest rights and four-fifths membership vote were applied without standards, benefiting existing members, discriminating against outside newspapers, and restraining local competition. Enjoin AP to cease such rights and votes and to void such by-law provisions.

II. Local News to AP Only:
The prohibition of members from giving their local news to any other agency than AP restrained national wire-service competition and abridged the public nature of news.
Enjoin AP to cease such prohibitions and to void such by-law provisions.

III. Wide World Photos:
Acquisition of Wide World Photos from the New York Times in 1941 gave AP such control over the national distribution of news photographs as to restrain national competition in news photography. Enjoin AP to divest itself of Wide World Photos and to void the 1941 contract for purchase.

IV. Canadian Press News Exchange:
Exclusive mutual news exchange agreements with the Canadian Press so excluded other American wire services from access to the news reports of CP as to restrain American competition among wires.
Enjoin AP to cease such mutual news exchange agreements with CP and to void the news exchange contract. [38]

Responding on November 25, 1942, the Associated Press made three points in its defense: (1) freedom of the press requires freedom of association and operational structure; (2) the product of AP operations contains a property right which the government cannot or should not regulate without abridging the First Amendment; and (3) the effect of the government's case, if successful, will be to create a monopoly of AP where one does not now exist.[39]

In a separate answer, the Chicago Tribune emphasized the inviolability of press freedom and the non-commercial nature of AP.

> The attempt of plaintiff . . . to construe the anti-trust laws of the United States in a fashion that places the press on a common level with commercial or business enterprises for the purpose of control and regulation is an assault upon the validity of the Bill of Rights and the other historical charters and precedents which have emancipated man from political servitude.
> AP is not engaged in any commercial business or in trade or commerce, nor is it engaged in interstate or foreign trade or commerce.[40]

Editorially the Tribune reacted viciously and politically, viewing the case solely as a New Deal power grab.

> The true purpose of the litigation is to show the newspapers of this country that they will take orders from Washington if they know what is good for them. . . . This suit may be regarded as a threat to the freedom of the press. The threat is the gravest which has arisen since the first amendment was adopted. Here we see the full force of government brought to bear with a view to demonstrating to all editors and all publishers that they must do what Washington tells them to do--or else.[41]

The AP board, though more reserved in its wording, incorporated the same idea in what must be taken as the organization's official viewpoint on the case.

> The Board feels . . . that the effort of the Department
> of Justice to make a public utility out of The Associated Press
> must be strenuously opposed, among other reasons in order
> to foreclose against the next step, if the Department is
> successful, namely, government regulation of a public utility. [42]

On October 6, 1943, a three-judge panel handed down a two-to-one

decision for the government on the first, second, and fourth charges by

the plaintiff. Judge Learned Hand, writing for the majority, said:

> In the production of news every step involves the con-
> scious intervention of some news gatherer, and two accounts
> of the same event will never be the same. . . . For this
> reason, it is impossible to treat two news services as inter-
> changeable, and to deprive a newspaper of the benefit of any
> service of the first rating is to deprive the reading public of
> means of information which it should have. [43]

Having thus followed the government's contention that a multiplicity of

voices, whether at the origin of news or between the origin and the local

outlet, was necessary to a democratic system, the court skirted the public

utility and monopoly questions emphasizing the by-law's negative effect on

local competition.

> Although . . . only a few members will have any direct
> personal interest in keeping out an applicant, the rest will
> not feel free to judge him regardless of the effect of his ad-
> mission on his competitors. Each will know that the time
> may come when he will himself be faced with the application
> of a competitor, and that will be true even as to those in
> whose "field" no opponent has as yet appeared. Unless he
> supports those who now object to the admission of their
> competitors, he will not in the future be likely to get their
> support against his own. [44]

In his dissent, Judge Thomas W. Swan made five points in support of

AP: (1) AP had not unreasonably restrained trade and thus did not qualify as

a monopoly; (2) news gathering is not affected with the public interest;

(3) determination of what is affected with the public interest is the business

of Congress and not the courts; (4) the court's majority has set the court up as a dictator in the business of revising AP's by-laws; and (5) a news report, with property rights attached, may be shared with whomever the producer of that report chooses.[45]

In effect, the court said that AP was not a monopoly and that adjustment of the AP-membership relationship to deny the latter use of the relationship for local self-interests would not make AP a monopoly. Moreover, the majority held that such adjustment was important not only to newspapers in general, but also to the public and the democratic process. News gathering is not a public utility in the same sense that telephone and telegraph companies are, the court said, but sufficient regulation of relationships is necessary in this case to maintain the First Amendment press freedom by opening previously closed channels of news accessibility.

AP and most of its members continued objecting to federal control of news content and association contracts, maintaining that AP was not a monopoly, that the court decision would make AP a monopoly, and that it was a breach of free speech to make AP a public utility. The board's official response to the decision read in part as follows:

> The decision of the statutory court in New York would subject the world's greatest news-gathering organization to suit and harrassment and to a perpetual injunction which would render it subject to future whims of administrative officials and continued supervision of the federal courts.
> The court found The Associated Press was not a monopoly. It found that it was not a common carrier. Yet the decision, if not appealed and overthrown, would impose a method of doing business upon The Associated Press which would hamper its efficiency and weaken its cooperative structure. There is no course open except to appeal from such intrusion.[46]

Both sides argued before the U.S. Supreme Court on December 5
and 6, 1944, and on June 18, 1945, the high court handed down a five-to-
three decision[47] affirming the lower court. The majority opinion, written
by Justice Hugo L. Black, employed as reasoning the so-called Social
Responsibility theory of the press which holds that government's principal
function, vis-a-vis the press, was to assist or force wherever possible
or necessary the maintenance or establishment of a multiplicity of communication channels to serve the public interest and the democratic system.[48]
Black established the government's role as protector of the First Amendment and then pointed out that in light of its membership practices, AP had
abridged that freedom for others.

> It would be strange indeed . . . if the grave concern for
> freedom of the press which prompted adoption of the First
> Amendment should be read as a command that the Government
> was without power to protect that freedom. The First Amend-
> ment, far from providing an argument against application of
> the Sherman Act, here provides powerful reasons to the con-
> trary. . . . Freedom to publish means freedom for all and not
> for some. Freedom to publish is guaranteed by the Constitu-
> tion, but freedom to combine to keep others from publishing
> is not. Freedom of the press from governmental interference
> under the First Amendment does not sanction repression of that
> freedom by private interests. The First Amendment affords
> not the slightest support for the contention that a combination
> to restrain trade in news and views has a constitutional im-
> munity.[49]

Justice Douglas, in his separate, concurring opinion, sought to use
the case as an opportunity to delineate activities concerning which antitrust
action was a valid remedy.[50] Justice Frankfurter's concurring decision
stressed the fact that although AP was impressed with the public interest
by virtue of the important product it distributed, it was not a public utility
in a legal sense.[51]

Dissenters for the most part followed Swan's dissent in the statutory court, emphasizing that AP was non-commercial, that destruction of competition and monopoly were not AP's purposes, that the court's majority was interferring with AP's use of its private property, and that the majority was setting AP up as a public utility.[52] Justice Roberts observed: "This is government by injunction with a vengeance."[53] Murphy dissented separately on the contention that the government had failed to prove its case, that the court had no precedent in this matter, and that the majority decision smacked of governmental intervention.[54]

Although several wealthy publishers sought unsuccessfully to reverse the high court's verdict by congressional action to amend the antitrust laws so as to exempt "mutual news gathering agencies,"[55] the AP by-laws were changed at a special meeting in mid-1945 to open regular membership to all newspaper applicants. In the following year, associate memberships were extended to include radio and television stations, non-voting newspapers, and all foreign news outlets.

In the final disposition of the case, only two of the government's four charges were remedied: revision of membership application procedures and nullification of the exclusive AP-CP news-exchange contract. The exclusive use of members' news by AP continues today as a feature of the AP-member relationship. (No such AP privilege is imposed upon associate members.) The court dismissed the government's plea for AP divestiture of Wide World Photos.

To some long-time AP members the 1945 decision still remains an
agonizing experience. One Southern editor and former AP director com-
mented on the decision while giving a historical account of AP's growth in
his state.

> At one time in this period the AP had some 30 mem-
> bers to less than a sparse half dozen for the other two
> (wire services). A membership in AP was a prized
> possession until the Roosevelt Supreme Court made it a five
> and ten cent store article. [56]

Others say that the court did not go far enough in limiting AP's control over
its members. The city editor of an Illinois daily wrote the following criticism of AP's exclusive control of his paper's news and over his personal
freedom of action.

> Since becoming affiliated with AP, it has been impressed
> on me that I may not serve as a "stringer" for anyone but AP.
> In other words, if there's a news item of state or national
> interest developing in the area, I may call it only to AP--or
> there are penalties of some sort. I feel rather strongly about
> this--for I feel I would have the "loyalty" to notify AP first in
> any event. From a personal standpoint, I feel this regulation
> tends to cause me not to turn in as many news items--when
> I may call only one news service. In other words, the little
> amount of extra dough you get is not worth the effort, where
> if you could call both services plus nearby metropolitan news-
> papers, this could be a nice source of additional income. [57]

Thus the membership remains at odds even today over the ideal terms of the
relationship, some calling it too loose and others sayint it is to stringent.

The net effect of the 1945 Supreme Court decision has been felt more
by the individual AP members than by the AP organization. The protest
right has been traced back to the long-outdated conditions of the 1890's when
AP badly needed members' financial and numerical support and when papers
committed themselves, and their future success, either to AP or to the old

UP in a fight to the death. A membership of the Series A variety gave AP added revenue, and the member, in turn, received a local-board position and a veto power over competitors' receipt of the AP report. In 1900 AP "repaid" these past supporters with protest rights but almost immediately began applying pressure to reduce the effectiveness of the franchise. In 1928 the franchise became universal, but the AP pressure continued. By 1942, the franchise was for members a little-used, last-resort measure, the presence of which was largely only a distant threat to the AP organization. In effect, it was by 1942 the members' only legal lever in relationships with AP (outside of cancellation of service, a move which most members felt would defeat their own purposes), and the courts had freed AP from the threat of this last membership leverage in 1945.

Legally, of course, bondholding remains another device by which individuals or blocs can exercise power vis-a-vis the AP organization, or more specifically the board of directors. And at the same time as the board and the administration were pressuring protest right holders into submission, the general manager and his administrative staff were beginning to edge the board out of power. Therefore, while bondholding continues to influence the election of directors, those directors no longer exercise the practical dominance they once did in the organization.

The question arose several times during the 1942-45 litigation over whether a federal government victory in the case would not in effect make a monopoly out of AP. Seeking an answer seems worthwhile, not to prove or disprove one side's contention, but to discover the actual impact of the decision

upon AP's membership and the wire service-subscriber relational dimensions. To provide an answer, the author turned to the International Year
Books of Editor & Publisher: The Fourth Estate, which are the only public
records of daily American newspapers that include wire-service affiliations. The complete tabulations of six years of affiliations (used in various
combinations for several inquiries in this chapter) are found in Table 19.
The affiliation summaries in Table 20 will provide an initial, aggregate
picture of affiliation changes. Seven-year periods before and after 1942
are represented in the tables by tabulations of 1935, 1942, and 1949. In
absolute figures, AP's membership was as follows: 1935, 1,179; 1942,
1,201; and 1949, 1,223. [58] According to Table 13, total newspapers declined 163 (or 8.3 per cent) between 1935 and 1942, and the total dropped
another seven newspapers (or 0.4 per cent) between 1942 and 1949. It appears as though AP had some slight increase over this universe, gaining
twenty-two newspaper members both before and after 1942. This is a pre-
1942 gain of 1.9 per cent and a post-1942 increase of 1.8 per cent. Moreover, the aggregate figures show no particular difference between the two
seven-year periods.

Another approach considers the relative growth and strength of wires
in terms of the various affiliation combinations. From this view point,
according to Table 20, AP showed a decline both in total memberships and
in those receiving AP alone. The UP and INS total newspaper clientele was
increasing simultaneously. Apparently, while a few newspapers were taking
advantage of the new open AP membership, many more papers were taking

advantage of wartime reader interest (in 1942) and of postwar prosperity

(in 1949) to supplement existing wire-service affiliations with new ones.

Note in Table 20 the across-the-board increases in wire combinations and

the simultaneous decline of one-wire or no-wire operations. As long as

three wires operated in the United States, AP was not able in these selected

years to gain much more than about 50 per cent saturation of the total news-

paper field.

A third investigation of these two seven-year periods (presented in

Table 21 as frequencies of individual change patterns) will be postponed

until a general discussion of overall patterns of affiliation changes. In

general, the court's decision seems not to have influenced AP's member-

ship to any significant extent. Not all newspapers would ever seek AP

membership if given the chance, and the decision came at an unrelated

turning point in American newspapering: the end of World War II when

combination affiliations began to rise and thus mitigated the possibility of

one-wire dominance in the United States.

Extra-legal relations in political interaction are those which con-

tribute to the image, reputation, and extra-contractual status of the com-

ponents. They operate principally within the psychological fields of

components and ordinarily in face-to-face or at least individual situations.

The following discussion points out that within the legal structure of wire

service-subscriber relationships, wires employ several types of devices

to influence the thoughts and actions of subscribers, i.e., to help retain

the dominant relational position created by the legal conditions described above. It should be noted that much of the extra-legal activity while

buttressing legal or power dominance, also is geared to influencing produc-

tion by increasing wires' actual market of outlet channels, vis-a-vis other

wires.

Primary within this dual wire-service thrust for political and pro-

ductive dominance is the shaping of the wire's image as a reputable, re-

liable service whose report is a necessary commodity. Essentially the

wire service has two subscribers: the daily news outlets which actually

receive the daily news reports, and the readers, listeners, or viewers

who ultimately depend on the reports for the daily information and opinions.

Both the wire and the outlets seek to make their respective publics believe

that their news reports are the most complete, objective, interpretative,

lively, exclusive, and so on. For the wires these one-step (vis-a-vis out-

lets) and two-step (vis-a-vis the public) attempts at attitude change are

simply advertising campaigns--praising and enhancing the product for in-

creased sales. The one-step campaign has always been an easy one;

political, productive, and communicative channels are already established

between the two and are subverted to handle the wire's advertising at times.

The two-step campaign, on the other hand, requires wire reliance upon out-

let cooperation (beyond the legal necessity of attribution by logotype) since

direct wire service-public relations are rare and confiscation of outlets'

time or space is legally impossible.

AP's constant, although somewhat unrealistic, emphasis upon its

cooperative structure, democratic processes, and egalitarian rate deter-

mination has made its job somewhat easier than UP's, INS's, or UPI's in terms of eliciting loyalty, sympathy, and strength in the wire-subscriber ties. AP, however, has not relied solely on this approach. Increasingly, in fact, these conditions obviously have not existed in AP and their continued use in advertising increasingly may tend to elicit suspicion, investigation, and rejection by members. Thus although these ideals are still presented, they are increasingly being replaced by AP's self-admiration for content improvements, technological developments, etc. (similar to competitors' messages from the beginning). The reports of the general managers in the Annual Volumes, beginning with Cooper have shown this tendency toward glossy self-adulation obviously designed to "sell" AP's ability, success, and improvement.

Use of membership totals and growth patterns of subscribers in new supplementary services is the wire's attempt to create a "band-wagon" effect among members. Such use is geared to creating membership optimism and strengthening existing psychological or contractual ties. (When membership figures are omitted from communiques to subscribers, there usually are related facts which indicate that the figures had declined in the previous year.) Both wires present these and other statistical indices of growth and size during annual reports in April to reach the larger, potential outlet-consumer market. Under the pretense of reporting to the members or subscribers, the wires' statements are covered by trade journals and thus reach the wider market as "factual" advertising. The content of and omissions from these reports reveal the wires' cognizance of their advertising value.

The Associated Press, however, until recently remained true to its early commitment to "non-commercial" news gathering by refraining from "hardsell" advertising in trade publications. AP's message was largely an exposition of its principles or ideals. Lately, however, AP has begun to equal (and on some occasions to surpass) UPI in commercial advertising efforts.

Within the spheres of present members or subscribers, however, AP has always had the edge on competitors in the number and diversity of extra-legal channels of pressure and psychological reinforcement. Many of these channels are maintained in the form of quasi-legal ties supposedly required by the cooperative structure of AP. By one means or another, however, both wires manage to maintain extra-legal connections which shape within the members or subscribers a positive, optimistic belief system with respect to the wire. Several of these connections are described below.

AP's Annual Volumes are directed toward the editors or publishers of member newspapers and have no equal in the UPI organization. Increasingly, as noted in Chapter IV, these reports have been structured to propagandize AP's operations rather than report actual conditions. Their format has swung from conservative to glossy and gaudy, and their emphasis has moved from legalistic policy and board minutes to promotional material. A review of the discussion of Annual Volumes in Chapter IV will illustrate this trend.

For the telegraph editors--the men who daily cut the wire and decide between AP and UPI--AP distributes the AP Log ("A Weekly Analysis of AP

News and Photo Coverage"). Here AP dwells upon the mechanical problems

of covering particular stories, applauds its staffers who did a good job over

the past week, notes changes in AP's filing and coverage procedures, and

tallies members' use of AP versus UPI on given stories in selected news-

papers. It is written with a shop-talk tone, as if the writer were himself

a telegraph editor (thus giving him the latitude of complimenting AP's staff

efforts). The weekly tally is again an attempt at the band-wagon influence,

the assumption being that selecting one wire over another may often be a

matter of habit in the stress and rush of getting wire copy ready for the news

columns. The Log also acts as an advertising vehicle for new features or

series being planned by AP. Advance warning about and descriptions of how

the new feature will be packaged and transmitted assure that the telegraph

editor will be more likely stopped by the feature's slug line when it appears

on the printer. UPI's Reporter performs the same function for UPI wire

editors, although not in as commercial and blatant a form as AP's Log.

AP's Managing Editors Association, started by Cooper in 1933, is

a channel directed at a third important local level of policy maker: the

managing editor. Formed as a channel for face-to-face exchange of ideas

between AP and its subscribers, Cooper describes it as . . .

> . . . a method by which representatives of all the "customers"
> who are the immediate users of the product meet in a large
> hall with the executives and representatives of the staff that
> turns out that product and with just one purpose in mind: to
> improve it! [59]

The "continuing studies" were begun in 1946 as a means of organizing

the APME into operating committees around specific subjects of investigation.

The so-called Blue Books and Red Books contain the reports of continuing studies and the APME convention minutes, respectively. They relay the APME's activities to the large majority of members who do not participate annually. The organization and the books provide another link of "cooperation" between the AP and its members. (It is probably no coincidence that shortly after these books appeared, the Annual Volumes' format was changed to complement them: pictures, soft cover, flashy typographical display, etc. In size and presentation, the Volumes might be called the "Green Books" in this triad of promotion.) An executive told the author that AP will use members' suggestions wherever possible and economically feasible, but AP will always listen to the membership's suggestions and gripes.[60] In addition to the contacts maintained via the organization between AP and its members, the APME apparently is an AP "feedback" channel, through which it can send up trial balloons for membership response and find out through members' comments and "investigations" how best to alter the product to increase its sales and usage.

Finally, face-to-face contacts are maintained most directly by traveling agents who visit member and non-member offices occasionally to gather "feedback" on their wire's image, to improve that image if possible, and perhaps to sell additional services. The author's experience with these agents has probably been similar to that of most wire editors. The representative arrives mid-morning asking how his wire is doing on a couple of the day's top stories. The wire editor's answers set the tone of the representative's approach. He will attempt to explain a bad situation or to exploit a good situation to the wire editor before moving onto the manag-ing editor's office either to make a sale or simply to re-establish personal contacts and show wire interest in the newspaper and its problems. Since these representatives personally contact all the newspapers, they reach many which do not participate in APME or AP's annual meeting. The face-to-face situation, of course, will in most cases have a more direct and positive effect upon all three levels of local decision makers than any amount of printed or group-meeting contacts. The representative serves as the principal contact between UPI and its clients.

In the final analysis, the legal structure of the relationship often pro-vides the opportunity for extra-legal pressures (which are principally exerted by the wires), while the extra-legal activities help to obliterate or cushion the real impact of political confinement (which increasingly has also originated with the wires). These trends and activities are largely attributable to the ingenuity of Kent Cooper who replaced the unstable though austere "establish-ment" atmosphere of AP membership with a more realistic commercial ap-proach to both the product and the membership.

Productive Interaction and Trends

Productivity as an interactional phase in the wire service-subscriber relationship is the existence of and changes in the actual wire service-outlet channels available for the communication product. It has been noted above that many of the extra-legal aspects of this relationship influence not only the power relations, but also the creative relations in that they help to

initiate, maintain, and strengthen the channels between wires and outlets.
Wires' images, reputations, creditability, and traditions and subscribers'
optimism, habits, and susceptibility are at stake in extra-legal pressures.
Thus, the discussion turns to trends in affiliation and clients' reasons for
their affiliation configurations.

UPI appears not to have discriminated in accepting subscribers;
the wire moved quickly into South America, Europe, radio, and television,
mindless of any traditional journalistic viewpoints and in a couple of cases
ignoring industry policy. AP, at least in its public statements, has reflected both a newspapering perspective and clubby selectivity in its membership practices (aside from the individual use of protest rights). The
AP board in 1919 described the due deliberation it took in passing on applications.

> It would have been a simple matter to increase the mem-
> bership by hundreds, but we welcome competition and aim only
> to encourage the growth of membership along the lines of the
> natural development of our news-gathering resources.[61]

The principle of cooperative newsgathering is emphasized in this statement,
even though in reality much of the organization's news-gathering function
had been taken over by its own permanent staff by 1919. AP did not let this
ideal die easily, however, and chose in later policy statements to alter the
emphasis to the good of the organization rather than anything more specific.
This broader concept is exhibited in the following board statement made in
1921.

> The Board continues to consider each application for
> membership with a view not only to the local situation but
> also to the general interests of the organization. It adopts
> no policy of forced growth.[62]

Use of more general criteria permitted the organization to accept more members, regardless of local duplication, quality of local news-gathering organizations, etc. Table 14 reveals that AP's growth has been relatively rapid and constant, and its rates of growth have been similar to UP's and UPI's where periods and types of outlets are comparable. By almost any criteria, it would be to AP's advantage to maintain a high total of outlets. And this appears, according to Table 14, to have occurred to AP officials.

The table leads to two important findings. First, AP moved rapidly into the broadcast and foreign fields beginning in 1945 when the decision was finally made to expand service. AP's eagerness seems to reveal a somewhat "commercial" motive which belies the board's statements above. Table 15 shows that AP's broadcast growth went from zero to 47.5 per cent saturation in two years, after which some large increases in AM radio and television outlets (see Table 13) forced AP's saturation downward. The opening of special radio service and the formation of state and regional radio associations have brought the saturation back up to about 46 per cent.

Second, increases in wire-service affiliations have not coincided with advances and declines in total outlets. Table 13 shows that between 1910 and 1921 total U.S. newspapers declined by 405; Table 14 shows AP's newspaper increase over the same period was 469. Again, between 1922 and 1931 total newspapers declined 110 while AP's newspaper total increased 124. Although some AP newspapers were in South and Central America (thus placing these AP figures in the total outlet column rather than the U.S. total column), the bulk of these additions came from the domestic newspaper field. Apparently, outlets increased as AP made available the hardcore news report and supplementary services more cheaply and rapidly. Thus, growth of subscribers seems to have been contingent upon the speed, quality, and cost of the service, and perhaps the relative financial stability of potential and actual subscribers (increasing over time with the decline of local competition) may have been a contributing factor.

Table 16 reveals the wires' inroads into the foreign field, indicating that here is where an increasing number of subscribers is now being recruited. In light of the Chapter V discussion on the instability of these foreign markets, the aggregate figures in Table 16 camouflage the problems of constantly shifting foreign clientele. AP and UPI are largely at the mercy of the whims of local news agencies, foreign governments, shifts in diplomatic relations, and transmission costs and arrangements in getting and serving these affiliations. A nation's newspapers and broadcast stations may be affiliates one day and the next be forced by their government to drop the American wire service. Moreover, the total number of nations served by American wires is misleading if the total picture excludes the necessity of sharing regions with three other major world wire services: TASS, Reuters, and Agence France-Presse.

In 1952, AP served 69 countries, and UP served 77, according to Table 16. Table 17, however, shows that even with the addition of INS, the American wires' influence was felt by only 62.6 per cent of the world's population, of which 54.6 per cent was influence shared with one, two, or three of these world competitors. TASS has the largest single bloc of unshared distribution market (30.9 per cent). The American wires, plus

Reuters and AF-P, must share distribution to 39. 8 per cent of the world's

population. Table 18 breaks this down as including large portions of

South America, Asia, and Europe. The American wires can count on only

slightly more than three-fourths of the distribution in their own home con-

tinent. Thus, although nearly half of AP's and UPI's subscribers are out-

side of the United States and are in more than one hundred foreign nations,

the total world picture is at best confining and unstable for them.

Tables 19 and 20 present the author's tabulation of wire affiliations

for newspapers in selected years. (Such personal tabulations are necessary

to avoid the wires' occasional secrecy, to weed out broadcast and "other"

outlets from wire-service totals, and to establish a standard long-term

definition of daily newspapers.) Because figures in Table 19 are difficult

to discuss meaningfully because of their number and diversity, temporal

trends and annual wire-service strengths will be depicted symbolically and

geographically in Figures 9, 10, 11, and 12.[63]

Figure 9 (see next page) shows the geographical distribution of affilia-

tion strength for AP and UPI during 1963. If AP and UPI concentrations of

25 per cent and less are removed from consideration (causing elimination

of twenty-one of the fifty states, according to Figure 9), the remaining

strength reveals some significant geographical patterns. In the Eastern

Division of twelve states, AP dominates in eight or two-thirds of the states;

UPI dominates only in West Virginia. In the Central Division, AP dominates

in half of the twelve states, UPI controls only Indiana. In the South, AP

dominates six of thirteen states (46.2 per cent), and UPI dominates only

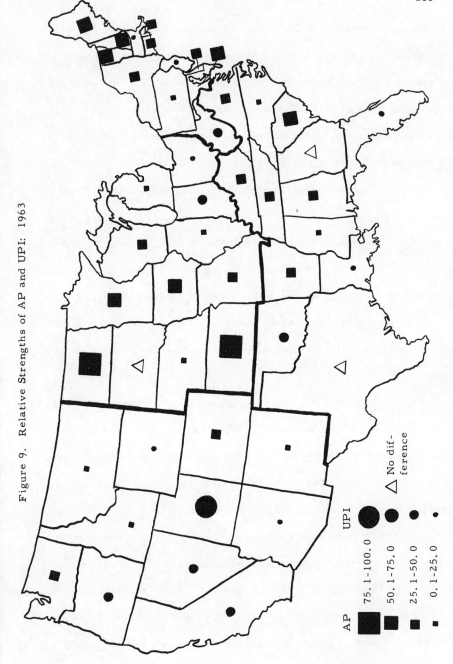

Figure 9. Relative Strengths of AP and UPI: 1963

Oklahoma. For these three divisions, AP controls twenty out of thirty-seven states or about 54 per cent; UPI dominates in three, for about 8.1 per cent. In the Western Division the picture is reversed: UPI controls four of eleven states (36.4 per cent) and AP controls two (18.2 per cent). In terms of total states AP far outdistances UPI in dominating the wire affiliation in the United States in 1963.

A small degree of geographical consistency is apparent in Figure 9. A band stretching east from California to Utah and north into Oregon is UPI territory. A strip of central states between North Dakota, Minnesota, and Wisconsin on the north and Kansas and Missouri on the south, is an AP region, as are New England (except for Massachusetts) and a Southern loop. After looking at trends which have led to this recent arrangement (Figures 10-12), territorial distribution and dominance will again be discussed.

Figures 10 and 11 each represent fourteen-year periods of changing affiliation patterns.[64] Increases of 15.1 per cent or more for either wire service between 1935 and 1949 occurred in only nine states (for AP--Idaho, New Mexico, Nebraska, Minnesota, Missouri, Tennessee, Maryland, and Maine; and for UP--Wyoming). If there is any regional concentration of such increases, it is in the central and western states (six out of nine states). For the period 1949-63, sixteen states had increases of 15.1 per cent or more (for AP--Washington, Colorado, Kansas, Iowa, Arkansas, Delaware, and New Hampshire; and for UP-UPI--Oregon, Utah, Arizona, Louisiana, Ohio, West Virginia, Florida, New Jersey, and Massachusetts). Only

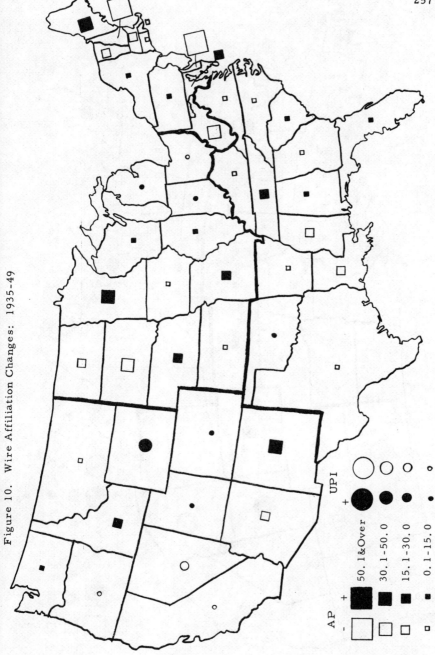

Figure 10. Wire Affiliation Changes: 1935-49

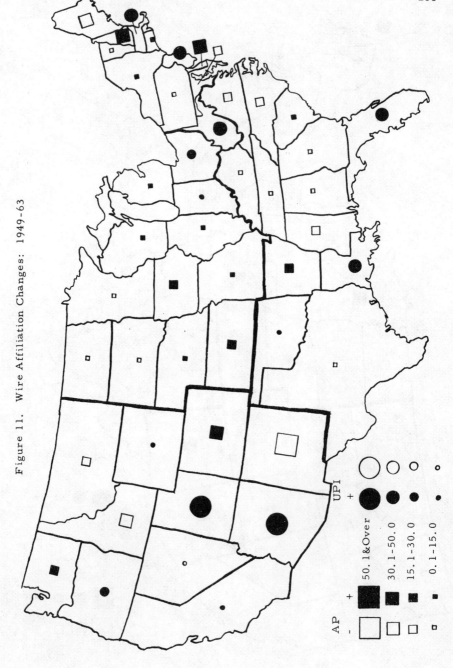

Figure 11. Wire Affiliation Changes: 1949-63

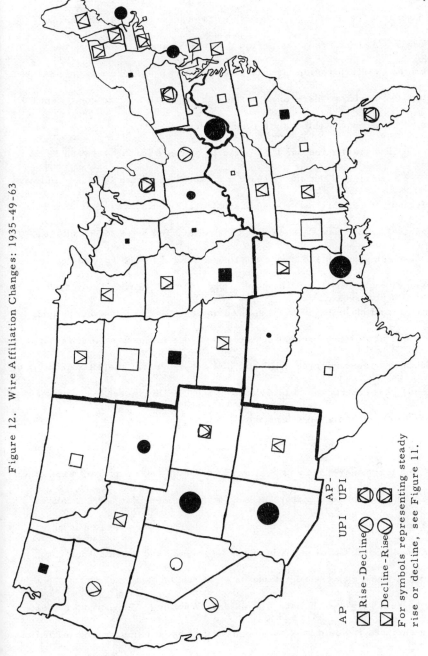

Figure 12. Wire Affiliation Changes: 1935-49-63

Arkansas appears in both periods with a large increase in affiliation for either wire, and for the latter period the largest group is found in the western and eastern regions (ten of sixteen states). In terms of increases over the two periods, there is no particular regional or state consistency nor any consistency within either wire service.

Affiliation declines of 15. 1 per cent or more for AP between 1935 and 1949 are found in ten states (Arizona, North and South Dakota, Louisiana, Mississippi, West Virginia, Delaware, Massachusetts, Vermont, and New Hampshire). Only Nevada showed a UP decline. Between 1949 and 1963, only Mississippi continued to decline for AP, but the wire showed declines in seven other states (Idaho, Montana, New Mexico, North Carolina, Virginia, Maryland, and Maine). UP-UPI showed no declines in the second period. AP clearly has experienced recent unstable relations in the East and West and in the South to a lesser degree. UP and UPI are unique for their fewer gains and declines, particularly the latter. Much of the UP-UPI increases between 1949 and 1963 was probably caused by the 1958 merger.

In Figure 12 the twenty-eight-year period is summarized, allowing small and large increases and declines to combine and counteract each other in creation of an overall picture of long-term trends. For AP, instances where increases of 15. 1 per cent or more occurred were limited to only four states: South Carolina, Missouri, Nebraska, and Washington. For UP-UPI, increases were registered in eight states: Massachusetts, New Jersey, West Virginia, Indiana, Louisiana, Wyoming, Utan, and Arizona. On the surface, it would look as though AP has been losing ground in affiliation

to UP and UPI, and to a small degree this is true. But this overlooks the
fact that in 1935 AP had 51.3 per cent of the total wire affiliations (1,179
in absolute figures), according to Table 20, and UP had only 37.4 per cent
(857 in total numbers). This is a very large cushion with which to operate,
and data show that in 1963 AP's 1,179 total had only been cut to 1,164 while
UP-UPI's 857 had only risen to 940. Thus, in aggregate figures, the picture
has not changed much in the last twenty-eight years.

As for declines, AP dropped in eight states: Montana, South Dakota,
Texas, Mississippi, Georgia, North Carolina, Virginia, and Alaska. UP-
UPI declined only in Nevada. AP's difficulty, apparently, is in the South;
UP-UPI's success has been in the South, but more in the West. Some factors
might be isolated to suggest reasons for these changes, e.g., the Western
growth of initially unstable newspapers, the declining economy in some rural
Southern sections, an over-saturation of newspapers and broadcast outlets
in some areas of the East, etc. It seems apparent, however, that no single
factor or set of related factors universally explains these affiliation conditions.
This is particularly true of the twenty-three states (46 per cent of the total)
in which AP or UP-UPI affiliations were not consistent throughout the twenty-
eight-year period, and the four states (8 per cent) whose inconsistency
involved both wire services alternately.

Some understanding of these trends and seeming inconsistencies can
be gained from an investigation of outlet-by-outlet affiliation changes during
the two periods. Table 21 presents the actual change patterns, rank ordered
for each period according to the frequency of each pattern. Given the eight

possible single and combination wire affiliations in the three tabulated
years when three wires operated (AP, UP, INS, AP-UP, AP-INS, UP-
INS, AP-UP-INS, and None), there are sixty-four possible change patterns
(including the eight patterns representing no change). Only those change
patterns which appeared at least once are included in Table 21, and since
affiliation was tabulated only once every seven years for this table, only
the "net" change of affiliation during each of the two seven-year periods
is shown. The number of change patterns appearing decreased from forty-
seven (73 per cent of sixty-four total possibilities) to forty-two (67 per
cent of the total) between the two periods. At least two-thirds of the
possible change patterns are represented, indicating a wide spectrum of
individual newspaper problems and solutions or personal dispositions and
choices.

It is first important to note that the rank order in Table 21 is somewhat dependent upon the affiliation category's original strength, i.e.,
"A-A" newspapers totaled 581 or 34.5 per cent in part because in 1935
there were 778 newspapers with AP-only affiliations. No other affiliation or combination could possibly total 581 on the table; the next highest
total is UP-only at 467 in 1935. But, on the other hand, the AP-only newspapers did have seven other alternatives, all but one (A-UI) appearing
somewhere on the table, although considerably lower in the rank order.
The first observation about this table, therefore, is that although many
patterns of change occurred, the preponderance of "changes" are reaffirmations of previous affiliations (as a seven-year net change pattern). In the

1935-42 column, such reaffirmations total almost 70 per cent; and in the
1942-49 column they total more than 78 per cent. Such high percentages
are due to the initial, high magnitude of some of these, particularly AP,
UP, AP-UP, AP-UP-INS, None, and INS. They are, however, also due
to a high level of continuing affiliations. Almost 75 per cent of the AP-only
newspapers in 1935 stayed with AP until 1942 (581 out of 778), and almost
82 per cent did the same between 1942 and 1949 (600 out of 735). Better than
65 per cent of the UP-only newspapers remained with UP alone between
1935-42 (305 out of 467), and better than 70 per cent did so between 1942-49
(320 out of 454).

Two trends appear in this fourteen-year period: (1) Tables 19 and
20 indicate that single-wire newspapers declined somewhat while combina-
tion-wire newspapers were increasing and that the wires' respective subscriber lists remained relatively stable throughout; and (2) Table 21 reveals
that period-long stability of existing affiliations was relatively great and that
(see "Difference" column) all but one (UI-UI) such reaffirmation showed
relatively large fourteen-year increases. In effect, the picture remains
relatively stable; only a few newspapers change affiliation and these changes
tend to cancel out each other, making trends, per se, almost non-existent
in the data.

The author has noted from his experience with these raw data, it
might be mentioned, that most frequently the same few newspapers will
shift affiliation several times, creating much of this small but persistent
underlying change. These newspapers are the exceptions rather than the rule.

It is, however, their activity which produces the long columns of relatively low frequency changes in Table 21. To illustrate this point, for 1935-42, the top nine entries included 79 per cent of the total newspapers and for 1942-49, the top nine entries totaled 83 per cent. Of the 79 per cent total for 1935-42, 68.2 per cent are affiliation reaffirmations. Of the 83 per cent total for 1942-49, 76.8 per cent are affiliation reaffirmations.

Up to this point aggregate affiliation data as indices of wire service-subscriber productivity have not revealed any discernible trends except for a slight increase in combination affiliations and a propensity of a few news-papers to continually change wire affiliations, while most maintain the same patterns. To break out of the aggregate-date confines and perhaps arrive at more meaningful findings requires careful scrutiny of individual cases. Two types of data on individual newspaper affiliation will be pre-sented: (1) reasons for long-standing wire-service affiliations expressed by newspapers' managing editors, and (2) reasons for recent affiliation changes, also given by managing editors. To gather the first type of data, the author constructed a stratified random sample of newspapers and solicited, by mail, managing editors' opinions of the wires in general and of their own affiliation. (The mechanics of this sample are described in Section I of Appendix C.) This stratified random sample, as Appendix C indicates, was accompanied by a mailing to managing editors of all newspapers with circu-lations of 100,000 and over. Responses to both sets of inquiries are sum-marized in Table 22.

In the first half of the table, responses are arranged according to respondents' wire affiliations. The editor usually will defend his affiliation, and so the question is not which wire seems best to him, but rather what are the reasons he gives for his affiliation. AP affiliates put greatest stress upon the wire's coverage and news report, a long tradition of affiliation, and the wire's organization (mostly the cooperative structure and strong state or regional organizations). The first and third were most frequently mentioned by small dailies (50,000 population and less) and the first and second reasons most frequently appeared for medium-sized papers (between 50,000 and 500,000 population). UPI affiliates noted coverage and news report and a long tradition as the two principal reasons for affiliation. Most of these occurred in small daily papers. Editors affiliated with both wires stressed expanded coverage, the complementary aspects of the wires' reports, and the fact that use of both and the content of both fill a specific need of the newspaper. Most of these affiliates, it appears, come from the medium and large dailies.

The responses reveal that editors may use the same reasons to support affiliation with either wire singly or both wires together. On the other hand, one finds editors explaining affiliation with the same wire in terms of diametrically opposed reasons. Personal opinions, past experiences, past teachers, single instances of wire activity, personality clashes, and probably many other factors apparently enter into the choice among affiliation alternatives. Also involved seems to be the momentary or long-term economic, competitive, mechanical, and labor conditions unique to each paper.

Specifically with respect to this latter group of factors, two relatively distinct groups of editors seem to be formed by the responses: (1)

(1) editors whose local conditions force them to make economics, "nuts-and-bolts," or competition their primary orientation; and (2) editors whose conditions permit a more subtle, qualitative evaluation. The former group visualizes the wires as a commodity of a quantitative or mechanical or monetary value to the newspaper. It helps fill up the news hole, one is less expensive than another, it was received in a package deal with our radio station, it moves sports news earlier, it helps us in our competition, etc. The author found many more of these statements originating with UPI-only editors and with a small group of competitive AP-UPI editors. The second group of editors discusses the qualitative aspects of his service, often stressing its worth to readers and to the community as a whole. Its writing is bright and colorful, its report is complete, it stresses interpretative reporting, regional coverage is excellent, readers must have all the news, the burden for community information is on us, etc. These are the feelings of an overwhelming number of large newspapers (100,000 circulation and over) and many small AP-only newspapers.

If the responses are taken as a whole, without regard to individual affiliations (see the second half of Table 22), this panel of working newspapermen visualize the two wires sometimes as clearly distinct and sometimes as undifferentiated. Figure 13 summarizes findings reported in Table 22 and adds, from the raw data, frequently mentioned specific reasons within each category.

Figure 13. Editors' Views of Wires' Characteristics
(Only most frequent categories and reasons)

Associated Press   United Press International

COVERAGE & REPORT (51.7%)*   COVERAGE & REPORT (49.2%)*
  It is complete   Regional coverage is good
  Regional coverage is good   Much interpretative reporting
  More accurate   Writing is good
  Less sensational   Stories are colorful
  It is the essential wire   It is the fill-in wire
                                          Makes more mistakes

WIRE ORGANIZATION (21.0%)   LONG TRADITION (25.4%)
  Strong state associations   Long-time subscriber
  Coop structure is good   UPI cooperates with us
  It is faster and larger   We were INS subscribers

LONG TRADITION (16.8%)   FILLS NEWSPAPER'S NEEDS (13.6%)
  Long-time subscriber   We have a small news hole
  AP cooperates with us   We are a small newspaper
                                          We are an evening paper

FILLS NEWSPAPER'S NEEDS (4.9%)   ECONOMICS-COMPETITION (11.8%)
  We need only one wire   UPI is less expensive
  Best wire for one-wire papers   We get package rate w/radio
  We are a small newspaper   We compete with an AP paper
  We are a large paper

ECONOMICS-COMPETITION (4.9%)
  AP costs less
  AP costs more
  We can afford only one wire.

---

* Percentages in parentheses are from Table 22 and indicate the relative
frequency of categories mentioned.

It has been noted that responses given for specific affiliations (whether sincere ones or rationalizations) originate in the individual respondent's perspective, values, and background. This is true whether one controls for the respondent's affiliation or for the wire service as the object of an overall response. With such a diversity of viewpoints to contend with, a wire service's mechanical usefulness, image, reputation, contractual costs, etc., must, therefore, be all things to all people. But since the wire must daily commit its entire being in public, on paper, and in the subscribers' offices, it must try to be as inoffensive as possible to the greatest number of people. Obviously, this in turn affects the quality of the wire's daily product, as well as the professional policies of its staff and the speed and progressiveness of policy changes.

Having thus considered the opinions and reasoning of editors content with their wire affiliation, the discussion turns to the more critical investigation of opinions and reasoning leading to a change in wire affiliations. These are more significant because, if they have been faithfully transmitted to the author, they represent sufficient reason for positively altering affiliation configurations. It remains, then, for the author to attempt to control for fidelity by using any additional data available to construct a situational backdrop for evaluating the responses. This is done in Section II of Appendix C, where responses of this type are summarized, discussed, and evaluated. In all, this category includes responses from ten managing editors or publishers whose papers were listed as having change wire affiliation between 1962 and 1963, according to the Editor and Publisher International

Year Books for those years. A total of thirty-eight such changes occurred;
the response, therefore, was 26.3 per cent.

The discussions in Appendix C seem to revolve around three fundamental motivational patterns initiating affiliation changes: (1) contraction
of operations, primarily for competitive and economic reasons (Kenosha
News, Ashland Times-Gazette, and Somerset American); (2) expansion of
operation, primarily for competitive and economic reasons (Burlington
Free Press, Oxnard Press-Courier, and the "Western newspaper"); and
(3) individual or isolated judgments, principally for qualitative, personal
reasons (Olean Times-Herald, Roseburg News-Review, and Red Wing Daily
Republican Eagle). The difference between the first two patterns is one of
perspective and an inclination either to the negative response by the paper to
its relations with environmental conditions (i. e., contraction of operations)
or to a positive response to these conditions (i. e., expansion of operations).

Two of the three papers apparently contracting operations dropped
two wires in favor of one of them; the third moved to a less expensive wire.
In all three cases, strong competition figures prominently, and each newspaper has shown circulation declines, vis-a-vis competitors' circulation,
and loss of some of its geographical field to competitors. This is competition not within the community but among relatively close communities. A
single-newspaper community is usually well saturated by that paper (unless
a neighboring metropolitan area has an influence upon the community), but
the fight for life is waged in the smaller towns and the rural areas between
the newspaper locations. Here the prize is the retail trade zone which not

only looks to the central community as the commercial focal point but requires news and advertising from that center of influence and orientation.
Ordinarily the battle over trade area circulation is not permanently won by
one newspaper. The momentary loser simply tightens his belt (as apparently is the case with the first group of three newspapers) and scouts
around for a circulation-building "gimmick" which will recapture lost
subscribers. Reasons given by the three responding newspapers in this
situation are: to concentrate on local news, to reduce costly wire-service
duplication, their new wire made them an attractive (financial) offer, the
decision was made without consulting editors, and the newspaper has
shifted to TTS shop operation.

On the other hand, the inquiry revealed three responding newspapers
apparently on the ascending side of their relations with neighboring competition. The Burlington Free Press seems to be moving to outstrip competitors who are already in a subordinate position. The other two newspapers
are taking positive steps to close the gap between themselves and presently
superior competition. Addition of a wire, or continued use of two wires, is
often advertised to readers as a reason for the paper's superiority over
competition (whether that superiority is real or not). Often the paper claims
a more complete and factual daily news picture because of its two-wire
service. One Illinois daily (in close competition with another local daily)
made the following assertions about its three-wire affiliation in an advertising supplement in 1951.

> Not one but all three of America's leading news services--
> the United Press, the Associated Press and International News
> Service!

The News-Gazette provides this unexcelled-in-the-
middle-west combination of news reports to bring you the
BEST coverage of state, national and world news--every
day.
It enables News-Gazette wire editors to choose the
best and latest stories from a COMPLETE news report
far more comprehensive than any other newspaper published
in east central Illinois affords.
It's why "Page One" of The News-Gazette is a recognized daily standout among Illinois newspapers.
It's expensive. But it gives News-Gazette readers the
best and most complete coverage. * * * We believe the
intelligent and news conscious readers of this community
deserve the best. [65]

Receiving all major wires is only the beginning, however. They

must be used to their fullest potential in the paper's news columns--a task

which is often overridden by production requirements, overworked staff

members, small news holes, a desire to be different from competition,

etc. The wire service itself becomes a "gimmick" for increasing circula-

tion as are the games, puzzles, features, prizes, magazine offers, etc.

The comment of the Burlington respondent sounds similar to the News-

Gazette's advertising pitch above.

The Free Press added the United Press International
teletypesetter trunk to its wire report in September of 1962.
It did this to give its readers news of national and world
events in greater depth.
We feel that our reading audience is becoming more
sophisticated and more interested in national and international
affairs. We are trying to keep abreast of this fortunate improvement in reader interest. [66]

The Oxnard paper added AP to its previous UPI-only affiliation "partly to

meet competition from a competing newspaper, the Ventura Star Free-Press,

which had both AP and UPI and which occasionally featured a good AP story

that we did not have."[67] The "Western newspaper" switched to the more ex-

pensive AP wire because "in a monopoly situation . . . the normally fuller coverage and greater accuracy of the AP offset the occasional earlier stories of the UPI. "[68] The discussion in Appendix C notes, however, that the publisher is apparently attempting to improve his state and regional coverage and to match the AP national news of his out-of-state competitor.

Editors' comments and affiliation changes in these first two patterns raise important questions about the possible correlation between affiliation and competition or the size of the community. Before moving to a discussion of the third motivational pattern, these questions will be explored through 1963 aggregate figures in Tables 23-25. The tables are based on the author's tabulation of affiliation patterns of seventy-three newspapers in thirty competitive situations and of 210 newspapers with circulations of 50,000 and over.

Tables 23 and 24 present affiliations of newspapers in true competitive situations. (Competition here is defined as two or more newspapers occupying either the morning or evening field of the same town. When both fields are competitive in one city, as for example in Chicago or New York City, two competitive situations are noted.) More than half of the seventy-three newspapers involved in local competition carry both major wire services, according to Table 23. There appears to be some correlation between the size of the newspaper's circulation and the affiliation: the larger the circulation, the more likely is the paper to receive both AP and UPI. This is particularly the case if UPI-only is considered the principal alternative to AP-UPI affiliation. Moreover, a comparison of percentages reveals that 100,000 circulation seems to be the breaking point between AP-UPI and

UPI-only affiliations. AP-only affiliations seem to take the middle ground, being more generally distributed among the various circulation strata.

Table 24 identifies dominant newspapers in competitive situations (so designated on the basis of circulation comparisons) as maintaining an AP-UPI affiliation two-to-one. Again, AP falls in the middle with UPI-only affiliates at the bottom. For subordinate participants in competitive situations, however, UPI-only affiliates are found in almost half of the cases. The correlation breaks down somewhat with AP-UPI second and AP-only third, but these two have a similar magnitude and many of the subordinate AP-UPI affiliates are found in the 100,000-and-over circulation brackets, according to raw data. There seems to be a general correlation between the wire affiliation on the one hand and the size of the newspaper and (to a lesser extent) its success in the competitive situation, on the other. Throughout these categories AP-UPI affiliates are numerous.

Table 25 turns the coin over and considers wire affiliations for newspapers with circulations of 50,000 and over in non-competitive situations. Again, a comparison of percentages reveals 100,000 circulation as the cutoff point between AP-UPI affiliates and AP-only or UPI-only affiliates. Comparing Tables 23 and 25 for newspapers with 50,000 circulation and over gives the following figures:

	Competition	No Competition
AP-UPI	71.1%	50.0%
AP-Only	17.8	31.0
UPI-Only	11.1	16.2
None	--	2.8
	100.0%	100.0%

There is a decline in AP-UPI affiliations in non-competitive situations, an opposite trend with AP-only affiliates, and a lesser increase for UPI-only and None. Large and medium-sized newspapers are included here, however, making competition not the only factor in operation. Clearly there is a dominance of AP-UPI affiliates in this group of newspapers, whether in competition or not. Also, it appears as though non-competitive and leading competitive papers which for some reason do not have the dominant AP-UPI configuration tend more toward making AP their single wire, rather than UPI. The general feeling among newspaper editors is that AP is the principal wire and UPI augments or supplements AP, if the local situation and the newspaper's budget permits a second wire.

The interplay of competition and newspaper size is delicate and does not always affect affiliation patterns the same way. Willoughby after studying competing small dailies in Washington, Indiana, concludes:

> There was negligible competition of ideas, and there were few opposing viewpoints for Washington, Indiana, readers to choose from.
> The Washington dailies not only resemble each other in makeup, typography and size, but also are very much alike in content. There seemed to be no essential differences between the two, and during the period covered two competitive daily newspapers did not appear to be necessarily better than one. [69]

Each paper operated at the time of this study with one wire service (not the same one), and part of Willoughby's conclusion is based on the finding that both papers use their separate affiliation to a similar degree, with similar emphasis, and for similar purposes.

Kearl, controlling for competition and newspaper circulation, discovers affiliation patterns similar to those found above by the author.

Kearl's findings, based on aggregate data, reveal that in the small-newspaper field Willoughby's case-study situation may not have been representative.

> . . . competition appears to be a spur toward increased availability of non-local news sources. Communities where competition has declined usually also experience a decline in press service availability. Communities where competition has increased see a correspondent increase in press service resources. [70]

For the larger cities, Kearl's conclusion includes the author's notation of strong AP-UPI affiliation.

> . . . larger dailies with a local monopoly or some modification of full competition are likely to have <u>somewhat greater</u> access to press services. However, a reduction in local competition seldom increased the number of press services reaching the community. It usually left the number unchanges. . . . [71]

Large newspapers in monopoly situations appear to have the money, the opportunity, and the predisposition to construct a better news picture, and to that end, to receive more wire reports. Publisher John Cowles notes:

> With only a small number of exceptions the best newspapers in America are those which do not have a newspaper competing with them in their local field. By best I mean the most responsible editorially, the fairest, the most complete, the most accurate, the best written, and most objective.
> Publishers and editors have, I believe, a deeper feeling of responsibility because they are alone in their field. [72]

It might be noted in passing that newspapers in non-competitive situations usually have larger news holes (because monopoly positions raise advertising rates, lower necessary advertising lineage, and reduce coverage of lesser local news events), and the prospect of having to fill these holes

will tend toward multiple wire-service receipt. The same conditions occur

in newspapers with large circulations where advertising rates are deter-

mined by the size of the readership rather than by an absence of competing

printed advertising media and where local (i. e., neighborhood or suburban)

news is confined to only one of several daily editions.

The third group of affiliation changes seems prompted by considera-

tions not directly related to competition, mechanics, costs, etc. Here the

responses are preoccupied with quality of the report (the Red Wing Daily

Republican Eagle). This is a personal value judgment made after individual

consideration of such questions as what is news, how should it be handled,

what is the role of interpretation or features, is accuracy or speed more

important, etc. Although some attention may also be given to quantitative,

mechanical problems (as for example the Olean Times-Herald) these are not

the principal reasons--nor are they evaluated locally in relation to local

competition, shop mechanics, etc., as was the case with the Somerset

American, for example.

While the first two groups acted primarily in response to external

conditions and forces, this group responds to the more isolated considera-

tions of quality and individual evaluation and choice. Thus, in Red Wing

the daily paper pays more for a "better" wire, and in Olean the paper with-

out external pressures determines that one wire satisfied its needs "better"

than the other. The Roseburg News-Review responded not to external forces

but to the internal revision of values which accompanied a change of manage-

ment. The new owner was a chain connected to one of the major wires.

The Roseburg situation raises the question of whether chain ownership in general has an effect upon wire-service affiliation. Using a
compilation of newspaper chains by Raymond B. Nixon,[73] the author
tabulated each chain newspaper's wire affiliation. Table 26 presents
the five major affiliation configurations emerging from this tabulation.
The 133 chains controlled 635 daily newspapers in the United States, or
36.1 per cent of the total 1,760 dailies in 1963. (These papers represented 44.8 per cent of the total daily morning and evening circulation
in the nation and 53.2 per cent of the Sunday circulation.) The "Recapitulation" in Table 26 reveals that almost 50 per cent of the chains (and an
equal percentage of newspapers involved) tended to use AP, either as a
dominant or an only wire, while about one-third did the same for UPI.
The larger the chain, however (as noted in the right-hand column of Table
26) the more mixed were the affiliations or the more likely the possibility
that the combined AP-UPI affiliation dominated the member papers. Raw
data show that large chains used all patterns of affiliations, as the following
list indicates.

AP Alone:
Harte-Hanks Newspapers (Texas), 11 papers
Lindsay-Schaub Newspapers (Illinois), 5 papers

AP With some UPI:
Lee Newspapers (Ill., Iowa, Mo., Nebr., & Wis.), 10 papers
John P. Harris Newspapers (Kansas & Iowa), 9 papers

UPI Alone:
Tracy McCraken Newspapers (Wyoming), 6 papers
McNaughton Newspapers (Illinois, Arizona & California), 5 papers

AP-UPI:
Hearst Newspapers (national), 11 papers
Booth Newspapers (Michigan), 9 papers

MIXED CHAINS--
AP Dominates:
   Newhouse Newspapers (national), 19 papers

UPI Dominates:
   John P. Scripps Newspapers (California & Washington),
                      6 papers
   Southwestern Publishing Co. (western states), 13 papers
   Scripps League Newspapers (western states), 18 papers
   H.C. Ogden Newspapers (West Virginia & New York),
                      12 papers

AP-UPI Dominates:
   John H. Perry Newspapers (Florida), 15 papers
   Ridder Publications (national), 15 papers
   Palmer Newspapers (Arkansas & Texas), 10 papers.

The tendency is for the small two- or three-newspaper "chains" to maintain a monolithic wire affiliation while the larger chains (even those with close present or past wire-service ties, such as Hearst, Scripps-Howard, Scripps League, and John P. Scripps) have a more diversified affiliation range. Part of this may be due to the fact that the larger the chain, the more diversified are the types of local and regional situations the chain's newspaper must accommodate. Also, the larger the chain, the larger the individual newspapers tend to be, and in light of previous findings the large-newspaper group is more inclined to use both wires.

Discussion and Conclusions

    Trends in the wire service-subscriber relationship appear to point toward increased wire domination of legal and extra-legal modes of exchange and a somewhat more limited subscriber dominance in productivity, the latter based primarily on individual rather than group motivation and modified by the wire's past performances and extent of extra-legal activity.

Subscribers have been left, legally, with only the contractual privileges of receiving the news report. While this has always been the extent of subscriber privilege in UP, INS, and UPI, the trend away from legal subscriber power has been apparent in AP. Past power for AP members was derived from local boards, protest rights, and stockholding or bondholding and has gradually been whittled away by external events (e.g., the 1945 Supreme Court decision) and by changes in internal conditions (e.g., loss of the board's power, extra-legal pressure to mitigate protest rights, etc.). The AP organization, on the other hand, has succeeded in having the exclusive-use-of-news section of the by-laws upheld by the Supreme Court; its locus of power has moved farther back into the organization, away from the board and the membership; and it has maintained the contractual prerogatives of collecting assessments, requiring logotype attribution to AP, enforcing its by-laws, and imposing punishments and fines.

Extra-legal pressures issue almost exclusively from the wires, reaching by one vehicle or channel or another every important decision-making level within actual or potential subscribers' organizations. AP's structure offers many more opportunities for such pressures than does UPI's, but both employ effective promotional departments. These pressures actually occur in a gray area between the political relations (upon which they depend for channels) and the productive relations (which they seek to establish, maintain, or strengthen).

These productive channels are the actual physical wire-outlet connections which when seen as a whole measure the "market" to which the wire can daily move its product. Establishment of such channels, it has been noted, depends primarily upon the individual editor or publisher and the local conditions confronting him. Several categories of forces affect these local decisions: (1) mechanical-quantitative versus professional-qualitative emphasis; (2) contraction versus expansion of operation, vis-a-vis local and area conditions; (3) small versus large newspaper disposition and budgetary considerations; (4) true local competition versus non-competition; (5) chain versus home ownership; (6) small-chain versus large-chain operation; and (7) a multitude of individual beliefs, judgments, and experiences regarding coverage and news reports, wire organizations, newspaper's traditional affiliation, etc.

In order to satisfy as many of these local forces as possible, the wire must remain inoffensive and uncommitted to radical or rapid changes. In general, this stance permits both wires to retain about three-fourths of their subscribers and members from year to year, largely to the wires' on-going promotional (i.e., extra-legal) activities. The smaller group of outlets which change affiliations appears to be predisposed to such frequencies of change. Part of the changes, however, occurs because of the inevitable annual appearance of new papers and suspensions. AP's edge in number of affiliates stems principally from its earlier start, its widely-advertised principles of cooperation and non-commercialism, and its lesser propensity to change quickly and to act daily with haste. This allows it to continue serving about 50 per cent of the U.S. newspapers and to be considered the "basic" wire by a majority of newspapers and chains. No competitor has overshadowed AP numerically since 1897, but the 1958

merger of UP and INS creates a formidable opponent. And in light of

UPI's close second place, the most recent trend toward multiple-wire

affiliations reveals some reduction of AP's individual standing as year-

by-year tabulations of regional UPI growth have noted.

Although the individual publisher and editor has initial power over

establishing the channel, the wires see to it, through whatever legal and

extra-legal means they have, that that channel is maintained. In an over-

whelming number of cases they are successful.

The fundamental condition of any relationship involves trends

toward subordination and superordination of relational contributors. The

following hypothesis from Chapter I asserts subscriber subordination in

the relationship described in this chapter.

4. The wire services have increasingly dominated the political
and productive relations with subscribers in the primary
environment.

Controls over the Associated Press originally existed for the sub-

scriber through local boards and the protest right, stocks and bondholding,

and representation on the board of directors. Local boards were replaced

by protest rights in 1900 and both were repelled (except as a legal threat

to AP) through continuous AP board and organizational pressure. The pro-

test right as a potential legal threat was abolished by the Supreme Court

in 1945. Representation on the board includes the additional votes a mem-

ber can cast by virtue of bondholding. (Sole control given to stockholders

was abolished in 1900, and this represents another loss of subscriber control over the wire, at least from the stockholders' viewpoint.) The board's loss of power to the general manager, and later to the administrative staff and through fragmentation (i.e., wider representation and limitation of tenure), has eliminated bondholding, voting, and board representation as effective controls over the organization.

Control by AP over subscribers includes effective pressure against protest rights (noted above), effective replacement of board power by general manager and administrative power, requirement of all local news exclusively (upheld by the Supreme Court), and use of the antagonism ruling (replaced in 1900 by prohibition of membership traffic with competing wires, which in turn was abolished by the attorney general in 1915). In effect, AP has overthrown initial newspaper control (which began actually in 1848) and dominates through internal control of policy and operations, requirement of local news exclusively, and through many more controlling and prohibitive provisions of news report contracts than exist for the subscribers (whose only contractual power is receipt of the news report). None of the original controls exercised by AP members were ever extended to the so-called commercial wire services, which have dominated from the start.

Extra-legal control is almost solely in the hands of the wires. Legal channels are used for promotion of the wire and both wires, in their own right, give service which is reasonable and have reputations which are generally recognized as good. Traveling agents, annual meetings, and weekly and annual publications reach all policy-making strata of the local subscribers, and reinforce existing affiliations or seek out new ones. The productive relationship which follows largely from the wire-controlled

extra-legal relationship is theoretically in the hands of the subscriber,

for he can initiate or cancel service when he wishes, and for essentially

individual or local reasons. But the wires remain uncommitted--all

things to all people--and thereby maintain about 70 per cent of their sub-

scribers over long periods of time. Wire control is also apparent in the

fact that each wire's reputation has been maintained sufficiently to cause

combination affiliations to rise in recent years. Part of this rise, how-

ever, must be attributed to outlets' declining competition and renewed

stability. Although the individual outlet has constant control over the

nature of its affiliations, the wires have experienced increasing client

totals and a high degree of clientele stability over time.

Footnotes

[1]Emery, op. cit., p. 345.

[2]Ibid., pp. 513-514.

[3]Ibid., pp. 670-671.

[4]Unesco, op. cit. (1964), compiled from national totals on pp. 69-369.

[5]Raymond B. Nixon and Jean Ward, "Trends in Newspaper Ownership and Inter-Media Competition," Journalism Quarterly, XXXVIII (Winter, 1961), pp. 3-14.

[6]Ibid., p. 4.

[7]Ibid., p. 7.

[8]Morris L. Ernst, The First Freedom (New York: The Macmillan Company, 1946), p. 68.

[9]Nixon and Ward, op. cit., p. 9.

[10]Ibid.

[11]Ibid., pp. 11-12.

[12]Ibid., p. 12.

[13]Sources for Figure 8 are Associated Press by-laws as they appear in various numbers of the Associated Press (Ill. & N.Y.) Annual Volumes; Rosewater, op. cit.; and Swindler, op. cit. The idea for Figure 8 comes from a chart in Swindler's article (p. 51), although the material presented in Figure 8 is in a different arrangement, with some additional entries and all updated material.

[14]Illinois AP, Volume, IV (1897), p. 4.

[15]Ibid., V (1898), p. 4.

[16]Ibid., VI (1899), p. 3.

[17]Ibid., II (1895), p. 6.

[18]Ibid., V (1898), pp. 180-181.

[19]Ibid., p. 360; VI (1899), p. 155; and VII (1900), p. 165.

[20]It will be remembered from Chapter III that the Laffan Agency was founded in 1888 by the Sun to supplement the paper's UP news report. The agency competed, to a limited extent, with AP until 1916 when Frank Munsey purchased the Sun, disbanded the agency, and combined the newspaper with the New York Press, an AP member. Mott, op. cit., p. 591.

[21]Swindler, op. cit., pp. 50, 52.

[22]U.S. v. A.P., et al., op. cit., sec. 116.

[23]New York AP, Volume, XVII (1917), p. 3.

[24]Ibid., XXIII (1923), p. 8.

[25]Rosewater, op. cit., pp. 303, 310.

[26]Hearst applied for AP memberships for his Chicago American and New York Evening Journal to the Illinois corporation in September, 1900. The application died on the table at AP's first New York annual meeting, and Hearst pressed for admission, seeking a writ of mandamus in the Illinois courts. The litigation dragged on until July 9, 1907, when the Circuit Court of Cook County sustained AP's motion for demurrer. Hearst's INS was founded two years later. Illinois AP, Volume, VIII (1901), p. 223, and New York AP, Volume, VIII (1908), p. 3.

[27]Cooper, op. cit. (1959), p. 197.

[28](Hearst interests), Shall The Individual Rights of Associated Press Franchise Holders Be Upheld? (New York: The Davidson Press, Inc., June, 1924), p. 19.

[29]Ibid., pp. 73, 78.

[30]Ibid., p. 3.

[31]Rosewater, op. cit., p. 309.

[32]Ibid., pp. 310-311.

[33]Cooper, op. cit. (1959), p. 191.

[34]U.S. v. A.P., et al., op. cit., secs. 122-123.

[35]New York AP, Volume, XLIII (1943), p. 41.

[36]United States v. Associated Press, et al., "Complaint," (New York: Southern Federal District Court, 1942), sec. 77.

[37]Ibid., passim.

[38]Ibid., secs. 52-54.

[39]United States v. Associated Press, et al., "Answer" (New York: Southern Federal District Court, 1942), passim.

[40]"Tribune and Col. McCormick Answer U. S. Charge in AP Suit," Editor & Publisher: The Fourth Estate, LXXV (November 21, 1942), p. AP10.

[41]The Associated Press, Member Editorials on the Monopoly Complaint (New York: The Associated Press, 1942), Illinois section.

[42]New York AP, Volume, XLIV (1944), p. 27.

[43]United States v. Associated Press, et al., 52 F. Supp. 362, 372 (1943).

[44]Ibid., 370-371.

[45]Ibid., 375-377.

[46]New York AP, Volume, XLV (1945), p. 4.

[47]The majority opinion was handed down by Justices Hugo L. Black, Stanley F. Reed, and Wiley B. Rutledge. Separate concurring opinions were written by Justices William O. Douglas and Felix Frankfurter. (All five were Roosevelt appointees.) Justice Owen J. Roberts wrote the dissenting opinion with Chief Justice Harlan F. Stone concurring. Justice Frank Murphy wrote a separate dissent. Justice Robert H. Jackson took no part in the decision because of his recent affiliation with the case through the Department of Justice.

[48]For the original pronouncement of this theory, see The Commission on Freedom of the Press, A Free and Responsible Press (Chicago: University of Chicago Press, 1947), and William E. Hocking, Freedom of the Press: A Framework of Principle (Chicago: University of Chicago Press, 1947). For a descriptive comparison between this and other press theories, see again Siebert, et al., op. cit., esp. pp. 73-103 and Jensen, op. cit. (1957), esp. pp. 292-320.

[49]Associated Press et al. v. United States, 326 U. S. 1; 65 S. Ct. 1416, 1420 (1945).

[50]Ibid., 1426-1427.

[51]Ibid., 1427-1429.

[52]Ibid., 1429-1443.

[53]Ibid., 1436.

[54]Ibid., 1438-1443.

[55]Illinois Congressman Noah M. Mason introduced H.R. 6301 ("a bill to amend antitrust laws relative to exempting mutual news gathering agencies") on May 3, 1946, according to the U.S. Congressional Record, 79th Cong., 2nd Sess., CXII (April 26 - May 22, 1946), p. 4455. The bill was referred to the House Judiciary Committee where hearings were conducted on May 23 and June 6, 1946. For a transcript of the testimony, see U.S. House of Representatives, Subcommittee II of the Committee on the Judiciary (79th Cong., 2nd Sess.), Hearings on a Bill to Amend Antitrust Laws Relative to Exempting Mutual News Gathering Agencies (Washington: Government Printing Office, 1946). The bill died in committee.

[56]Personal letter to the author. (Emphasis added.)

[57]Personal letter to the author.

[58]These totals are gained from national totals of various affiliation combinations given in Table 19 (Appendix B). It will be noted that these totals do not match those claimed by AP in Table 14 (Appendix B). In fact, discrepancies are marked, as the following recapitulation includes:

Year	AP Total	E&P Total	U.S. Court*
1935	1,359	1,179	---
1942	1,262	1,261	1,247
1949	1,723	1,223	---
1958	1,763	1,217	---
1962	1,729	1,178	---
1963	1,750	1,164	---

* U.S. v. A.P., et al., "Findings of Fact, etc." op. cit.

In fairness to AP, the author points out that AP totals are U.S. outlets minus broadcast outlets. Thus, these totals include many outlets other than newspapers. The difference of fourteen between the E&P totals and the court's findings may be caused by the fact that in several places newspapers with the same name publish both morning and evening editions, and thus are counted twice in E&P totals. AP memberships after 1937, however, were registered in the newspaper's name, and therefore such two-edition papers were probably counted only once by the court as it studied AP's records.

[59]Cooper, op. cit. (1959), p. 205.

[60]Interview by the author, December 27, 1963, in the executive offices of the Associated Press, New York City.

[61]New York AP, Volume, XIX (1919), p. 7.

[62]Ibid., XXI (1921), p. 4.

[63]In Figures 9, 10, 11, and 12, the author portrays the relative strength of the two leading American wire services (AP and UP or UPI) for the years or periods indicated. To determine "relative strength," the following method was used. Each wire's total affiliates in each state were rendered as a percentage of the state's total newspapers. The smaller percentage was subtracted from the larger, and the remainder was called the "relative strength" of the dominant wire, vis-a-vis the other, in that state. (Because several newspapers in one state may receive both wires, the sum of the wires' percentages may exceed 100 per cent. This adds to, rather than detracts from, the relative nature of the presentations.)

[64]In Figures 10, 11, 12 where trends are depicted, the above method was employed for the years opening and concluding the periods indicated. Trends were then determined by subtracting the smaller from the larger year and noting whether the trend was a rise or decline over the period. If a state went from 25 per cent AP to 15 per cent UP, the symbols would show a UP rise of 40 per cent.

[65]Champaign-Urbana News-Gazette, March 31, 1951, Supplement, p. 1, col. 8.

[66]Personal letter to the author.

[67]Personal letter to the author.

[68]Personal letter to the author.

[69]Wesley F. Willoughby, "Are Two Competing Dailies Necessarily Better than One?" Journalism Quarterly, XXXI (Spring, 1955), p. 204.

[70]Bryant Kearl, "Effects of Newspaper Competition on Press Service Resources," Journalism Quarterly, XXXV (Winter, 1958), p. 64.

[71]Ibid.

[72]John Cowles, "Fewer Papers Mean Better Papers," Nieman Reports, V (July, 1951), p. 3.

[73]Raymond B. Nixon, "Groups of Daily Newspapers Under Common Ownership," Editor & Publisher: The Fourth Estate, International Year Book, XLIII (1963), pp. 310-312.

CHAPTER VII

WIRE-SERVICE RELATIONS WITH NEWS SOURCES

> Things have changed since I was
> last in Washington. Now, suddenly,
> all the diplomats talk like news-
> paper men and all the newspaper
> men talk like diplomats.
> -- A. F. Dobrynin (1962)

This chapter continues the discussion of relations between wire
services and their primary environment begun in Chapter VI by considering
the dynamics of wire service-news source interaction. Again the relationship is divided into political and productive spheres, although the distinction
is a difficult one to make in this case and is compounded by the fact that
productive interaction brings this study dangerously close to a discussion
of the product emerging from such interaction.

There are three principal problems involved in investigating this
relationship within the purview of this study. First, data are difficult to
gather regarding both momentary conditions and long-term trends of the
relationship s contributors. The scope of an international wire service requires data representing a wide diversity and distribution of individual reporters and sources. Moreover, the fact that these are individuals and not
corporations raises substantive as well as procedural problems of data
collection not easily solved. Besides these difficulties, the number, distribution, and actual individuals on both sides are constantly changing
requiring a sequence of samples to measure trends--an undertaking too
far-reaching for this study.

289

Second, several aspects of the interaction between reporters and news sources proceed on levels of symbolic and relational abstraction which are impossible to quantify. Although quantification alone should not define the boundaries of description, it should be a jumping-off point. Third, existing speculative, historical, and anecdotal literature (the bulk of scholarly endeavor in this area) is outdated, sketchy, or concerned with the press as a whole. With the exception of Chapters II and III these discussions have at least begun with an empirical base. Even if this paper relied entirely upon library materials, the literature in this area would not be a definitive source.

Reporter and News Source Trends

As noted above, previous studies of the components of this relationship have encountered one of several pitfalls, due primarily to the nature of the subject matter. Of the four outstanding studies of correspondents,[1] only those by Theodore Kruglak and Leo C. Rosten distinguish between wire-service personnel and the press corps in general. Rosten, however, makes only brief passing references to wire correspondents in a book which is now considered out of date. Although Kruglak limits his investigation to correspondents in Western Europe, his study is more contemporary and more thorough. It is probably an asset to have Kruglak's information available as opposed to something on domestic correspondents. The latter are not dissimilar from most news reporters in training, background, income, etc., because of the influence of the American Newspaper Guild, an influence not felt by some wire reporters abroad. Kruglak's responses

include 104 (or 61.5 per cent) of the 169 full-time Americans and

foreigners working for AP, UP, and INS in Western Europe in 1955. This

total wire-service corps is 59.1 per cent of the total full-time press corps

representing U.S. media in that area.[2]

Kruglak describes wire-service correspondents in Western Europe

as follows: they are either from the Midwest (52 per cent) or the East (33

per cent); about half of them are married; they have the highest percentage

of non-journalistic backgrounds (13 per cent); almost 26 per cent of them

have less than five years of journalistic experience; 60 per cent are on their

first foreign assignment and almost 39 per cent have been on their present

assignment less than one year; one-fourth of them can speak a foreign lan-

guage well; more than half are under the age of 36; 42 per cent makes less

than $6,000, and only 28 per cent makes more than $8,000.[3]

Kruglak is critical of the wire-service correspondents' lack of

general journalistic background.

> . . . there are more correspondents without a well-rounded
> background in the news agency ranks than in the other media.
> * * * The picture of the inexperienced American news agency
> correspondents which emerges is that of a reporter who has
> had less than five years experience in journalism, has been
> in Europe or in his present post for less than a year, has little
> knowledge of the language of the country in which he works,
> and is underpaid by American standards.[4]

Kruglak follows up his critical evaluation of the wires' foreign staff with

four suggestions for improvement.

> . . . the news agencies have a high turnover of European
> personnel, due primarily to their policies of paying wages
> below those prevalent in the other media. The news agencies

can revise their hiring and employment practices in accordance with the following principles:

1. The hiring of inexperienced personnel should not be eliminated entirely . . . but there should be a better balance between the inexperienced and experienced correspondents.

2. Salaries cannot be based on local considerations alone. There should be graduated scales in keeping with experience and ability. A news agency correspondent embarking on his second tour of duty in Europe should receive greater financial incentive to remain in Europe and with the agency.

3. The non-American correspondents should not be treated as second-class citizens, especially in pay and privileges. At the same time, the non-American correspondents should be given greater opportunity to obtain an American background.

4. The news agency Elite should be given greater inducements, financial and otherwise, to remain in the news agency field and in Europe. [5]

The foreign press corps in general (and particularly outside of wire services) is well-paid and professional with a high socio-cultural standing both in society and within the occupation, according to Kruglak. Yu and Luter give this profile of the foreign correspondent in general.

. . . a correspondent is likely to be: A man in his late thirties or early forties. A native of a city of the Midwest or Middle Atlantic region. A college graduate. (Only 5 per cent of the group received no college training. Fifty-seven per cent hold at least one college degree; a third of these have two degrees or more.) Experienced in journalism (17 years, ten as a foreign correspondent). A Democrat or independent. In the upper echelon of salaries in journalism. (the median falls in the $12-$15,000 range). [6]

Although ten years can change correspondents' conditions somewhat, the marked differences between these two descriptions require some consideration. It should be noted that Kruglak included non-American correspondents for U.S. media; Yu and Luter did not. This, in itself, will account for some of the difference. There seems, however, to be good reason to generalize that wire-service personnel abroad are of lesser caliber than their colleagues. As will be seen, the physical and productive size of the wires creates very large staffs abroad, and this demand causes the wires to lower their standards in order to man their foreign posts.

The bulk of the news handled by all media (and wires in particular) concerns political and governmental events. The press-government relationship has traditionally been the focal point for practical and philosophical considerations of press freedom or constraint, of public opinion, and of democratic institutions. Government and politics, therefore, constitute the single most important primary field component in the wire service-news source relationship discussed here.

Recent trends in government, unlike those of correspondents at home or abroad, are well documented and widely known. For purposes of this study, these trends can best be presented by relying upon the observations of past and present journalists close to the scene. Although government and politics are never stagnant institutions in the American experience, their twentieth-century changes have been sporatic, presenting overt evidence of trends only under crisis stresses. Most journalists, whether because of personal concurrence or dissent, note the advent of the New Deal as the start of a governmental and political revolution in the United States which is unmatched in this century. It continues in extended form today at all levels of government. Perhaps the most insightful investigation of the journalists's government has been done by Douglass Cater, who describes the New Deal changes and their influences on journalists.

The Great Depression and the accompanying New Deal
ushered in a new era of Washington journalism. It created
news in quantity and complexity that threatened for a time
to overwhelm the poor correspondent. The first Hundred Days
of the Roosevelt Administration caused him severe growing
pains. Such strange new subjects as banking and monetary
policy, labor relations, and the rest suddenly had to be added
to his vocabulary and, hopefully, his understanding.
The New Deal years produced qualitative as well as
quantitative change in Washington reporting. News production
became a bigger business than ever, geared to year-round
output. Gone were the days when the reporter left Washington
with the adjournment of Congress. Reporting grew compart-
mentalized, the reporter became something of a specialist,
often as expert as the official. . . . News was too fast breaking, too diverse, too complicated to permit the former loose
arrangements. The press forsook its old carefree ways just
as government did. [7]

The government was entering into new and more diversified areas of

policy-making and debate; the so-called alphabet agencies or bureaucratic

appendages growing out of executive and legislative necessity or expediency

multiplied rapidly to serve an ever-widening range of public needs and de-

sires. The accompanying power shifts (in this case in Washington) were

away from open debate and locally-based considerations of principle and

representation and toward the private conference and obscurely-based con-

siderations of finance and pragmatic national interest. Max Lerner depicts

the power shift.

There has been a shift from Congressional to Presidential and administrative power, a shift from formal
policy-making to budget-making power which often has
carried policy-making with it, a shift from local and state
power to Federal power. Similarly there has been a shift
of power from the churches, the universities, and the lawyers
to the Big Press and the opinion industries, from the farmers
and small-industry groups to the big corporate industries,
from the owners to the managers of industry, from civilians
to the military. [8]

And while the general emphasis on federal direction and control increased, the same intra-governmental shifts appeared in the state and local levels with the rise of administrative branches in each state capital, broader state controls and services emulating federal programs, and the growing role of managerial and professional expertise.

Although Washington is not the total governmental beat for the wires, it is a model of most American governmental institutions today and suffers as such only from its unique size and occasional extremes. Found in this model is the trend toward the impersonality of a policy-making machine programmed by an unseen, unheard professional operating within the closed bureaucratic sanctuaries. Budgeted good will, public opinion, and imagery circumvent the budget-controlled "authoritative allocation of values" which affects not only the citizenry in this country, but much of the world's population. Less and less of significance is exposed to public scrutiny by government officials. Cater, in another work, lists three principal characteristics of Washington politics.

> The first is that the public dialogue is usually more ferocious than the private one. The politicians feel compelled to stage a blood-and-guts spectacle even when, behind the scenes, they are prepared to arrive amicably at arrangements.
> A second condition . . . is that the important battles in Washington are seldom merely clashes of personality; they are clashes in which policy and personality have become inextricably mixed.
> (Third) when one considers the extraordinary interests and ambitions that congregate in Washington, it is remarkable how rare and how relatively petty have been the instances of genuine corruption. * * * White House politics has been played on a higher level than courthouse politics, even when the occupant of the White House was formerly a courthouse politician. [9]

The impact of these characteristics is felt first by the press and then through the press by the public, which, according to Cater, still relies upon "fictional myths" for understanding Washington occurrences. The press has not countermanded these myths.

The meager empirical base for this section is found in Tables 27-30 (see Appendix B). Growth of the AP and UP-UPI domestic and foreign news-gathering structures is sketched in Table 27 in terms of the number of domestic and foreign bureaus. It will be remembered from previous chapters that AP's original structure called for cooperative news gathering by member newspapers to save AP the added expense of a large staff. It was enough, AP thought, to staff bureaus in a few key centers in the United States and abroad. Almost immediately AP was aware that its network of newspaper-stringers was not sufficient. The newspapers had their own problems or competition to combat, their news judgment was not always in tune with national news perspectives, local news-gathering abilities and facilities were not always up to reporting a major event for a national wire, and sometimes the newspaper assigned the least adept local reporter to maintain the paper's AP link. It is noted in Chapter V in connection with internal productive relations how AP's changeover to a full-time national staff of reporters brought economic stress to the organization but in the long run created a more stable news-gathering situation. Table 27 shows that between 1894 and 1927 AP's total bureaus nearly quadrupled, due only in part to the impetus of World War I (bureaus fell short of being doubled between 1912 and 1920). Growth was as large in the foreign field as in the

United States, although AP continued to rely primarily upon Reuters, Havas, and Wolff for its international report.

It is interesting to note that UP's total bureaus only doubled between 1909 and 1933, even though UP did not rely on member-stringers and a world news exchange cartel. If, however, a comparable period (twenty-four years) is computed for AP, the bureau growth is about the same as UP's--about double. The news-gathering structures of both services, therefore, expanded at about the same rate, apparently responding simi-larly to the increased needs of subscribers for news, to new definitions of news, and to new types of news-generating situations (e.g., World War I). The difference between the wires, however, shows up in the fact that in 1928 about 65 per cent of UP's bureaus were domestic while about 81 per cent of AP's were domestic. With the help of the world new agency cartel, AP was able to concentrate on domestic news gathering. But even today the distinction exists between the wires, although to a lesser extent: AP's domestic bureaus in 1962 were about 66 per cent of the total while UPI's were about 58 per cent. (It is noted below that UPI's foreign staff is numerically larger than AP's.) As a final note, UP-UPI reports a 200 per cent increase in its total bureaus between 1933 and 1963, while AP shows an increase of only about 53 per cent. There will be more to say about the UP-UPI figures shortly.

Tables 28, 29, and 30 show the 1963 distribution of foreign corres-pondents among employers and bureau locations, and with respect to Americans versus foreign nationals, respectively. The tables are based on John Wilhelm's "census" of foreign correspondents for U.S. news media,[10]

but are original here because their emphasis and organization differ from

Wilhelm's essentially raw data. Reliability in such a census is always diffi-

cult to achieve, owing to momentary conditions of world news events,

presence of correspondents on special, short-term assignments abroad,

employers stretching employee totals, etc. Wilhelm uses as his basic

total, "the number of American foreign correspondents working for America

media."[11] This included 515 Americans and 718 foreign national for a total

of 1,233 full- or part-time correspondents in 1963. Yu and Luter call

Wilhelm's definition liberal and assert that "his respondents include a num-

ber of correspondent who are not working for news media."[12] They guess

that there are between 350 and 450 full-time American foreign correspondents.

All criteria for such a study are personal in the long run and are useful only

so far as they relate to the data gathered under their purview. In this case

the field of foreign correspondents within which AP and UPI staffers will be

viewed appears to be an extremely broad one, based on choices which permit

almost any American medium affiliate to be counted. Yu and Luter are proper

to call Wilhelm on his liberal definition of American correspondents, yet

their own survey is unrealistic for failing to account for the foreign nationals

whose copy often dominate the wire-service reports on specific foreign news

events.

It is doubtful that Wilhelm's "liberal" definition of correspondents

affects AP and UPI as much as it does many pseudo-news units listed in

Table 28. Thus the wires' total of 577 correspondents or 47 per cent of a

"liberal" total would probably be more imposing if that total were more conservative. In addition, by employing nearly half of the foreign press corps, the wires (along with only a few other employers) contribute greatly to the concentration of foreign news coverage for the U.S. public in a few organizations. The top five organizations include about two-thirds of the total foreign correspondents; the top eight account for about three-fourths of the reporters; and the top ten employers have a total combined staff of 1,001 or about 82 per cent of the census total. These top ten include both wire services, four magazine organizations, two newspaper services, and two radio-television networks. Together they probably are the principal sources of news for most Americans. The wires dominate this ten-employer field with 57 per cent of the total correspondents.

Table 29 lists the eighty bureau sites used by Wilhelm to locate the 1,233 correspondents. Immediately it is apparent that AP and UPI have most of these sites covered to some extent. The wire-to-total percentages shown in the table distribute themselves along a normal curve with the 40-to-60 per cent range receiving about one-third of the bureaus, and most of these being the important news-gathering or news-relaying points (e.g., London, Tokyo, Buenos Aires, West Berlin, Moscow, etc.). Table 29 suggests that the wires' strategy in foreign news coverage calls for broad and thin staff distribution with heavy concentrations   in key, widely scattered centers.

The vast dimensions of world news coverage grow more complicated as important conflicts and diplomatic maneuvers occur increasingly in the developing nations while a constant vigil must be maintained in the old, established capitals. Transmission facilities and traditional wire-service bureau arrangements dictate continued location of large staff concentrations in the older capitals, but budgets do not permit duplication of these staffs in the remote but potentially newsworthy capitals of emerging Asia, Africa, and South America. In calm times these regions are covered primarily by foreign nationals or beginning Americans whose principal job is to file initial stories of flare-ups in diplomatic or military affairs. Subscribers and other news media assume this to be a primary function of the wires. Then all media, including the wires, move in their more experienced reporters from the nearest well-staffed bureau or relay point to take over the major news covering job. Subscribers expect this also of their wire service, as do those other media outlets not critically interested or strategically capable of sending their own reporters.

These demands of subscribers, including other media outlets and the increasing complexity of foreign coverage are constantly weighed against the costs of and funds available for such operations. The postwar decline in significant foreign news coupled with a general negative U.S. reaction to foreign affairs prompted the wires to reduce their foreign staffs and adjust budgets to accommodate other types of activity. Max Grossman noted in 1947 that AP had gone from 150 European correspondents on VE-Day to forty-two in August of 1946. UP at the peak of the war had 120 front-line reporters, but in 1947 its European staff numbered sixty-five. [13] Grossman

points out the budgetary and additudinal factors involved.

> . . . the major problem confronting foreign correspondents
> is domestic in origin. I mean by that that the lack of play
> being given foreign news by most of our newspapers at home
> has had a corollary in the decrease in the number of foreign
> correspondents in Europe and other overseas news centers.
> Bureau chiefs overseas told me bluntly that they were
> being obliged to lay off correspondents because of budget re-
> ductions and also because newspapers back home are not
> printing adequate amounts of foreign news. [14]

Kruglak's observation that the wire services use inexperienced and inex-

pensive staff personnel provides the clue to how wires have kept costs down

while expanding foreign news staffs to meet the increasingly difficult task of

world news coverage in recent years. Discussion of Table 30 (below) also

makes this clear.

One curious finding in Table 29 is that AP reporters are in seventy-

four bureau locations (as compared with fifty-seven foreign AP bureaus ac-

cording to Table 27) and UPI reporters man in seventy-three bureaus (as

compared with UPI's claim to 110 foreign bureaus). No definitive explana-

tion exists for these reverse discrepancies. It might be suggested, however,

that Wilhelm counted full- and part-time correspondents' locations as

bureaus, while AP counted only full-time staffs as bureaus, and UPI has

pushed the limit of its criteria to amass a large total. Wilhelm notes that

the Journalism Quarterly editor had asked him for organizational totals in

his summation but that he discounts their validity.

> I had shrunk from giving the organization total because
> the well-known "numbers game" between major competing
> wire services had become somewhat meaningless. The UPI
> recently claimed 247 staff correspondents in Latin America

> alone. The AP now refuses to give such figures at all, as
> they are torn between straining categories or showing up
> with a lesser figure. [15]

The question of the data's reliability must remain unresolved for lack of

wire-service cooperation.

Table 30 shows that AP and UPI maintain their large staff distri-

butions by employing many foreign nationals who ordinarily do not expect

as large a salary as do Americans. In terms of the number of Americans

serving on foreign staffs, AP and UPI are in a minority among news media.

While a rough correlation is prevalent in raw data between the staff size

and the percentage of foreign nationals (the smaller the staff, the fewer the

foreigners, particularly at the low end of the spectrum), several of the

large organizations (not AP and UPI) are dominated by Americans (see for

example the percentages of Americans for U.S. News and World Report,

the American Broadcasting Company, the New York Herald-Tribune, the

New York Times, the Chicago Tribune, Time, and Christian Science

Monitor, Newsweek, and National Broadcasting Company).

An important question is raised here as to whether foreign nationals

should report news for American companies and audiences. Americans

abroad probably have somewhat less understanding of the social, cultural,

and political events and general background they encounter unless their

assignments are extended ones (and even this is no guarantee). Foreign

nationals, on the other hand, can apply personal socio-cultural background

and insights to the events they report if they are assigned to either their own

country or the region including their native land. Such assignments to

native countries are avoided by the wires to reduce reporters' personal
involvement in or alienation from affairs of state. Language barriers in
many smaller countries, however, can be overcome only with assignments such as these. In any event, the foreign national is less equipped
to report the news to an American audience because of the same socio-
cultural differences which impede American understanding of foreign
politics. Often American rewrite men will adjust the foreigner's copy to
fit American consumption and thereby obliterate cultural nuances which
would have added realism and depth to the account and might have been
educational if not informative to American audiences. In the final analysis, the question of Americans versus foreign nationals has no answer
given the present structure of wires and their labor force. This remains
as one of the most vital and crucial areas of inquiry requiring immediate
attention, particularly as it affects international communications and the
framing of global human goals and needs.

Another debate centers on the impact on the wires' news reports of
news-exchange agreements between AP or UPI and other world or national
wire services. It will be recalled that AP was a member of the four-party
world cartel from 1887 to 1934, exchanging news and dividing the world for
distribution with Reuters, Havas, and Wolff. Two features of AP's world
news-gathering operation must, however, be noted: (1) before 1934 AP
did not rely solely upon the incoming reports of these three European news
agencies for all of its world news (as the tabulation of AP foreign bureaus
notes in Table 27), and (2) after 1934, AP continued to rely on foreign news

services as some of its news sources. Both periods surrounding 1934 have been discussed in Chapter V in connection with the mounting costs of foreign coverage and the mounting desires of AP to move into territory outside cartel jurisdiction. UP's go-it-alone policy has constantly kept it away from contracts with Reuters, Havas, and Wolff, but it too has signed news exchange agreements with foreign national services.

Agreements between AP or UP-UPI and foreign national agencies include one-way or reciprocal exchange of all or part of the parties' reports, sometimes without consideration. In 1953 Unesco counted 139 news agencies as existing at one time or another between 1835 (the first appearance of Havas) and 1953. Forty-five had suspended operation while ninety-four were still delivering a news report. Of those still operating, six were world-wide agencies, seventy-six were national services, and twelve were "specialized" services (e. g. , the Associated Negro Press and Katholische Internationale Presseagentur). [16] In that year AP had news exchange contracts with ten agencies (in addition to agreements with Reuters and Agence France-Presse); UP had contracts with fifteen; and INS had them with two. [17]

In 1964, Unesco found 183 existing world, national and specialized news agencies, [18] of which AP had news exchange contracts with twenty-four. [19] (Comparable data were not available for UPI in this Unesco source.) AP contracted with 12. 8 per cent of the total news agencies in 1953 and 13. 1 per cent in 1964. These percentages are small, but consideration of only contractual arrangements is deceiving. Most full- or part-time foreign correspondents for both AP and UPI rely heavily on the national or world news agencies operating in their assigned region. Whether they read those agencies' wires directly or get them indirectly through the local press outlets, these agencies provide the correspondent with news tips, background material, and sometimes complete stories.

The theory that once a news item is printed or transmitted in one locale makes it public knowledge everywhere is strictly observed by all national and international news organizations. The fact that many of these foreign national wires are either subsidized by their governments or are actual governmental departments not only does not seem to bother the American wires and correspondents but often is thought to be an asset as the only direct informational "pipeline" into otherwise inaccessible governmental offices. In some cases the possibility of propaganda must be accepted as a fact of life if any news is to be gathered and disseminated. In the following sections the impact of various governmental impingements on the press will be noted as affecting the news report. These too are "facts of life" for the wires and must be tolerated if a report is to be produced daily. As long as one wire adheres to the theory outlined above, others will have to follow suit or face the dreaded fate of being beaten on a bulletin.

Political Interaction and Trends

The interaction between government and the press proceeds on at least two levels: the legalistic, formalistic level and the extra-legal, politico-economic level.[20] Each level relies on the other in part for its shape and substance, and each, in turn, influences the other by its on-going patterns of interaction and change.

The legalistic level of press-government interaction may itself be subdivided into areas in which one component may initially have a primary interest but which ultimately draw both contributors into interaction. Some of these areas are: access to public records, public officials, the public attention, and the public news columns; decision-making as regards public policy or corporate policy; freedom of speech, of fair comment and criticism, and of individual action; public interest, public order, public opinion, and public morality; invasion of privacy; libel or slander; private property rights; and so on. Since AP and UPI gather news throughout the world, no specific governmental-journalistic situation is any more characteristic of the wires than any other. Any number of formulas for governmental control and press freedom can be found, and the major American wire services must operate within most of them. Some make the press part of government financially and/or structurally, others maintain an absolute separation of press and government; some private press systems are closely restricted by the government, other governmental press units have some freedom to criticize officials. The legalistic conditions which frame the relationship in a given country may be found in constitutional provisions; statutory laws; special legislation; executive or monarchic orders; court interpretations; common law precedents; socio-cultural history; or the daily whims of small and large officials.

The relationship, however, does have some rather definite universal implications both for governments and the wires. A legal balance must ultimately be found between the needs and requirements of both contributors, particularly recently as wires have tended to be more international in their operations and officials have tended increasingly to recognize the propa-

ganda, diplomatic, or image-building potential of international communi-

cation. The relationship must embrace each component's peculiar type

of relational needs and contributions: for the press, a desire to know and

to ask and a need to be correct, and for the government, a need to tell

and to maintain civil order and a desire to control. Each formula, regard-

less of how "authoritarian," "libertarian," or "socially responsible" it is,

will finally (and usually to some extent legalistically, or at least formal-

istically) settle pragmatically upon a compromise which serves both parties

to some extent (although neither party completely) and reflects the socio-

cultural backgrounds from which each has arisen. (Reflection upon the

diversity of socio-cultural backgrounds prevalent between American wires

and foreign governments will reveal how trying this process of compromise

can sometimes be and how often it is inconvenient or downright intolerable

from one of the parties' socio-cultural perspective.)

The legal status of AP and UPI, therefore, is different in every

country in which they gather news, and the news reports they distribute

show the signs of favoritism for news coming from easily accessible govern-

ments and a quiet acquiescence for the handouts and constraints of less

accessible or more belligerent establishments. The multitude of formal

statuses makes AP and UPI everything from critical observers (in an

"objective interpretational" sense) to governmental mouthpieces (by

"cooperative" necessity). This must automatically be the case since wire-

service competition and the demands of subscribers require a "complete" news report each day and since news is as likely to occur in totalitarian

states as in free societies.

But some of the suppressive measures or cooperative propagandiz-

ing occurs in its subtlest and most influential forms at the extra-legal,

politico-economic level. Although more numerous in other countries, such

practices do not escape usage or attempts at usage in the United States.

In 1917, AP General Manager Melville E. Stone was approached informally

by the U.S. Department of State. Stone reported the incident to the AP

board of directors as follows.

> I may say that I was asked to go to Washington some
> time ago. The United States was very anxious to soften the
> asperity toward us that was evident in South America, and
> the State Department asked me to employ the editors of al-
> most every leading paper in South America on handsome
> salaries as correspondents of The Associated Press, and I
> was told that we could pay them handsome amounts whether
> they sent us any news or not and that the government would
> recoup us for anything that we paid. I said:
> "Well, that means subsidy."
> "Well," they said, "The Associated Press would not be
> suspected of anything of the kind, because its reputation is
> such that it would not be."
> And I very promptly replied that its reputation would not
> be such if we undertook a thing of that kind.
> The government is moved by what they conceive to be a
> perfectly proper point of view -- that they want something
> more than a mere news report to go back and forth between
> these countries. They want some sort of illuminating
> service from the United States to indicate that this country
> is not money-grabbing or territory-grabbing. [21]

In addition to subsidies, a world or national wire service may encounter

bribes, trade union pressures, preferential arrangements for the use of

telegraphic and radio facilities, personal governmental favoritism, etc.

Indirectly, pressures upon newspaper and broadcast subscribers may affect

the wires. The above pressures operate on the outlets, as well as opportunities presented by newsprint allocations, incorporation procedures,
licensing practices, official advertising, and machinery quotas.

Because of the multiplicity of legal and extra-legal relations existing worldwide, the Americans wires must assume a multilateral posture
with respect to their news sources. The relationship may be odious for
wire correspondents, but they must make the best of it in order to get
what little news the relationship will yield. Other correspondents may accept the reasons for suppression (and perhaps even the purposes and
principles of the regime) and work positively within such suppression.

Eugene Lyons is perhaps the leading example of a wire-service
correspondent who accepted an adverse news situation and performed as
a publicist for the regime. Moscow bureau chief for United Press beginning
in 1928, Lyons recalls his early feelings toward Russian censorship.

> Except for the attendent physical annoyances, the censor-
> ship did not seem to me at all stringent. Most of my dis-
> patches passed muster so easily that I could only wonder why
> certain of my colleagues fussed and fumed at the restraint.
> The editorial changes suggested by Rthstein, Fodolsky, or
> another of the censors, were usually, I thought, reasonable
> and often positively helpful. Sometimes I felt they had saved
> me from cabling implied criticisms of the Soviet regime into
> which I had been betrayed by an extravagant adjective or a too
> literal reading of the news.
> No censorship anywhere seems harsh to a reporter who
> agrees enthusiastically with the viewpoint of the censors. . . .
> I collaborated with the Press Department in rewording a piece
> of news so as to take the sting out of it. . . . I wrote a num-
> ber of feature stories, in fact, on the mildness of the Soviet
> censorship as compared to the stringency of those in Italy and
> other countries. [22]

Born in Russia, though raised and educated in New York City, Lyons had worked for TASS before joining UP.[23] Lyons describes his early personal

approach to the Stalin government.

> It was through an emotional haze that I viewed the new
> Bolshevik world around me. My early dispatches out of
> Moscow were laudatory, though toned down to conceal
> my bias.[24]

But this was early in Lyons' Moscow tour of duty; by the early 1930's he

became disillusioned with the Stalinist policies and became a bitter opponent

of the regime. In November, 1930, Lyons was selected for a rare inter-

view with Stalin, but within a couple of years Lyons had been expelled for

an uncensored report of a Soviet-Japanese incident.[25] The previously dis-

cussed connections between several rightist Latin American countries and

news disseminators in the United States (including INS and UPI, to a lesser

degree) show the extent to which cooperative news relations can influence

the flow of supposedly "objective" news reports.[26] For Lyons, cooperation

was based on a philosophic commitment (or at least a cultural compatability),

while relations between INS and UPI and the Latin regimes were apparently

prompted by monetary considerations.

On the other hand, a news agency or an individual correspondent

may assume the role not of publicist, but of antagonist to the local regime.

UPI vice-president Earl J. Johnson recently charged TASS with being a

government publicity agency.

> Tass wears the outer garments of a regular news service
> but operates in the main as a department of the Soviet govern-
> ment. Yet the deeply rooted American concept of press freedom,
> combined with diplomatic expediency, has put Tass men in this
> country on a par in many respects with reporters for UPI or AP.
> The Russian agency is not a news service at all in the
> American sense. It is the voice of the Soviet regime. It reacts

officially to moves and statements by other governments and
is the right arm of Soviet propaganda. Its correspondents
abroad are believed to report primarily for the guidance of
the home government and, of course, they are servants of
the Soviet regime. [27]

Henry F. Schulte, former UPI bureau chief in Madrid, reports

that a leading American newspaper with a large foreign staff sent a re-

porter into Spain to write a two-week series on conditions in that country.

When told that it would take longer than two weeks to become well ac-

quainted with the country, the reporter said that he did not want to know

Spain; he had been sent "to get the Franco regime." [28]

Aside from these cooperative or antagonistic power relations between

government and the press, activities of wire services and governments

sometimes assume a triangular structure, involving an American wire,

American governmental agencies, and a foreign government. Diplomatic

protocol dictates a balanced press representation between diplomatically

reciprocating nations. Thus, representatives of the Spanish press (and

particularly Spain's national news service, Agencia Efe) are allowed in

certain numbers in the United States in return for a similar number of

United States journalists in Spain. Although diplomatic immunity is not ex-

tended to reporters, although they often must obtain governmental work

permits, and although their stay is based on personal visas and their

activities must conform with the foreign governments conception of press

freedom, American correspondents abroad do have recourse through their

own government's diplomatic channels when a foreign government threatens

to or actually does expel, confine, or arrest them.

Schulte reports, for example, that American correspondents receive two types of protection from the U.S. government: (1) a guarantee
of safety in the foreign country, even though the correspondent is subject
to the foreign nation's laws, and (2) help getting the correspondent into the
country. Reprisal through diplomatic channels by alteration of reporter
allotments is the principal recourse for a breach of safety or a denial of
entrance. Schulte's personal experience with Franco over the threat of
expulsion from Spain is illustrative of the far-reaching ramifications in
power relations between wire-service correspondents and foreign governments when the two disagree. Schulte describes the situation and comments
on its implications.

> Franco was holding a parade in Madrid and press repre-
> sentatives were relegated to a box next to Franco's and near
> the diplomatic corps. From that position I couldn't have seen
> how the public was reacting to the parade. So I sent a boy to
> the box, and I covered the parade from a position on the street
> among the parade-watchers. When some secret police came by,
> the crowd whistled, which is the same in Spain as the Bronx
> cheer is in the United States. I reported this in the fifteenth or
> sixteenth paragraph of my cover story.
> The London desk moved the incident up to the eighth para-
> graph and the New York desk made a lead out of it. I was
> called in by the government as a result and was threatened with
> expulsion, which meant taking my press card and visa. But
> there is a lot of bad publicity connected with expelling a news-
> man. Every newspaper in the world goes to bat for the re-
> porter. It would hurt Spain's image in the halls of Congress
> where foreign aid is voted, and it would mean American retalia-
> tion by withdrawing visas of Spanish correspondents in the
> United States. It doesn't bother the individual because there is
> a lot of money in it for him in magazine articles, lectures, and
> so forth.[29]

Schulte was not expelled. Before Spanish officials decided on a course of
action, he had returned to the United States and left UPI's staff.

Many other instances of triangular press-government relations
could be presented, but only a few more will be given to illustrate the
range of relations, from informality to absolute seriousness. During
the reign of terror which accompanied Stalin's 1937 purges and collecti-
vization of agriculture and industry in Russia, U.S. Ambassador Joseph
E. Davies relied upon a small band of American correspondents in Moscow
for advice and information. Davies recalls his relationship with the newsmen.

> Every evening after the trial, the American newspaper-
> men would come up to the Embassy for a "snack" and beer
> after these late night sessions and we would "hash" over the
> day's proceedings. Among these were Walter Duranty and
> Harold Denny of the New York Times, Joe Barnes and Joe
> Phillips of the New York Herald-Tribune, Charlie Nutter and
> Dick Massock of the Associated Press, Norman Deuel and
> Henry Shapiro of the United Press, Jim Brown of the Inter-
> national News. They were an exceptionally brilliant group of
> men. I came to rely upon them. They were of inestimable
> value to me in the appraisal and estimate of men, situations,
> and Soviet developments. * * * Shapiro . . . was a lawyer,
> a graduate of the Moscow law school. His knowledge of Soviet
> law was most helpful. The other men were all very familiar
> with Soviet conditions, personalities, and Russian psychology.
> * * * As a matter of fact, I have come to think of them more
> or less as "unofficial colleagues."[30]

Not only do press-government relations operate informally through
such personal contacts as these, but also through the feeding of press dispatches to officials, sometimes the first news of the occurrence which the
official receives. Cater describes the informational role of wires in a
U.S. decision-making process.

> In times of critical congressional debate, when the hour
> for voting draws near, the rooms outside the chambers became
> a beehive of whispered consultation between press and politi-
> cian. News tickers in the Capitol and White House lobbies

transmit the last-minute communiques. The hastily torn off
teletape rushed to the Senate floor is a familiar sight during
the final frenzied assaults on the enemies' strongholds. As
each congressional fight reaches its crisis, one is made
sharply aware of the pervasive influence on news and newsmen. [31]

Ben H. Bagdikian throws penetrating light on the role of the wire services

in informing public officials of other officials' activities.

> On fast-breaking news, The Associated Press and
> United Press International can beat almost every method
> available to the government, short of the DEW line. AP
> and UPI teleprinters operate in the White House, in the
> Pentagon, (where Secretary McNamara sees thirty or so
> takes in a typical day), and AP, UPI, and Reuters have
> tickers in the Secretary of State's quarters. Tickers also
> operate behind the chamber of Congress.
> The need for accuracy is obvious. On August 3, 1961,
> wire services (using suppositions shared by the police) in-
> accurately reported that two Cubans were in the process of
> hijacking an American jet airliner in Texas. Members of
> Congress kept running back to the tickers all afternoon and
> some worked themselves into such fury that they proposed
> resolutions all but declaring war on Cuba. The hijackers
> turned out to be a pair of Americans from Arizona. [32]

Fett was informed by a UP source that one of six UP subsidiary

operations in 1948 was the Washington City News Service, which was de-

scribed as follows: "A summary of government reports, local news and

highlights . . . sent daily to 100-odd government offices, executives and

special correspondents in the nation's capital." [33] AP's Washington City

News Service, operating under the auspices of the Press Association, Inc.,

performs the same service, totalling 145 subscribers in 1960. [34]

Serious triangular relations, of course, develop at critical stages

in foreign relations, such as military incidents, diplomatic upheavals, and

all-out war. Often at times like these, the U.S. government is not in a

position to aid or support the wire services because (1) the government is principally concerned with its own status and prestige in the situation, and

(2) wire-service personnel have no diplomatic immunity.

The outbreak of full-scale war presents a wire service with unique

and often not easily remedied situations. Diplomatic guarantees and pro-

tections are meaningless when belligerents sever diplomatic relations,

often leaving foreign correspondents stranded and at the mercy of the

enemy. American journalistic tradition, of course, dictates close sur-

veillance at or near the front lines by war correspondents, but this often

proves disastrous for correspondents and wires as the following collage of

AP reports and observations during World War II will illustrate.

> The Associated Press building in London was bombed
> once and finally destroyed by fire and water so that it is no
> longer habitable. * * * The removal of the remaining Ameri-
> cans from Berlin was under consideration as well as tentative
> plans for the pooling of news at Berlin by the three news
> services, in event the American representatives of these
> agencies departed the country. * * * A dozen staffers . . . .
> were under polite but definitely protective custody in Axis
> countries, awaiting the outcome of inter-governmental
> negotiations for their evacuation. . . . The group included
> staffers in Berlin, Rome, Tokyo, Shanghai, and Indo-China.
> * * * The London staff has been doubled in preparation for
> coming events [i.e., the Normandy invasion]. * * * The
> story was finally released, with only one minor deletion on
> military security grounds. * * * Under mandatory censorship
> regulations in the battle areas, plus voluntary censorship at
> home . . . news obviously has been handled under vigilant,
> constant restriction. * * * Again, there was a serious lack of
> adequate facilities for the big staff of correspondents assigned
> to the North African expedition. This was due in some measure,
> however, to such unforeseen events as the sinking of a ship
> loaded with radio transmitting equipment. * * * Edward H.
> Crockett . . . died when the British warship he was on was
> torpedoed in the Mediterranean. * * * A total of 179 persons
> served as AP war correspondents during the war. [35]

Sometimes the peacetime perils of a single wire-service correspondent

arouses considerable public sympathy and official government assistance as for example the case of AP's Prague bureau chief, William N. Oatis,

arrested by the Czech government in 1951. Frank Starzel reports on

governmental response to the Oatis affair.

> The Associated Press has made and continues every
> effort to obtain Oatis' release. It has been joined by the United
> States Government, senators, congressmen, newspapers,
> scores of organizations and hundreds of private citizens. The
> State Department has instituted a series of economic and dip-
> lomatic measures in retaliation and has been seeking every
> avenue to pave the way for his release.
> These efforts were not confined to the United States.
> Oatis' arrest aroused indignation throughout the free world.
> Secretary of State Dean Acheson denounced Oatis' arrest in
> a speech before the United Nations. It was brought up at a
> U. N. meeting in Geneva and subject to inquiry by the Council
> of Europe. [36]

Clearly the relationships between the international press and the

multitude of governments is delicate, multi-dimensional, multilateral,

and sometimes even formally or informally diplomatic. It varies for the

American wire service from country to country. But as long as AP and UPI

are committed to the international collection and distribution of news, they

must tolerate and cooperate with the various legal and extra-legal pressures,

threats, and confinements they encounter. They have learned to accept

their various relationships with governments, but the size and content of

the resulting AP and UPI reports inevitably show the effects of propaganda,

partial coverage, inaccessibility, and favoritism.

Productive Interaction and Trends

The formulation and transmission of meaning among wire-service

reporters and their news sources has undergone radical changes because of both components in recent years. Many of the governmental changes affect the frequency and content of interaction, yet the very growth of governmental news sources has made the wires' transmission load greater. Of the eighty-one employers listed in Table 28, AP and UPI stand alone in terms of the volume and diversity of news daily gathered and distributed. Cater makes this point with respect to the Washington situation.

> Backbone of the industry and, to a certain extent, its central nervous system are the giant wire services with a labor force large enough to monitor every major news out- let in the capital and to maintain a steady outgoing flow of words. The wire-service employee . . . is the bucket boy for the never ceasing stream of news that may be scooped up at any hour of day or night and poured into print by the far-flung distributors.[37]

The constant interplay of symbols and euphemisms between reporters and news sources evolves toward a compromise between each component's needs and desires of semantic presentation. The news source wants news to be acceptable to the public and positive for his image (or at least non- commital and inoffensive), while the reporter must satisfy his reader and editor with conflict, drama, and volume. Cater observes the distinction.

> . . . the official and the reporter are moved by funda- mentally different compulsions. The official's first response to a newsworthy event is assimilative. He attempts to relate it to the broad body of record on which he precariously builds his policies. The reporter's first impulse, on the other hand, is distributive: he seeks to communicate the news- worthy event as speedily and widely as possible.[38]

Motivation for the wire-service reporter originates largely in AP-UPI competition which demands a large number of bulletins, elongated treatment of stories, frequent updating of copy, and preoccupation with speed. James Fixx's description of the wires' "quarterbacks," Francis T. Leary, UPI managing editor, and Samuel G. Blackman, AP general news editor, points

out how the rivalry to beat the opposition becomes a prime daily target.

> In the running rivalry between the AP and UPI, few
> stories are written, edited, or put on a wire without at
> least a moment's instinctive speculation about what the
> opposition is likely to be up to, and few joys are greater
> than coming up with a clear winner. . . .[39]

This drive forces reporters to move stories before they are complete or

backgrounded or sometimes even checked for accuracy, even though the

public and the official want the copy to be complete, explanatory, and above

all accurate.

A case of the wires' rivalry and undue speed affecting the accuracy

and impact of a news story is the U. S. Supreme Court's decision in June of

1962 to ban prayers in public schools. The uproar that followed the de-

cision prompted William Hachten to analyze the press coverage in relation

to that reaction. Justice Tom C. Clark criticized the press for initial

coverage that was too brief while wire-service reporters defended their

stories as accurate and factual. [40] After noting that the Court's wording

could have been more direct, Hachten went on to hold the press primarily

accountable for much of the initial misunderstanding and reaction.

> The initial wire-service stories, while factual, accurate,
> and objective, were too brief to counter squarely the two
> most widespread misconceptions about the decision: first,
> that it had in one stroke banned all religious observance from
> public life or education; second, that it was a decision that
> had taken a position against religion in general.
> Later in the day, the wire services, in their effort to
> follow up an obviously "hot" story, worked on a first-come,
> first-served basis in selecting persons for comment. There
> was balance in the choice of clergymen, but not in congressional
> comment, which was heavily loaded with southerners. . . .
> However, the wire services must bear responsibility on
> this point. The news-gathering processes gave them ample

opportunity to balance their stories and to include informed
comments. The press need not be a mere transmission belt
for the reckless. [41]

This criticism focuses attention on wire reporters' preoccupation

with speed, competition, and making one news event produce several

stories. The wire-service reporter, more than other American journal-

ists, has learned to "package" the news to serve three functions: (1) to

use a given news event as much and in as many different ways as is possible,

both in one report (e. g., side-bars, background sketches, boxes, etc.) and

over several days (e. g., the over-night, the follow-up, the reaction story,

etc.); (2) to keep the wire filled with new or changing copy (to keep the sub-

scribers both happy and inclined to use that wire); and (3) to keep up with

the opposition. Cater notes the mechanical, split-second packaging of news

items on the distribution side.

> For the wire-service employee, the news is like fluid,
> to be portioned out in bulletins, and leads, and "takes."
> It is capable of being bottled in any quantity. Its production
> is more determined by the technical than by internal factors
> of the news itself. The great Associated Press "A" wire
> that binds the nation can carry an optimum sixty words a
> minute. News from Washington or London or Hong Kong
> moves onto it according to tightly scheduled "budgets,"
> scarsely less methodically prepared than a big department
> store's allotment of display space to shoes and hats and
> women's lingerie. [42]

In another place, Cater quotes a wire-service reporter who describes how

the wires' packaging requirements affect his activities and judgments.

> A central fact of life for the wire service reporter in
> Washington is that there are a great many more afternoon
> than morning papers in the United States. This creates a
> problem because the early afternoon paper on the East Coast
> goes to press between 10 and 10:30 a.m. --before the "news
> development" of the day. It means the wire service reporter

must engage in the basically phony operation of writing the "overnight"--a story composed the previous evening but giving the impression when it appears the next afternoon that it covers that day's events.

Our job is to report news but it also is to keep a steady flow of news coming forward. Every Saturday morning, for example, we visit the Congressional leaders. We could write all the stories that we get out of these conferences for the Sunday a. m. 's but we don't. We learn to schedule them in order to space them out over Sunday's and Monday's papers. [43]

While packaging may involve either the long-term treatment of one story or the relative handling of several stories on one day's wire, there is also a wire-service procedure for a single developing story. Ault and Emery in a textbook describe some of the techniques used to update a developing wire story.

Experienced wire service rewrite men soon learn the trick of inserting a "platform" paragraph high in the original story onto which they can rest the pickup paragraph at the end of the new lead, so the transition reads smoothly. They learn to avoid allusions whose meaning is lost if a new lead is placed on top of the story and to avoid burying an important angle from the earlier story under several paragraphs of new lead material. Another trick they acquire is to keep the story in focus, so that the later but lesser developments do not smother the main elements of the new situation. Ideally, a developing story can be "topped" two or three times with new leads, yet will appear to the reader in his newspaper as though it was all written at one time. [44]

Daniel Boorstin calls these practices of re-hashing, withholding, and creating via interviews "the production of pseudo-events--in all kinds of packages, in black-and-white, in technicolor, in words, and in a thousand other forms."[45] He relates what makes a good Washington correspondent in the mid-twentieth century and how the reporter must forsake traditional journalistic tenets of accuracy and objectivity.

Nowadays the test of a Washington reporter is seldom his skill at precise dramatic reporting, but more often his adeptness at dark intimation. If he wishes to keep his news channels open, he must accumulate a vocabulary and develop a style to conceal his sources and obscure the relation of a supposed event or statement to the underlying facts of life, at the same time seeming to offer hard facts. Much of his stock in trade is his own and other people's speculation about the reality of what he reports. He lives in a penumbra between fact and fantasy. He helps create that very obscurity without which the supposed illumination of his reports would be unnecessary. A deft administrator these days must have similar skills. He must master "the technique of denying the truth without actually lying.'[46]

As Boorstin indicates, the public official also has a role in this growing process of news packaging. Aside from the general framework provided by the legal and extra-legal confinements imposed by the relationship, the official for his part takes a positive position in news distribution. The rise of a publicity-conscious officialdom has called for public relations men attached to every type of governmental unit. (Estimates place the number of Washington information officers at about three thousand, or about twice the size of the press corps there.[47]

In addition to those designated as information officers, the governmental hierarchy itself must also be accessible to reporters. And it is at this level of high executives and congressmen that the reporter usually finds his most valuable news sources and stories, although he often must sacrifice specific statements, names of news sources, and concrete verb constructions in his final copy. Devices such as the secret or background briefing, the news leak, the unsigned speculation, or the interview-generated news story and the news conference are a few of the more prominent means by which high officials achieve their ends: to solicit public opinion or reaction to present or future governmental policy, to gain public attention and acceptance, to formulate a public opinion conducive to a planned future policy course, to bluff or threaten foreign or domestic opponents publicly, or simply to boast of accomplishments.

Although the procedures and instances of administrative and legislative "news management" are legion, two examples will suffice. President Franklin D. Roosevelt was known for the "help" he gave reporters in preparing their copy. At a 1939 press conference with war tensions mounting in Europe, Roosevelt is quoted as having told reporters:

> I want to get something across, only don't put it that way. In other words, it is a thing that I cannot put as direct stuff, but is background. And the way--as you know I very often do it--if I were writing the story, the way I'd write it is this--you know the formula: "When asked when he was returning (to Washington), the President intimated that it was impossible to give any date; because while he hoped to be away until the third or fourth of March, information that continues to be received with respect to the international situation continues to be disturbing. Therefore it may be necessary for the President to return (to the capital) before the third or fourth of March. It is understood that this information relates to the possible renewal of demands by certain countries, these demands being pushed, not through normal diplomatic channels but, rather, through the more recent type of relations; in other words, the use of fear or aggression."[48]

Although this is an extreme case, it illustrates the type of meaningless "news" which public officials will often ask the press to distribute, without understanding or concern for the necessity of a news peg and of the hardcore factual base on which a news story is supposed to be built. Yet the image must be maintained of an active, concerned public official, and the public attention must constantly be courted through the so-called news dispatches, which in the final analysis emerge solely from the official's disposition to give the "news" and to structure its contents and shape.

Congress is also eager to maintain its public image, to emit illusions of principled activity, and to keep the public spotlight trained on it. Many congressmen try and fail at the art of attracting and holding the interest of newsmen, largely because of their lack of inside information and of a central location in the power structure of Congress. Occasionally, however, a congressman with nothing more than some questionable or partial information on scandelous, subversive, or sensational conditions gains the spotlight. This was the case with Senator Joseph McCarthy. Richard Rovere, a Washington reporter during the McCarthy witch-hunt era, describes the senator's tactics.

> He knew how to get into the news even on those rare occasions when invention failed him and he had no unfacts to give out. For example, he invented the morning press conference called for the purpose of announcing the afternoon press conference. The reporters would come in--they were beginning, in this period, to respond to his summonses like Pavlov's dogs at the clang of a bell--and McCarthy would say that he just wanted to give them the word that he expected to be ready with a shattering announcement later in the day, for use in the papers the following morning. This would gain him a headline in the afternoon papers: "New McCarthy Revelations Awaited in Capital." Afternoon would come, and if McCarthy had something, he would give it out, but often enough he had nothing, and this was a matter of slight concern. He would simply say that he wasn't quite ready, that he was having difficulty in getting some of the "documents" he needed or that a "witness" was proving elusive. Morning headlines: "Delay Seen in McCarthy Case--Mystery Witness Being Sought."[49]

Conceivably any personality in government can prey upon the press's two most vulnerable characteristics--objectivity and competition--just as McCarthy did, because it is always difficult to determine where reporting

ends and exploitation begins. Ordinarily no determination is made at all,
and the newsmen and their employers are dragged forward by the escalating
effects of repeated official activity interacting with media deadlines, competition, and need for speed. The judging of an individual item's inherent
news value is directed not as much by whether it is news as by questions
of where or when to carry it in relation to other copy. The reliance on
officials by newsmen, and by trigger-happy wires in particular, is constant
and almost slave-like. The wire reports' prime characteristic is quasi-
official, semantic intimation and speculation. In the extreme condition of
national crises when governmental policy becomes the focal point of public
attention, the media become conveyor belts for whatever official is currently
acting or reacting. Discussing such "periods of high social tension" within
the framework of social values and communication's role in value formation,
Carey concludes:

> . . . in periods when intermediate structures are weakened
> or eroded, individuals are attached directly to national
> centers of organization and communication. And, in such
> periods, intermediate communication systems, themselves,
> become extensions or reflections of the national centers. [50]

Ultimately, to a greater or lesser degree, the public official decides
whether to release the news, and if so, when, what, how much, to whom,
and under what circumstances. The American wire service finds itself
constantly being violated by the news managers but increasingly playing
a vital role in domestic and international politics and communication. It
is usually the first to report a news event and often remains the only or
principal source of information, background, and interpretation upon

which the public (and sometimes even many public officials) will form

opinions and perhaps take action.

Yet despite this power, wire-service reporters--and the press

corps in general--find their role made no easier by the officials upon

whom they must rely for their information. Within these narrowing

boundaries, the reporter, however, remains an individual committed to

a journalistic tradition which hopefully may sustain some degree of his

autonomy. This last vestige of journalistic integrity in a relationship

which increasingly subordinates the press to government is described by

Walter Lippmann.

> Much might be said about the personal relations between
> politicians and newspapermen. They are invariably delicate
> and difficult. For obviously they must be close: correspondents
> must see much of the men they write about. Yet if they do,
> they soon find themselves compelled to choose between friend-
> ship and the ties of loyalty that come from companionship on the
> one hand, the stern embarrassing truth on the other. This is the
> unpleasant side of newspaper work and I have never heard of
> any way of avoiding it. When a personal friend becomes a public
> man, a predicament soon arrives in which friendship and pro-
> fessional duty are at odds. [51]

Discussion and Conclusions

Trends in the wire service-news source relationship point increas-

ingly toward news-source domination, particularly for government news

which constitutes the bulk of the wires' daily reports. The wires are no

different from the press in general in this respect, but their volume,

diversity, organizational size, and speed make them the most prominent

journalistic component of the changing press-government relationship.

This increasing domination by government stems from its physical growth, its increasing policy diversity and complexity, and its shifts in power away from open operation and public involvement. Internationally, governmental trends have been toward more news capitals, increased multilateral diplomatic relations, and a continuously high level of diversity in legal and extra-legal foreign controls over the press. The key concepts in the relationship are, for the news sources, politico-cultural necessity and, for the wires, productive-civilian reaction. They apply in all realms: legal (political), extra-legal, and productive interaction.

Both at the legal and extra-legal levels, officials, responding to cultural determinants and political necessities, have determined or are determining daily the extent of press freedom or restraint. Laws, edicts, constitutional provisions, court decisions, etc., shape the formalistic nature of the press and its relations with government. These relational forms affect and are affected by whatever extra-legal pressures seem appropriate to governmental officials in terms of the government's cultural history and daily necessity. In both cases, the press can either accept these forms and pressures as a citizen or subject or melt away. The home government may assist and support these citizen-newsmen abroad, formally or informally, but seldom is this the case at home, except on the government's terms only.

In terms of productivity, the governmental machinery shapes all aspects of the news in response to its relationships with the domestic citizenry and the world population. Again, the press reacts, scurrying to collect the important items dropped here and there by officials, and falling back on the ever-present stream of governmental handouts for copy at other times. The more critical the national or international crisis, the more the press reacts by acquiescence, in effect turning over its channels completely to officialdom.

Although trends point to governmental dominance of the relationship with the press, some areas of compromise are found within the legal, extra-legal, and productive prerogatives of governmental control. Officials want to report, to control, to maintain civil order, to create a positive image, to mold public opinion, and to speculate publicly. For this they need a press organization, and the wires' foreign and domestic dimensions make them prime targets for officials with news. The press, on the other hand, wants to know, to ask, to be correct, to handle news involving drama and conflict, to gain clients' reliance, and to beat the competition. For this the press looks increasingly to government. The agreement reached between news sources and the wires, in most cases is not only a compromise of rights and duties, or desires and needs, but is a cooperative exchange based on mutual tolerance. The wire-service news report shouts to an objective observer the silence of some countries' officials by their perpetual absence and whispers the deluge of the faithful daily news-makers. Nameless news sources, carefully fragmented and obscured facts, and speculation are the prime characteristics of the product born of this cooperative compromise, and the net effect is the obliteration of meaningful news and the construction of pseudo-events or half-news.

The key question here, as in Chapter VI, concerns trends toward superordination and subordination of relational contributors.

> 5. The wire services have been increasingly dominated by news sources in the political and productive relations with the news sources in the primary environment.

The control of government (assumed here as the principal news source for the wires) over the press has always been fairly complete, in the formal sense. (Informal or extra-legal publishing or opinionating is constantly prevalent, but in most cases does not have nearly as great an influence upon society's communication and the government-press relationship as does the daily routine press production.) Even in the granting of absolute press freedom, government maintains control over the relationship, for what is given can be taken away.

Thus, whether one considers the wires in their national or international context, governmental control, based on one or another traditional, socio-cultural background, has continuously affected the wires' position generally and subordinated their role in their relationship with government sources in particular. The thrust of the above hypothesis, however, is that this wire-service subordination has tended over time to increase, and a number of findings in the present chapter support this contention. Growing wire-service size, speed, and volume have made them more useful to governmental sources wishing to reach the public. Growing governmental services and size have made the wires more vital to the increased number of sources wishing to reach the public. Less openness and more preoccupation with image-building or swaying public opinion have made the wires an ideal medium for the greater volume of shear public relations material

pumped out by governmental sources. AP's reduced reliance upon mem-

bers and terminated ties with the world cartel make it (along with UPI)

more objective and thus more inclined to carry whatever the governmental

news source wants publicized.

Thus, the compromise between wire service and news source

over productive matters is increasingly couched in terms of the latter's

legal and extra-legal controls or prerogatives over the former, including

whether to release an item, and if so, how.

_____

Footnotes

[1] The first study of note on correspondents was Leo C. Rosten's
The Washington Correspondents (New York: Harcourt, Brace and Company,
1937), which describes the backgrounds and practices of Washington cor-
respondents. See specific wire-service descriptions on pages 115-126.
Theodore E. Kruglak's The Foreign Correspondents (Geneva: Librairie E.
Droz, 1955), is limited to correspondents in Western Europe but contains
many helpful statistics about the backgrounds of wire-service personnel.
A smaller, less comprehensive survey to quantify foreign correspondents'
backgrounds (without specific reference to wire services) is J. William
Maxwell's "U.S. Correspondents Abroad: A Study of Backgrounds," Journalism Quarterly, XXXIII (Summer, 1956), pp. 346-348. In the process at
this writing is an inquiry conducted by the Columbia Graduate School of
Journalism. A report of early findings (responses by full-time American
foreign correspondents to a questionnaire) is Frederick T. C. Yu and
John Luter, "The Foreign Correspondent and His Work," Columbia Journalism Review, III (Spring, 1964), pp. 5-12. If this initial article is indicative
of the entire Columbia project, the inquiry will not differentiate among
correspondents' employers.

[2] Kruglak, op. cit., pp. 130-131.

[3] Ibid., passim.

[4] Ibid., p. 70.

[5] Ibid., p. 117.

[6] Yu and Luter, op. cit., p. 7.

[7] Douglass Cater, The Fourth Branch of Government (Boston:
Houghton Mifflin Company, 1959), pp. 94-95.

[8] Max Lerner, America As a Civilization (New York: Simon and
Schuster, 1957), p. 397.

[9] Douglass Cater, Power In Washington (New York: Random House,
1964), pp. 241-242.

[10] John Wilhelm, "The Re-Appearing Foreign Correspondent: A
World Survey," Journalism Quarterly, XL (Spring, 1963), pp. 147-168.

[11] Ibid., p. 148.

[12] Yu and Luter, op. cit., p. 5.

[13] Max R. Grossman, "Some Contemporary Problems of Foreign Correspondence," Journalism Quarterly, XXIV (March, 1947), pp. 37-38.

[14] Ibid.

[15] Wilhelm, op. cit., p. 150.

[16] Unesco, op. cit. (1953), pp. 15-17.

[17] Ibid., pp. 48, 50, 61.

[18] Unesco, op. cit. (1964), pp. 373-377.

[19] Ibid., p. 168.

[20] The dichotomy employed here is suggested in the International Press Institute's Government Pressures on the Press (Zurich: The International Press Institute, 1955). Several of the ideas introduced in this discussion of press-government relations, however, have been formulated by the author.

[21] Cooper, op. cit. (1956), pp. 139-140.

[22] Eugene Lyons, Assignment in Utopia (New York: Harcourt, Brace and Company, 1937), p. 110.

[23] John Hohenberg, Foreign Correspondence: The Great Reporters and Their Times (New York: Columbia University Press, 1964), pp. 317-318.

[24] Lyons, op. cit., p. 96.

[25] Hohenberg, op. cit., pp. 318-320.

[26] See Wechsler, op. cit.

[27] Earl J. Johnson, "Tass A Soviet Department Within the United States," The Overseas Press Bulletin, XVIII (October 12, 1963), p. 4.

[28] Interview by the author, Fall of 1963.

[29] Ibid.

[30] Joseph E. Davies, Mission to Moscow (London, 1943), pp. 180-181, 227, quoted in Kruglak, op. cit., p. 98.

[31] Cater, op. cit. (1959), pp. 14-15.

[32]Ben H. Bagdikian, "Washington Letter: The Morning Line," Columbia Journalism Review, I (Fall, 1962), p. 28.

[33]Fett, op. cit., p. 28.

[34]New York AP, Volume, LXI (1961), p. 56.

[35]Ibid., XLII (1942), pp. 4, 35, 61; XLIII (1943), pp. 74, 77; XLIV (1944), p. 53; XLV (1945), pp. 53, 68, 72; and XLVI (1946), p. 115.

[36]Ibid., LII (1952), p. 100.

[37]Cater, op. cit. (1959), p. 3.

[38]Ibid., p. 17.

[39]James F. Fixx, "Quarterbacking a Nation's News," Saturday Review, XLVI (August 10, 1963), p. 48.

[40]William A Hachten, "Journalism and the Prayer Decision," Columbia Journalism Review, I (Fall, 1962), pp. 4-5.

[41]Ibid., pp. 7-8.

[42]Cater op. cit. (1959), p. 3.

[43]Ibid., pp. 108, 110.

[44]Ault and Emery, op. cit., p. 221.

[45]Daniel J. Boorstin, The Image (New York: Atheneum Press, 1962), p. 36.

[46]Ibid., p. 34.

[47]Cater, op. cit. (1959), p. 5.

[48]Boorstin, op. cit., pp. 20-21.

[49]Richard Rovere, quoted in ibid., pp. 21-22.

[50]Carey, op. cit., p. 187. Carey cites Thomas J. Bennett, Government Publicity and Democratic Press Theory (Urbana, Ill.: unpublished University of Illinois Ph.D. thesis, 1962), p. 218, for an empirical assist on this conclusion.

[51]Walter Lippmann, "Notes on the Freedom of the Press," (April 25, 1936, Today and Tomorrow), The Essential Lippmann, Clinton Rossiter and James Lare, eds., (New York: Random House, 1963), p. 410.

Chapter VIII

CONCLUSIONS

> We receive letters of criticism
> from newspaper readers these days
> as well as from telegraph editors.
> This is a new development. * * *
> They still are not well informed
> about the role of U.P.I. and AP,
> but they do know what the initials
> stand for.
>   -- Earl Johnson (1962)

This thesis has attempted to describe the current conditions of the

major American wire services and to indicate the historical trends in pro-

cesses and relationships which have led up to these conditions. Primarily

an exercise in descriptive investigation, this study has been aimed at

drawing together scattered research on the wires, introducing previously

unreported data, and providing an empirical and theoretical base upon

which subsequent research may rest.

In this chapter, the findings of this study are briefly summarized,

hypotheses are discussed, and areas of future investigation are introduced.

In the historical account of wire-service development, the 1890's

are selected as the turning point in the wires' character and condition.

Prior to this decade "early development and instability" were the keynotes

for the wires. The rise of daily newspapers, a revision in the news con-

cept (leading to the "penny press"), improvements in transportation and

communications, and a more aggressive seeking of news led to institu-

tionalization of the press and provided the backdrop and general impetus

for the emergence of the first American wire service, the New York

333

Associated Press, in 1848 as a group effort within the press institution.
The NYAP appeared in response to four immediate problems or conditions:
problems within newspapers' dealings with the telegraph industry, the illustrative success of foreign news agencies, a revision of editors' thinking
about local competition (particularly in New York City), and the difficulties
developing over coverage of the Mexican War.

Throughout this pre-1890's period, the NYAP continually tried to
control news gathering in the United States by limiting its own membership, imposing tight restrictions on clients and regional satellites, and
entering mutual assistance agreements with telegraph companies and
foreign news agencies. Because of these latter agreements, the NYAP's
news report grew to be a vital, desirable component of nineteenth-
century American journalism. The controlling New York editors, however,
considered it primarily as their exclusive property, contributing to their
newspapers first and foremost, yielding added revenue for them, and enhancing their reputations.

Friction over control of news gathering and content of the report
was inevitable under such circumstances, and despite the above mentioned
NYAP attempts to maintain control, conflict developed among AP organizations (originating primarily within the more liberal Western Associated
Press) and was fostered by differing opinions over how to handle growing,
competitive wires and telegraph companies. NYAP's self-preservation
measures closely paralleled those of the well-established trusts and monopolistic industrial empires of the American social and cultural environment

of the time, and its continually improving news report gave the wire an additional source of institutional strength vis-a-vis reformers, journalistic revolutionists, and cyclical swing toward the ideological adjustment of industry prevalent at times elsewhere in American life.

AP's 1893 reorganization successfully alleviated internal facionalism as a source of instability, and the ensuing victory over the old UP established AP as a national wire and eliminated external competition as a threat to internal stability. Although competition inevitably was to arise again, AP's broad base of local support, continued reliance upon the world cartel and members for gathering news, and well-established ties with telegraph companies allowed it to concentrate upon improving service and introducing the flood of technological advances which have appeared since that time.

Threats of instability are increasingly non-existent within the respective organizations. Threats stemming from the wires' industrial and scientific suppliers and partners had declined but are beginning to re-develop in new and broader forms. Governmental threats have been infrequent: one in 1900 was circumvented by a change of state for AP, and one in 1945 has provided greater internal AP stability than had existed previously while not altering AP's operation appreciably. The post-1893 era has been a period of continuous technological growth, improvement of the news reports, and expansion of services and clientele, based on increasing internal emphasis on commercialism and the corollary of producing and distributing a product geared to market demands. Such an emphasis has developed partially because of the environmental events which have made

the report lively and salable and partially because of increasing environ-

mental pressure for market-oriented operation and the development of

large-scale organizational structure to support such an operation.

Political maturation in the wires (particularly the AP) has developed

by progressive stages of submerging the processes of naming policy-makers

and of policy-making increasingly within the stable administrative structure

of the organization. From control of AP by wealthy, stockholding or bond-

holding newspapers, the locus of power has shifted to the general manager,

and finally to the administrative staff itself. These shifts are the result of

the self-perpetuating nature of growing bureaucratic systems, the increasing

commercial emphasis of wire operations (beginning with Cooper's propensity

for expansion, technological innovation, and development of supplementary

services in response to market demands), and the increasing fragmentation

of board power, brought on largely by membership desires to democratize

representation. The growth of bureaucratic spheres of influence and self-

interest in the wires parallels general industrial development in the United

States. Both in the wires and in industry in general, the day of the great

leader has passed. Now the assets and procedures of industrial production

and distribution have become so well established that executive, operational,

and departmental personnel may come and go without disturbing the on-going

productive and political processes. Moreover, in this climate policy-making

increasingly involves questions of what the market will bear or what tech-

nical devices are feasible and profitable rather than what is journalistically

a tenable approach to news gathering in a democratic society where daily
flow of information and comment is vital to the body politic.

In productive maturation, the market orientation clearly emerges
under Cooper's so-called positive policy of budgeting to accommodate
emergencies and innovation as well as routine operation. While Stone and
Martin operated from essentially journalistic viewpoints, budgeting only
for routine matters and largely disregarding innovation and expansion,
Cooper and his successors have sought to maintain the loyalty of mem -
bers and staffers and to expand the numbers of both by greatly expanding
economic outlays and by searching out new areas of content and distribution.
The consumer newspaper and the consumer public have become the principal
targets of wire-service operations.

Relations with the wires' two primary environmental components,
in both the political and productive realms of interaction, have tended to
develop with opposing allocations of strength: the wires dominating relations with clients or subscribers and being dominated in relations with
news sources (particularly government). In addition to losing power over
policy-making through the board of directors, AP subscribers have lost
their protest rights, while the wire maintains exclusive control over local
news and over use of the report through by-law and contractual provisions.
Dominance is maintained through the extra-legal channels of frequent
personal contacts and through an extensive promotional program which
utilizes "official" publications and meetings. Although clients determine
affiliations largely on the basis of personal perspective or local problems,

the wires offer little choice, except in specific news coverage instances.
Thus, the prerogative which clients might exercise in "casting consumer
votes" for one wire or another is mitigated by the wires' overriding similarity and inoffensiveness. The fact that most affiliations remain stable
over time bears this out. Increases in two-wire affiliations reflect increased client stability more than choices presented by the wires, except
at the story-by-story level.

The wires as individuals without diplomatic immunity are dominated by the various legal and extra-legal controls imposed by governments and officials responding to their individual socio-cultural traditions
and the necessities of maintaining civil order. Although the wires may
take a position, vis-a-vis a government, ranging from publicism to antagonism, the ultimate determinant of whether news will be given to the wire
is the predisposition of the government or official, who also determines
how that news is to be released. Because government increasingly is the
primary source of wire-service news and because the wires increasingly
present the government with broad, effective channels of publicizing news
and comment, some sort of compromise must be worked out between the
two. In the end, however, this compromise is largely limited by the all-
pervasive traditions and necessities of governing within a given society and
under a particular philosophic framework.

In this brief summary, as in the chapters it represents, are found
the confirmations for the five hypotheses outlined in Chapter I and discussed in various places throughout the study. These hypotheses will be
restated briefly below.

1. The wire services have been found to have attained the status of social institutions over time, having begun as a group effort within another social institution, the newspapers. The wires, therefore, solve a unique problem for society, that of national and international news collection and distribution, by reliance upon relatively standard patterns of belief and action, in the sense that their political and productive processes (and the belief system inherent in those processes) exhibit relatively broad spatial and temporal consistency. The outgrowth of necessity in the parent-institution of newspapers, the wires have become the unchallenged occupants of this domain of social communication, developing their own patterns of growth and structure and having their own individual effect upon society. Thus, they have taken their place with such communicative institutions as advertising, newspapers, television, etc., in the transmission of messages from one segment of society to another. And such transmission, because of its broad dimensions, might ultimately prove to render the wire-service institution as more central to social communication than these other institutions.

2. Wire-service patterns of operation have continually resembled those of the wires' social and cultural environment, due not only to reciprocal wire-environment reliance and assistance contingent upon on-going interaction but also to the changing requirements impinging upon all institutional operation. The wire services, therefore, must be viewed, along with all other communication institutions, as an adjunct of the industrial order in this society with standardized patterns of belief and action developing continuously around commercial and economic consideration and necessity.

3. With the exception of certain new productive problems connected with innovation and market saturation, the wires have attained
political and productive stability within their standardized patterns of
operation. At one level, this means that the wires have exhibited an
increasing bureaucratization paralleling that of American industry in
general and have increasingly budgeted and innovated to achieve specific
market-oriented goals in production and distribution of the news report.
At another level, this indicates that the wires (with the exception noted
above) have successfully reduced the threat of endogenous or exogenous
stresses upon or blockage of standardized action patterns.

4. The wire services have increasingly dominated their subscribers in both the political and productive spheres of activity. While
UP, INS, and UPI have always demonstrated a large degree of such
dominance, AP's cooperative structure has undergone successive alteration to bring it closer to its competitors in this regard. This primarily
one-way flow of news and power leaves the local outlets (and, indeed,
many national news organizations and governmental establishments) at
the mercy of the wires' definition of news values. While local publishers
and broadcasters may still hold prerogatives of affiliation and story-by-
story selection, the wires afford them little choice in either instance.
Supplemental press associations offer respectable and diverse alternatives,
but the wires, in terms of speed and volume, continue to be essential to
local news outlets while supplemental press services are only what their
name implies.

5. News sources, particularly those in government, have increasingly dominated the wires in both political and productive interaction.
Government as the ultimate or authoritative allocator of values for the
maintenance of society must control the press as an individual citizen,
with all the assumptions and ramifications which "citizen" carries in
various socio-cultural environments. The wires' broad dimensions and
domination over subscribers, however, make them appealing, if not vital,
targets for governmental news, comment, and propaganda. In one sense,
the wires must allow themselves to be the tools of government if they are
to secure any news at all, while in another sense, the wires find themselves the national and international carriers of on-going dialogues within
the cold war, in particular, and in all facets of ideological and institutional conflict, in general.

Confirmation of the last two hypotheses places the wires in the
position of "brokers of symbols," passing on meaning from the dominant
news sources to the subordinate local outlets. Brought about largely by
the desire to compile a complete daily news report and to expand service
of all kinds to as broad a field of markets and consumers as possible, this
broker role brings the wires toward the passive, distributive stance of
a telegraph or telephone system in communication phenomena.

These observations are not meant as the final explanation of wire-
service operation in this country. On the contrary, they point the way to
future investigation of more detailed wire-service data. The author suggests that such investigation might proceed along several fronts, for

example: actual and potential controls by wires over the content of local

outlets, possible bias in the news report and the shortcomings of objec-

tive and interpretative reporting by the wires, the whole problem of

Americans covering and understanding foreign news events, and the effect

upon society's communication channels--and ultimately upon society's

beliefs and values--of two huge and continually expanding corporations.

Each route of investigation has many turns and important ramifications for

a democratic society's on-going flow of information. Initial probes or

speculation have appeared with respect to some of these considerations,

and a few will be presented below.

Teletypesetter has presented the researcher with an impetus for

concern about the mounting control of the wires over local outlets' con-

tent. Cutlip notes that "where a paper goes over completely to use of

wire tape, the amount of wire news is apt to increase at the expense of

local news."[1] Cranford considers TTS a fundamental innovation in news-

paper production.

> Few developments in journalistic technology since the
> invention of the Linotype machine and rotary presses ap-
> pear to have affected newspaper production as have recent
> refinements of the Teletypesetter method of automatic
> typecasting.[2]

Moreover, the proposed computerization of the TTS system will heighten

wire-service control by delivering a "tailor-made" report to the news-

paper office, a report which the wire editor can assume is suited for his

paper's individual readership without any editing or selection.

In a more general sense, the wires make telegraph editors' work easy by selecting and then "budgeting" certain stories in this selection

for top play. Gieber comments on the power of wire-service selection.

> The press association has become the recommender
> of news to the wire editor and thus the real selector of
> telegraph news. The wire editor evaluated the news ac-
> cording to what the AP sent him.
> If the reader got vital information about the workings
> of his democratic political system one day and a plethora
> of crime and accident news the next, it was due to the nature
> of the channels of press association news and the "open
> gateway" of the newspaper. [3]

Breed quotes the managing editor of an Ohio daily with a circulation of

90,000 on the usefulness of the wires' daily budgets.

> It is used religiously. It immediately enables you to
> look forward to what's coming--makes makeup easier.
> You can almost make up your paper without seeing the
> news--just by using the budget. [4]

Most of these studies are now at least ten years old and even at their

writing were limited in scope to small regions or even to individual cases.

A thorough and broad-scoped updating of this literature is in order, as is

a reappraisal of the so-called "gatekeeper" studies[5] for possible refine-

ment and reorientation under systems theory.

Some preliminary studies by the author support the contention that

bias does seem to exist in the news report. Different vocabularies appear

to be used when describing the United States or its allies and the Com-

munist bloc. A detailed content analysis of the news reports is necessary.

Study of the wire copy emphasis--perhaps along procedural-substantive

or conflict-agreement continua as suggested by George Gerbner[6]--will

help reveal the framework within which the wires visualize and describe

important domestic and international events.

Consideration of the values inherent in the report is also required,
values implied by vocabulary, emphasis, so-called objective selection and
reporting of events, and interpretation or speculation. Whether these
values tend toward change or toward reinforcement of existing belief
patterns, their dimensions should be delineated. In this connection, the
wire services as the nation's largest collector and distributor of news and
comment take on an all-pervasive role in constructing and transmitting
the signals which instruct the public and shape its reactions to events.
Carey notes this role for the media in general.

> Most mass media content takes on the form of a social
> ceremony as it celebrates the values which the national com-
> munity holds in common and the most generalized of these
> values, seemingly, is a cathetic commitment to the norms
> of democratic politics--to the rules of how the society should
> operate. [7]

Robert H. Sollen, a California wire editor, comments on the bias he has
detected in the wires' news reports.

> The press services have a greater tendency to support
> and justify State Department cold war policy than to research,
> analyze, and report international relations in a detached
> manner. There is nothing patriotic about patriotic reporting,
> if by that we mean compromising the facts or the essential
> story to maintain a favorable national image. [8]

Questions of covering foreign news are more difficult to examine and
understand. Cultural differences make both Americans abroad and foreigners writing for U.S. consumption untenable alternatives, at least in
theory. But now, more than at any other time in the history of this nation,
Americans must understand the nature and implications of foreign affairs.
Yet it seems, as Heilbroner points out, that the nation is no closer to such
understanding and in fact may have slipped further away from it.

When we think back over the past few years, what strikes
us is the suddenness of [history's] blows, the unannounced
descent of its thunderbolts. Wars, revolutions, uprisings have
burst upon us with terrible rapidity.

Reading the morning newspaper has become an act no
longer anticipated with mild pleasure but with uneasy sus-
pense. The bewildering turnabouts of fortune, the abrupt
shifts of expectations, the awareness of the innumerable
microscopic factors by which our destiny may be affected,
all conspire to make of our encounter with history a frighten-
ing and disorienting ordeal.[9]

Arnold Beichman, a long-time reporter and critic of the press,

suggests that part of the trouble stems from the fact that American

dailies do a "sloppy job covering the news."

Instead of learning from continual failure, they are full
of self-congratulations at the marvellous job they are doing
and, equally sodden with self-commiseration that nobody
appreciates the great performance it is.[10]

But Beichman notes that part of the fault lies with the reporter at the scene

(often a wire-service correspondent) where stultifying, bland accounts are

written.

I watched some of my colleagues reporting the late
unpleasantness at the United Nations when Nikita Khrushchev
decided to instruct the Assembly in Marxism-Leninism.
The daily stories often resembled the reports of a tennis
match (he won the first set, we won the second set, deuce
on the third game); then you added up the score, forgetting
the "barbarous multitudes" whose heads were swivelling
from one court to the other trying to keep up.[11]

These observations and assertions are only hypotheses at the

moment, but they must ultimately be incorporated into a theory of wire-

service operation and tested under rigorous conditions. The areas of

possible investigation are many and varied, but in light of the institutional,

maturational, and relational status of the wires, the findings are important.

Footnotes

[1]Scott M. Cutlip, "Content and Flow of AP News--From Trunk to TTS to Reader," Journalism Quarterly, XXXI (Fall, 1954), p. 444.

[2]Robert J. Cranford, "Effects of the Teletypesetter Upon Newspaper Practices," Journalism Quarterly, XXIX (Spring, 1952), p. 181.

[3]Walter Gieber, "Across the Desk: A Study of 16 Telegraph Editors," Journalism Quarterly, XXXIII (Fall, 1956), p. 432.

[4]Warren Breed, "Newspaper 'Opinion Leaders' and Processes of Standardization," Journalism Quarterly, XXXII (Summer, 1955), p. 283.

[5]See Gieber, op. cit.; David Manning White, "The 'Gate Keeper': A Case Study in the Selection of News," Journalism Quarterly, XXVII (Fall, 1950), pp. 383-390; and Wilbur Schramm, "The Gatekeeper: A Memorandum," Mass Communications (2nd ed.; Urbana, Ill.: University of Illinois Press, 1960), pp. 175-177.

[6]George Gerbner, "Press Perspectives in World Communication: A Pilot Study," Journalism Quarterly, XXXVIII (Summer, 1961), pp. 313-322.

[7]Carey, op. cit., p. 175.

[8]Robert H. Sollen, "Nationalistic Bias in Reporting the Cold War," Editor & Publisher: The Fourth Estate, XCLV (July 8, 1961), p. 64. (A reprint of a speech.)

[9]Robert L. Heilbroner, The Future as History (New York: The Grove Press, Inc., 1959), p. 13.

[10]Arnold Beichman, "Report from America," Encounter, XVL (March, 1961), p. 87.

[11]Ibid., p. 90.

APPENDICES

Appendix A

WIRE-SERVICE HISTORY IN ENVIRONMENTAL PERSPECTIVE
(Chapters II & III)

Year	Wire Services: American, (FOREIGN) American Media	(INVENTIONS) Social-Cultural Environment
	A. Pre-Wire Service Media & Techniques	
1690	1st Amer. npr.	Locke's Civil Government
1702		1st daily npr in English (London)
1704	1st continuous Amer. npr	
1710		John Wise: congregational liberty
1718		1st daily npr in German (Ausburg)
1725	1st npr in New York City	
1731		1st magazine (in present sense)
1732	1st foreign language npr in U.S.	
1734	John Peter Zenger trial	
1735		Jonathan Edwards: relig. revival
1739		Hume's Human Understanding
1740		Enlightened Despots begins
1741	1st Amer. magazine	
1747		Franklin's electric experiments
1750		Romanticism begins in W. Europe
		Physiocrats
		Lit & art Classicalism ends
1754		French & Indian War
1756		Seven Years' War
1760		"1st" Industrial Revolution
1762		Rousseau's Social Contract
1763		Treaty of Paris
		Seven Years' War ends
1764		Parliament: "Sugar Act"
1765	Parliament: Stamp Act	
1767		Townsend Acts passed

Appendix A (continued)

(INVENTIONS)

Year	Wire Services: American, (FOREIGN) American Media	Social-Cultural Environment
1770		Boston Massacre
1773		Factory System begins
		Boston Tea Party
1774		1st Continental Congress
		Parliament: "Intolerable Acts"
1775		Lexington & Concord Battles
1776	Virginia Bill of Rights	Declaration of Independence
		State constitutions
		Smith's Wealth of Nations
1777		1st daily npr in Paris
		Articles of Confederation
		Vermont ends Slavery
1780	Npr advertising increases	Western land ceded to Union
		Romanticism begins in E. Europe
1781		Art. of Confederation ratified
		Kant's Critique of Pure Reason
1783	1st daily npr in Amer.	Revolutionary War ends;Amer.free
	Mercantile & Pol. nprs rise	Moves to strengthen central govt.
1784	Harbor activity in Boston	
	1st successful daily npr in US	
1785	Massachusetts taxes nprs	NW Ter. Land Ordinance
	2-column cuts, large type used	
	1st npr beyond Alleghanies	
1786		Virginia: religious freedom
		Shay's Rebellion
1787	1st "Federalist Paper" printed	Constitutional Convention
		Northwest Ordinance
1789	Bill of Rights adopted	Constitution in effect
	Fenno's Gazette of the U.S.	Washington is 1st Pres. (Fed.)
		French Revolution
		Mercantilism ends

Appendix A (continued)

Year	Wire Services: American, (FOREIGN)	American Media	Social-Cultural Environment (INVENTIONS)
1790		News handled in taverns, inns, coffee houses, ordinaries. "country" nprs increase	Funding & Assumption Acts; Burke's Reflections on Fr. Rev.; Utilitarianism - Bentham; Power-driven factory machinery
1791		Freneau's National Gazette	1st Bank of United States
1792			Washington re-elected (Fed.)
1793			U.S. neutral to European war
1794		The Farmer's Weekly Museum	(1st SEMAPHORE LINE-France); Whisky Rebellion
1796		Editorials signed by editors	Enlightened Despots ends; John Adams, Pres. (Fed.)
1798		Fed. Congress: Alien & Sedition Acts	Ky. & Va. Resolutions
1799			Fr. Revolution ends-Napolean
1800		National Intelligencer appears; Duane called before Senate	Jefferson, Pres. (Dem-Rep.); (ELECTRIC BATTERY)
1801			End of: Physiocrats, Romanticism, Enlightenment, Deism
1803			Marbury v. Madison; Louisiana Purchase
1804			1st French Empire
1805			Lewis & Clark Expedition
1807		Stereotyping Process	(FULTON'S STEAMBOAT)
1808		Fourdrinier Paper Process	Embargo Act; Madison, Pres. (Dem-Rep.)
1811	Topliff boards ships		
1812			Fr. Semaphore: 1,000 miles of lines; Madison re-elected (Dem-Rep.); War between U.S. &England

Appendix A (continued)

Year	Wire Services: American, (FOREIGN)	American Media	(INVENTIONS) Social-Cultural Environment
1813	Willington boards ships	"Columbian Press" invented	
1814		1st npr in Illinois Cylinder press developed Steam-powered printing press	Treaty of Ghent (WHITNEY'S COTTON GIN) Congress of Vienna
1815	Sandy Hook-New York City Semaphore		Battle of New Orleans, Waterloo
1816			Monroe, Pres. (Dem-Rep.) 2nd Bank of United States
1817			Richardo's Prin. of Pol-Economy
1819			Unitarian Church founded Panic of 1819
1820			McCulloch v. Maryland Monroe re-elected (Dem-Rep.) Missouri Compromise
1821	NYC nprs share expense of news		Hegel's Philosophy of Right
1822	NYC nprs meet ships, jointly, alone		Sante Fe Trail opened
1823	NY Statesman Washington reporter		Monroe Doctrine
1824			John Q. Adams, Pres. (no party) (ELECTROMAGNETISM)
1825		Steam-driven cylinder press (the Napier press)	U.S. govt Express Post Erie Canal completed
1826		NY Enquirer founded	(PHOTOGRAPHY - France) Amer. Temperance Society
1827	NY Journal of Commerce&Courier meet ships in own boats;rivalry NY "Morning Association"founded NY Enquirer Washington Reporter	NY Journal of Commerce founded NY Morning Courier founded	Indians moved west of Miss. R.

Appendix A (continued)

Year	Wire Services:American, (FOREIGN)	American Media	(INVENTIONS) Social-Cultural Environment
1828	NY Journal of Commerce schooner		Jackson, Pres. (Dem) Amer. Peace Society founded Railroad construction begins
1829	NY Courier-Enquirer clipper boat	Courier & Enquirer merge	
1830	"Morning Association" Courier- Enquirer & Journ. of Commerce receiving Washington, D.C., news		Mormon Church founded (1st LOCOMOTIVE in U.S.) July Revolution in France Romanticism ends in Europe Nativist Movement begins
1831	6 news boats at war in NY harbor		Jackson re-elected (Dem)
1832	Craig meets ships at Halifax, uses carrier pigeons Courier-Enquirer has irregular pony news from Philadelphia	Hoe enlarges Napier press	(MAGNETIC TELEGRAPH by Morse) Free Public School movement Pres. nominating conventions
1833	NY Journ. of Commerce sets up regular Philadelphia pony run Above pony run extended to Wash- ington, D.C. later in year. NY Sun meets ships, uses pigeons	NY Sun founded Start of Penny Press Era 1st npr in Chicago	Amer. Antislavery Society founded German Unification begins
1834	Nprs started using rail lines (ACENCE HAVAS founded)		
1835	NY Herald uses boats & express NY Journ. of Commerce & Courier- Enquirer use "black ponies"	NY Herald founded NY Sun's Moon Hoax	Anti-abolition riots in North Abolitionists gain free speech in Massachusetts
1836	NY Sun & Transcript join for news express from Washington Courier & Enquirer & Herald join for locomotive express from Wash- ington Nprs begin exchanging proofs.	NY Express founded Phil. Public Ledger founded	Van Buren, Pres., (Dem) (ELECTROMAGNETIC TELEGRAPH) U.S. Govt express mail service

Appendix A (continued)

Year	Wire Services:American,(FOREIGN)	American Media	Social-Cultural Environment (INVENTIONS)
1837	Three NYC harbor cooperatives: 1)Courier-Enquirer & Journ. of Commerce (2 nprs) 2)Express,Mercantile Advertiser & Gazette (3 nprs) 3)Commercial Advertiser,Evening Star & American (3 nprs) NY Herald ran its own boat NY Sun met important arrivals	Baltimore Sun founded Lovejoy murdered in Illinois	Horace Mann school reforms (Morse Patents TELEGRAPH) Plank Roads begun Panic of 1837 Ralph Waldo Emerson's address at Harvard (break from Europe)
1838	NY Herald met ships at Montauk Pt.		1st transatlantic steamboat Chartist Movement in England
1839	Bennett, 1st foreign correspondent		(PRACTICAL PHOTOGRAPH)
1840			Harrison, Pres. (Whig)
1841	NY Evening Post has correspondents in Paris and London	NY Tribune founded	Liberty Party (abolitionist) Commonwealth v. Hunt rise of trade unions in U.S.
1843			(PRUSSIAN TELEGRAPH LINE) U.S. Telegraph Approp. Bill
1844	1st telegraph news dispatch		(1st Public TELEGRAPH LINE-England) (1st Public Telegraph in U.S.)
1845			Polk, Pres. (Dem) "Manifest Destiny" 1st used Know-Nothing Party founded Texas annexed (1st FRENCH TELEGRAPH LINE)
1846	NY nprs all carry "Telegraph News" Telegraph: Portland, Me.;Buffalo, N.Y.; & Harrisburg, Pa.	1st npr on Pacific Coast Hoe's rotary printing press	Mexican War begins
1847	NYC Independent Reporters Bureau Telegraph:St. Louis & Charleston, S.C.	Chicago Tribune founded	1st women's college in U.S.

Appendix A (continued)

Year	Wire Services: American, (FOREIGN) B. Local Organization and Early Growth	American Media	Social-Cultural Environment (INVENTIONS)
1848	NY Associated Press founded, 1 political npr-Express 2 mercantile nprs-Courier-Enquirer & Journ. of Commerce 3 penny nprs-Sun, Tribune, Herald Dr. Jones, NYAP General Manager Phil. Ledger is 1st NYAP client Telegraph: Chicago & Milwaukee	Most nprs were AMs	Taylor, Pres. (Whig) Free-Soil Party appears Gold in California Mexican War ended Feb. Revolution in France; start of 2nd French Republic Italian Unification begins Marx's Communist Manifesto Chartist Movement Ends
1849	(WOLFF TELEGRAPHEN BUREAU founded)		
1850		National typographical union	Fr. Semaphore System ended Compromise of 1850 Popular reforms included: utopianism anti-Catholicism Mormonism Perfectionism Millerism spiritualism Shakerism prohibitionism nativism vegetarianism pacifism antipauperism feminism abolitionism
1851	Craig, NYAP General Agent NYAP revises contracts, methods NY Times, 7th NYAP member (REUTERS, LTD. founded)	NY Times founded	
1852	Many telegraph companies, much duplication of systems	Washington Evening Star founded	(DUPLEX TELEGRAPH-Austria) Stowe's Uncle Tom's Cabin 2nd French Empire begins Pierce, Pres. (Dem)
1853	NYAP ends local, regional competition		Republican Party replaces Whigs (WOOD PULP PAPER) Crimean War begins

Appendix A (continued)

Year	Wire Services: American, (FOREIGN) American Media		Social-Cultural Environment (INVENTIONS)
1855	Western Union organized; gives exclusive service to NYAP		Whitman's Leaves of Grass Thoreau's Walden Industrial expansion is rapid
1856	NYAP reorganized, expanded		Buchanan, Pres. (Dem)
1857			Dred Scott decision
1858	1st Atlantic cable (failed)		Pikes Peak gold rush 1st oil well (Titusville)
1859	NY World gets NYAP membership replacing Courier-Enquirer	1st formal interview (Greeley & Brigham Young)	Mill's On Liberty Darwin's Origin of Species
1860	Amer. Telegraph Co. absorbed by Western Union		Lincoln, Pres. (Rep) Dems split in convention South Carolina secedes 1st evidence of large cities Western Pony Express "2nd" Industrial Revolution
1861			Civil War begins Morrill Tariff Act passed Russian serfs emancipated

C. Regional Organization & Drive for Stability

Year	Wire Services		Social-Cultural Environment
1862	Western AP formed (15 representatives from Pa., Ohio, Ind., Ill., Mich., Mo., &Ky.)		Civil War continues Homestead Act passed Pacific Railway Act passed Railroad land grants
1863			Civil War continues Emancipation Proclamation (1st BESSEMER STEEL PLANT) National Banking Act passed
1864			Civil War continues Lincoln re-elected (Rep)

Appendix A (continued)

Year	Wire Services: American, (FOREIGN)	American Media	Social-Cultural Environment (INVENTIONS)
1865	WAP incorporated in Michigan	Web printing press developed	Civil War ends
	War increases telegraph system		13th Amendment
			Southern "Black Codes"
1866	Simonton, NYAP General Agent		Ku Klux Klan organized
	NYAP-WAP agreement, partnership		"Radicals" in Congress
	Successful Atlantic cable		Austro-Prussian war
1867	NYAP-WAP get exclusive contract		Reconstruction Acts passed
	with Western Union		Tenure of Office Act passed
	Northwestern AP incorporated in		Range-cattle industry begins
	Illinois; NY State AP in NY.		Marx's Das Kapital
	New England AP founded		2nd English Reform Act
1868		Web perfecting press	Pres. Johnson impeached
			Grant, Pres. (Rep)
			(TYPEWRITER)
			14 Amend. in effect
			Tweed Ring in NYC
1869	Hasson News Assn. formed for PMs		15th Amend. sent to states
			Transcontinental RR completed
1870	Hasson renamed Amer. Press Assn.	NY Times & Harper's campaign against NYC Tweed Ring	Impressionism begins
			Franco-Prussian War
1871	APA incorporated in Pennsylvania		Law of Papal Guaranties
1872			Grant re-elected (Rep)
1873		1st daily illustrated npr	Depression begins
			Silver demonetized
1875			Credit Mobilier & Whisky Ring
			(Bell's TELEPHONE)
			Germ theory of disease
			3rd French Republic begins
1876		Chicago Daily News founded	Hayes, Pres. (Rep)-Dispute
			War with Sioux Indians
			(INTERNAL COMBUSTION ENGINE)

Appendix A (continued)

Year	Wire Services: American, (FOREIGN)	American Media	(INVENTIONS) Social-Cultural Environment
1877	APA reorganized as National Assoc. Press Company		(Edison's PHONOGRAPH) Granger Cases Federal troops leave South Railroad strikes
1878		Pulitzer buys St. Louis Dispatch merges it with Post	Greenback Party at peak Knights of Labor organized Bland-Allison Act passed Congress of Berlin Standard Oil trust formed Greenbacks redeemed in gold George's Progress & Poverty
1879	AP's 1st leased wire (Washington to New York)		Garfield, Pres. (Rep)
1880		More PM than AM nprs Halftone engraving developed	
1881	Postal Telegraph Co. organized		Civil Service Act passed
1882	Wm. H. Smith, AP General Agent UP formed, incorp. in NY State; took over APA & NAPC movement; Included: Boston Globe, Phil. Public Ledger, NY Daily News, Chicago Herald, Detroit News.		Triple Alliance appears
1883	Commercial Cable Co. organized	Pulitzer buys NY World (AP npr)	Cleveland, Pres. (Dem)
1884	AP's 2nd leased wire (Chi-NYC)	Typewriter used in npr office	Mugwump Revolt in GOP 3rd English Reform Act
1885	UP duplicating AP news service	Mergenthaler Linotype	(A. C. TRANSFORMER) Farm prices decline
1886			Amer. Fed. of Labor formed 14th Amend protects corporations Chicago strikes & riots Final defeat of S. W. Indians

Appendix A (continued)

Year	Wire Services: American, (FOREIGN)	American Media	Social-Cultural Environment (INVENTIONS)
1887	AP-Havas-Reuters-Wolff cartel UP incorporated in Illinois		(PHONOGRAPH RECORD) Interstate Commerce Act passed Farmers Alliance grows Dawes Act - Indian policy
1888	NY Sun sets up Laffan News Bureau		Harrison, Pres. (Rep)
1890		2/3rds of nprs are PMs	Sherman Antitrust Act End of U.S. frontier McKinley Tariff passed
1891	WAP probes NYAP-UP stock exchange Southern AP founded	Munsey begins chain building Halftones sent by wire	
1892	NYAP-UP agreements disclosed; WAP moves to control organization NY Sun & Tribune leave AP, join UP AP (National) incorporates in Ill., absorbs several regional APs.	NYC: 9 AMs, 7 PMs, 13 foreign- language, & 14 class nprs.	Cleveland, Pres. (Dem) People's Party formed Mesabi iron-ore range (COLOR PHOTOGRAPH)
	D. National Organization & Rise of Competition		
1893.	AP included most of nprs in Phil. & Baltimore, & NY World Stone, AP General Manager AP signs exclusive contract with Reuters, Havas & Wolff AP-UP agreements sought; UP un- willing; AP-UP competition be- comes keen.		Depression begins (Edison's MOVIE MACHINE)
1894	Russo-Japanese War covered by AP	Wm. L. McLean buys Phil. Bulletin	(MOTION PICTURE PROJECTOR) Pullman strike;Coxey's Army Populist Movement grows Russo-Japanese War Electricity used for factories
1895	Wireless telegraph developed	Marconi radio signals	

Appendix A (continued)

Year	Wire Services: American, (FOREIGN)	American Media	Social-Cultural Environment (INVENTIONS)
1896	Height of AP recruitment, raiding in UP's eastern territory	NY World & Journal (Pulitzer & Hearst) begin Yellow Journalism	McKinley, Pres. (Rep.) / Bryan, Dem & Populist nominee
1897	UP declares bankruptcy / NY Sun avoids AP, enlarges Laffan / Scripps-McRae Press Assn. formed / Scripps News Assn. formed	Corbett-Fitzsimmons fight movies	
1898	Publishers Press Assn. formed / AP's extensive coverage of war / AP criticized for war coverage / AP-Inter-Ocean dispute begins		Spanish-American War / Puerto Rico, Guam, Hawaii & Philippines acquired by U.S.
1899		Yellow Journalism at its peak	Philippine Insurrections / Boar War begins / China Open-Door policy by U.S. / McKinley re-elected (Rep) / Boxer Rebellion (China)
1900	AP affected with public interest says Illinois Supreme Court in Chicago Inter-Ocean case / AP incorporates in New York State	8 chains control 27 nprs.	
1901			TR involved in coal strike / U.S. Steel formed
1902			1st state workmen's compensation law
1903		"The Great Train Robbery" 1st motion picture telling story / 1st telephone wirephoto- Germany	Panama revolt aided by U.S.
1904			Roosevelt, Pres. (Rep) / Corollary to Monroe Doctrine / Entente cordiale appears / Russo-Japanese War / Lochner v. New York
1905			Russian Revolt / Einstein theories disclosed

Appendix A (continued)

Year	Wire Services: American, (FOREIGN)	American Media	Social-Cultural Environment (INVENTION)
1906			Human voice sent by radio
			Hepburn Act & Pure Food and Drug Act passed
1907	United Press Associations formed; established for PMs; included:		
	Scripps-McRae Press Assn.		
	Scripps News Service		
	Publishers Press Assn.		
1908	Howard, UP General Manager		Taft, Pres. (Rep)
			Bosnian Crisis
1909	International News Service formed		Payne-Aldrich Tariff
	(Hearst service for AM nprs)		Lenin's Materialism & Empirio-Criticism
	National Press Association formed		
	(Hearst service for PM nprs)		
	Farrelly, INS-NPA operations chief		
1910	Hearst forms International News Photos	12 Chains control 50 nprs.	
	Morkrum Co. develops teletype		
1911	Hearst merges INS &NPA		Standard Oil dissolved
1912	Howard, UP Pres. & Gen. Mgr.	Radio Act (licensing)	Wilson, Pres. (Dem)
	AP creates traffic dept.		Balkan Wars
1913			16th & 17th Amends. ratified
			Federal Reserve & Underwood Tariff Acts passed

E. International Organization & Technological Impetus

1914	La Nacion asks for AP service	End of Yellow Journalism	Clayton Antitrust Act passed
	AP introduces teletype in NYC	1st commercial use of radio	World War I begins in Europe
	AP-50,000 miles of leased wires		
	UP-15,000 miles of leased wires		

Appendix A (continued)

Year	Wire Services: American, (FOREIGN)	American Media	(INVENTIONS) Social-Cultural Environment
1915	AP allows nprs to use other wires UP uses teletype outside of NYC		Germans sink Lusitania
1916	UP starts Latin Amer. service Munsey buys NY Sun; Laffan News Bureau dies; Sun combined with Press (an AP npr)	Munsey begins consolidations 1st broadcast of news	Wilson re-elected (Dem) U.S. offers war mediation
1917	INS denied British & French cables Hearst forms Universal Service for AM service Amer. Press Assn. bought by Western Newspaper Union (a mat & plate serv.)	Espionage Act passed	U.S. enters WWI Russian Revolution begins
1918	Howard (UP) & Cooper (AP) travel Latin Amer. recruiting clients War coverage improves wire copy UP's false armistice (Howard) (ROSTA founded in RUSSIA)	Sedition Act passed	WWI Armistice signed Wilson's 14 Points
1919	La Prensa receives UP service	Whitney v. Calif. (Clear & Present Danger) 1st major U.S. tabloid (NY News) NY Times forms Wide World Photos	Versailles Peace Conference Weimar Republic formed
1920	UP begins service for AMs Hawkins, UP President	1st radio patent pool cartel Pioneer radio stations created WWJ, 1st npr-owned station (Detroit News)	Harding, Pres. (Rep) Prohibition in effect Red Scare in U.S. Women Suffrage in effect Dewey's Reconstruction in Philosophy
1921	F. R. Martin, AP General Manager UP begins service to Europe		

Appendix A (continued)

Year	Wire Services: American, (FOREIGN)	American Media	Social-Cultural Environment (INVENTIONS)
1922	AP prohibits clients from broad-casting AP news on radio	Amer. Society of Npr Editors	Post War prosperity begins Insulin Discovered Fascist revolt in Italy
1923	Bickel, UP President	Time begins new magazine trend Picture televised (NYC-Phil.)	Scandals in government; Harding dies in office. Ku Klux Klan reaches peak
1924	Acme Newspictures formed as UP & NEA subsidiary	Tabloid Journalism at its peak AT&T telephotography	Coolege, Pres. (Rep) Immigration Act passed 1st Labor Govt. in Britain Lenin's death; Stalin accedes
1925	Cooper, AP General Manager AP uses bylines, livlier copy AP relaxes broadcast rules (ROSTA renamed TASS-in RUSSIA)	Gitlow v. New York (bad tend.) 60 chains control 300 nprs.	Scopes trial in Tennessee Locarno Agreements
1926	Teletypesetter developed	NBC organized 1st of Book Clubs appear AT&T begins limited national wirephoto service Radio-AT&T cartel (doom for Western Union)	Whitehead's Science & the Modern World
1927		2nd NBC Network (Blue) formed Radio Act of 1927 (limited licensing to 3 years) United Independent Broadcaster is formed (later becomes CBS)	Lindbergh flies Atlantic Sacco, Vanzetti executed
1928	Morkrum-Kleinschmidt teletype AP inaugurates AP Newspictures AP-UP-INS give radio news scripts INS serving AMs;Universal Service gives supple. &spec. services.	1st Disney animated cartoon Regular TV schedule, Schenectedy	Hoover, Pres., (Rep) Stock market at its peak Kellogg-Briand Pact

Appendix A (continued)

Year	Wire Services: American (FOREIGN)	American Media	(INVENTIONS) Social-Cultural Environment
1929	AP-UP-INS radio service enlarged 1st npr experiment with TTS	Armstrong develops FM radio Coaxial cable developed	Stock market collapse 1st USSR 5-Yr Plan 2nd Labor Govt. in Britain
1930		Npr. Ad. revenue:$860,000,000 90 AM Stns affiliated with nprs. AT&T acquires Teletype Corp. Npr circulation: 40,000,000 Npr. Ad. revenue:15% below'29 Npr. Ad. revenue:24% below'29	Bank failures increase Smoot-Hawley Tariff Penicillin discovered
1931	TTS used on practical basis	Near v. Minnesota	Hoover freezes war debts Britain off gold standard Japan seizes Manchuria 2nd British Labor Govt. ends Spanish Monarch overthrown
1932	Hellschreiber invented	Npr Adv. revenue:40% below'29	Roosevelt, Pres. (Dem) Reconstruction Finance Corp. Bonus Army ejected from Capital 15 million unemployed Britain ends free trade
1933	"Biltmore agreement" ends AP-UP-INS supply of radio news CBS begins forming own news staff "Biltmore agreement" sets up Press Radio Bureau (Pact between: AP, UP, INS, ANPA, CBS&NBC) (WOLFF reorganized by Hitler as DNB)	Npr Adv. revenue:45% below'29 Npr circulation:12% below'30 Amer. Npr Guild founded	Nat'l Industrial Recovery Act Ag Adjustment Act TVA, CCC created "Lameduck" Amendment Prohibition repealed Bank holiday U.S. off gold standard "Good Neighbor" policy
1934	AP ends cartel with Reuters, Havas. Transradio Press Service formed (to compete with Press Radio Bureau)	Television becomes prevalent Communications Act - FCC Mutual Broadcasting System formed	Nazis seize Weimar Republic Additional New Deal legislation.

Appendix A (continued)

Year	Wire Services:American(FOREIGN)	American Media	Social-Cultural Environment (INVENTIONS)
1935	AP begins Wirephoto Service INS begins Soundphoto Service Baillie, UP President UP & INS supply news to radio Last of Morse equipment disappears		NRA & AAA invalidated Social Security, NLRB & WPA CIO breaks with AFL 1st Amer. Neutrality Act Italo-Ethiopian war
1936	UP begins NEA-Acme Telephoto	Scripps Chain Dominance ends NY Times begins Wire Photos Life starts new magazine trend	Roosevelt re-elected (Dem) Rhineland remilitarized Spanish Civil War begins Berlin-Rome Axis Militarists win in Japan
1937	NLRB v. AP decided for NLRB	Npr Adv. revenue:$630,000,000 Npr. circulation:41,500,000 Hearst Chain dominance ends	Court packing fight Economic recession Auto & Steel strikes Japan invades China
1938	Robt.McLean, AP President AP begins pony Wirephoto UP, ANG sign contract	St. Louis Post-Dispatch facsimile	"Parity" established Wages & Hours Bill passed Nazis overrun Austria Munich Agreement
1939	AP allows news broadcast on sponsored programs AP sends 1st color Wirephotos	1st regular TV broadcasts	Repeal Amer.Arms Embargo Nazi-Soviet agreement Nazis invade Poland League of Nations ends Franco reigns in Spain (ATOMIC FISSION)
1940	AP: 285,000 miles of leased wire UP: 176,000 miles of leased wire Transradio Press Serv. serves 175 Stations, 50 Nprs (Fr.Govt.buys HAVAS as tool)	250 Stns affiliated with nprs Keystone Broadcasting Co. 1st sponsored TV news broadcast	Roosevelt re-elected (Dem) Selective Service Act France defeated in 6 weeks Nazis invade Denmark & Norway Destroyers-bases deal with Britain

Appendix A (continued)

Year	Wire Services: American (FOREIGN)	American Media	Social-Cultural Environment (INVENTIONS)
1941		Full commercial TV authorized	Lend-Lease Act passed
			Nazis invade Russia
			Atlantic Charter
			Japan attacks Pearl Harbor
			World War II
1942	Chi. Sun brings antitrust action against AP for non-admission	NBC's Blue Network made separate	
	Dist. Court upholds US in US v AP		
1943			Teheran Conference
			Cairo Conference
1944	AP's False D-Day flash		D-Day invasion of Europe
	(AGENCE FRANCE-PRESSE formed from old HAVAS)		Dumbarton Oaks Conference
			Roosevelt re-elected (Dem)
1945	Supreme Court upholds US in US v. AP	Old Blue Network (NBC) becomes ABC	Nazi surrender, May 7
			2 atomic bomb drops
	AP amends membership bylaws	War casualties: 37 reporters	Japanese surrender, Aug. 15
	AP's premature armistice flash	killed, 112 wounded	Yalta Conference
	UP's false Japanese armistice		United Nations formed
			3rd Labor Govt. in Britain
			Potsdam Conference
1946	AP opens assoc. membership to Radio		Peron reigns in Argentina
			Cold War begins
			4th French Republic
1947			Marshall Plan announced
			Truman Doctrine - rearm
			Taft-Hartley Law passed
			Communist coup in Hungary
			Reds seize Czechoslovakia
1948	Starzel, AP General Manager	Great TV expansion begins; No. of sets increased by 1 million during the year.	Berlin blockade, airlift
			Truman, Pres. (Dem)
1949			USSR has atomic device
			NATO created
			Reds win Chinese Civil War

Appendix A (continued)

(INVENTIONS)

Year	Wire Services:American(FOREIGN)	American Media	Social-Cultural Environment
1950	AP's premature Inchon landing	Interpretative-objective dispute	Korean War begins
1951	AP, UP, INS develop TTS circuits UP begins daily news film service for TV	Dennis v. U.S. (gravity of evil) War casualties: 17 killed while reporting	Korean Armistice Gen. MacArthur recalled
1952	UP begins world newsphoto service TTS wires going to 600 nprs UP converts overseas radio transmission from Morse to printer	End TV freeze; many new stations	Eisenhower, Pres. (Rep) Hydrogen bomb
1953	INS involved in foreign PR work UP begins facsimile photo service for television stations	Color TV authorized by FCC (CBS) ABC enters TV field	Korean treaty signed USSR hydrogen explosion Stalin dies Anti-Red riots in E. Berlin
1954	UP extends facsimile to nprs.		Brown v. Topeka McCarthy anti-Red hearings Reds win in Indochina SEATO organized
1955	Bartholomew, UP President	DuMont TV network dissolved	AFL-CIO merger Anti-polio vaccine Warsaw Pact signed 1st "Summit" meeting (Geneva)
1956	1st transatlantic telephone cable		Eisenhower re-elected (Rep.) Hungarian revolt
1957			1st U.N. police force 1st man-made satellite (USSR) Little Rock school crisis
1958	UP absorbs INS; result is UPI	Mutual & Keystone are "service networks" furnishing "feeds"	1st U.S. satellite 1st domestic jet air service Khrushchev gains power in Russia
1959		Rigged TV quiz shows probed	Castro gains power in Cuba

Appendix A (continued)

Year	Wire Services:American(FOREIGN)	American Media	Social-Cultural Environment (INVENTIONS)
1960		Echo I, passive com. satellite	Kennedy, Pres. (Dem)
			1st Fr. nuclear explosion
			U-2 incident ends summit
1961			Gagarin, 1st man in space
1962		114-day NYC npr strike	Court's prayer decision
		Kennedy proposes satellite co.	Stock exchange slump
		AT&T's Telstar launched	Ol' Miss integrated
			Geneva Disarmament talks
1963	AP stock lists computerized.		

Appendix B

STATISTICAL TABLES
(Chapters IV-VII)

Table 1. Board Representation of City Sizes: Selected Years

2.22*   1892-1893

   8*- M. H. de Young, San Francisco Chronicle
  - - William A. Collier, Memphis Appeal-Avalanche 64,495*
  16 - James E. Scripps, Detroit Tribune & Evening News
   9 - Frederick Driscoll, St. Paul Pioneer Press**
  11 - Eugene H. Perdue, Cleveland Leader
   2 - Washington Hesing, (Chicago) Illinois Staats Zeitung
  14 - Albert J. Barr, Pittsburgh Post
   5 - Charles W. Knapp, St. Louis Republic
   2 - Victor Lawson, Chicago Record & Daily News
67/36 - 1.86   2.22   .36 - 64,495

1.12   1900-1901

  16 - Frank B. Noyes, Washington Evening Star
   1 - Don C. Seitz, New York World
  12 - Albert J. Barr, Pittsburgh Post
   4 - Charles W. Knapp, St. Louis Republic
  13 - Thomas G. Rapier, New Orleans Picayune
  10 - M. H. de Young, San Francisco Chronicle
   1 - Whitelaw Reid, New York Tribune
   3 - W. L. McLean, Philadelphia Evening Bulletin
   8 - George Thompson, St. Paul Dispatch**
  11 - Charles P. Taft, Cincinnati Times-Star
   6 - Charles H. Grasty, Baltimore Evening News
   5 - Stephen O'Meara, Boston Journal
  41 - Harvey W. Scott, Portland Oregonian
   1 - Herman Ridder, New York Staats-Zeitung
   2 - Victor Lawson, Chicago Daily News
134/120 - 1.12   1.12   .00 - 0

1.94   1910-1911

  16 - Frank B. Noyes, Washington Evening Star
   3 - W. L. McLean, Philadelphia Evening Bulletin
  17 - W. R. Nelson, Kansas City Star**
   1 - Adolph S. Ochs, New York Times
  - - A. C. Weiss, Duluth Herald 78,466
   5 - Charles H. Taylor, Boston Globe

Table 1 (continued)

```
15 - Thomas G. Rapier, New Orleans Picayune
 1 - Herman Ridder, New York Staats-Zeitung
28 - Harvey W. Scott, Portland Oregonian
 2 - Victor Lawson, Chicago Daily News
 8 - Albert J. Barr, Pittsburgh Post
 - - Charles Hopkins Clark, Hartford Courant. . . .  98,915
 4 - Charles W. Knapp, St. Louis Republic
31 - Clark Howell, Atlanta Constitution
 - - V. S. McClatchy, Sacramento Bee                 44,696
131/78 - 1.68                1.94           .26 -222,077 - 74,026
```

3.87   1920-1921

```
14 - Frank B. Noyes, Washington Evening Star
 2 - Victor Lawson, Chicago Daily News
45 - R.M. Johnston, Houston Post
66 - W.H. Cowles, Spokane Spokesman-Review
29 - D.E. Town, Louisville Herald
 - - Frank B. McLennan, Topeka State Journal. . .   50,022
33 - Clark Howell, Atlanta Constitution
 - - V.S. McClatchy, Sacramento Bee . . . . . . .   65,908
46 - Charles Hopkins Clark, Hartford Courant
 9 - Charles A. Rook, Pittsburgh Dispatch
 5 - Elbert H. Baker, Cleveland Plain Dealer
 3 - W.L. McLean, Philadelphia Evening Bulletin
 1 - Adolph S. Ochs, New York Times
 - - A.C. Weiss, Duluth Herald . . . . . . . . . .   98,917
27 - John R. Rathom, Providence Journal
280/78 - 3.59               3.87           .28 - 214,847 - 71,616
```

4.35   1930-1931

```
15 - Frank B. Noyes, Washington Evening Star
31 - Clark Howell, Atlanta Constitution
 6 - Elbert H. Baker, Cleveland Plain Dealer
 - - Stuart H. Perry, Adrian (Mich.)Telegram . .    13,064
30 - J.R. Knowland, Oakland Tribune
51 - Richard Hooker, Springfield (Mass.)Republican
 1 - Adolph S. Ochs, New York Times
74 - B.H. Anthony, New Bedford (Mass.)Standard
 3 - Robert McLean, Philadelphia Evening Bulletin
10 - Frederick E. Murphy, Minneapolis Tribune**
69 - W.H. Cowles, Spokane Spokesman-Review
 - - Frank P. McLennan, Topeka State Journal. . .   64,120
 7 - E. Lansing Ray, St. Louis Globe-Democrat
 - - Frederick I. Thompson, Mobile Register . . .   68,202
 2 - Robert R. McCormick, Chicago Tribune
299/78 - 3.83               4.35           .52 - 145,386 - 48,462
```

Table 1 (continued)

3.40   1940-1941

  3 - Robert McLean, Philadelphia Evening Bulletin
 12 - Frank B. Noyes, Washington Evening Star
  9 - Frederick E. Murphy, Minneapolis Times-Tribune**
  7 - Paul Patterson, Baltimore Sun
 16 - E.H. Butler, Buffalo News
  - - Josh L. Horne, Rocky Mount (N.C.) Telegram.   25,568
 67 - W.H. Cowles, Spokane Spokesman-Review
  8 - E. Lansing Ray, St. Louis Globe-Democrat
  - - Stuart H. Perry, Adrian (Mich.) Telegram. . .   14,230
  2 - Robert R. McCormick, Chicago Tribune
 15 - George B. Longan, Kansas City Star**
 17 - L.K. Nicholson, New Orleans Times-Picayune
 29 - J.R. Knowland, Oakland Tribune
  6 - Paul Bellamy, Cleveland Plain Dealer
 54 - John Cowles, Des Moines Register
 28 - Clark Howell, Atlanta Constitution
 41 - E.K. Gaylord, Oklahoma City Oklahoman
  - - Houston Harte, San Angelo (Tex.)Standard. . .   25,802
314/120 - 2.62   3.40   .78 - 65,600 - 21,867

2.69   1950-1951

  3 - Robert McLean, Philadelphia Evening Bulletin
  8 - E. Lansing Ray, St. Louis Globe-Democrat
 17 - L.K. Nicholson, New Orleans Times-Picayune
 15 - Roy A. Roberts, Kansas City Star**
 24 - Palmer Hoyt, Denver Post
  - - Stuart H. Perry, Adrian (Mich.)Telegram. . .   18,383
  2 - John S. Knight, Chicago Daily News
 27 - J.R. Knowland, Oakland Tribune
  7 - Paul Bellamy, Cleveland Plain Dealer
  1 - Arthur Hays Sulzberger, New York Times
 32 - Paul Miller, Rochester (N.Y.) Democrat & Chronicle
 10 - Robert B. Choate, Boston Herald
 38 - James M. North, Jr., Fort Worth Star Telegram
  - - Harry F. Byrd, Jr., Winchester (Va.) Star. .   13,841
  9 - Benjamin M. McKelway, Washington Star
  4 - Norman Chandler, Los Angeles Times
 34 - James E. Chappell, Birmingham Age-Herald
  - - O.S. Warden, Great Falls (Mont.) Tribune. .   39,214
231/120 - 1.93   2.69   .76 - 71,438 - 23,813

Table 1 (continued)

6. 65   1960-1961

   8 - Benjamin M. McKelway, Washington Star
  47 - John R. Reitemeyer, Hartford Courant
   1 - Richard W. Clarke, New York Daily News
   - - Raymond L. Spangler, Redwood City Tribune. . 46,290
  75 - W. H. Cowles, Spokane Spokesman-Review
   - - Henry D. Bradley, St. Joseph (Mo.) Gazette . . 79,673
   4 - Robert McLean, Philadelphia Evening Bulletin
  71 - Kenneth MacDonald, Des Moines Tribune
  18 - John W. Runyon, Dallas Times-Herald
   - - Millard Cope, Marshall (Tex.) News Messenger 23,846
  77 - Franklin D. Schurz, South Bend Tribune
   - - Hugh N. Boyd, New Brunswick (N. J.) Home News 40, 139
   - - Harold A. Fitzgerald, Pontiac (Mich.) Press . 82,233
 113 - Bernard H. Ridder, Jr., Duluth News-Tribune
   3 - W. D. Maxwell, Chicago Tribune
  22 - George W. Healy, Jr., New Orleans Times-Picayune
   - - Max E. Nussbaum, Moultrie (Ga.) Observer . 15,764
  39 - Paul Miller, Rochester (N. Y.) Times-Union
478/78 - 6. 13   6. 65   . 52 - 287,945 - 47,991

---

* Numbers on the left are indices of the city's population ranking in a rank
order of all urban places over 100,000 population, according to the appropriate U. S. Census reports. The total of these index numbers is divided
by the sum of the first n numbers, where n is the total number of cities represented by a population of 100,000 or more. Thus, if 15 such cities were
represented (as is the case of the boards during 1900-1901, 1940-1941, and
1950-1951), the quotient would be 1. 00, if those 15 cities were the 15 most
populous in the United States, according to a rank order. The larger this
quotient, therefore, the more diversified and the less populous (and the
more representative) are the cities represented on the board. The numbers on the right are the actual population totals for cities of less than
100,000 population. These are totaled, averaged (number on the extreme
right), rounded to the nearest thousand, made a decimal number, and subtracted from 1. 00. In effect, the smaller the average, the larger the
difference between that average and 100,000 (or, by conversion, 1. 00) and,
therefore, the larger the final index number on the right for cities of less
than 100,000 population. The index numbers on the left and right are
added to give the final index of representation on the board. The larger
that final index, the more representative is the board of smaller communities.
    The important underlying assumption here is that an evenly dis-
persed city representation on the board (in terms of population and number
of cities) is reflective of an equally even dispersement of the U. S. population

Table 1 (continued)

among cities of various sizes and of the even dispersement of the various-
sized cities themselves. The U.S. Census figures below indicate that
population dispersement among cities has been relatively equal between
1890 and 1950 while the number of smaller cities (i.e., those with populations of less than 100,000) have greatly outnumbered their larger counterparts. (Population distribution among cities with daily newspapers follows
a similar pattern as figures in Appendix C will reveal.)

| | % of Total Population | | No. of Urban Places | |
| | Over | Under | Over | Under |
Year	100,000	100,000	100,000	100,000
1890	15.4	19.7	28	1,320
1900	18.7	21.0	38	1,699
1910	22.1	23.6	50	2,212
1920	25.9	25.3	68	2,654
1930	29.6	26.6	93	3,072
1940	28.9	27.6	92	3,372
1950	29.5	29.5	107	3,916

SOURCE: United States Bureau of the Census, Historical
Statistics of the United States: Colonial Times to 1957
(Washington: Government Printing Office, 1960), p. 14.

** Directors from newspapers in either St. Paul or Minneapolis are considered here as representing both cities, and their ranking is based on the
combined St. Paul-Minneapolis population. The same is true for directors
from newspapers in either Kansas City, Mo., or Kansas City, Kan.

SOURCES: various numbers of the Associated Press (Illinois and New
York) Volumes and U.S. Bureau of the Census, Abstract of the
Eleventh Census: 1890 (Washington: Government Printing Office,
1896), pp. 34-37, 88; Abstract of the Twelvth Census: 1900 (1904),
pp. 100-102; Abstract of the Fourteenth Census: 1920 (1923), pp.
50-51ff; Abstract of the Fifteenth Census: 1930 (1933), pp. 22-24ff;
Abstract of the Sixteenth Census: 1940 (1943), p. 32ff; Characteristics of the Population, United States Summary: 1950 (1953),
pp. 46-47; and Characteristics of the Population, United States
Summary: 1960 (1964), p. 50ff.

Table 2. Board Representation of Newspapers: 1893-1964
(Rank ordered by years)

Yrs.

Yrs.			
68 - Washington Star		9 - Duluth News Tribune	
65 - Philadelphia Bulletin		Houston Post	
48 - New Orleans Times-Picayune		New York Daily News	
44 - Atlanta Constitution		New York World	
43 - Spokane Spokesman-Review		Oklahoma City Oklahoman	
40 - New York Times		Worcester (Mass.) Telegram	
39 - Cleveland Plain Dealer		8 - Cleveland News	
36 - Kansas City Star & Times		Denver Post	
35 - Chicago Daily News		Des Moines Tribune	
30 - Adrian (Mich.) Telegram		Great Falls (Mont.)Tribune	
29 - Chicago Tribune		Minneapolis Journal	
Hartford Courant		St. Paul Dispatch	
Oakland Tribune		Waterbury (Conn.)Republican	
St. Louis Globe-Democrat		7 - Birmingham News	
24 - St. Louis Republic		Boston Journal	
20 - Baltimore Sun		Dallas Herald	
Pittsburgh Post		Dayton Daily News	
18 - Birmingham Age-Herald		Fort Worth Star-Telegram	
San Francisco Chronicle		Louisville Herald	
17 - New York Staats-Zeitung		Providence Journal	
16 - Topeka State Journal		St. Paul Pioneer Press	
15 - Rocky Mount (N.C.) Telegram		5 - Marshall (Tex.)News-Messenger	
14 - Sacramento Bee		New Brunswick (N.J.)Home News	
13 - Buffalo News		New York Tribune	
Los Angeles Times		Philadelphia North American	
Pontiac (Mich.) Daily Press		Rochester (N.Y.)Times-Union	
Portland Oregonian		St. Joseph (Mo.) Gazette	
Rochester (N.Y.) Democrat-Chronicle		South Bend Tribune	
12 - Minneapolis Tribune		4 - Cincinnati Volksblatt	
Winchester (Va.) Evening Star		Cleveland Leader & News-Herald	
11 - Baltimore News		Detroit Tribune & News	
Boston Globe		Moultrie (Ga.) Observer	
Boston Herald		3 - Cincinnati Times-Star	
Des Moines Register		Dallas News	
Duluth Herald		Holyoke (Mass.)Transcript-	
Pittsburgh Dispatch		Telegram	
New York Evening Post		Hutchinson (Kan.) News	
San Angelo Standard		Phoenix Gazette	
10 - Lawrence (Kan.) Journal World		Springfield (Mass.) Union	
Louisville Courier-Journal		2 - Atlanta Journal	
Miami Herald		Brooklyn Eagle	
New Bedford (Mass.) Standard		Chicago Inter-Ocean	
Redwood City Tribune		Davenport Times	
Springfield (Mass.) Republican		Decatur (Ill.) Herald	

Table 2 (continued)

Denver Republican
Memphis Appeal-Avalanche
Memphis Commercial Appeal
Muskegon (Mich.) Chronicle
New Orleans States
Savannah News
Syracuse Herald
1 - Albany Knickerbocker News
Augusta Chronicle
Boise Statesman
Boston Traveler
Charleston (S.C.) News &Courier
Cincinnati Enquirer
Columbus (Ohio) Dispatch
(Chicago) Ill. Staats-Zeitung
Little Rock Gazette
Milwaukee Journal
Omaha Bee
Portland (Me.) Express & Advertiser
(Denver) Rocky Mountain News
St. Louis Post-Dispatch
Salt Lake City Tribune
Syracuse Post-Standard
Wausau (Wis.) Record Herald
Woonsocket (R.I.) Evening Call

SOURCE: various numbers of the Associated Press (Illinois and New York) Volumes.

Table 3.   Board Representation of Cities: 1893-1964
(Rank ordered by years)

Yrs.

93 - New York City		St. Paul		St. Joseph, Mo.
70 - Philadelphia	14 -	Sacramento		South Bend
68 - Washington	13 -	Buffalo	4 -	Detroit
67 - Chicago		Los Angeles		Memphis
54 - St. Louis		Pontiac, Mich.		Moultrie, Ga.
51 - Cleveland		Portland, Ore.	3 -	Holyoke, Mass.
50 - New Orleans		Springfield, Mass.		Hutchinson, Kan.
46 - Atlanta	12 -	Winchester, Va.		Phoenix
43 - Spokane	11 -	Denver		Syracuse
36 - Kansas City		San Angelo	2 -	Brooklyn
35 - St. Paul-Minneap.	10 -	Dallas		Davenport
31 - Baltimore		Lawrence, Kan.		Decatur, Ill.
Pittsburgh		Miami		Muskegon, Mich.
30 Adrian, Mich.		New Bedford, Mass.		Savannah, Ga.
Boston		Redwood City	1 -	Albany, N.Y.
29 - Hartford	9 -	Houston		Augusta
Oakland		Oklahoma City		Boise
25 - Birmingham		Worcester, Mass.		Charleston, S.C.
20 - Duluth	8 -	Cincinnati		Columbus, Ohio
Minneapolis		Great Falls, Mont.		Little Rock
19 - Des Moines		Waterbury, Conn.		Milwaukee
18 - Rochester, N.Y.	7 -	Dayton		Omaha
San Francisco		Fort Worth		Portland, Me.
17 - Louisville		Providence		Salt Lake City
16 - Topeka	5 -	Marshall, Texas		Wausau, Wis.
15 - Rocky Mount, N.C.		New Brunswick, N.J.		Woonsocket

SOURCE: Various numbers of the Associated Press (Illinois & New York)
Volumes.

Table 4. Board Representation of States: 1893-1964
(Rank ordered by years)

Yrs.

130 - New York (1)*	25 - Alabama (29)	Idaho (42)
101 - Pennsylvania (2)	21 - Iowa (11)	Maine (34)
95 - Missouri (12)	17 - Kentucky (20)	Nebraska (35)
84 - California (5)	15 - North Carolina (16)	South Carolina (31)
69 - Illinois (4)	13 - Oregon (31)	Utah (45)
68 - Dist. of Col. (48)	12 - Virginia (14)	0 - Alaska (50)
67 - Ohio (6)	11 - Colorado (21)	Delaware (49)
65 - Massachusetts(10)	10 - Florida (18)	Hawaii (51)
55 - Minnesota (14)	9 - Oklahoma (26)	Mississippi (30)
53 - Georgia (23)	8 - Montana (27)	Nevada (47)
50 - Louisiana (33)	Rhode Island (40)	New Hampshire (41)
49 - Michigan (9)	5 - Indiana (7)	New Mexico (38)
43 - Washington (17)	New Jersey (28)	North Dakota (44)
42 - Texas (3)	4 - Tennessee (22)	South Dakota (39)
38 - Connecticut (19)	3 - Arizona (37)	Vermont (43)
31 - Maryland (36)	2 - Wisconsin (13)	West Virginia (24)
29 - Kansas (8)	1 - Arkansas (25)	Wyoming (46)

* Numbers in parentheses indicate the states' rank order, according to the average membership in AP during 1895, 1900, 1918, 1932, 1942, 1958, and 1963. Sources of state memberships are AP's Annual Volumes for the first four years and Table 19 (Editor & Publisher International Year Books) for the last three.

SOURCE: Various numbers of the Associated Press (Illinois & New York) Volumes.

Table 5. Director Longevity on AP's Board: 1893-1964
(Rank ordered by years)

Yrs. Director and Newspaper	Pres	Exec	Veep
53 - Frank B. Noyes, Washington Star	38	53	
43 - Clark Howell, Atlanta Constitution		14	1
40 - Robert McLean, Philadelphia Bulletin*	19	40	2
34 - Victor F. Lawson, Chicago Daily News & Record	6	32	
33 - W.H. Cowles, Spokane Spokesmen-Review			2
30 - Adolph S. Ochs, New York Times		30	
29 - E. Lansing Ray, St. Louis Globe-Democrat		23	3
28 - Stuart H. Perry, Adrian (Mich.) Telegram		16	5
J.R. Knowland, Oakland Tribune			
25 - W.L. McLean, Philadelphia Bulletin		14	
24 - Charles W. Knapp, St. Louis Republic	1/2**	24	
21 - Robert R. McCormick, Chicago Tribune		1	1
20 - Albert J. Barr, Pittsburgh Post			
18 - Paul Patterson, Baltimore Sun		17	3
Paul Bellamy, Cleveland Plain Dealer		15	1
E.H. Baker, Cleveland Plain Dealer		10	
M.H. de Young, San Francisco Chronicle			
L.K. Nicholson, New Orleans Times-Picayune			
17 - Charles Hopkins Clark, Hartford Courant		17	3
Thomas G. Rapier, New Orleans Picayune			1
16 - Herman Ridder, New York Staats-Zeitung			
15 - Benjamin M. McKelway, Washington Star*	5 1/2	14	1/2
14 - Frank P. McLennan, Topeka State Journal			2
V.S. McClatchy, Sacramento Bee			
13 - Paul Miller, Rochester Democrat & Chronicle*	1	10	3
Josh L. Horne, Rocky Mount (N.C.) Telegram			1
12 - Harry F. Byrd, Jr., Winchester (Va.) Evening Star*		8	2 1/2
Frederick E. Murphy, Minneapolis Tribune			
11 - E.H. Butler, Buffalo News		4	2
Charles A. Rook, Pittsburgh Dispatch		10	
Roy A. Roberts, Kansas City Times		2	
Harvey W. Scott, Portland Oregonian			
A.C. Weiss, Duluth Herald			
10 - Raymond L. Spangler, Redwood City Tribune		2	1
George B. Longan, Kansas City Star			2
W.R. Nelson, Kansas City Star & Times			2
Palmer Hoyt, Portland Oregonian			
9 - Robert B. Choate, Boston Herald		8	1
Arthur Hays Sulzberger, New York Times		8	1
John S. Knight, Miami Herald		7	2
Charles H. Grasty, Baltimore News		6	1 1/2
George F. Booth, Worcester Telegram		6	
B.H. Anthony, New Bedford Standard.		5	1

Table 5 (continued)

	Pres	Exec	Veep
John R. Reitemeyer, Hartford Courant		5	
Bernard H. Ridder, Jr., Duluth News Tribune		4	1
Mark Ethridge, Louisville Courier-Journal		3	1
Harold A. Fitzgerald, Pontiac (Mich.) Daily Press		2	4
Richard W. Clarke, New York Daily News		2	1
W.H. Cowles, Spokane Spokesman-Review (2nd term)		2	1
Norman Chandler, Los Angeles Times			4
John Cowles, Des Moines Register			2
Dolph Simons, Lawrence (Kan.) Journal World			1
Frederick I. Thompson, Birmingham Age Herald			
James E. Chappell Birmingham Age Herald			
E.K. Gaylord, Oklahoma City Oklahoman			
8 - Kenneth MacDonald, Des Moines Tribune*		3	1
Nathaniel R. Howard, Cleveland News			
H.V. Jones, Minneapolis Journal			
George Thompson, St. Paul Dispatch			
O.S. Warden, Great Falls (Mont.) Tribune			
7 - Frederick Driscoll, St. Paul Pioneer-Press		7	
Richard Hooker, Springfield (Mass.)Republican		3	
George W. Healy, Jr., New Orleans Times-Picayune*		1	
R.M. Johnston, Houston Post			2
W.D. Maxwell, Chicago Tribune*			
James M. North, Jr., Fort Worth Star Telegram			
James W. Runyon, Dallas Times Herald*			
D.E. Town, Louisville Herald			
6 - Stephen O'Meara, Boston Journal		3	1
Gen. Charles H. Taylor, Boston Globe		4	4
John R. Rathom, Providence Journal		4	
Houston Harte, San Angelo Standard			6
James M. Cox, Jr., Dayton Daily News			1
5 - Whitelaw Reid, New York Tribune		4	
Franklin D. Schurz, South Bend Tribune*		3	
Clayton McMichael, Philadelphia North American		2	
Hugh N. Boyd, New Brunswick (N.J.) Daily Home News*			
Millard Cope, Marshall (Tex.)News-Messenger*			
Frank E. Gannett, Rochester (N.Y.) Times-Union			
4 - John Norris, New York World		1	
Henry D. Bradley, St. Joseph (Mo.) Gazette*			1
L. Markbreit, Cincinnati Volksblatt			
Max E. Nussbaum, Moultrie (Ga.) Observer*			
Eugene H. Perdue, Cleveland Leader & News-Herald			
James E. Scripps, Detroit Tribune & Evening News			
3 - W.J. Pape, Waterbury (Conn.) Republican		3	5
Oswald Garrison Villard, New York Evening Post		3	
S.S. Carvalho, New York World		2	
Eugene C. Pulliam, Phoenix Gazette*		2	

Table 5 (continued)

	Pres	Exec	Veep
Wright Bryan, Cleveland Plain Dealer*			
William Dwight, Holyoke (Mass.)Transcript-Telegram*			
Albert P. Langtry, Springfield (Mass.) Union			
W.Y. Morgan, Hutchinson News			
2 - William Penn Nixon, Chicago Inter-Ocean	2		
D.D. Moore, New Orleans Times-Picayune			2
Charles P. Taft, Cincinnati Times-Star			1
William A. Collier, Memphis Appeal-Avalanche			
Arthur Jenkins, Syracuse Herald			
1 - Frederick Roy Martin, Providence Journal		1	
Don C. Seitz, New York World		1	
W.D. Brickell, Columbus Dispatch			
Harry T. Grant, Milwaukee Journal			
Washington Hesing, Chicago Illinois Staats-Zeitung			
Irwin R. Kirkwood, Kansas City Star			
William F. Knowland, Oakland Tribune*			
Victor F. Ridder, New York Staats-Zeitung			
Gene Robb, Albany Knickerbocker News & Times-Union*			
Walter A. Strong, Chicago Daily News			
1/2 - Jerome D. Barnum, Syracuse Post Standard			
Edward P. Call, New York Evening Post			
Edward Rosewater, Omaha Bee			

---

* Directors serving on the board at this writing. (Members of 1964-65 board.)
** The symbol 1/2 refers to all board or office terms of less than one year.

SOURCE: Various numbers of the Associated Press (Illinois & New York) Volumes.

Table 6. Turnover of Directors: 1901-1963
(Numbers are director changes)

Yr.	Dir. Changes			
1901 - 1	1917 - 1	1933 - 2	1949 - 1
1902 - 1	1918 - 0	1934 - 2	1950 - 4**-14
1903 - 2	1919 - 1	1935 - 2	1951 - 4**
1904 - 0	1920 - 0 - 11	1936 - 0	1952 - 4 **
1905 - 1	1921 - 2	1937 - 0	1953 - 0
1906 - 1	1922 - 1	1938 - 0	1954 - 2
1907 - 0	1923 - 3**	1939 - 1	1955 - 0
1908 - 1	1924 - 2	1940 - 2 - 10	1956 - 1
1909 - 1	1925 - 0	1941 - 2	1957 - 3**
1910 - 1 - 9*	1926 - 1	1942 - 0	1958 - 0
1911 - 1	1927 - 3**	1943 - 4**	1959 - 3**
1912 - 2	1928 - 1	1944 - 1	1960 - 3**-20
1913 - 1	1929 - 1	1945 - 0	1961 - 4**
1914 - 2	1930 - 0 - 14	1946 - 0	1962 - 0
1915 - 1	1931 - 0	1947 - 1	1963 - 2
1916 - 2	1932 - 1	1948 - 1	

---

* The additional numbers are ten-year totals of directorship turnovers.
** Indicates years in which directorship turnovers were 50 per cent or
more of the possible turnover for one year.

SOURCE: Various numbers of the Associated Press (Illinois & New York)
    Volumes.

Table 7. History of Administrative Posts: 1892-1964

Stratum & Position	Earliest Year	Latest Year	Total Years	No. of Men in Post	Total Man-Years
Executive Positions					
General Manager	1892	1964	72*	6	72**
Assistant General Manager	1894	1964	68	17	137 1/2
Executive or Administrative Assistant	1926	1964	14	9	21
Deputy General Manager	1962	1964	2	1	2
Operational Chiefs					
News Department Chief	1912	1964	46	9	74
General News Supervisors	1920	1943	19	12	43
Traffic & Membership	1912	1954	40	8	45
Promotion & Personnel	1942	1954	12	5	22
Department Editors					
Markets & Election Superintendent	1922	1964	39	7	39
Foreign News Editor	1927	1964	37	8	38
Feature or Newsfeature Editor	1927	1964	37	5	37
Newsphoto Editor	1927	1964	37	6	39
Wide World Photo Editor	1940	1964	23	5	23
Sports Editor	1927	1964	37	5	37
Special Services	1938	1942	4	1	4
News Editor, World Service	1946	1964	18	4	19
Radio News Editor	1947	1964	17	2	17
Executive Clerk	1943	1961	18	1	18

* "Total Years" will equal the difference between "Earliest Year" and "Latest Year" for positions which have been continuous. For intermittent positions, this total will be somewhat less than the difference.

** "Total Man-Years" refers to the number of years occupants have devoted to the position. This total cannot be less than "Total Years," but where two or more men have occupied a position simultaneously, this will be larger than "Total Years."

SOURCE: Various numbers of the Associated Press (Illinois & New York) Volumes.

Table 8. Longevity of Administrative Personnel: 1892-1964
(Rank ordered by years)

Yrs.	Administrator, Highest Position**	Gen. Mgr.	Exec.	Oper.	Dept. **
36	- Kent Cooper, general manager	23	28	8	
35 1/2	-Alan J. Gould, assistant general manager		10	21	11***
35	- Melville E. Stone, general manager	28	28		
33	- Lloyd C. Stratton, assistant general manager		25		4
26	- J. M. Wing, Newsfeature general editor*				26
	F. A. Resch, Newsphoto editor*				26
23	- C. E. Honce, assistant general manager		9	14	
21	- Frank J. Starzel, general manager	14	20	1	
19 1/2	-Oliver S. Gramling, assistant gen. mgr.		15 1/2	4	
19	- Jackson S. Elliott, assistant gen. mgr.		15	4	
18	- T. R. Smits, Sports Editor*				18
	Hugh V. Kelly, executive clerk				18
17 1/2	-Charles S. Diehl, general manager	1/2	17 1/2		
17	- Harry T. Montgomery, deputy gen. mgr*		10	4	3
16	- Ben Bassett, foreign news editor*				16
	Paul Michelson, general news editor		16		
15	- L. A. Brophy, general business editor				15
14	- Wes Gallagher, general manager*	2	10	4	
	W. J. McCambridge, assistant gen. mgr.		4	10	
13 1/2	- L. F. Curtis, supt. of markets & elections				13 1/2
13	- John A. Aspinwall, radio news editor*				13
	J. M. Kendrick, executive assistant		1	8	4
	T. H. O'Neil, general news supervisor			9	4
12	- Frederick Roy Martin, general manager	4	12		
	M. A. White, general news editor		12		
11	- C. A. Jagger, assistant gen. mgr.		4		7
	L. M. Thomason, personnel chief		11		
10	- Max Desfor, Wide World Photos editor*				10
9	- Milton Garges, executive assistant		3	6	
8	- W. F. Brooks, executive assistant		2	3	3
	Norris A. Huse, Newsphoto editor				8
	Paul Miller, assistant gen. mgr.		8		
	Stanley M. Swinton, assistant gen. mgr. *		2		6
6	- Glenn Babb, foreign news editor				6
	Samuel G. Blackman, gen. news editor*		6		
	John Evans, foreign news editor				6
	Paul Sanders, world service news editor				6
5	- Charles E. Kloeber, news dept. chief		5		
	Leo M. Solomon, Wide World Photos editor				5
	Howard Townsend, Wide World Photos editor				5
4	- Herbert Barker, sports editor				4
	L. P. Hall, traffic chief		4		
	Wilson Hicks, feature editor				4

Table 8 (continued)

Yrs.	Administrator, Highest Position**	Gen. Mgr.	Years as: Exec.	Oper.	Dept. **
	Byron Price, executive news editor		4		
	Charles S. Smith, foreign news editor			4	
	George Turner, general news supervisor		4		
3 -	W. L. Beale, Jr., Washington News editor				3
	Paul Cowles, executive assistant	3			
	Paul Friggens, executive assistant	2	1		
	Dale C. Harrison, gen. news supervisor		3		
	E. Blanton Kimbell, research & development mgr.				3
	George Naeder, gen. news supervisor		3		
	Smith Reavis, foreign news editor			3	
	Orlo Robertson, sports editor			3	
	Watson S. Sims, world service news editor*			3	
	Edward Stanley, Newsphoto editor			3	
2 -	H.C. Beaty, general news supervisor		2		
	Robert J. Cavagnaro, executive representative	1			1
	J.F. Chester, gen. business editor				2
	Dewitt Mackenzie, foreign news editor				2
	W.T. McCleary, Feature Editor				2
	Nate Polowetzky, general business editor				2
	S.P. Richardson, general news supervisor		2		
	J.M. Roberts, foreign news editor				2
	J.L. Springer, Wide World Photos editor				2
	Milo M. Thompson, special assignments				2
	E.T. Wolford, traffic chief		2		
1 1/2-	Keith Fuller, assistant general manager*	1 1/2			
	Louis J. Kramp, assistant gen. manager*	1 1/2			
1 -	H.W. Blakeslee, Newsphoto editor				1
	Daniel DeLuce, executive assistant*	1			
	Victor Hackler, executive assistant*	1			
	J.N. Lodge, general news supervisor			1	
	Pugh Moore, executive representative	1			
	A.L. Murphy, Newsphoto editor				1
	Robert D. Price, Newsfeature news editor				1
	William Henry Smith, general manager	1	1		
	James F. Tomlinson, gen. business editor*				1
	A.L. Uhl, foreign news editor				1

* Administrative personnel serving AP at this writing.
** The "Highest Position"(not the most recent position in all cases) is determined by the order of strata and executive positions shown in Table 8. No particular order is given to positions in the Operational and Departmental strata.

Table 8 (continued)

*** The total years in all three strata, indicated at the right, may not in all cases equal the total number of administrative years (on the left). Where these totals are not equal, the individual has served in positions in two strata simultaneously.

SOURCE: Various numbers of the Associated Press (Illinois & New York) Volumes.

Table 9. Mobility and Longevity of Personnel: 1892-1964

Strata	Tot. Men	Tot. Yrs.	Avg. Yrs.	Range	Top Men
Departmental	35	237 1/2	6.50	1-26	Resch & Wing
Operational	14	75	5.36	1-16	Mickelson
Executive	12	85	7.08	1-35	Stone
Dept. -Oper.	1	13	13.00	13	O'Neil
Dept. -Exec.	4	54	13.50	2-33	Stratton
Oper. -Exec.	9	158 1/2	17.61	3-36	Cooper
Dept-Oper-Exec	4	73 1/2	18.38	8-35 1/2	Gould

SOURCE: Data in Table 8.

Table 10. Annual AP Revenue and Membership Growth:
1893-1964

Year	Annual Revenue	% Rise-Decline**	% Rise-Decline Of AP Membership*	
			Tot.	U.S.
1893[a]	$ 280,508	- - -	220.0%	
1894	992,348	- - -	84.1	
1895	1,193,051	20.3%	4.2	
1896	1,227,819	2.9	5.3	
1897	1,605,866	30.8	63.9	
1898	1,905,725	18.7	3.5	
1899	1,935,796	1.6	-3.2	
1900[b]	1,474,580	- - -	5.7	
1900-1[c]	1,492,901	- - -	-2.3	
1901-2	2,077,690	- - -		
1902-3	2,113,085	1.7		
1903-4	2,193,397	3.8		
1904-5	2,278,298	3.9		
1905-6	2,364,159	3.8		
1906-7	2,485,854	5.2		
1907[d]	1,284,213	- - -		
1908	2,613,686	- - -		
1909	2,639,752	1.0		
1910	2,728,888	3.4		
1911	2,792,626	2.3	3.6	
1912	2,958,030	2.3	4.3	
1913	3,093,409	4.6	3.3	
1914	3,137,952	1.5	1.6	
1915	3,171,410	1.1	-0.1	
1916	3,241,428	2.2	11.3	
1917	3,478,394	7.3	7.6	
1918	3,788,178	8.9	4.3	
1919	4,452,879	17.6	7.6	
1920	5,372,090	20.6	3.0	
1921	5,623,975	4.7	1.0	
1922	5,989,293	6.5	-7.0	
1923	6,651,850	11.1	2.3	
1924	7,043,777	5.9	-1.1	
1925	7,567,363	7.4	0.9	
1926	8,149,834	7.7	1.8	
1927	8,641,623	6.0		
1928	9,045,633	4.7		
1929	9,660,908	6.8	2.7	
1930	10,255,028	6.1	1.3	
1931	10,071,562	-1.8	0.6	
1932	9,002,981	-10.6		
1933	7,865,800	-12.6		
1934	8,087,714	2.8	1.9	

Table 10 (continued)

Year	Annual Revenue	% Rise-Decline**	% Rise-Decline Of AP Membership* Tot.	% Rise-Decline Of AP Membership* U. S.
1935	$ 9,404,213	16.3	1.4	
1936	10,370,232	10.3	1.6	
1937	10,746,269	3.6	2.4	
1938	11,061,208	2.9		
1939	11,013,228	-0.4		
1940	11,304,909	2.7		
1941	11,491,511	1.7	8.0	1.2%
1942	11,916,860	3.7	8.3	-0.2
1943	11,768,437	-1.3	3.5	-0.7
1944	12,616,668	7.2	9.6	-1.2
1945	16,650,630	32.0	24.4	2.7
1946	18,928,152	13.7	24.0	2.4
1947	20,389,816	7.7	21.7	102.4
1948	22,365,973	9.7	8.7	0.3
1949	23,500,824	5.1		4.6
1950	23,647,156	0.6		0.3
1951	24,651,797	4.3		2.9
1952	26,893 390	9.1		1.8
1953	28,162,843	4.7		3.0
1954	29,440,959	4.5	0.6	4.1
1955	30,339,950	3.1		4.1
1956	31,876,168	5.1		3.6
1957	32,977,527	3.5		2.3
1958	34,394,894	4.3		5.8
1959	35,568,863	3.4		4.9
1960	38,547,443	8.4		1.6
1961	40,128,292	4.1		3.3
1962	42,451,846	5.8		2.4
1963	44,030,275	3.7		

* Percentages of membership rise or decline are for total members and associate members of AP. These percentages and the absolute figures they represent are in Table 14.

** Percentages of revenue rise or decline are for annual changes, based on the preceding year's total.

[a]Five-month period from Aug. 1 to Dec. 31, 1893.

[b]Nine-month period from Jan. 1 to Sept. 30, 1900.

[c]Nine-month period from Oct. 1, 1900, to June 30, 1901. The Associated Press operated on fiscal years beginning July 1 for the years 1901-2 through 1906-7. At all other times the AP financial statements represented calendar years.

[d]Six-month period from July 1 to Dec. 31, 1907.

SOURCE: Various numbers of the Associated Press (Illinois & New York) Volumes, general manager's report for 1893-1912, and the auditing committee's report, 1913-1963.

Table 11. Conditions of Annual AP Expenses: 1893-1963

388

Year	Annual Expenses	% Rise-Decline*	Annual Gain/Loss	Year	Annual Expenses	% Rise-Decline*	Annual Gain/Loss
1893[a]	$ 356,238	---	$-75,734	1922	$6,012,856	11.1	$-23,563
1894	1,126,095	---	-133,747	1923	6,377,654	6.2	274,196
1895	1,227,335	8.8	-34,283	1924	7,068,392	10.8	-24,615
1896	1,265,121	3.3	-37,301	1925	7,567,363	7.1	0
1897	1,520,545	19.7	85,320	1926	8,051,739	6.3	98,095
1898	1,889,697	24.3	16,027	1927	8,641,623	7.3	0
1899	1,797,517	-4.8	138,279	1928	9,042,731	4.6	2,902
1900[b]	1,395,663	---	78,916	1929	9,660,908	6.9	0
1900-1[c]	1,440,575	---	52,325	1930	10,023,367	3.7	231,661
1901-2	1,934,732	---	142,958	1931	10,065,315	0.4	6,246
1902-3	1,999,441	3.6	113,644	1932	8,879,223	-11.7	123,758
1903-4	2,257,377	13.0	-63,979	1933	7,820,458	-11.9	45,342
1904-5	2,321,577	2.7	-43,279	1934	7,916,450	1.3	11,263
1905-6	2,253,705	-3.0	110,453	1935	9,262,253	15.9	141,959
1906-7	2,370,914	5.3	114,940	1936	10,093,116	9.0	277,116
1907[d]	1,378,921	---	-94,708	1937	10,746,269	6.6	0
1908	2,605,657	---	8,028	1938	11,061,208	2.9	0
1909	2,697,157	3.4	-57,404	1939	11,081,321	0.2	-68,092
1910	2,742,492	1.5	-13,603	1940	11,179,535	0.9	125,373
1911	2,846,812	4.0	-54,186	1941	11,372,774	1.7	118,737
1912	2,908,295	2.1	49,734	1942	11,305,577	-0.5	611,282
1913	2,883,853	-1.0	209,555	1943	11,686,822	3.4	81,614
1914	3,149,135	9.4	-11,182	1944	12,276,754	5.0	339,913
1915	3,197,412	1.6	-26,001	1945	16,997,706	38.4	-347,076
1916	3,199,781	0.1	41,646	1946	18,913,846	11.2	14,305
1917	3,383,960	5.6	94,433	1947	20,308,660	7.4	81,155
1918	3,940,766	16.6	-152,588	1948	22,269,044	9.7	96,928
1919	4,449,898	12.9	2,981	1949	23,471,336	5.4	29,487
1920	5,191,143	16.6	108,946	1950	23,666,669	0.9	-19,513
1921	5,409,941	4.2	214,034	1951	24,693,645	4.3	-41,847

Table 11 (continued)

Year	Annual Expenses	% Rise-Decline*	Annual Gain/Loss
1952	$26,895,913	8.5	-2,523
1953	28,024,697	4.2	138,145
1954	29,348,228	4.7	92,731
1955	30,374,048	3.5	-34,098
1956	31,984,704	5.3	-108,535
1957	33,213,044	3.8	-235,517
1958	34,708,014	4.5	-313,120
1959	35,988,239	3.6	-419,376
1960	38,338,131	6.5	209,312
1961	39,945,307	4.2	182,985
1962	42,356,308	6.0	-95,538
1963	44,050,353	3.9	20,078

* Percentages of expenditure rise or decline are for annual changes, based on the preceding year's total.

a-dSee footnotes a-d of Table 10.

SOURCES: Various numbers of the Associated Press (Illinois & New York) Volumes, general manager's report for 1893-1912, and the auditing committee's report, 1913-1963.

Table 12. Annual AP Expenses by Operational Categories:
1893-1963
(Thousands of Dollars)

Year	Incoming* Service	%**	Foreign Service	%	Leased-Wire Service	%	Salaries	%	General Expenses	%
1893[a]	$ 29	---	$ 39	---	$219	---	$ 50	---	19	---
1894	124	---	113	---	636	---	192	---	54	---
1895	122	-1.6	114	0.9	742	16.7	191	-0.5	51	-5.6
1896	118	-3.3	119	4.4	782	5.4	188	-1.6	48	-5.9
1897	129	9.3	138	16.0	922	5.1	219	16.5	94	95.8
1898	112	-14.7	415	200.7	1024	11.1	232	5.9	87	-7.4
1899	138	23.2	289	-30.3	1033	0.8	246	6.0	76	-12.6
1900[b]	106	---	205	---	819	---	189	---	68	---
1900-1[c]	103	---	209	---	828	---	207	---	93	---
1901-2	151	46.6	258	23.4	1173	41.7	272	31.4	74	-20.4
1902-3	142	-6.0	262	1.6	1215	3.6	287	5.5	74	0.0
1903-4	152	7.0	331	26.3	1334	9.8	300	5.2	424	473.0
1904-5	147	-3.3	380	14.8	1386	3.9	309	3.0	400	-5.7
1905-6	137	-6.8	278	-26.9	1417	2.2	318	2.9	411	2.8
1906-7	151	10.2	272	-2.2	1502	6.0	333	4.7	101	-75.4
1907[d]	62	---	147	---	909	---	171	---	57	---
1908	200	---	278	---	1609	---	363	---	114	---
1909	189	-5.5	280	0.7	1639	1.9	387	6.6	101	-11.4
1910	182	-3.7	216	-22.9	1725	5.2	445	15.0	128	26.7
1911	204	12.1	240	11.1	1764	2.3	474	6.5	123	-3.9
1912	217	6.4	238	-0.8	1804	2.3	509	7.4	138	12.2
1913	177	-18.3	224	-5.9	1856	2.9	502	-1.4	122	-11.6
1914	157	-11.3	430	92.0	1898	2.3	520	3.6	139	13.9
1915	153	-2.5	519	20.7	1860	-2.0	527	1.3	132	-5.0
1916	147	-3.9	542	4.4	1831	-1.6	541	2.7	135	2.3
1917	129	-12.2	565	4.2	1974	7.8	544	0.6	168	24.4
1918	118	-8.5	801	41.8	2279	15.5	587	7.9	153	-8.9
1919	164	39.0	747	-6.7	2740	20.7	647	10.2	148	-3.3
1920	212	29.3	707	-5.4	3305	20.6	812	25.5	151	2.0
1921	226	6.6	631	-10.7	3467	4.9	922	13.6	159	5.3
1922	240	6.2	730	15.7	3825	10.3	1046	13.4	166	4.4
1923	524	118.3	703	-3.7	4548	18.9	366	-65.0	230	38.6
1924	589	12.4	703	0.0	4936	8.5	384	4.9	257	11.7
1925	612	3.9	695	-1.1	5327	7.9	388	1.0	296	15.2
1926	649	6.0	695	0.0	5818	9.2	398	2.6	323	9.1
1927	638	-1.7	715	2.9	5971	2.6	419	5.3	270	-16.4
1928	665	4.2	683	-4.5	6229	4.3	386	-7.9	285	5.7
1929	1128	69.6	803	17.6	6583	5.7	289	-25.1	301	5.6
1930	996	-11.7	814	1.4	7062	7.3	294	1.7	322	7.0
1931	1011	1.5	881	8.2	6825	-3.4	286	-2.7	271	-15.8
1932	1088	7.6	618	-29.9	6187	-9.3	253	-11.5	230	-15.1

Table 12 (continued)

Year	Incoming* Service		Foreign Service		Leased-Wire Service		Salaries		General Expenses	
1933	$1521	38.9	548	-11.3	4923	-20.4	233	-7.9	262	13.9
1934	1563	3.7	680	24.1	4912	-0.2	240	3.0	246	-6.1
1935	1856	18.7	797	17.2	5571	13.4	245	2.1	276	12.2

Year	Dom. News Collection		For. News Collection		News Distribution		Admin. Salaries		Supplemental Services	
1936	$1961	5.7	780	-2.1	4163	-25.3	$236	-3.7	$2252	---
1937	2342	19.4	766	-1.8	4472	7.4	192	-18.6	2319	3.0
1938	2425	3.5	758	-1.0	4588	2.6	197	2.6	2241	-3.4
1939	2421	-0.2	1014	33.8	4584	-0.1	221	12.2	2284	1.9
1940	2453	1.3	1047	3.3	4719	2.9	228	3.2	2201	-3.6
1941	2480	1.1	1142	9.1	4829	2.3	216	-5.3	2182	-0.9
1942	2403	3.1	1088	-4.7	4661	-3.5	217	0.5	2430	11.4
1943	2677	11.4	1547	42.2	4105	-11.9	235	8.3	2427	-0.1
1944	2800	4.6	2002	29.4	4220	2.8	275	17.0	2486	2.4
1945	2910	3.9	3539	76.8	6144	45.6	397	44.4	3170	27.5

Year	Domestic News Collection & Distribution		Foreign News Collection & Distribution		Admin. Salaries		Supplemental Services	
1946	$10,010	---	$3,962	---	$449	13.1%	$3,887	22.6%
1947	11,232	12.2%	3,702	-6.6%	472	5.1	4,288	10.3
1948	12,602	12.2	3,836	3.6	481	1.9	4,796	11.8
1949	13,066	3.7	3,907	1.9	501	4.2	5,291	10.3
1950	13,610	4.2	3,309	-15.3	513	2.4	5,383	1.7
1951	14,304	5.1	3,276	-1.0	564	9.9	5,663	5.2
1952	16,111	12.6	3,365	2.7	594	5.3	5,963	5.3
1953	16,431	2.0	3,368	0.1	603	1.0	6,580	10.3
1954	17,378	5.8	3,474	3.1	631	4.6	6,936	5.4
1955	17,701	1.9	3,639	4.7	646	2.4	7,089	2.3
1956	18,460	4.3	4,068	11.8	686	6.2	7,735	9.1
1957	18,737	1.5	4,444	9.2	738	7.7	8,148	5.3
1958	19,167	2.3	4,811	8.3	757	2.6	8,448	3.7
1959	19,770	3.1	4,850	0.8	787	4.0	8,878	5.1
1960	20,850	5.5	5,442	12.2	817	3.8	9,555	7.6
1961	21,060	1.0	5,859	7.7	851	4.2	10,362	8.4
1962	22,096	4.9	6,693	14.2	854	0.4	10,589	2.2
1963	22,438	1.5	6,805	1.7	825	-3.5	11,210	5.9

a-dSee footnotes a-d of Table 10.

* The Associated Press has used three sets of operational categories since 1893. The first set (1893-1935) divides expenditures as follows: Incoming News Service--local agencies, outside correspondents, telegraph tolls, miscellaneous messages, markets, and shipping (the domestic newsgathering

Table 12 (continued)

operation); Foreign News Service--European offices, correspondents, foreign news contracts, and cable tolls (the foreign news-gathering operation); Leased-Wire Service--operator and messenger salaries, extra operator service, rental of wires, telegraph tolls, auxiliary services, manfold supplies, typewriter exchanges and repairs, and incidentals (the distribution of the news report); General Expenses--general office expenses, telephone charges, furniture and fixtures, stationery and printing, postage, newspapers and books, traveling expenses, legal expenses, and taxes; and Salaries--between 1893 and 1908 included "agents, editors and executives," and after 1909 included "Correspondents, editors, executives, superintendents, and retired list."

After 1935, the AP did not break down its two subsequent sets of operational categories into items. In the text of this study the author has assumed the contents of these categories on the basis of AP's general statements with regard to operations which bear these category names.

** Decimal numbers are percentages of annual category rise or decline, based on the preceding year's category total.

SOURCE: Various numbers of the Associated Press (Illinois & New York) Volumes, general manager's report for 1893-1912, and auditing committee's report for 1913-1963.

Table 13. Growth of United States Daily News Outlets: 1783-1964

Year	Total Nprs		Year	Total Nprs		Year	Total Nprs	
1783	1	---	1880	909	(a)	1900	2190	0.5
1790	8	700.0*	1881	956	5.2	1901	2220	1.4
1800	24	200.0	1882	1028	7.5	1902	2284	2.9
1810	26	8.3	1883	1119	8.9	1903	2307	1.0
1820	42	61.5	1884	1197	7.0	1904	2344	1.6
1830	65	54.8	1885	1207	0.8	1905	2326	-0.8
1840	138	112.3	1886	1260	4.4	1906	2381	2.4
1850	254	84.1	1887	1394	10.6	1907	2398	0.7
1860	387	52.4	1888	1515	8.7	1908	2414	0.7
1868	519	34.1	1889	1522	0.5	1909	2427	0.5
1870	574	10.6	1890	1662	(a)	1910	2433	0.2
1871	594	3.5	1891	1726	3.9	1911	2418	-0.6
1872	525	-11.6	1892	1836	6.4	1912	2435	0.7
1873	647	23.2	1893	1905	(b)	1913	2442	0.3
1874	678	4.8	1894	1988	4.4	1914	2457	0.6
1875	718	5.9	1895	2056	3.4	1915	2447	-0.4
1876	738	2.8	1896	2135	3.8	1916	2461	0.6
1877	709	-3.9	1897	2136	0.04	1917	2410	-2.1
1878	719	1.4	1898	2174	1.8	1918	2166	(c)
1879	812	12.9	1899	2179	0.2	1919	2078	-4.1

Year	Total U.S. Outlets		Total Nprs		Total AM Stations**		Total FM Stations**	Total TV Stations**
1920	2042	-1.7	2042	-1.7				
1921	2029	-0.6	2028	-0.7	1	---		
1922	2063	1.7	2033	0.2	30	(d)		
1923	2592	25.6	2036	0.1	556	(d)		
1924	2544	-1.9	2014	-1.1	530	-4.7		
1925	2579	1.4	2008	-0.3	571	7.7		
1926	2529	-1.9	2001	-0.3	528	-7.5		
1927	2630	4.0	1949	-2.6	681	29.0		
1928	2616	-0.5	1939	-0.5	677	-0.6		
1929	2550	-2.5	1944	0.3	606	-10.5		
1930	2560	0.4	1942	-0.1	618	2.0		
1931	2535	-1.0	1923	-1.0	612	-1.0		
1932	2517	-0.7	1913	-0.5	604	-1.3		
1933	2510	-0.3	1911	-0.1	599	-0.8		
1934	2512	0.1	1929	0.9	583	-2.7		
1935	2535	0.9	1950	1.1	585	0.3		
1936	2605	2.8	1989	2.0	616	5.3		
1937	2629	0.9	1983	-0.3	646	4.9		
1938	2625	-0.2	1936	-2.4	689	6.7		
1939	2610	-0.6	1888	-2.5	722	4.8		
1940	2643	1.3	1878	-0.5	765	6.0		

Table 13 (continued)

Year	Total U.S. Outlets		Total Nprs		Total AM Stations**		Total FM Stations**		Total TV Stations**	
1941	2677	1.3*	1857	-1.1	817	6.8	1	---	2	---
1942	2644	-1.2	1787	-3.8	851	4.2	2	100.0	4	100.0
1943	2609	-1.3	1754	-1.8	839	-1.4	12	500.0	4	0.0
1944	2668	2.3	1744	-0.6	875	4.3	43	258.3	6	50.0
1945	2685	0.6	1749	0.3	884	1.0	46	7.0	6	0.0
1946	2730	1.7	1763	0.8	913	3.3	48	4.3	6	0.0
1947	2943	7.8	1769	0.3	1027	12.5	140	191.7	7	16.7
1948	3758	27.7	1781	0.3	1586	54.4	374	167.1	17	142.9
1949	4407	17.3	1780	-0.1	1877	18.3	700	87.2	50	194.1
1950	4653	5.6	1772	-0.4	2051	9.3	733	4.7	97	86.0
1951	4754	2.2	1773	0.1	2198	7.2	676	-7.8	107	10.3
1952	4828	1.6	1786	0.7	2297	4.5	637	-5.8	108	0.9
1953	4883	1.1	1785	-0.1	2357	2.6	616	-3.3	125	15.7
1954	5161	5.7	1765	-1.1	2487	5.5	560	-9.1	349	179.2
1955	5359	3.8	1760	-0.3	2635	5.6	553	-1.3	411	17.8
1956	5533	3.2	1761	0.1	2790	5.9	540	-2.4	442	7.5
1957	5730	3.6	1755	-0.3	2974	6.6	530	-1.9	471	6.6
1958	5936	3.6	1751	-0.2	3156	6.1	537	1.3	492	4.5
1959	6129	3.3	1755	0.2	3287	4.2	578	7.6	509	3.5
1960	6374	4.0	1763	0.5	3416	3.9	678	17.3	517	1.6
1961	6619	3.8	1761	-0.1	3507	2.7	821	21.1	530	2.5
1962	6918	4.5	1760	-0.1	3653	4.2	960	16.9	545	2.8
1963	7161	3.5	1754	-0.3	3770	3.2	1081	12.6	556	2.0
1964					3897	3.4	1146	6.0	564	1.4

* Decimal numbers are percentages of annual medium rise or decline, based on the preceding year's medium total.

** Figures are for AM, FM, and television stations in operation rather than those holding operating licenses.

[a]Sources leave a 14-month gap in figures. An annual rate tabulation is unrepresentative.

[b]Sources leave a 15-month gap in figures. An annual rate tabulation is unrepresentative.

[c]A change in source and counting criteria makes annual rate tabulation impossible.

[d]The initial growth of radio in 1922-23 was so rapid and annual rates of increase so large that space does not permit their inclusion in the column. The rate for 1922 is 2900.0 per cent and for 1923, 1753.3 per cent.

SOURCES: For newspapers -- 1783-1860, Lee, op. cit., p. 717; 1868-1879, George P. Rowell & Co. data in ibid., pp. 720-721; 1880-1917, N.W. Ayer & Son data in ibid., pp. 722-723; and 1918-1963, Editor

Table 13 (continued)

& Publisher: The Fourth Estate, International Year Book,
XLIII (1963), p. 215.

For AM, FM and television Stations -- 1921-1944, United States
Bureau of the Census, Historical Statistics of the United States:
Colonial Times to 1957 (Washington: Government Printing Office,
1960), p. 491; and 1945-1964, United States Bureau of the Census,
Statistical Abstract of the United States: 1964 (85th ed.; Washington: Government Printing Office, 1964), p. 519.

Table 14. Growth of Wire-Service Subscribers: 1892-1964

| Year | ASSOCIATED PRESS | | | | UNITED PRESS (UPI) | | | | INS |
	Total	%Rise-Decline*	U.S.	% of US Outlets**	Tot.	%Rise-Decline*	U.S.	% of US Outlets**	Total
1892	63	---	63	3.4%					
1893	207	228.6	207	10.9					
1894	381	84.1	381	19.2					
1895	397	4.2	397	19.3					
1896	418	5.3	416	19.5					
1897	685	63.9	637	29.8	150^a		150^a	7.0%	
1898	709	3.5	658	30.3					
1899	686	-3.2	625	28.7					
1900	725	5.7	655	29.9					
1901			612	27.6					
1902									
1903			662	28.7					
1904			691	29.5					
1905			710	30.5					
1906									
1907					369	(146.0)***	369	15.4	
1908	774	(6.8)	767	31.8					
1909					392	(6.2)	392	16.2	
1910	801	(3.5)							
1911	830	3.6							
1912	866	4.3			491	(25.3)	491	20.2	
1913	895	3.3			500	1.8	500	20.5	
1914	909	1.6							
1915	908	-0.1			625	(25.0)	625	25.5	
1916	1011	11.3							
1917	1088	7.6							400
1918	1135	4.3							
1919	1221	7.6			745	(19.2)			
1920	1258	3.0			780	4.7			
1921	1270	1.0							
1922	1181	(b)							
1923	1208	2.3			867	(11.2)			
1924	1195	-1.1							
1925	1206	0.9			1032	(19.0)			
1926	1228	1.8			1100	6.6			
1927									
1928	1246	(1.5)			1150	(4.5)			
1929	1280	2.7			1170	1.7			
1930	1297	1.3			1317	12.6			600
1931	1305	0.6							
1932									
1933	1315	(0.8)			1240	(-5.8)	900	35.9	
1934	1340	1.9							

Table 14 (continued)

Year	ASSOCIATED PRESS				UNITED PRESS (UPI)				INS
	Total	% Rise-Decline*	% of US U.S.	Outlets	Tot.	% Rise-Decline	U.S.	% of US Outlets	Total
1935	1359	1.4			1360	(9.7)			
1936	1381	1.6							900
1937	1414	2.4							
1938									
1939					1715	(26.1)			
1940	1578	(11.6)	1249	47.3	1400	-18.4			900
1941	1705	8.0	1264	47.2					
1942	1846	8.3	1262	47.7					
1943	1910	3.5	1253	48.0					
1944	2094	9.6	1238	46.4					
1945	2604	24.4	1271	47.3					
1946	3229	24.0	1302	47.7	2529	(79.6)			1075
1947	3931	21.7	2635	89.5	2689[c]	6.3			
1948	4274	8.7	2648	70.5	2997[c]	11.5			1100
1949			2771	62.9	3219[c]	7.4			
1950			2788	59.9	3342	3.8			
1951	5564	(30.2)	2859	60.1	3469	3.8			
1952			2910	60.3	3533	1.8	2344	48.6	
1953	6750	(21.3)	2997	61.4	3736	5.7			
1954	6791	0.6	3120	60.5	4541	21.5			3000
1955			3249	60.6	4515	-0.6			
1956			3365	60.8	4654	3.1			
1957			3443	60.1	4833	3.8			3000
1958	7275	(7.1)	3641	61.3	5063	4.8			
1959			3820	62.3	5628[d]	11.2			(d)
1960			3882	60.9	5366	=4.7	3652	57.3	
1961			4012	60.6	6409	19.4			
1962	8000	(10.0)	4109	59.4	6546	2.1			
1963			4130	57.7					
1964					5846.	(-10.7)			

* Percentage of total subscriber rise or decline are for annual changes, based on the preceding year's total.

**Percentages of total daily United States outlets (newspaper and broadcasting) are computed on the basis of total outlets listed in Table 13.

***Annual rates of growth or decline in parentheses are for periods of two or more years and represent the net change during the space in time left by a gap in available data.

aThe 1897 United Press total is for the three news agencies controlled by Scripps (Scripps-McRae Press Association, Scripps News Association, and Publishers' Press Association), according to Lee, op. cit., pp. 536-537.

bIn 1922 the Associated Press altered its method of tabulating memberships. Prior to 1922 AP counted Sunday newspapers as separate memberships; after that year Sunday papers were considered separate memberships only if they had no affiliation with weekday morning or evening AP members.

Table 14 (continued)

^cUnited Press reports that these figures represent newspapers and radio and television stations receiving "direct service" from UP. Larger totals for these three years are also given as including a "client wire service and radio network" e.g., "magazines, radio commentators, steamships, and executive offices." These larger totals are: 1947, 4,327; 1948, 4,327; and 1949, 4,538.

^dThe year 1959 marks the first totals for United Press International after the UP-INS merger.

SOURCES: Various numbers of the Associated Press (Illinois & New York) Volumes; Editor & Publisher: The Fourth Estate, "ANPA-AP Convention Issue" LXXVIII-XCVII (1945-1964); Lee, op. cit.; Mott, op. cit.; and various mimeographed wire-service pamphlets.

Table 15. Growth of Broadcast Stations & AP Subscribers: 1945-1963

Year	US Total*	% Rise-Decline**	AP Total	% Rise-Decline**	% of US Total
1945	936	- - -	0		
1946	967	3.3	0		
1947	1,174	21.4	456	- - -	38.8
1948	1,977	68.4	940	106.1	47.5
1949	2,627	32.9	1,048	11.5	39.9
1950	2,881	9.7	1,068	1.9	37.1
1951	2,981	3.5	1,126	5.4	37.8
1952	3,042	2.0	1,185	5.2	39.0
1953	3,098	1.8	1,264	6.7	40.8
1954	3,396	9.6	1,376	8.9	40.5
1955	3,599	6.0	1,501	9.1	41.7
1956	3,772	4.8	1,606	7.0	42.6
1957	3,975	5.4	1,702	6.0	42.8
1958	4,185	5.3	1,878	10.3	44.9
1959	4,374	4.5	2,042	8.7	46.7
1960	4,611	5.4	2,122	3.9	46.0
1961	4,858	5.4	2,263	6.6	46.6
1962	5,158	6.2	2,380	5.2	46.1
1963	5,407	4.8	?		

* U.S. Totals are for AM, FM, and television stations as
listed in Table 13.
** Percentages of rise or decline are for annual changes,
based on the preceding year's total.
SOURCES: Various numbers of the Associated Press (Illinois
& New York) Volumes, and U.S. Bureau of the Census,
Statistical Abstract of the United States: 1964 (85th ed.;
Washington: Government Printing Office, 1964), p. 519.

Table 16. Number of Nations Served by AP, UP, and UPI: 1893-1964

Year	AP	UP	Year	AP	UP	Year	AP	UP	Year	AP	UPI
1892			1910			1928			1946	54	61
1893			1911	3		1929		45	1947	55	
1894			1912	3		1930		44	1948	64	
1895			1913			1931			1949	67	68
1896	2		1914			1932	5		1950	73	69
1897	3		1915			1933			1951	72	
1898	3		1916			1934			1952	69	77
1899	3		1917			1935		49	1953	68	
1900	4		1918	4		1936			1954		
1901			1919			1937			1955	68	
1902			1920	13		1938			1956	70	
1903			1921			1939		52	1957	70	
1904			1922			1940		50	1958	73	
1905			1923			1941			1959		92
1906			1924			1942			1960	79	
1907			1925		36	1943			1961		103
1908			1926			1944	38		1962	87	111
1909			1927			1945	49		1963	100	
									1964		114

SOURCES: Same as for Table 14.

Table 17. Relative Influence of World News Agencies
(Based on Population)

World News Received Primarily from:	% of World	CUMULATIVE			
		TASS	AP-UP-INS	Reut	AF-P
TASS	30.9	30.9			
AP-UP-INS	8.0		8.0		
Reuters	2.7			2.7	
Agence France-Presse	1.8				1.8
AP-UP-INS & Reuters	3.6		3.6	3.6	
AP-UP-INS & AF-P	2.8		2.8		2.8
Reuters & AF-P	0.7			0.7	0.7
AP-UP-INS, AF-P & Reuters	39.8		39.8	39.8	39.8
AP-UP-INS, AF-P, Reut. &TASS	8.4	8.4	8.4	8.4	8.4
No world news agency	1.3				
Totals	100.0	39.3	62.6	55.2	53.5

SOURCE: Unesco, News Agencies: Their Structure and Operation (Paris: Georges Lang, 1953), p. 197.

Table 18. Zones of Influence of World News Agencies
(Based on Population)

World News Received Primarily from:	Afr.	N.A.	S.A.	Asia*	Eur.*	Oce.	USSR
TASS				36.3	22.5		100.0
AP-UP-INS		77.6	11.1	0.6		4.2	
Reuters	27.9			0.7	0.1		
Agence France-Presse	17.0	0.3	**	0.4	0.2	0.5	
AP-UP-INS & Reuters	16.8	2.2	0.4	2.1	2.7	80.6	
AP-UP-INS & AF-P	8.6		17.7	2.3			
Reuters & AF-P	8.7		0.2				
AP-UP-INS, AF-P & Reuters	14.8	18.4	70.6	41.1	72.6		
AP-UP-INS, AF-P, Reut. &TASS				15.3	1.9		
No world news agency	6.2	1.5	**	1.2	**	14.7	
Totals	100.0	100.0	100.0	100.0	100.0	100.0	100.0

* Not including the U.S.S.R.
**Less than 0.1 per cent.

SOURCE: Same as Table 17.

Table 19. Wire Affiliation Configurations by States: Selected Years

State	1935 AP	UP	INS	AP UP	AP INS	UP INS	AP UP INS	None	1942 AP	UP	INS	AP UP	AP INS	UP INS	AP UP INS	None
Ala.	11	3	3	3	2	0	0	1	12	1	1	1	0	0	4	1
Alaska	5	0	0	1	0	0	0	0	5	1	0	0	0	0	0	0
Ariz.	8	1	0	2	0	0	0	0	5	1	0	2	0	0	2	0
Ark.	12	7	0	10	0	0	0	8	10	13	1	13	0	0	0	2
Calif.	21	66	5	20	4	2	11	9	16	65	2	18	6	4	14	1
Colo.	10	9	0	8	0	0	1	1	10	10	0	3	0	0	3	1
Conn.	19	6	1	3	0	0	0	0	17	5	2	1	0	0	3	0
Del.	2	0	0	0	0	0	0	0	0	0	0	0	0	0	2	0
D.C.	1	1	1	1	0	1	0	0	1	1	0	0	0	1	1	0
Fla.	26	7	0	6	0	0	2	2	25	3	2	4	2	1	3	0
Ga.	14	6	1	5	0	1	0	0	12	7	0	2	2	0	3	0
Hawaii	1	2	0	0	1	0	0	2	0	2	0	2	0	0	0	0
Idaho	11	5	0	1	0	0	0	1	10	3	0	3	0	0	0	0
Ill.	30	29	6	7	3	2	8	13	34	28	5	8	4	1	8	2
Ind.	26	34	9	11	4	4	2	14	21	35	11	11	1	3	9	4
Iowa	18	5	8	5	2	0	6	0	20	7	5	6	0	0	5	2
Kan.	43	1	0	4	0	0	0	9	43	4	0	2	0	0	1	8
Ky.	18	2	2	3	1	1	0	3	18	2	1	2	0	0	4	3
La.	8	0	0	5	0	0	2	1	7	3	0	6	0	0	0	0
Maine	8	1	0	0	0	0	2	0	8	0	0	0	0	0	2	0
Md.	9	0	0	2	0	0	1	0	11	0	0	0	0	0	1	0
Mass.	23	4	8	8	5	2	2	9	16	10	9	8	2	1	6	4
Mich.	22	18	1	4	0	0	10	2	18	18	0	11	1	1	5	0
Minn.	18	8	0	5	0	0	2	0	20	4	0	5	0	0	2	0
Miss.	12	2	0	2	0	0	1	1	13	5	0	0	0	0	3	1
Mo.	18	11	0	6	2	1	0	18	23	11	0	5	2	2	2	11
Mont.	10	1	0	7	0	0	0	0	10	1	0	6	0	0	0	0
Nebr.	4	8	0	2	0	0	5	3	5	8	0	5	0	0	3	1
Nev.	1	7	0	0	0	0	0	0	0	6	0	2	0	0	0	0
N.H.	8	0	0	0	0	0	0	1	8	1	0	0	0	0	0	1
N.J.	15	2	2	5	0	2	3	4	16	3	1	4	0	2	4	2
N.M.	8	2	0	1	0	0	0	1	10	1	0	2	1	0	1	0
N.Y.	47	22	4	26	2	3	1	12	44	21	2	16	1	2	11	7
N.C.	23	6	0	6	0	0	0	3	26	5	0	9	0	0	2	0
N.D.	10	0	0	1	0	0	0	0	10	0	0	2	0	0	0	0
Ohio	21	41	20	10	4	2	9	6	13	33	17	10	3	1	18	10
Okla.	18	25	0	10	0	0	1	11	16	26	0	10	0	0	4	2
Ore.	7	11	0	7	0	0	0	0	7	8	1	4	1	0	1	0
Penn.	44	44	20	10	5	8	6	10	44	38	15	13	2	4	15	4
R.I.	5	0	1	3	0	0	0	0	4	0	1	1	0	0	2	0
S.C.	7	1	0	6	0	0	2	0	12	0	0	0	0	0	4	0
S.D.	12	3	0	0	0	0	0	1	12	2	0	1	0	0	0	1
Tenn.	10	6	1	6	0	0	2	1	12	4	0	5	0	0	4	0

Table 19 (continued)

State	AP	UP	INS	AP UP	AP INS	UP INS	AP UP INS	None	AP	UP	INS	AP UP	AP INS	UP INS	AP UP INS	None
Texas	47	27	5	20	4	0	9	13	29	28	4	24	5	0	13	12
Utah	1	2	0	3	0	0	0	1	0	3	1	1	0	0	2	0
Vt.	8	0	0	0	0	0	0	1	9	0	0	1	0	0	0	0
Va.	25	3	0	1	0	0	0	1	25	3	0	3	0	0	0	0
Wash.	14	9	1	8	1	0	0	0	7	6	0	12	1	0	0	0
W.Va.	20	4	0	3	0	1	2	2	21	3	0	5	1	0	0	1
Wis.	15	13	0	11	1	0	0	2	17	12	0	10	1	0	0	3
Wyo.	4	2	0	2	0	0	0	0	3	3	0	4	0	0	0	0
Totals	778	467	99	270	41	30	90	167	735	454	81	263	36	23	167	84

1949   1958

State	AP	UP	INS	AP UP	AP INS	UP INS	AP UP INS	None	AP	UP	INS	AP UP	AP INS	UP INS	AP UP INS	None
Ala.	9	2	0	7	0	0	2	0	10	1	0	5	1	0	2	0
Alaska	4	1	0	0	0	0	0	0	4	1	0	1	0	0	0	0
Ariz.	6	2	0	1	2	0	2	1	7	3	0	1	0	0	2	0
Ark.	11	7	0	12	0	0	2	3	14	4	0	6	0	0	8	3
Calif.	17	55	1	21	6	3	20	2	20	51	0	34	3	2	13	2
Colo.	9	11	0	4	1	0	1	1	11	8	0	5	0	0	1	1
Conn.	14	5	0	4	0	0	3	0	14	3	0	2	0	0	6	0
Del.	0	0	0	0	0	0	2	0	1	0	0	2	0	0	0	0
D.C.	1	1	0	1	0	0	1	0	1	1	0	0	0	0	1	0
Fla.	21	3	1	4	7	0	4	0	19	4	1	10	2	0	5	1
Ga.	8	4	0	7	0	0	8	1	9	4	3	5	3	2	4	0
Hawaii	0	1	1	1	0	0	1	0	2	1	0	1	0	1	0	0
Idaho	10	1	0	2	0	0	2	0	7	2	0	5	0	0	0	0
Ill.	31	23	5	15	1	1	10	5	37	21	3	10	2	1	5	4
Ind.	19	33	13	11	2	6	7	2	18	24	15	6	7	3	11	1
Iowa	21	9	2	9	0	0	2	2	28	6	1	4	3	1	1	0
Kan.	39	4	0	4	1	0	0	7	40	2	0	3	1	0	2	5
Ky.	17	4	1	4	1	0	2	1	16	3	0	3	0	1	3	1
La.	6	3	0	6	2	0	0	1	4	6	0	3	3	0	3	0
Maine	8	0	0	2	0	0	0	0	7	0	0	2	0	0	0	0
Md.	9	0	0	0	2	0	1	0	9	0	0	0	2	0	1	0
Mass.	15	5	8	10	2	2	8	3	14	12	3	8	3	1	7	4
Mich.	17	19	0	10	1	2	5	0	21	16	0	13	2	0	3	0
Minn.	21	3	0	0	2	0	4	0	20	2	0	4	0	0	2	1
Miss.	10	4	0	3	0	1	1	2	10	4	0	1	2	1	2	0
Mo.	25	7	0	3	0	0	8	11	27	10	1	2	4	0	5	8
Mont.	7	1	0	7	0	0	0	2	6	4	0	7	0	0	0	1
Nebr.	7	7	0	1	1	0	5	0	9	6	0	1	1	0	3	0
Nev.	0	4	1	2	0	0	1	0	1	5	0	1	0	0	1	0
N.H.	6	1	0	2	0	0	0	1	7	1	0	1	0	0	0	0
N.J.	14	2	1	1	2	4	5	1	12	3	0	2	2	3	3	0
N.M.	12	0	0	1	1	0	1	0	7	6	0	2	2	0	1	0

Table 19 (continued)

State	AP	UP	INS	AP UP	AP INS	UP INS	AP UP INS	None	AP	UP	INS	AP UP	AP INS	UP INS	AP UP INS	None
N.Y.	41	14	3	20	2	2	12	5	49	14	3	12	2	1	11	3
N.C.	26	7	0	9	0	0	2	0	21	7	0	13	2	1	1	1
N.D.	9	0	0	3	0	0	0	0	10	0	0	0	1	0	0	0
Ohio	23	29	17	6	3	2	17	6	30	34	14	2	5	4	8	1
Okla.	11	25	1	11	1	1	3	2	12	27	0	8	2	2	1	0
Ore.	7	10	0	2	1	0	1	0	4	11	0	4	1	0	1	1
Penn.	46	36	9	11	5	4	13	5	49	37	4	8	5	2	14	6
R.I.	3	0	1	1	0	0	2	0	3	0	1	3	0	0	0	0
S.C.	6	0	0	4	2	0	4	0	13	1	0	2	2	0	0	0
S.D	5	4	0	3	0	0	0	0	7	4	0	1	0	0	0	0
Tenn.	14	2	0	8	0	0	5	0	12	4	0	4	3	0	4	0
Texas	33	19	2	25	4	4	14	12	37	32	3	22	6	0	10	1
Utah	0	2	0	1	1	0	2	0	0	2	0	0	0	1	2	0
Vt.	8	1	0	0	0	1	0	0	8	1	0	0	0	1	0	0
Va.	24	2	0	5	2	0	0	0	24	1	0	0	7	1	0	0
Wash.	9	4	0	12	1	1	0	0	11	4	0	11	1	0	0	0
W.Va.	15	14	0	1	1	0	0	0	8	14	0	3	3	0	2	0
Wis.	16	11	0	10	2	0	0	3	20	7	0	9	2	0	0	0
Wyo.	4	5	0	0	0	0	0	0	2	7	0	0	0	0	0	0
Totals	694	407	67	287	59	34	183	79	732	421	52	251	85	29	149	45

	1962 AP	UPI	AP UPI	None	AP	UPI	AP UPI	None
Ala.	12	1	6	1	10	3	7	1
Alaska	4	1	1	0	4	1	1	0
Ariz.	4	5	4	1	4	5	4	1
Ark.	15	6	12	1	16	5	12	1
Calif.	15	53	54	7	13	51	54	7
Colo.	12	7	5	0	13	6	5	0
Conn.	14	1	10	0	13	2	10	0
Del.	1	0	2	0	1	0	2	0
D.C.	1	1	1	0	1	1	1	0
Fla.	12	7	21	4	12	13	20	4
Ga.	9	8	12	0	9	9	12	0
Hawaii	2	1	1	1	2	1	1	1
Idaho	7	4	3	1	7	4	3	1
Ill.	35	23	19	3	35	24	20	3
Ind.	20	43	21	5	18	43	21	7
Iowa	31	6	4	3	30	6	5	3
Kan.	43	3	4	1	44	3	4	2
Ky.	16	4	5	1	16	4	5	1
La.	4	5	9	1	4	5	9	1
Maine	6	0	3	0	6	0	3	0
Md.	9	0	3	0	9	0	3	0

Table 19 (continued)

State	AP	UPI	AP UPI	None	AP	UPI	AP UPI	None
Mass.	10	17	21	3	10	16	19	3
Mich.	19	16	17	1	20	15	17	1
Minn.	18	2	6	2	19	1	6	2
Miss.	7	5	4	2	7	6	4	2
Mo.	31	7	7	7	32	7	9	4
Mont.	5	4	5	2	5	4	5	2
Nebr.	9	6	5	0	9	6	5	0
Nev.	1	6	1	0	1	4	2	0
N.H.	7	0	2	0	7	1	1	0
N.J.	8	7	10	2	7	10	9	2
N.M.	7	9	3	0	9	7	3	0
N.Y.	45	13	28	2	46	14	27	2
N.C.	24	13	9	1	22	14	9	1
N.D.	8	0	1	1	9	0	1	1
Ohio	29	48	13	6	28	49	13	7
Okla.	13	24	11	3	12	25	11	3
Ore.	6	11	4	3	5	13	3	1
Penn.	47	43	22	5	49	42	21	5
R.I.	4	1	2	0	4	1	2	0
S.C.	12	1	4	0	12	1	4	0
S.D.	7	6	0	0	6	6	0	1
Tenn.	16	4	8	0	14	5	8	0
Texas	57	28	29	3	57	28	28	4
Utah	0	3	2	0	0	3	2	0
Vt.	7	1	0	0	6	1	1	0
Va.	21	5	4	2	21	6	3	2
Wash.	14	2	9	2	14	2	9	1
W.Va.	7	17	6	1	7	17	6	1
Wis.	18	6	11	3	18	7	10	3
Wyo.	4	6	0	0	4	6	0	0
Totals	734	490	444	80	727	503	437	84

SOURCE: Editor & Publisher: The Fourth Estate, "International Year Book Number," LXVII (Jan. 26, 1935), LXXV (Jan. 31, 1942), LXXXII (Jan. 31, 1949), and XCI (Feb. 28, 1958); and International Year Book, XLII (1962), and XLIII (1963).

Table 20.   Trends in Domestic Wire Affiliations: Selected Years

Affiliation

Combinations:*	1935	1942	1949	1958	1962	1963
AP only	40.0%	39.9%	38.3%	41.4%	42.0%	41.5%
UP only	24.1	24.6	22.5	23.9	---	---
INS only	5.1	4.4	3.7	3.0	---	---
UPI only	---	---	---	---	28.0	28.7
AP-UP	13.9	14.3	15.8	14.2	---	---
AP-INS	2.1	1.9	3.3	4.8	---	---
UP-INS	1.6	1.2	1.9	1.7	---	---
AP-UP-INS	4.9	9.1	10.1	8.4	---	---
AP-UPI	---	---	---	---	25.4	25.0
None	8.6	4.6	4.4	2.6	4.6	4.8
	100.0	100.0	100.0	100.0	100.0	100.0

Wire Totals:**

AP	51.3%	49.7%	49.4%	49.9%	55.8%	55.3%
UP	37.4	37.6	36.8	37.2	---	---
INS	11.3	12.7	13.8	12.9	---	---
UPI	---	---	---	---	44.2	44.7
	100.0	100.0	100.0	100.0	100.0	100.0

Npr. Changes:***

Deaths	---	36.4	18.9	16.0	22.0	15.0
New Papers	---	22.3	14.1	13.2	17.8	21.0
Net Change	---	-14.1	-4.7	-5.0	-4.3	3.0
Mergers	---	5.0	3.1	2.4	5.0	3.0
Intervening Yrs.		7	7	9	4	1

* 100 Per cent is based on the distribution of affiliation configurations among the total number of newspapers in the United States in the years shown.

** 100 per cent is based on the total number of subscriber-wire service connections in the United States in the years shown. Papers receiving both AP and UP, therefore, are counted twice.

*** Numbers are annual averages based on totals in each category for the intervening period between the selected years, divided by the number of intervening years. "Mergers" include only those arrangements between newspapers by which one paper loses its identity. Newspaper "deaths" includes such losses of identity by merger.

SOURCE: Data in Table 19, and additional data from sources cited in Table 19.

Table 21. Trends in Affiliation Changes: 1935-42 & 1942-49

\%	Total	Change*	\%	Total	Change*	\%	Change*
\multicolumn{3}{} 1935 - 1942			1942 - 1949			Difference	
34.5	581	A-A	34.7	600	A-A	4.1	AUI-AUI
18.1	305	U-U	18.5	320	U-U	3.5	AU-AU
7.3	123	AU-AU	10.8	187	AU-AU	0.6	AUI-AU
3.9	65	A-AU	6.9	119	AUI-AUI	0.5	U-A
		AU-AUI	3.1	54	N-N		A-AI
3.0	51	N-N	2.8	49	I-I	0.4	U-U
		AU-A	2.5	44	A-AU		UI-AUI
2.8	47	AUI-AUI	1.9	33	U-A		AI-AI
2.5	42	I-I	1.8	32	AUI-AU	0.3	I-I
1.7	28	N-U	1.6	27	A-U		AU-U
1.6	27	U-AU	1.5	26	AU-AUI	0.2	A-A
1.5	26	A-U	1.4	25	AU-A		AU-AI
1.4	23	U-A	1.4	24	AI-AI	0.1	N-N
1.3	22	I-U	1.2	20	U-AU		A-U
		A-AUI	1.0	17	A-AI		I-A
1.2	21	AUI-AU	0.9	15	U-UI		U-UI
1.2	20	N-A	0.8	14	AU-U		AUI-AI
1.0	16	AI-AI	0.6	11	N-U		I-AU
0.8	14	U-I	0.6	10	UI-AUI		AU-UI
0.7	12	UI-UI	0.5	9	A-AUI		UI-AU
0.7	11	UI-U	0.5	8	UI-UI		N-AI
0.6	10	AI-AUI			AI-AUI	0.0	(15 entries)
		AUI-A			N-A	-0.1	AI-AUI
		N-I	0.4	7	I-A		U-N
0.5	9	A-AI			N-I		AI-AU
		A-N	0.3	6	U-UI		I-N
0.5	8	U-AUI			U-N		I-AUI
		AU-U	0.3	5	AU-AI		AU-I
0.4	7	U-N	0.2	4	U-I		AI-I
0.3	6	I-A			AUI-A		UI-I
0.3	5	I-UI			AUI-AI		AUI-UI
0.2	4	U-UI	0.2	3	A-N		N-AU
0.2	3	I-N	0.1	2	I-AU	-0.2	UI-UI
		AI-A			I-AI		N-I
		AI-AU			I-UI		I-UI
		UI-AUI			AU-UI		U-AUI
0.1	2	A-I			AI-AU		AI-A
		I-AUI			UI-AU	-0.3	A-N
		AU-AI			N-AI	-0.4	U-AU
0.1	1	U-AI	0.1	1	A-I		AUI-A
		I-AI			U-AI	-0.6	U-I
		AU-I			I-N	-0.7	N-A
		AI-I					UI-U

Table 21 (continued)

%	Total	Change	%	Total	Change	%	Change
		UI-I				-0.8	A-AUI
		AUI-AI					I-U
		AUI-UI				-1.1	N-U
		N-AU				-1.4	A-AU
						-1.6	AU-A
						-2.4	AU-AUI
100.0	1684		100.0	1731			

* Changes do not include those caused by new newspapers, mergers, or suspensions. Symbols used above are defined as follows: A - AP, U - UP, I - INS, and N-None.

SOURCES: Same as for Table 19.

Table 22.   Managing Editors' Opinions on Wire Services

I. RESPONSES DIVIDED BY EDITORS' AFFILIATIONS

Population Strata:*	6	5	4	3	2	1	Total
AP-Alone Affiliations							
AP POSITIVE							
Coverage & Report	45.2	36.7	38.4	46.4	---	---	42.1
Fills Npr's Needs	---	13.3	15.4	3.6	---	---	6.9
Long Tradition	19.3	20.0	23.1	28.6	---	---	22.8
Econ.-Competition	9.7	3.3	7.7	7.1	---	---	6.9
Wire Organization	22.6	26.7	15.4	14.3	---	---	20.6
Best for Readers	3.2	---	---	---	---	---	1.0
	100.0	100.0	100.0	100.0			100.0
	(31)**	(30)	(13)	(28)	(0)	(0)	(102)
UPI NEGATIVE							
Coverage & Report	60.0	50.0	---	100.0	---	---	55.6
Wire & Npr's Needs	---	50.0	---	---	---	---	11.1
Econ.-Competition	20.0	---	100.0	---	---	---	22.2
Wire Organization	20.0	---	---	---	---	---	11.1
	100.0	100.0	100.0	100.0			100.0
	(5)	(2)	(1)	(1)	(0)	(0)	(9)
BOTH WIRES ARE							
GOOD	100.0	100.0	---	---	---	---	33.3
AP&UPI DUPLICATE	---	---	100.0	100.0	---	---	66.7
	(1)	(1)	(1)	(3)	(0)	(0)	(6)
Grand Total	37	33	15	32	0	0	117
Strata Distribution	31.6	28.2	12.8	27.4	---	---	100.0
UPI-Alone Affiliations							
UPI POSITIVE							
Coverage & Report	33.3	---	---	---	50.0	---	32.5
Fills Npr's Needs	20.0	100.0	---	---	---	---	20.0
Long Tradition	30.0	---	---	50.0	50.0	---	32.5
Econ.-Competition	16.7	---	---	50.0	---	---	15.0
	100.0	100.0		100.0	100.0		100.0
	(30)	(2)	(0)	(2)	(6)	(0)	(40)
AP NEGATIVE							
Wire & Npr's Needs	50.0	---	---	---	---	---	40.0
Econ.-Competition	50.0	---	---	---	---	---	40.0
Wire Organization	---	---	---	---	100.0	---	20.0
	100.0				100.0		100.0
	(4)	(0)	(0)	(0)	(1)	(0)	(5)

Table 22 (continued)

Population Strata:*	6	5	4	3	2	1	Total
BOTH WIRES ARE							
GOOD	33.3	---	---	---	---	---	33.3
AP & UPI DUPLICATE	66.7	---	---	---	---	---	66.7
	(3)	(0)	(0)	(0)	(0)	(0)	(3)
Grand Total	37	2	0	2	7	0	48
Strata Distribution	77.1	4.2	---	4.2	14.5	---	100.0

AP-UPI Affiliations

BOTH POSITIVE	6	5	4	3	2	1	Total
Coverage & Report	---	50.0	50.0	33.8	25.0	42.8	34.5
Fills Npr's Needs	---	12.5	---	37.5	40.0	14.3	33.6
Long Tradition	---	25.0	25.0	12.5	10.0	28.6	14.3
Best for Readers	---	12.5	25.0	16.2	25.0	14.3	17.6
		100.0	100.0	100.0	100.0	100.0	100.0
	(0)**	(8)	(4)	(80)	(20)	(7)	(119)
AP POSITIVE	---	71.5	50.0	71.1	63.6	---	68.3
UPI POSITIVE	---	28.5	50.0	28.9	36.4	---	31.7
		100.0	100.0	100.0	100.0		100.0
	(0)	(7)	(4)	(38)	(11)	(1)	(60)
EITHER IS GOOD	---	---	---	38.5	33.3	---	35.3
AP & UPI DUPLICATE	---	---	---	7.7	33.3	100.0	17.6
WIRE COMP. IS GOOD	---	---	---	53.8	33.3	---	47.1
				100.0	100.0	100.0	100.0
	(0)	(0)	(0)	(13)	(3)	(1)	(17)
Grand Total	0	15	8	131	34	8	196
Strata Distribution	---	7.7	4.1	66.8	17.3	4.1	100.0

II. RESPONSES DIVIDED BY OPINION CATEGORIES

Population Strata:*	6	5	4	3	2	1	Total
AP POSITIVE							
Coverage & Report	45.2	42.9	46.7	60.0	71.4	---	51.7
Fills Npr's Needs	---	11.4	13.3	1.8	---	---	4.9
Long Tradition	19.4	17.1	20.0	16.4	---	---	16.8
Econ. -Competition	9.7	2.9	6.7	3.6	---	---	4.9
Wire Organization	22.6	25.7	13.3	18.2	28.6	---	21.0
Best for Readers	3.2	---	---	---	---	---	0.7
	100.0	100.0	100.0	100.0	100.0		100.0
	(31)	(35)	(15)	(55)	(7)	(0)	(143)

Table 22 (continued)

Population Strata:*	6	5	4	3	2	1	Total
UPI POSITIVE							
Coverage & Report	33.3	50.0	50.0	69.2	70.0	---	49.2
Fills Npr's Needs	20.0	50.0	---	---	---	---	13.6
Long Tradition	30.0	---	---	23.1	30.0	---	25.4
Econ.-Competition	16.7	---	50.0	7.7	---	---	11.8
	100.0	100.0	100.0	100.0	100.0		100.0
	(30)	(4)	(2)	(13)	(10)	(0)	(59)
AP-UPI POSITIVE							
Coverage & Report	---	50.0	50.0	33.8	25.0	42.9	34.5
Fills Npr's Needs	---	12.5	---	37.5	40.0	14.3	33.6
Long Tradition	---	25.0	25.0	12.5	10.0	28.5	14.3
Best for Readers	---	12.5	25.0	16.2	25.0	14.3	17.6
		100.0	100.0	100.0	100.0	100.0	100.0
	(0)	(8)	(4)	(80)	(20)	(7)	(119)
BOTH WIRES ARE GOOD	50.0	100.0	---	8.3	50.0	---	23.8
AP&UPI DUPLICATE	50.0	---	100.0	91.7	50.0	100.0	76.2
	100.0	100.0	100.0	100.0	100.0	100.0	100.0
	(4)**	(1)	(1)	(12)	(2)	(1)	(21)
AP NEGATIVE							
Wire & Npr's Needs	50.0	---	---	---	---	---	40.0
Econ.-Competition	50.0	---	---	---	---	---	40.0
Wire Organization	---	---	---	---	100.0	---	20.0
	100.0				100.0		100.0
	(4)	(0)	(0)	(0)	(1)	(0)	(5)
UPI NEGATIVE							
Coverage & Report	60.0	50.0	---	100.0	---	---	55.6
Wire & Npr's Needs	---	50.0	---	---	---	---	11.1
Econ.-Competition	20.0	---	100.0	---	---	---	22.2
Wire Organization	20.0	---	---	---	---	---	11.1
	100.0	100.0	100.0	100.0			100.0
	(5)	(2)	(1)	(1)	(0)	(0)	(9)
SUMMARY OF RESPONSES:							
AP Positive	41.9	70.0	65.2	34.2	17.5	---	40.2
UPI Positive	40.5	8.0	8.7	8.1	25.0	---	16.6
AP-UPI Positive	---	16.0	17.5	49.7	50.0	87.5	33.4
Both Good-Duplicate	5.4	2.0	4.3	7.4	5.0	12.5	5.9

Table 22 (continued)

	6	5	4	3	2	1	Total
AP Negative	5.4	---	---	---	2.5	---	1.4
UPI Negative	6.8	4.0	4.3	0.6	---	---	2.5
	100.0	100.0	100.0	100.0	100.0	100.0	100.0
	(74)	(50)	(23)	(161)	(40)	(8)	(356)
Strata Distribution	20.8	14.0	6.5	45.2	11.2	2.3	100.0
Total Respondents	19	12	6	44	12	2	95
Avg. Statements per Respondant	3.89	4.17	3.83	3.66	3.33	4.00	3.75

* Population strata are divided as follows:
    6 - 25,000 and less
    5 - 25,001 to 50,000
    4 - 50,001 to 100,000
    3 - 100,001 to 500,000
    2 - 500,001 to 1,000,000
    1 - 1,000,001 and over.

** Numbers in parentheses are the total $\underline{n}$ represented by the 100.0 per cent under which they appear.

SOURCE: Mailed responses to a letter inquiry based on a stratified random sample conducted by the author during the Summer and Fall of 1963. See Appendix C, Section I for details.

Table 23. Wire Affiliations of Competitive Daily Newspapers

Circulation Strata	AP-UPI		AP Only		UPI Only		None		Total
500,001 and Over	8	100.0*	-		-		-		8
100,001 to 500,000	24	72.7	6	18.2	3	9.1	-		33
50,001 to 100,000	-		2	50.0	2	50.0	-		4
25,001 to 50,000	2	28.6	2	28.6	3	42.8	-		7
25,000 and Less	3	15.8	6	31.6	8	42.1	2	10.5	19
not available	1		-		1		-		2
Totals	38	52.1	16	21.9	17	23.3	2	2.7	73

* Decimal numbers indicate the percentages which the adjacent absolute numbers are of the total in the extreme right-hand column.
SOURCE: Editor & Publisher: The Fourth Estate, International Year Book, XLIII (1963), pp. 17-279.

Table 24. Wire Affiliations of Dominant & Subordinate Competitors
(30 Competitive Situations)

Wire Affiliation	Dominant Competitors		Subordinate Competitors	
AP-UPI	20	66.7%	8	26.7%
AP Only	8	26.7	7	23.3
UPI Only	2	6.7	14	46.7
None	-	---	1	3.3
Totals	30	100.0	30	100.0

SOURCE: Same as Table 23.

Table 25. Wire Affiliations in One-Newspaper Cities
(50,000 circulation and over)

Circulation Strata	AP-UPI		AP Only		UPI Only		None		Total
500,001 and Over	3	60.0*	-		2	40.0	-		5
100,001 to 500,000	45	60.0	21	28.0	7	9.3	2	2.7	75
50,000 to 100,000	57	43.8	44	33.8	25	19.2	4	3.1	130
Totals	105	50.0	65	31.0	34	16.2	6	2.8	210

* Decimal numbers indicate the percentages which the adjacent absolute numbers are of the total in the extreme right-hand column.
SOURCE: Same as Tables 23 and 24.

Table 26. Wire Affiliations of Chains & Chain Newspapers

Chain Configurations	Total Chains		Total Nprs.		Average Nprs. per Chain	
AP Chains	42		157		3.74	
AP Alone		20		65		3.25
AP W/some UPI		22		92		4.18
UPI Chains	30		116		3.87	
UPI Alone		20		59		2.95
UPI w/some AP		10		57		5.70
AP-UPI Chains	16		69		4.31	
Mixed Chains	44		291		6.61	
AP Dominates		17		131		7.71
UPI Dominates		10		79		7.90
AP-UPI Dominates		5		53		10.60
No dominant wire		12		28		2.33
Chains without wires	1		2		2.00	
	133		635		4.77	

RECAPITULATION

AP Alone	20	16.7%	65	10.7%	3.25
AP Basic Wire	22	18.3	92	15.2	4.18
AP Dominates Mixed Chain	17	14.2	131	21.7	7.71
AP-UPI Basic & Dominates	21	17.5	122	20.2	5.81
UPI Dominates mixed Chain	10	8.3	79	13.0	7.90
UPI Basic Wire	10	8.3	57	9.4	5.70
UPI Alone .	20	16.7	59	9.8	2.95
	120*	100.0	605*	100.0	5.04

* Excludes "Mixed Chains - No Dominant Wire" and "Chains without wires" totals.

SOURCE: Editor and Publisher: The Fourth Estate, International Year Book, XLIII (1963), pp. 17-279; and Raymond B. Nixon, "Groups of Daily Newspapers Under Common Ownership," ibid., pp. 310-312.

Table 27. Growth of AP, UP, and UPI Bureau Systems: 1894-1963
(Only years where data are available)

	AP BUREAUS			UP-UPI BUREAUS		
Year	Total	U.S.	For.	Total	U.S.	For.
1894	22	21	1			
1895	24	23	1			
1896	24	23	1			
1897	24	23	1			
1898	25	24	1			
1899	25	24	1			
1900	28	24	4			
1901	30	26	4			
1902	31	27	4			
1903	33	27	6			
1904	34	28	6			
1905	35	29	6			
1906	36	30	6			
1907	38	29	9			
1908	40	30	10		12	
1909	41	31	10	27	21	6
1910	42	32	10			
1911	46	36	10			
1912	46	36	10			
1913	46	35	11			
1914	47	36	11			
1915	49	38	11		24	
1916	60	48	12			
1917	63	50	13			
1918	67	52	15			
1919	68	54	14			
1920	85	65	20			
1921	86	69	17			
1922	88	71	17			
1923	86	73	13		50	
1924	86	75	11			
1925	94	83	11			
1926	93	79	14			
1927	108	86	22			
1928	100	81	19	79	51	28
1929	104	85	19			
1930	108	86	22			
1931	109	91	18			
1933				81	51	30
1939						40
1944						42
1945			38			52
1946						58

Table 27 (continued)

Year	AP BUREAUS			UP-UPI BUREAUS		
	Total	U.S.	For.	Total	U.S.	For.
1947			49			67
1948						68
1949	151	99	52	148	80	68
1951				160		
1957				205	110	
1958				210		
1959				220	122	98
1960			50	234	140	94
1961				248		
1962	167	110	57	261	151	110
1963				264		

SOURCES: Same as for Table 14.

Table 28. Total Foreign Correspondents Abroad: 1963
(By employer)

Total Correspondents

302-UPI (24.5%*)	Army Times	Booth Nprs
275-AP (22.6%*)	MBC	Continental Press
90-McGraw-Hill	TV News	Burroughs
75-N.Y.Times	UPI Newspictures	IPI
66-Time-Life	2-NEA	OPC Bulletin
60-NBC	Free Europe Press	Progresso (N.Y.)
38-CBS	Reporter	Movie Life
36-Newsweek	This Week	Sat. Evening Post
30-Christ. Sci. Monitor	Radio Press Interntl	High Fidelity Magazine
29-Time	Ridder Nprs	Free World Forum
19-ABC	Petroleum Weekly	Atlantic Monthly
15-Fairchild	Amer. Negro Press	Com. &Fin. Chronicle
14-NANA	Pittsburgh Courier	Sports Illustrated
US News&World Rpt	1-Washington Star	Billboard
13-UPI Movietone	St. Paul Dispatch	Motion Picture
12-Chicago Tribune	Mich. State Journal	Nation
N.Y.Herald-Trib.	Worchester Telegram	Travel Agent
9-Chicago Daily News	Pittsburgh Press	Travel Magazine
Baltimore Sun	Kansas City Star	True
Hearst Headline	Cleveland Plain Dlr.	Fortune
8-Washington Post	Toledo Blade	Metrotone
7-N.Y.Daily News	Long Island Advocate	Day Morgen Journal
Wall St. Journal	Milwaukee Journal	Cotton Trade Journal
Journ. of Commerce	Raleigh News	WBNX (N.Y.)
6-Worldwide Press	Charlotte Observer	Interfilm
Copley Nprs	Ashevl. Citizn-Times	Milburn McCarty Assoc.
5-Bus. Internatl.	Greensboro News	African-Amer. Institute
Vision	Chester News-Journ.	Fox Telenews
4-L.A. Times	Daily American	Monitor News
Westinghouse	Miami Herald	Voice of America
3-Minneap. Star-Trib.	Miami News	Foreign News Service
S.F. Chronicle	Seattle Post	Sporting News
Religious News	Overseas News Agy.	Look
Universal Trade	Keystone Press	Quigby Publications
Telemats	Jewish Telegraphic	Esquire
New Yorker	Macnes	American Red Cross
Variety	N.Y. Post	American Exporter

* Wire-service percentages represent wire's portion of the total 1,233 foreign correspondents included in this list.

SOURCE: John Wilhelm, "The Re-Appearing Foreign Correspondent: A World Survey," Journalism Quarterly, XL (Spring, 1963), pp. 154-168.

Table 29. Geographical Distribution of Correspondents: 1963
(Rank ordered by bureau locations)

Total Location	AP	UPI	Wire%*	Total Location	AP	UPI	Wire%*
183-London	43	42	46.4	Johannesburg	3	2	55.6
95-Tokyo	23	15	40.0	8-Frankfurt	3	5	100.0
66-Paris	8	6	21.2	Nairobi	1	1	25.0
64-Rome-Milan	7	6	20.3	Managua	1	2	37.5
52-Buenos Aires	14	17	59.6	San Juan	1	2	37.5
34-Bonn	5	6	32.4	7-Accra	-	2	28.6
29-Copenhagen	12	10	75.9	Quito	1	2	42.9
26-Ankara-Istanbul	7	2	34.6	Seoul	2	1	42.9
Rio de Janeiro	4	4	30.8	Singapore	4	1	71.4
25-Vienna	3	1	16.0	6-Belgrade	2	1	50.0
Helsinki	3	17	80.0	Tel Aviv	-	1	16.7
24-Amsterdam	10	9	79.2	Tangier-Rabat	1	2	50.0
Mexico City	4	4	66.7	5-Dublin	1	1	40.0
23-Oslo	9	12	91.3	Lagos-Enugu	2	1	60.0
22-Stockholm	6	8	63.6	Guatemala City	1	1	40.0
20-Hongkong	2	2	20.0	Colombo	1	1	40.0
19-West Berlin	6	5	57.9	Djakarta	2	1	60.0
18-Sydney	2	12	77.8	4-Teheran	1	1	50.0
16-Moscow	4	3	43.8	La Paz	1	1	50.0
Bogata	2	11	86.7	St. Thomas	1	1	50.0
15-Geneva-Zurich	3	2	66.7	Kuala Lumpur	1	1	50.0
Leopoldville	1	2	20.0	3-San Jose	1	1	66.7
Brussels	5	3	53.3	Kingston	-	-	---
New Delhi	3	2	20.0	Bombay	1	1	66.7
Karachi	1	8	60.0	Inverscargill	-	-	---
14-Madrid	2	6	57.1	2-Baghdad	1	1	100.0
Montevideo	5	7	85.7	Amman	1	1	100.0
Manila	2	2	28.6	Damascus	1	1	100.0
Bangkok	4	4	57.1	Algiers	1	1	100.0
Taipei	2	2	28.6	Addis Ababa	1	1	100.0
12-Lima	4	4	66.7	Salisbury	1	-	50.0
Santiago	2	4	50.0	Santo Domingo	1	1	100.0
11-Beirut	4	2	54.5	San Salvador	1	1	100.0
Cairo	4	4	72.7	Port-au-Prince	1	1	100.0
Panama City	3	1	36.4	Aukland	1	1	100.0
10-Lisbon	3	3	60.0	Wellington	1	1	100.0
Caracas	2	4	60.0	1-Hamburg	1	-	100.0
Saigon	2	2	40.0	Munich	1	-	100.0
9-Athens	2	2	44.4	Luxembourgh	-	-	---
Warsaw	2	3	55.6	Tegucigalpa	-	-	---

* Wire percentages indicate the percentage of total foreign correspondents in a given location which are employed by AP and UPI.
SOURCE: Same as for Table 28.

Table 30. Americans Percentage of Total Correspondents: 1963
(Only employers with 3 or more correspondents)

% of
Americans

100. 0 - Westinghouse (4)*
 Minneap. Star-Trib. (3)
 Army Times (3)
 MBC (3)
88. 9 - Chicago Daily News (9)
87. 5 - Washington Post (8)
85. 7 - Wall St. Journal (7)
 N. Y. Daily News (7)
78. 6 - US News & World Rpt (14)
75. 0 - L. A. Times (4)
73. 7 - ABC (19)
66. 7 - N. Y. Herald-Trib. (12)
 Hearst Headline (9)
 Worldwide Press (6)
 Copley Nprs (6)
 S. F. Chronicle (3)
 Universal Trade (3)
 New Yorker (3)
 Variety (3)

 TV News (3)
60. 0 - N. Y. Times (75)
58. 6 - Time (29)
58. 3 - Chicago Tribune (12)
57. 1 - Journal of Commerce (7)
56. 7 - Christ. Sci. Monitor (30)
55. 6 - Baltimore Sun (9)
52. 8 - Newsweek (36)
51. 7 - NBC (60)
50. 0 - NANA (14)
47. 4 - CBS (38)
47. 0 - Time-Life (66)
43. 3 - McGraw-Hill (90)
40. 0 - Vision (5)
33. 3 - Fairchild (15)
28. 0 - AP (275)
24. 5 - UPI (302)
20. 0 - Bus. Internatl. (5)
 7. 7 - UPI Movietone (13)

* Numbers in parentheses are the employers' total number of
foreign correspondents.

SOURCE: Same as for Tables 28 and 29.

APPENDIX C
SELECTION AND MECHANICS OF TWO SAMPLES USED IN
THIS STUDY

I. Random Sample of Managing Editors' Opinions on Wire Services

The random sample of opinions on wire services expressed by managing editors was conducted in connection with the Chapter VI discussion of the wire service-subscriber relationship.

A universe of 1,760 newspapers (morning, evening, and "all day" dailies) was established with the help of the "Ready Reckoner," a composite tabulation by states of U.S. daily newspapers and their circulations, appearing in the Editor & Publisher: The Fourth Estate, International Year Book for 1963 (Vol. XLIII), p. 14. The Reckoner also provided a division of total newspapers into six strata based on corporate city populations. This stratification of the universe had the following dimensions.

Population Strata	Daily Newspapers Total	Per Cent	Total Circulation	Average Circulation
1,000,001 and Over	31	1.8%	13,272,942	428,159
500,001 to 1,000,000	48	2.7	9,833,793	204,871
100,001 to 500,000	206	11.7	17,354,470	84,245
50,001 to 100,000	216	12.2	6,859,793	31,758
25,001 to 50,000	302	17.2	5,389,041	17,845
25,000 and Less	957	54.4	7,193,145	7,521
	1,760	100.0		

It could be argued that stratification according to circulation might be more realistic for purposes of grouping similar types of newspapers. There is, however, no available tabulation in terms of circulation, and to perform such a tabulation would be time-consuming and would give rise to the possibility of tabulation errors. On the other hand, population and circulation, while not positive correlates in every instance, do show some degree of

correlation, as one can note from the "Average Circulation" column in
the above table.

Population stratification and randomness of individual newspaper
choices became, therefore, the two principal criteria in selecting two
samples of one hundred newspapers each. The selection process involved
blindly pointing to newspaper entries on pages 17 to 279 of the Year Book
for 1963. The entries are arranged alphabetically by city names within
an alphabetical listing of states (including Alaska, Hawaii, and the District
of Columbia). The entries, moreover, are consecutively listed in four
columns per page with full- or partial-page advertisements appearing in
conjunction with specific entries rather than in a predetermined order.
Finally, each newspaper's entry has a length dependent upon the amount of
information and the number of staff members the paper submitted to the
Year Book. Consequently, randomness of choice was secured by blind pointing, alphabetical listings, continuous and haphazard placement, and varying
lengths of entries. Since one hundred newspapers were to be selected from
262 pages of entries (or one paper for every 2 1/2 pages with twelve pages
left over), it was decided to pick from pages approximately 2 1/2 pages apart.
The additional twelve pages would make up for those few instances when an
advertisement would occupy the page location at which a selection was to be
made. To avoid the bias connected with either beginning on page 17 (and
Alabama automatically) or skipping the first 2 1/2 pages, the author opened
the book at random, marked the spot, and worked back and then forward
from that spot by 2 1/2-page intervals.

The number of sample newspapers in each population stratum was determined by rounding off the percentages in the table on the first page to the nearest whole number, the sum then equaling one hundred. Each successive newspaper selected was placed in the appropriate stratum on the basis of the population of the city in which it was published, and such placement continued until each stratum was filled. By the end of the process of skipping 2 1/2 pages and making a selection, some strata were filled and selections had to be discarded. When this occurred, the author simply moved down the column to the next entry and the next, until he found one which would fill a vacancy in a stratum. Although no particular attempt was made to make the sample representative of geographic distributions among the four regional divisions used in Figures 2 and 9-12, it can be assumed that the randomness of state placement in the Year Book and of the selection process tended to produce such a distribution. (Had attention been paid to geographic location, either stratification or randomness would have been jeopardized.) A brief discussion of geographic distribution appears later in this section.

One sample was drawn in August, 1963, with letters of inquiry mailed to each newspaper's managing editor (as named in the newspaper's Year Book entry) on August 27, 1963. A second sample of one hundred newspapers was constructed in late September, 1963, with letters sent on October 10, 1963. The author's return address and the body of the letter were mimeographed while the inside address and salutation were added by typewriter. Each letter was individually signed in ink. The author identified himself and the nature of his study in the opening paragraph. Next he referred to his source (the <u>Year Book</u>) and indicated having noted that the paper had a particular wire-service affiliation (added by typewriter) which had not changed in the last year. Following is the third paragraph which presents the managing editor with a series of "open-ended" questions about why this affiliation is maintained, what the precise service is, and the editor's opinions with respect to the major American wires.

> I am writing to ask if you would be kind enough to indicate briefly what factors, both yours and the wire services', (economic, quality of service, orientation of news coverage, special contractual arrangements with wire services, competition, circulation, etc.) have caused you to maintain this alignment over the past year. Also, would you please indicate what types of service you subscribe to (trunk line, "side lines," state or regional lines, etc.) and what secondary or supplementary newsgathering service you also receive. Any statements of you opinion on the relative merits of AP's and UPI's service would aid considerably in evaluating the wire service-newspaper relationship in the United States.

As the figures below indicate, response to this type of unstructured questioning was 25 per cent over the two samples. In retrospect, the author feels that he might have elicited a larger response had he enclosed self-addressed stamped envelopes, mailed "prod" letters to those not responding, and added a one- or two-page collection of specific questions to be answered by checking appropriate blanks. For a number of reasons, however, the author was not able to follow up these possibilities. Looming large among the reasons were a lack of money and a shortage of time. In a more positive way, however, the author was interested in seeing the type and extent of editors' responses to an "open-ended" inquiry about company policy and personal opinions. The size and distribution of the

two responses were as follows:

Population Strata	Total Sample	Sample 1 Response No.	Sample 1 Response %	Sample 2 Response No.	Sample 2 Response %	Response to Combined Samples No.	Response to Combined Samples %	Dif.
1,000,001 and Over	2%	1	3.6	1	4.5	2	4	2%
500,001 to 1,000,000	3	3	10.7	2	9.1	5	10	7
100,001 to 500,000	12	3	10.7	4	18.2	7	14	2
50,001 to 100,000	12	4	14.3	2	9.1	6	12	-
25,001 to 50,000	17	9	32.1	3	13.6	12	24	7
25,000 and Less	54	8	28.6	10	45.5	18	36	-18
	100%	28	100.0	22	100.0	50	100	

The author actually approached this inquiry in two steps. The first

sample was initially considered to be the only one, but the figures above

reveal how unrepresentative the response is of the various strata. All of

the second stratum contacts (500,001 to 1,000,000 population) responded

while only eight of the fifty-four contacts in the 25,000 or less stratum (or

14.8 per cent) replied. These disparities seemed to suggest another at-

tempt at securing representation of the newspaper universe. Thus, the

second sample was selected. Here a truer response of some strata was

obtained, but others were under-represented (especially the two strata em-

bracing the 25,001 to 100,000 population cities). Another reason for at-

tempting a second mailing was that it was feared that the late-August in-

quiries had been ignored either in the rush of the traditional "back-to-

school" editions or in the absence of vacationing managing editors. The 28

per cent response of the August mailing, however, proved to be the larger

of the two. When the two sample responses are combined, the bottom

stratum remains greatly under-represented.

It seems significant, however, that many editors or managing editors of small-town newspapers do not respond to such an inquiry as this. Perhaps the biggest reason for this may be simply that they are too busy with the day-to-day mechanics of newspapering to take the time to write. Other reasons, however, are also worth considering, in light of the types of responses received. Principally, it appears as though many of the small-town editors who did respond had trouble formulating affiliation reasons and personal opinions beyond the areas of relative cost of the wires and somewhat outdated stereotypes of the wires' images. While a few respondents gave insightful evaluations, many more in small towns were relatively superficial in their treatment of this subject. One can guess that wire quality and the possibility of affiliation changes ordinarily do not occupy the minds of a large percentage of small-town editors.

While similar types of responses can be found among the larger-population strata, the tendency (particularly in the three strata over 100,000 population) was to discuss affiliation and opinion in a more complete, thoughtful, even penetrating way. The author, for example, found it much more difficult to categorize the responses of big-city managing editors because they were more complex, less dogmatic or polarized than those of the small-town respondents. Partially this is due, of course, to the fact that they are being asked to defend their paper's affiliation, and the preponderance of newspapers in cities of 100,000 population and over receive both AP and UPI. But in another sense, such a situation would permit comparisons and evaluations between both wires, while the one-wire

newspaper editor will see only one news report ordinarily. Since many

of these big-city managing editors wrote insightful discussions of the

wires and since the first sample had shown that they were more inclined

to respond much more to the author's inquiry, he decided to poll managing

editors of all newspapers with circulations of 100,000 or more, except

for those used in either sample. This "supplementary survey" meant

mailing an additional ninety-one inquiries of the type described above.

This was done on October 10, 1963, along with Sample 2, and the responses

totaled forty-four (or a very good 48.4 per cent response). When the cir-

culation-based "supplementary survey" is converted to population strata,

the overall distribution is as follows:

| | Total Responses | |
Population Strata	No.	Per Cent
1,000,001 and Over	11	11.7
500,001 to 1,000,000	17	18.1
100,001 to 500,000	29	30.8
50,001 to 100,000	7	7.4
25,001 to 50,000	12	12.8
25,000 and Less	18	19.2
	94	100.0

This is the distribution of responses which form the basis for data in

Table 22 (see Appendix B.)

In addition to population representation of the responses is con-

sideration of geographic and affiliation representation. Although neither

was a criterion in the sample selections, their tabulation and presenta-

tion here reveals additional dimensions of the total response. Geographic

distribution figures are as follows:

Division*	Universe No.	%	Sample 1 No.	%	Sample 2 No.	%	Suppl. S. No.	%	Combined No.	%	Resp. Dif.
East	393	22.4	3	10.7	2	9.1	12	27.3	17	18.1	-4.3
Central	576	32.6	14	50.0	13	59.1	13	29.5	40	42.5	9.9
West	295	16.8	5	17.9	3	13.6	11	25.0	19	20.2	3.4
South	496	28.2	6	21.4	4	18.2	8	18.2	18	19.2	-9.0
	1760	100.0	28	100.0	22	100.0	44	100.0	94	100.0	

* For the composition of these divisions, see Figures 2 or 9-12. The District of Columbia is included in the Eastern Division, and Alaska and Hawaii are in the Western Division.

Responses divided according to respondants' wire affiliations are as follows:

Wire Affil.	Universe No.	%	Sample 1 No.	%	Sample 2 No.	%	Suppl. S. No.	%	Combined No.	%	Resp. Dif.
AP	727	43.4	15	53.5	9	40.9	9	20.4	33	35.1	-8.3
UPI	503	30.4	5	17.9	7	31.8	-	---	12	12.8	-17.6
AP-UPI	437	26.2	8	28.6	6	27.3	35	79.6	49	52.1	25.9
	*1667	100.0	28	100.0	22	100.0	44	100.0	94	100.0	

* The 93-newspaper difference between this total and the 1,760 universe used elsewhere in this section is caused by two factors: (1) the deletion from this tabulation of newspapers receiving no wire service report, and (2) the fact that Editor & Publisher counts "all day" newspapers in both the morning and evening columns, thus counting them twice in the newspaper total. (The above tabulation by the author, however, counts "all day" papers only once.)

Western and Central newspapers responded generally in greater numbers than did Eastern and Southern papers. There is no apparent reason for this, but it does introduce some small amount of section bias in the total response. The two stratified random samples elicited relatively representative affiliation responses. Taken together, the two samples yielded the following response: AP, 48%; UPI, 24%; and AP-UPI, 28%. The one notable shortage is for UPI affiliates (which, of

course, in turn will affect the other two affiliation categories), either
with or without supplementary survey. Also noted in the text of Chapter
VI in connection with UPI newspaper editors' greater propensity to negative,
economic comments, this trend appears indicative of a secondary role assumed by UPI even in the minds of UPI-only newspaper editors. Because
of these affiliation disparities, Table 22 includes a division of opinions
among affiliation categories.

II. Intensive Study of One-Year Affiliation Changes

Editor & Publisher International Year Books for 1962 and 1963
(Vols. XLII and XLIII) reveal by comparison affiliation changes for thirty-
eight U.S. newspapers. The aggregate scope of these wire-service changes
along several dimensions is presented below.

Population Strata	Changes in Affiliation No.	%	1963 Universe
1,000,001 and Over	0	- - -	1.8%
500,001 to 1,000,000	0	- - -	2.7
100,001 to 500,000	4	10.5	11.7
50,001 to 100,000	6	15.8	12.2
25,001 to 50,000	9	23.7	17.2
25,000 and Less	19	50.0	54.4
	38	100.0	100.0%

From. . . Population Strata	A to: AU	U	N	U to: AU	A	N	AU to: A	U	N	N to: AU	A	U	Tot.
100,001 to 500,000	1							2		1			4
50,001 to 100,000				2			1	3					6
25,001 to 50,000	3	1	2		1			2					9
25,000 and Less		8			7		2	2					19
	4	9	2	2	8		3	9		1			38

There is disproportionately high degree of change manifest in the
smaller population categories, as compared with the 1963 distribution of

newspapers among the six population strata. The breakdown of changes
in terms of wire-service affiliations before and after the changes shows
no particular trends. Both wires gained several newspapers and lost a
similar number. In terms of net change, AP lost nine newspapers, and
UPI gained three. The discussion will return to these figures later.

In an attempt to better understand the mechanics of wire service-
newspaper relations (as they relate to changes in the basic physical connection between the two components), the author wrote the publishers or
managing editors of these newspapers on May 16, 1963. After noting the
affiliation change, according to the Year Books, the author asked the
addressee "to indicate briefly what factors, both yours and the wires',
(economic, quality of service, special contractual arrangements with the
wires, competition, circulation, etc.) prompted this change of affiliation
during the year." The addressee was also given the opportunity to express
his opinion as to "the relative merits of AP's and UPI's service."

The thirteen responses (a response of 34.2 per cent) were distributed
as follows.

Population Strata	Responses No.	%	Change Universe
100,001 to 500,000	1	7.7	10.5%
50,001 to 100,000	2	15.4	15.8
25,001 to 50,000	4	30.8	23.7
25,000 and Less	6	46.1	50.0
	13	100.0	100.0%

The response was generally representative of the total universe of
affiliation changes, according to the population strata. In retrospect, the
low response is probably due to such things as the author's failure to enclose

self-addressed, stamped envelopes, to use follow-up or "prod" letters,
and to formulate easily answered questionnaire sheets. This, however,
is an "intensive" study of specific cases and representativeness of
responses (although fairly faithful) is not very important. Nor is the size
of the response important, if the cases responding are completely described and apparently representative of the various types of motivational
and situational configurations producing affiliation change. (As the text of
Chapter VI indicates, this response was indeed illuminating about wire
affiliation changes and does, in fact, present a wide field of situations.)

One discouraging note is that three of the thirteen responses indicated that the change of affiliation had not occurred, claiming that the
Year Book's wire-service notations were in error. This three-out-of-
thirteen ratio is very high, but the author believes that most of the errors
in the Year Books were corrected by these letters, since it is easier for a
publisher to write and correct the record (claiming no change in affiliation)
than it is for him to write and explain why a change was made. The author
is aware of the fact that some of his most important raw data come from
these Year Books and that these responses cast doubt upon many of the findings in this study, but he hastens to point out that at present there is no
other public listing of daily newspapers which includes their affiliations.

Thus, the ten remaining responses which do explain changes in
wire service affiliations compare as follows with the adjusted universe of
change.

Population Strata	Responses No.	%	Change Universe
100,001 to 500,000	-	---	8.6%
50,001 to 100,000	2	20.0	17.2
25,001 to 50,000	3	30.0	22.8
25,000 and Less	5	50.0	51.4
	10	100.0	100.0

The elimination of these three responses affects the representativeness of the remaining responses only in the top population stratum, but again such representation is not as crucial as the extent and type of information elicited.

The remainder of this section is devoted to presentation of two types of raw data: (1) Editor & Publisher Year Book notations on other changes in the entries for the twenty-five non-responding newspapers whose wire affiliation changed between 1962 and 1963, and (2) the ten responses paraphrased and summarized and compared with Year Book notations on concurrent changes and discussed in light of the total apparent local situation.

Other changes for twenty-five non-responding newspapers may or may not be indicative of reasons for the affiliation change, but they are the only available supplementary data.

Other Changes (from Year Book)	25,000 & Less	25,001-50,000	50,001-100,000	100,001-500,000	Total
Total newspapers changing wires	13	5	4	3	25
Advertising rate increase	2	1	2	2	7
News stand price increase	3	2	1	-	6
Circulation decrease	3	1	1	1	6
Personnel changes	20	6	8	1	35
Owner-publisher	2	-	1	-	3
Editor-in-chief	2	-	1	-	3
Exec. or Mng. editor	4	1	2	-	7
Advertising manager	5	2	1	-	8
Circulation manager	5	1	2	-	8
General business manager	2	2	1	1	6
Many on editorial staff	2	-	-	-	2
Changed supplementary services	-	-	1	1	2
Moved into new office	1	1	-	-	2
No change other than wire	1	1	-	-	2
Nprs with local competition	-	-	2	-	2

These figures for those newspapers which showed affiliation changes but which did not respond to the author's inquiry seem not to indicate any particular factors which universally accompany a change in wire service. Personnel changes are frequent throughout newspapering, particularly on advertising and circulation staffs, so this would not seem to be significant, particularly since a connection between such changes and a wire-service policy must at best be indirect. The raw data indicate, however, that all but two newspapers appeared somewhere in these factors with changes. Also, it is noteworthy that all but one paper showed changes in only a few categories and did not show changes simultaneously in two or more of the economic indices, i.e., changes in advertising rate, subscription rates, and circulation figures. Apparently each newspaper had a particular regional, state, or local problem or condition with which to contend, and its own situation, as shown in these indices, reflects that particular problem. Advertising rate increases ranged from 4.5 to 16.6 per cent; subscription rate increases ranged from 14.3 to 66.7 per cent; and circulation in one year fell off from 0.1 to 30.9 per cent.

To fit these changes with wire affiliation changes is practically impossible, except by sheer guesswork. Not only does one not know whether these changes are healthy or last-ditch efforts, but one also cannot tell from a distance whether the local situation makes a particular wire change a move toward more expensive or more economical service. As a final point, these affiliation changes may not be geared to such aggregate alterations in the paper's condition at all, but rather to personal feelings or beliefs of staffers, perhaps not even top-ranking editors and owners.

The following summaries of the ten responses indicate the types of pressures and considerations behind a wire-service change. The responses are presented in descending order of circulation, as of 1963. Each response presentation is divided into three parts: reasons given by the respondent for the wire-service change, supplementary data on concurrent changes available in Editor and Publisher Year Books, and the author's discussion of the situation.

1. Burlington (Vt.) Free Press; AP to AP-UPI; Circ.: 33,839; Pop.: 35,531.

REASONS: (a) to give readers news of national and world events in greater depth, and (b) paper is de-emphasizing limited-interest news and emphasizing general-interest news. "We feel that our reading audience is becoming more sophisticated and more interested in national and international affairs. We are trying to keep abreast of this fortunate improvement in reader interest."

E&P: Free Press is a home-owned morning newspaper with no Sunday edition. Its competition, the Vermont News, discontinued evening publication on May 30, 1961, becoming a Sunday-only newspaper and carrying UPI only. The circulation of the Free Press has increased about 1,000 in the last two years, now at 34,204, while the News has fluctuated around 11,000 since its change to Sunday only.

AUTHOR: Burlington, with a 1962 estimated population of 36,028 is the largest city in Vermont and occupies a relatively isolated corner in northwestern Vermont. The Free Press is one of two morning papers in the state (the other with more than 20,000 circulation is the Herald at Rutland in southwestern Vermont) and appears to dominate the morning field in the northern part of the state.
Control by the Free Press of this area appears to be unchallenged, except for the failing efforts of the News which has carried UP and UPI at least since 1958. All other papers are in neighboring counties and are much smaller.
Apparently the Free Press, its glowing comments about readership notwithstanding, has moved to make itself a statewide newspaper, similar to the Milwaukee Journal in Wisconsin. Its competition, then, is not the Sunday News but rather the Rutland Herald, the only

other morning paper in Vermont and, along with Burlington, the only other city with a retail trade zone of 100,000 or more population in the state. The fact that the Herald has received AP only probably goes a long way to explain why the Free Press has sought to move beyond duplication of the former's wire with the addition of UPI.

2. Kenosha (Wis.) <u>News</u>; AP-UPI to UPI; Circ.: 25,241; Pop.: 67,899.

REASONS: (a) to concentrate more heavily on local news, (b) to provide readers with wire photos, (c) new contract with UPI includes Unifax (photo) service, (d) to reduce costly duplication. "We have no complaint over the arrangement nor did we have any complaint with the service provided by AP in the past. For us, the change was a matter of economics."

E&P: The News made the following increases between 1962 and 1963: daily subscription, 7 cents to 10 cents; weekly subscription, 40 cents to 45 cents; maximum advertising rate, 15 cents to 18 cents; minimum advertising rate, 14 cents to 17 cents; and "Independent-Republican" to "Independent." Changes were also made in the posts of executive vice-president, secretary, treasurer, and comptroller, most of these being promotions within the organization.

AUTHOR: The statement that the change "was a matter of economics" appears to be an accurate one from all indications. Kenosha is located in the extreme southeastern corner of Wisconsin, a state dominated by newspapers from Chicago, Milwaukee, and St. Paul-Minneapolis. The News is wedged in between the Racine Journal-Times (10 miles north) and the Waukegan-North Chicago (Ill.) News-Sun (17 miles south). All three papers are evening editions, and the Kenosha News, among the three, has the lowest circulation (about 7,000 below the other two), the lowest advertising rate (from 2 cents to 8 cents per line below them), and the lowest retail trade zone population (although the city itself is larger by about 12,000 population than Waukegan). Of the two, the Racine Journal-Times is the stronger competitor for the News, since statelines do, in fact, impose limitations on papers' advertising and circulation ranges in some areas. While the Waukegan News-Sun uses AP and UPI, the Racine Journal-Times uses only AP. And with the latter as the larger threat to Kenosha's paper, the News appears to have dropped that wire which duplicates the competitor's service. The question of having to drop a wire seems supported by the general subordinate position of the News and its 1962-63 moves to increase revenue. The paper feels the financial pinch of nearby competition and of a confining trade and reading area.

3. Olean (N.Y.) Times-Herald; UPI to AP; Circ.: 17,589; Pop.: 21,868.

REASONS: (a) to receive Pennsylvania report less expensively (AP decided to move an abbreviated Pennsylvania report on the paper's
New York State wire at no extra cost. With UPI, the paper had
to have two machines, one for New York State news and another
for the Pennsylvania wire.); (b) AP's coverage of New York State,
particularly the western region, is more extensive than UPI's;
and (c) AP opens earlier and moves sports and state copy first,
all of which benefits the paper's mechanical and news-handling
operations to a greater extent. The writer comments that AP's
dominance in New York State is probably due to a traditional and
fruitful relationship which AP enjoys with member newspapers.
"Most papers 'protect' AP rather than UPI when regional news
develops. Also, AP bureaus that I am familiar with have had
more manpower than competing UPI bureaus. AP also seems to
have an edge on facsimile picture quality, although I understand
improvements by UPI since then have overcome the deficiency."
"I cannot see where either AP or UPI seriously outdistance each
other. Unfortunately, they both continue to have a preoccupation
with spot news at the expense of depth reporting."

E&P: The only 1962-63 changes were a change in advertising rates from
12 cents to 14 cents per line and addition of a new treasurer.
The paper receives the Gannett News Service reports for an over-
night view of governmental news in Albany, the New York state
capital.

AUTHOR: The Times-Herald appears to have taken advantage of a wire-
service decision which seems tailor-made to solve the paper's
problem of serving Pennsylvania residents who constitute about
20 per cent of the papers total circulation. The community, about
five miles from the New York-Pennsylvania state line, is in southwestern New York State and has as its chief competition the
Salamanca (N.Y.) Republican-Press, an evening paper with only
4,055 circulation. Between 1962 and 1964 the Times-Herald's
circulation has increased 5.8 per cent while the Republican-Press
circulation has gone up only 2.8 per cent. Salamanca's trade zone
is only 8,404, while Olean's is 25,303.
Across the state line, the Bradford (Pa.) Era, a morning paper,
operates about fifteen miles away from Olean. Its morning publication, however, probably does not impinge excessively upon the
Times-Herald's 20 per cent circulation in that state.
In short, the Times-Herald appears to be a healthy newspaper
whose circulation is increasingly rapidly and whose field is almost
unchallenged. The paper has raised its advertising rate 2 cents
per year for the past three years and recently raised its daily price
from 7 cents to 10 cents. It appears to be building, and in so doing

it has taken advantage of a change in wire-service policy to afford
itself better state and even two-state coverage, which is ideal for
its situation. The editor talks at length of qualitative characteristics
of the respective wires, and his choice of dropping UPI and
adding AP does not appear based on competitive or "gimmick"
motivation since both the Republican-Press and Era are AP-only
papers. If the editor had wanted to use the wire for a promotion
gimmick during either an expansion or contraction period, he would
have either added AP to UPI or stayed with the unique UPI wire.

4. Oxnard (Calif.) <u>Press-Courier</u>; UPI to AP-UPI; Circ.: 15,254; Pop.:
    40,265.

REASONS: (a) to receive AP's sports wire on tape; (b) to supplement UPI's
    report; and (c) to meet competition (the Ventura Free-Press has both
    AP and UPI). The writer comments that both wires are good and
    that each has features and good writers which are by no means dupli-
    cated in the other wire.

E&P: Advertising rate increased from 11 cents to 12 cents, and a new city
    editor was named.

AUTHOR: The Oxnard Press-Courier, along with its two potential competi-
    tors in Ventura County, the Ventura Star-Free Press and the Santa
    Paula Chronicle, all operate under the shadow of the giant dailies
    operating southeast of them in neighboring Los Angeles County, but
    within this threesome some curious conditions exist. Oxnard, the
    largest of the three cities with the largest retail trade area, has a
    newspaper which is about 9,000 circulation below the Ventura paper.
    It is difficult to explain why this should be so; the only outward dif-
    ference is that the Star-Free Press has AP, UPI, and NEA and the
    Press-Courier had only UPI and now only AP and UPI.
    The E&P figures on circulation reveal that the Oxnard paper has in-
    creased 16.8 per cent in the last three years while the Ventura paper
    has gained only 3.8 per cent. (The Santa Paula Chronicle's circula-
    tion is only 4,119 and thus is not in the same league with the other
    two Ventura County papers.)
    The respondent has willingly acknowledged that an attempt to match
    competition has led to the addition of AP. And this, connected with
    a hike in advertising rates and an increase in circulation of large
    proportions, seems to point to an expansion program to regain
    some ground lost to Ventura somewhere along the way. The Oxnard
    Press-Courier is speculating with added wire service and expanded
    revenue in an attempt to meet the Ventura paper, a member of the
    six-newspaper John P. Scripps chain.

5. Roseburg (Ore.) <u>News-Review</u>; AP to UPI; Circ.: 11,909; Pop.: 11,467.

REASONS: (a) to fall in line with Scripps League policy ("The majority of
Scripps League papers use the UPI service."); (b) to get "a more
flexible service in connection with volume"; (c) to get less restrictive
contractual arrangements. The writer believes that the two wires
are comparatively equal on "larger matters." "In most areas UPI
has a little edge, it would seem, in 'local' news. While that may
not presently be true in Oregon, it seems to be improving. UPI . . .
is more colorful in its reporting, though not as rigidly bound to detail as is the AP. I regard both news services and their personnel
most highly."

E&P: Circulation declined from 12,277 to 11,909, a drop of about 3 per
cent. Daily price has doubled, going from 5 cents to 10 cents.

AUTHOR: The writer begins his response by pointing out that the News-
Review was purchased by the Scripps League in 1960. (The respondent, in point of fact, was editor of the newspaper prior to its
purchase by the League chain.) It appears as though the first reason
given is, in fact, the principal reason (except, of course, for the
fact that UPI should come more cheaply to Scripps League newspapers). Of the eighteen Scripps League newspapers in 1963, eleven
carried UPI only, five received AP only, and one each received AP-
UPI and no wire. One of those eleven is the Roseburg News-Review.
To go one step further, Roseburg is the seat of Douglas County,
Oregon, and except for some infringement by the Eugene Register-
Guard in the northern part, the county is dominated by the Roseburg
paper. In short, it is a "safe" little paper, isolated by geographic
conditions and commanding dominance as the only daily newspaper
within the county. It is obvious why this should be a property worth
purchasing by a seven-state West Coast chain: it is a uncontested
moneymaker. And so in the past three years the price has risen
from 5 cents to 10 cents and the advertising rate has gone from 13
cents to 14 cents. In part, the chain's directive to drop AP and add
UPI may be aimed at aiding UPI in Oregon, which according to the
respondent's comments is in a building process.

6. Ashland (Ohio) <u>Times-Gazette</u>; AP to UPI; Circ.: 9,173; Pop.: 17,419.

REASONS: (a) UPI made an attractive offer financially; (b) UPI promised
to protect the Times-Gazette in nearby towns where the paper has
a "quasi-competition" with another paper (probably the Mansfield
News-Journal, carrying AP and UPI about 14 miles away); and
(c) UPI offered Unifax (photo) service at a reduction if the paper
took it for one year.

E&P: The president and publisher was named editor between 1962 and 1963, the old editor disappeared, the city editor was named managing editor (a new position), and a new city editor was found in the editorial staff.

AUTHOR: Economics is obviously the principal factor in this decision; the respondent makes that quite clear above in the reasons he lists for the change. The Ashland Times-Gazette is one of two Koehl Chain newspapers, the other being the Galion Inquirer (also an evening paper and operating in the second county to the west, or 31 miles away), a UPI newspaper for many years. Both Koehl papers are relatively small operations (less than 10,000 circulation) in small retail trade zones (less than 20,000 population). The Mansfield paper (owned by the two-newspaper Horvitz Chain along with the Lorain Journal) is a larger paper with circulation of 35,000 in a trade area of 80,000 population. Both Horvitz papers are AP-UPI papers, leaving no competitor room for different coverage within the wire-service framework.

As noted above, however, economics seems to have been the principal motivation, along with the competitive situation (to be taken up in a moment). The personnel changes noted in E&P seem to have contributed to the change. The respondent, a news executive, makes the following statement: "When our contract with AP was about to expire, UPI made us what the publishers considered to be a financially attractive offer. Editorial executives were not consulted about this change." The decision, therefore was made without consideration for the quality of the wire. Competition for the Ashland paper appears to mean keeping the Mansfield paper out of its county. This seems to be a newspaper losing some its grip upon its county, grasping for economic advantage and the promise of protection by a wire in a competitive area.

7. Red Wing (Minn.) Daily Republican Eagle; UPI to AP; Circ.: 8,508; Pop.: 10,528.

REASONS: (a) AP has a distinctly superior Minnesota bureau (coverage has more depth, accuracy, interpretation, broader news base, larger and better staff); (b) AP has a more conservative treatment of national and international news ("I'm a firm believer in conservative accuracy in news and in the long run, I think AP has the edge for consistent reporting."); (c) to get both Minnesota and Wisconsin news on TTS tape, which is important for the paper's mechanical operation (UPI offers TTS only for Wisconsin news; the Minnesota UPI report is delivered only by all-cap printer); and (d) to take advantage of AP's strong cooperative news-gathering structure among newspapers in southeastern Minnesota ("UPI must depend on stringers many of them with small radio stations and largely inexperienced. At present, there is only a single one-wire service newspaper in the state that subscribes to UPI, the Stillwater Gazette.").

E&P: Daily price went from 7 cents to 10 cents between 1962 and 1963. A new circulation director was named, and the respondent was named managing editor and city editor.

AUTHOR: The key to this switch, apparently, is found in the following statement by the respondent: "One of my first thoughts upon taking over this position 11 months ago was that a review was due on the paper's wire service. (My background includes three years on the St. Paul Pioneer Press, where I sat on the wire desk regularly and handled both AP and UPI side by side.)" This statement reveals concern for qualitative features of the wires' reports, and this qualitative viewpoint is supported by the four reasons listed above.
Red Wing, the county seat of Goodhue County, is about 45 miles southeast of the Twin Cities along the Mississippi River. Although living in the shadow of St. Paul-Minneapolis dailies, the paper is the only daily in Goodhue County and has no competition for two Minnesota counties along the river and for three Wisconsin counties directly across the river. The Red Wing retail trade zone, according to ABC, extends well beyond the Goodhue County boundaries, totaling 46.5 thousand persons. The newspaper seems to command dominance in the area. The nearest small-town newspaper competition is located in Faribault (the News, with a circulation of 7,410) 52 miles southwest.
Thus, if competition is not a factor and circulation been maintained (ABC circulation totals increased from 8,383 to 8,508 between 1962 and 1963), a propensity to save money in the absence of competition might account for the change. The respondent, however, points out that AP costs the paper $112.15 per week while UPI cost it $98.43. The change must have been motivated by the respondent's own qualitative appraisal of the wires' reports.

8. "A Western newspaper"; UPI to AP; Circ.: 7,539; Pop.: 23,786.

NOTE: The respondent asked that the source of this information not be identified.

REASONS: (a) AP in this state does a substantially better job on local news; (b) "In a monopoly situation the normally fuller coverage and greater accuracy of AP offset the occasionally earlier stories of the UPI"; and (c) the paper had been with AP for 20 years before switching to UPI eight years ago because "of a problem involving personality, and also because of the lower charge."

E&P: A drop in circulation from 7,910 to 7,539 between 1962 and 1963. Other changes are personnel, as follows: new comptroller, new classified advertising manager, new city editor, and several editorial staff changes.

AUTHOR: This evening paper, along with another one in the next county to the south, control the sparsely populated northwestern corner of a western state. Both are owned by the same man (and are the only two papers in this chain), and although both papers have switched from UPI to AP, the publisher wrote with regard to only one of them (even though the author contacted each newspaper separately with an inquiry). The western paper's circulation declined 9.5 per cent between 1962 and 1963 and the sister paper's circulation fell off 6.3 per cent. Their combined circulation of 11,403 supposedly covers counties in that corner of their state which have a combined population of 95.4 thousand persons. Moreover the western newspaper's letterhead reveals with a circulation map that its distribution area extends into the next state to the north and even into a community with a daily newspaper (receiving AP since 1958) whose circulation has increased 6.2 per cent between 1962 and 1963. Finally, the state as a whole is experiencing annual population increases of about 5.5 per cent and its only metropolitan morning and evening newspapers show a combined circulation increase of 13.2 per cent between 1962 and 1963.

Apparently, this Western newspaper and its sister paper are experiencing a period of stagnation while the state and competitive and nearby metropolitan newspapers show substantial growth patterns. The paper pays more for AP than it did for UPI, and the respondent's reasons stress improved coverage of state and local news, yet personnel changes and the papers' reverse condition, vis-a-vis their environment, leads the author to suspect that the change of wires may be due partially to the fact that the respondent's "monopoly situation" is decaying somewhat in terms of revenue. The wire change seems like a move to improve the papers' position, vis-a-vis competition; it is an expansion move (and one taken for these tactical reasons, rather than for inherent, qualitative AP characteristics since "a problem involving personality" caused severance of AP ties eight years ago).

9. Somerset (Pa.) American; AP-UPI to AP; Circ.: 5,838; Pop.: 6,347.

REASONS: (a) AP's TTS wire is the more useful for the paper's automatic composing setup, (The paper switched to TTS composition in 1959 when it started taking AP's TTS Pennsylvania wire); (b) UPI's two-wire setup in Pennsylvania (a trunk and a sports-state wire) is more difficult to handle and must be set manually; and (c) the change in affiliation occurred in 1962 because that was when the five-year contract with UPI expired; it would have happened earlier if that had been possible.

"We run the (AP) tape direct from the reperforator into the Linotype from the time the wire opens at 3 (p.m.) until 10:30 (p.m.). Then tape is sent back for only the type we plan to use."

E&P: Between 1962 and 1963, circulation declined from 5,985 to 5,838 (a drop of 2.5 per cent), the price increased from 5 cents to 7 cents, and the advertising rate increased from 5 1/2 cent to 6 1/2 cents. A new president and a new city editor were named.

AUTHOR: The respondent's reasons and additional comments point principally to securing a wire service which meshes with the paper's mechanical system. In fact, this emphasis on mechanics seems to pervade the operation, with wire copy indiscriminantly fed into the composing room for 7 1/2 hours with apparently little or no editing. On the surface, this seems to be the reason for the decision to drop UPI: composing arrangements are in invariable factor and use of a wire service must conform to this factor with AP coming closer than UPI. In fact, use of AP and introduction of TTS are synonymous and UPI is a carry-over arrangement from manual composition days. Probing more deeply, the American's closest morning competition is the Bedford Gazette (UPI) and the Cumberland (Md.) News (AP-UPI). Both have increased their circulations by more than 5 per cent since 1958 while the American's circulation has declined 4.5 per cent since that time. The closest evening paper, the Connellsville Courier, has increased circulation by 1.1 per cent since 1958 and had a 2.9 per cent increase between 1962 and 1964. By comparison, therefore, the American experiences a declining trend, the reverse of its nearest competitors.
The switch to TTS composition is a far greater expenditure for the paper than the receipt of a wire service, perhaps greater even than receipt of two wires in the long run. Such a switch was made for reasons not apparent in the data and prior to the period under consideration. Obviously, however, it does remain the principal criterion on which to choose a wire service, primarily because of the expense wrapped up in backshop, TTS equipment. Whether competition is a factor cannot be ascertained, although competitors do show quite opposite trends from those of the American.

10. Iowa City (Iowa) Daily Iowan; AP to AP-UPI; Circ.: 4,773; Pop.: 33,443.

REASONS: (a) current budget allots $6,000 to wire services; this permits receipt of UPI for six months. (AP is the paper's principal wire; the paper is an AP member.); and (b) receiving both wires is beneficial to the paper's staff members.

AUTHOR: The Daily Iowan is a college newspaper published at the University of Iowa by university students with faculty supervision. Although the paper sells advertising and subscriptions, it is partially subsidized through university funds. Therefore, this change in affiliation is responsive to conditions not normally prevalent in a newspaper's economic, competitive, and perspective conditions. It is not discussed in the text of Chapter VI.

A discussion of these case studies is presented in Chapter VI. One final point is worth noting. The thirty-five newspapers showing affiliation changes compare with total newspapers on the basis of geographic distribution in the following way.

Division	Total Newspapers	Change of Affiliation	Responses
East	22.4%	22.9%	30.0%
Central	32.6	· 25.7	40.0
West	16.8	25.7	30.0
South	28.2	25.7	---
	100.0%	100.0%	100.0%

Changes in affiliation for 1962-63 were higher in the West and lower in the Central division than the distribution of newspapers would indicate. Responses from the East, Central, and West were pushed above their actual representativeness by the absence of responses from the South.

BIBLIOGRAPHY

Alisky, Marvin, and Barash, Robert. "Radio News Values of Teletypesetter Copy," Journalism Quarterly, XXXIV (Summer, 1957),
349-354.

"AP Denies Monopoly Charges in Answer to Government Suit," Editor &
Publisher: The Fourth Estate, LXXV (Nov. 21, 1942) AP7-AP9.

Associated Press, The. (Illinois Corporation) Annual Volumes.
Chicago: The Associated Press, I-VIII (1894-1901).

Associated Press, The. (New York Corporation) Annual Volumes.
New York: The Associated Press, I-LXIV (1901-1964).

_____. AP Reference Book. 1st rev. New York: The Associated
Press, 1949.

_____. APME Blue Books. New York: The Associated Press, 1947-
1958.

_____. APME Red Books. New York: The Associated Press, I-XVII
(1948-1964).

_____. The Associated Press. New York: mimeographed Associated
Press pamphlet, n.d.

_____. How The Associated Press Collects News Abroad. New York:
mimeographed Associated Press pamphlet, n.d.

_____. Member Editorials on the Monopoly Complaint. 2 vols.
New York: The Associated Press, 1942-43.

_____. The Torch is Passed. New York: The Associated Press, 1963.

_____. What Makes a Good Newspaper. New York: The Associated
Press, n.d.

_____. Writing for the AP. New York: The Associated Press, 1959.

_____. Your AP. New York: The Associated Press, 1958.

Associated Press, et al. v. United States. 326 U.S. 1-60 (1945). 64 S.Ct.
1058 (1944). 65 S.Ct. 1416-1443 (1945). 66 S.Ct. 6-7 (1945).

Ault, Phillip H., and Emery, Edwin. Reporting the News. New York:
Dodd, Mead & Co., 1959.

Bagdikian, Ben H. "Washington Letter: The Morning Line," Columbia Journalism Review, I (Fall, 1962), 26-28.

Baillie, Hugh. High Tension. New York: Harper & Brothers Publishers, 1959.

Barnes, Arthur M., and Lyness, Paul I. "How the Wire Services Reported the Rutledge Murder Trial: A Study in Taste," Journalism Quarterly, XXVIII (Spring, 1951), 161-178.

Barnes, Peter. "The Wire Services in Latin America," Nieman Reports, XVII (March, 1964), 3-8.

Beichman, Arnold. "Report from America," Encounter, XVI (March, 1961), 87-92.

Benet, Stephen Vincent. "The United Press," Fortune Magazine, VII (May, 1933), 67-72, 94, 97, 98, 100, 102, 104.

Boorstin, Daniel J. The Image. New York: Atheneum Press, 1962.

Breed, Warren. "Newspaper 'Opinion Leaders' and Processes of Standardization," Journalism Quarterly, XXXII (Summer, 1955), 277-284.

Brown, Charles H. News Editing and Display. New York: Harper & Brothers Publishers, 1952.

Bureau of Media Research, Indiana University. The Impact of TTS: Preliminary Report. Bloomington, Ind.: a mimeographed report, 1954.

Carey, James W. Communication Systems and Social Systems: Two Economic Postulates Applied to a Theory of Communication Systems. Urbana, Ill.: unpublished Ph.D. thesis, University of Illinois, 1963.

Carter, W.F. "The Dwindling Morse Tribe," The AP World, XIX (Spring, 1964), 22-27.

Cater, Douglass. The Fourth Branch of Government. Boston: Houghton Mifflin Co., 1959.

_____. Power in Washington. New York: Random House, 1964.

Chafee, Zechariah, Jr. Government and Mass Communications. 2 vols. Chicago: University of Chicago Press, 1947.

Champaign-Urbana (Ill.) News-Gazette, The. Promotional supplement, LVI (March 31, 1951).

Colangelo, Joseph G., Jr. "How to Fold a Newspaper," The Reporter, XXX (January 16, 1964), 45-47.

Commager, Henry Steele, and Morison, Samual Eliot. The Growth of the American Republic. 2 vols. 5th ed. New York: Oxford University Press, 1962.

Commission on Freedom of the Press. A Free and Responsible Press. Chicago: University of Chicago Press, 1947.

Cooper, Kent. Barriers Down. New York: Farrar & Rinehart, Inc., 1942.

_____ Kent Cooper and the Associated Press. New York: Random House, 1959.

_____. The Right to Know. New York: Farrar, Straus and Cudahy, 1956.

Cowles, John. "Fewer Papers Mean Better Papers," Nieman Reports, V (July, 1951), 3-5.

Cranford, Robert J. "Effects of the Teletypesetter Upon Newspaper Practices," Journalism Quarterly, XXIX (Spring, 1952), 181-186.

Cutlip, Scott M. "Content and Flow of AP News -- From Trunk to TTS to Reader," Journalism Quarterly, XXXI (Fall, 1954), 434-446.

Danielian, N.R. A.T.&T.: The Story of Industrial Conquest. New York: The Vanguard Press, 1939.

Diehl, Charles S. The Staff Correspondent. San Antonio: The Clegg Company, 1931.

Editor & Publisher: The Fourth Estate. "Convention Edition." LXXVIII-XCVII (1945-1964).

_____. "International Year Book Numbers." LXVII (January 26, 1935); LXXV (January 31, 1942); LXXXII (January 31, 1949); and XCI (February 28, 1958).

Editor & Publisher: The Fourth Estate. International Year Books. XLII-XLIV (1962-1964).

Emery, Edwin. The Press and America. 2nd ed. Englewood Cliffs, N.J.: Prentice-Hall, Inc., 1962.

Ernst, Morris L. The First Freedom. New York: The Macmillan Co., 1946.

Erwin, Ray. "AP Finds Smaller Papers Oppose 11-Pica TTS Tape," Editor & Publisher: The Fourth Estate, XC (April 27, 1957), 21, 140.

_____. "Standard 11-Pica Meets Opposition in ANPA," Editor & Publisher: The Fourth Estate, XC (April 27, 1957), 13-14, 142.

Faris, Barry. "The Role of the Wire Services," The Quill, XLVII (December, 1959), 15-16.

Fett, Ronald R. America's Role in International News Exchange: A Study of the AP, UP, INS, and "Voice of America" Since World War II. Urbana, Ill.: unpublished master's thesis, University of Illinois, 1949.

Fixx, James F. "Quarterbacking a Nation's News," The Saturday Review, XLVI (August 10, 1963), 48-49.

Flesch, Rudolf. The AP Writing Handbook. New York: The Associated Press, 1951.

Gewehr, Wesley M., Gordon, Donald C., Sparks, David S., Stromberg, Roland N., and Crosman, Herbert A. (eds.). American Civilization: A History of the United States. New York: McGraw-Hill Book Company, 1957.

Gieber, Walter. "Across the Desk: A Study of 16 Telegraph Editors," Journalism Quarterly, XXXIII (Fall, 1956), 423-432.

Gramling, Oliver. AP: The Story of News. New York: Farrar and Rinehart, Inc., 1940.

Grossman, Max R. "Some Contemporary Problems of Foreign Correspondence," Journalism Quarterly, XXIV (March, 1947), 37-42.

Hachten, William A. "Journalism and the Prayer Decision," Columbia Journalism Review, I (Fall, 1962), 4-9.

Hacker, Andrew. (ed.). The Corporate Take-Over. New York: Harper & Row, Publishers, 1964.

Heilbroner, Robert L. The Future as History. New York: The Grove Press, 1959.

Hendrix, Hal, Kelly, Frank K., Lyford, Joseph P., and Marlens, Al. "The News from Latin America," Columbia Journalism Review, I (Fall, 1962), 49-58.

Hocking, William E. Freedom of the Press: A Framework of Principle. Chicago: University of Chicago Press, 1947.

Hofstadter, Richard. Great Issues in American History. 2 vols. New York: Vintage Books, 1958.

Hohenberg, John. Foreign Correspondence: The Great Reporters and Their Times. New York: Columbia University Press, 1964.

International News Service. International News Service. New York: mimeographed International News Service pamphlet, 1946.

International Press Institute. The Flow of the News. Zurich: International Press Institute, 1953.

_____. Government Pressures on the Press. Zurich: International Press Institute, 1955.

_____. Professional Secrecy and the Journalist. Zurich: International Press Institute, 1962.

Jensen, Jay W. Liberalism, Democracy and the Mass Media. Urbana, Ill.: unpublished Ph.D. thesis, University of Illinois, 1957.

_____. "A Method and a Perspective for Criticism of the Mass Media," Journalism Quarterly, XXXVII (Spring, 1960), 261-266.

Johnson, Earl J. "Tass A Soviet Department Within the United States," The Overseas Press Club Bulletin, XVIII (October 12, 1963), 4.

Jones, Alexander. Historical Sketch of the Electric Telegraph: Including Its Rise and Progress in the United States. New York: G.P. Putnam, 1852.

Jones, Robert L., Troldahl, Verling C., and Hvistendahl, J.K. "News Selection Patterns from a State TTS-Wire," Journalism Quarterly, XXXVIII (Summer, 1961), 303-312.

"Justice Department in Civil Suit Charges AP is Monopoly," Editor & Publisher: The Fourth Estate, LXXV (November 21, 1942), AP5-AP6, AP15-AP19.

Kearl, Bryant. "Effects of Newspaper Competition on Press Service Resources," Journalism Quarterly, XXXV (Winter, 1958), 56-64.

Key, V.O. Politics, Parties and Pressure Groups. 5th ed. New York: Thomas Y. Crowell Company, 1964.

Kobre, Sidney. Foundations of American Journalism. Tallahassee: Florida State University, 1958.

Kruglak, Theodore E. The Foreign Correspondents. Geneva: Librairie E. Droz, 1955.

Lee, Alfred McClung. The Daily Newspaper in America. New York: The Macmillan Company, 1937.

Lerner, Max. America as a Civilization. 2 vols. New York: Simon and Schuster, 1957.

Lippmann, Walter. The Essential Lippmann. Clinton Rossiter and James Lare, eds. New York: Random House, 1963.

Lyons, Eugene. Assignment in Utopia. New York: Harcourt, Brace and Company, 1937.

Maxwell, J. William. (ed.). The Foreign Correspondent: His Problems in Covering the News Abroad. Iowa City: State University of Iowa, 1954.

_____ "U.S. Correspondents Abroad: A Study of Backgrounds," Journalism Quarterly, XXXIII (Summer, 1956), 346-348.

"M.E.S." His Book. New York: Harper and Brothers Publishers, 1918.

Morison, Samuel Eliot. An Hour of American History. Rev. ed. Boston: Beacon Press, 1960.

Morris, Joe Alex. Deadline Every Minute: The Story of United Press. Garden City, N.Y.: Doubleday & Company, Inc., 1957.

Mott, Frank Luther. American Journalism. 3rd ed. New York: The Macmillan Company, 1962.

Nafziger, Ralph O. International News and the Press: An Annotated Bibliography. New York: The H.W. Wilson Company, 1940.

Nimmo, Dan D. Newsgathering in Washington. New York: Atherton Press, 1964.

Nixon, Raymond B. "Groups of Daily Newspapers Under Common Ownership," International Year Book. Editor & Publisher: The Fourth Estate, ed. XLIII (1963), 310-312.

Nixon, Raymond B., and Ward, Jean. "Trends in Newspaper Ownership and Inter-Media Competition," Journalism Quarterly, XXXVIII (Winter, 1961), 3-14.

Park, Robert E. "The Natural History of the Newspaper," Mass Communications. Wilbur Schramm, ed. 2nd ed. Urbana, Ill.: University of Illinois Press, 1960. Pp. 8-23.

Peterson, Theodore B. Magazines in the Twentieth Century. 2nd ed. Urbana, Ill.: University of Illinois Press, 1964.

Pett, Saul. "How The Associated Press Covered the Kennedy Tragedy," The AP World, XVIII (Winter, 1963-64), 3-6.

Rideing, William H. "The Metropolitan Newspaper," Harper's Monthly, LVI (December, 1877), 43-59.

Rosewater, Victor. History of Cooperative News-Gathering in the United States. New York: Appleton and Company, 1930.

Rosten, Leo C. The Washington Correspondents. New York: Harcourt, Brace and Co., 1937.

Schramm, Wilbur. "The Gatekeeper: A Memorandum," Mass Communications. 2nd ed. Urbana, Ill.: University of Illinois Press, 1960. Pp 175-177.

Shall the Individual Rights of Associated Press Franchise Holders Be Upheld? New York: The Davidson Press, Inc., 1924.

Siebert, Fred S., Peterson, Theodore B., and Schramm, Wilbur. Four Theories of the Press. Urbana, Ill.: University of Illinois Press, 1956.

Sollen, Robert H. "Nationalistic Bias in Reporting the Cold War," Editor & Publisher: The Fourth Estate, XCIV (July 8, 1961), 64-65.

Stempel, Guido H., III. "Uniformity of Wire Content of Six Michigan Dailies," Journalism Quarterly, XXXVI (Winter, 1959), 45-48.

Stone, Melville E. Fifty Years a Journalist. Garden City, N.Y.: Doubleday, Page & Company, 1921.

Swindler, William F. "The AP Anti-Trust Case in Historical Perspective," Journalism Quarterly, XXIII (March, 1946), 40-57.

Swinton, Stanley M. AP International Operations. New York: mimeographed Associated Press pamphlet, n.d.

Taylor, Howard B., and Scher, Jacob. Copy Reading and News Editing. New York: Prentice-Hall, Inc., 1951.

Thompson, Robert Luther. Wiring a Continent. Princeton: Princeton University Press, 1947.

"Tribune and Col. McCormick Answer U. S. Charges in AP Suit," Editor & Publisher: The Fourth Estate, LXXV (November 21, 1942), AP10-AP11, AP19-AP21.

United Nations Educational, Scientific and Cultural Organization. News Agencies: Their Structure and Operation. Paris: Georges Lang, 1953.

_____. World Communications: Press, Radio, Television, Film. Amsterdam: Drukkerij Holland N. V., 1964.

United Press International. United Press International. New York: mimeographed United Press International pamphlet, n. d.

United States Bureau of the Census. Abstract of the Eleventh Census: 1890. Washington: Government Printing Office, 1896.

_____. Abstract of the Twelfth Census: 1900. Washington: Government Printing Office, 1904.

_____. Abstract of the Fourteenth Census: 1920. Washington: Government Printing Office, 1923.

_____. Abstract of the Fifteenth Census: 1930. Washington: Government Printing Office, 1933.

_____. Abstract of the Sixteenth Census: 1940. Washington: Government Printing Office, 1943.

_____. Characteristics of the Population, United States Summary: 1950. Washington: Government Printing Office, 1953.

_____. Characteristics of the Population, United States Summary: 1960. Washington: Government Printing Office, 1964.

_____. Historical Statistics of the United States: Colonial Times to 1957. Washington: Government Printing Office, 1960.

_____. Statistical Abstract of the United States. 85th ed. Washington: Government Printing Office, 1964.

United States Congress (79th Cong., 2nd sess.). Congressional Record, XCII (April 26 - May 22, 1946).

United States House of Representatives. Subcommittee II of the Committee
on the Judiciary (79th Cong., 2nd sess.). Hearings on a Bill to
Amend Antitrust Laws Relative to Exempting Mutual News Gathering Agencies. Washington: Government Printing Office, 1946.

United States v. Associated Press, et al. 52 F. Supp. 362-377 (1943).

_____. "Answer." New York: Southern Federal District Court, 1942.

_____. "Complaint." ibid.

_____. "Findings of Fact and Conclusions of Law." New York:
Southern Federal District Court, 1944.

_____. "Judgment." New York: Southern Federal District Court,
1942.

Van Horn, George. "Analysis of AP News on Trunk and Wisconsin
State Wires," Journalism Quarterly, XXIX (Fall, 1952), 426.

Villard, Oswald Garrison. "The Press Today: II. The Associated Press,"
The Nation, CXXX (April 23, 1930), 486-489.

_____. "The Press Today: III. The United Press," The Nation, CXXX
(May 7, 1930), 539-542.

Von Bertalanffy, Ludwig. "General System Theory," General Systems:
Yearbook of the Society for the Advancement of General Systems
Research, I (1956), 1-10.

_____. "General System Theory -- A Critical Review," ibid., VII
(1962), 1-20.

Wechsler, James A. "Propaganda in the Press: A Study in Suppression,"
The Progressive, XXVII (August, 1963), 10-15.

Westley, Bruce. News Editing. Cambridge, Mass.: The Riverside Press,
1953.

White, David Manning. "The 'Gate Keeper': A Case Study in the Selection
of News," Journalism Quarterly, XXVII (Fall, 1950), 383-390.

White, Llewellyn. "Ragtime to Riches," Mass Communications. Wilbur
Schramm, ed. 2nd ed. Urbana, Ill.: University of Illinois Press,
1960. Pp. 43-69.

White, Llewellyn, and Leigh, Robert D. "The International News-Gatherers," Mass Communications. Wilbur Schramm, ed. 2nd ed.
Urbana, Ill.: University of Illinois Press, 1960. Pp. 76-94.

Wilhelm, John. "The Re-Appearing Foreign Correspondent: A World Survey," Journalism Quarterly, XL (Spring, 1963), 147-168.

Willoughby, Wesley F. "Are Two Competing Dailies Necessarily Better than One?" Journalism Quarterly, XXXII (Spring, 1955), 197-204.

Yu, Frederick T.C., and Luter, John. "The Foreign Correspondent and His Work," Columbia Journalism Review, III (Spring, 1964), 5-12.

VITA

Richard Allen Schwarzlose was born March 18, 1937, in Chicago, Illinois, and attended public schools in Chicago, Urbana, and Champaign, Illinois. He received his Bachelor of Science degree in Journalism from the University of Illinois in 1959.

In that same year he was admitted to the Graduate College of the same institution where he received an A.M. in Political Science in 1960. He was a teaching assistant in the Department of Journalism during 1962-63 and was appointed instructor in the College of Journalism and Communications in 1963. During the 1964-65, he was a research assistant with the Office of Community Development of the University of Illinois.

Between 1955 and 1962 he served in various reporting and editing capacities for the Champaign-Urbana News-Gazette. His previous scholarly work is Minnesota Electoral Behavior As Analyzed By "Significant" Party Configurations, his master's thesis in 1960.

DISSERTATIONS IN BROADCASTING

An Arno Press Collection

Bailey Robert Lee. **An Examination of Prime Time Network Television Special Programs, 1948 to 1966.** *(Doctoral Thesis, University of Wisconsin, 1967)* 1979

Burke, John Edward. **An Historical-Analytical Study of the Legislative and Political Origins of the Public Broadcasting Act of 1967.** *(Doctoral Dissertation, The Ohio State University, 1971)* 1979

Foley, K. Sue. **The Political Blacklist in the Broadcast Industry:** The Decade of the 1950s. *(Doctoral Dissertation, The Ohio State University, 1972)* 1979

Hess, Gary Newton. **An Historical Study of the Du Mont Television Network.** *(Doctoral Dissertation, Northwestern University, 1960)* 1979

Howard, Herbert H. **Multiple Ownership in Television Broadcasting:** Historical Development and Selected Case Studies. *(Doctoral Dissertation, Ohio University, 1973)* 1979

Jameson, Kay Charles. **The Influence of the United States Court of Appeals for the District of Columbia on Federal Policy in Broadcast Regulation, 1929-1971.** *(Doctoral Dissertation, University of Southern California,1972)* 1979

Kirkley, Donald Howe, Jr. **A Descriptive Study of the Network Television Western During the Seasons 1955-56 to 1962-63.** *(Doctoral Dissertation, Ohio University, 1967)* 1979

Kittross, John Michael. **Television Frequency Allocation Policy in the United States.** *(Doctoral Dissertation, University of Illinois, 1960)* 1979

Larka, Robert. **Television's Private Eye:** An Examination of Twenty Years Programming of a Particular Genre, 1949 to 1969. *(Doctoral Dissertation, Ohio University, 1973)* 1979

Long, Stewart Louis. **The Development of the Television Network Oligopoly.** *(Doctoral Thesis, University of Illinois at Urbana-Champaign, 1974)* 1979

MacFarland, David T. **The Development of the Top 40 Radio Format.** *(Doctoral Thesis, University of Wisconsin, 1972)* 1979

McMahon, Robert Sears. **Federal Regulation of the Radio and Television Broadcast Industry in the United States, 1927-1959:** With Special Reference to the Establishment and Operation of Workable Administrative Standards. *(Doctoral Dissertation, The Ohio State University, 1959)* 1979

Muth, Thomas A. **State Interest in Cable Communications.** *(Doctoral Dissertation, The Ohio State University, 1973)* 1979

Pearce, Alan. **NBC News Division:** A Study of the Costs, the Revenues, and the Benefits of Broadcast News and **The Economics of Prime Time Access.** *(Doctoral Dissertation, Indiana University, 1972)* 1979

Pepper, Robert M. **The Formation of the Public Broadcasting Service.** *(Doctoral Dissertation, University of Wisconsin, 1975)* 1979

Pirsein, Robert William. **The Voice of America:** A History of the International Broadcasting Activities of the United States Government, 1940-1962. *(Doctoral Dissertation, Northwestern University, 1970)* 1979

Ripley, Joseph Marion, Jr. **The Practices and Policies Regarding Broadcasts of Opinions about Controversial Issues by Radio and Television Stations in the United States.** *(Doctoral Dissertation, The Ohio State University, 1961)* 1979

Robinson, Thomas Porter. **Radio Networks and the Federal Government.** 1943

Sadowski, Robert Paul. **An Analysis of Statutory Laws Governing Commercial and Educational Broadcasting in the Fifty States.** *(Doctoral Thesis, The University of Iowa, 1973)* 1979

Schwarzlose, Richard Allen. **The American Wire Services:** A Study of Their Development as a Social Institution. *(Doctoral Thesis, University of Illinois at Urbana-Champaign, 1965)* 1979

Smith, Ralph Lewis. **A Study of the Professional Criticism of Broadcasting in the United States. 1920-1955.** *(Doctoral Thesis, University of Wisconsin, 1959)* 1979

Stamps, Charles Henry. **The Concept of the Mass Audience in American Broadcasting:** An Historical-Descriptive Study. *(Doctoral Dissertation, Northwestern University, 1956)* 1979

Steiner, Peter O. **Workable Competition in the Radio Broadcasting Industry.** *(Doctoral Thesis, Harvard University, 1949)* 1979

Stern, Robert H. **The Federal Communications Commission and Television:** The Regulatory Process in an Environment of Rapid Technical Innovation. *(Doctoral Thesis, Harvard University, 1950)* 1979

Tomlinson, John D. **International Control of Radiocommunications.** 1945

Ulloth, Dana Royal. **The Supreme Court:** A Judicial Review of the Federal Communications Commission. *(Doctoral Dissertation, University of Missouri-Columbia, 1971)* 1979